Conversations with Tocqueville

Conversations with Tocqueville

The Global Democratic Revolution in the Twenty-first Century

EDITED BY AURELIAN CRAIUTU
AND SHELDON GELLAR

LEXINGTON BOOKS

A division of
ROWMAN & LITTLEFIELD PUBLISHERS, INC.
Lanham • Boulder • New York • Toronto • Plymouth, UK

LEXINGTON BOOKS

A division of Rowman & Littlefield Publishers, Inc.
A wholly owned subsidiary of The Rowman & Littlefield Publishing Group, Inc.
4501 Forbes Boulevard, Suite 200
Lanham, MD 20706

Estover Road, Plymouth PL6 7PY, United Kingdom

British Library Cataloguing in Publication Information Available

Library of Congress Cataloging-in-Publication Data

Conversations with Tocqueville: the global democratic revolution in the twenty-first
century / edited by Aurelian Craiutu and Sheldon Gellar.
    p. cm.
  Includes bibliographical references and index.
  ISBN 978-0-7391-2301-0 (cloth: alk. paper)
  ISBN 0-7391-2301-7 (cloth: alk. paper)
  ISBN 978-0-7391-2302-7 (pbk.: alk. paper)
  ISBN 0-7391-2302-5 (pbk.: alk. paper)
  ISBN 978-0-7391-3524-2 (e-book)
  ISBN 0-7391-3524-4 (e-book)
  1. Democracy. 2. Democracy—History—21st century. 3. Tocqueville, Alexis de,
1805-1859. I. Craiutu, Aurelian. II. Gellar, Sheldon.
  JC423.C7165 2009
  321.8—dc22

                                                                          2008048287

Printed in the United States of America

*To Lin and Vincent Ostrom and all those affiliated with the
Workshop in Political Theory and Policy Analysis
who, through their passion, generosity, and dedication, have created
a genuine intellectual and friendly community in Bloomington*

Contents

Preface

The current era is an appropriate time to reexamine the analytical theory of Alexis de Tocqueville, who was born more than 200 years ago in 1805. The 150th anniversary of his death will occur in 2009. While Tocqueville wrote in a different era, he wrote for all of us and not just for his contemporaries. His analytical theory—which is elucidated in this volume—is a long-lasting contribution to political theory. Tocqueville's *Democracy in America* is a still a fun and interesting read, but the contemporary reader tends to ask several core questions: Is the emergence of democracy in what became the United States of America but a single chapter in the unfolding of human existence in *one* country? Or, does it represent an important phase of development in the emergence of *all* mankind?

Reading the chapters in this excellent book edited by Aurelian Craiutu and Sheldon Gellar leads one to conclude that Tocqueville was contributing to our understanding of the unfolding of human existence among *all* of mankind. This leads one to ask some key questions: What are the principles that apply to the unfolding reality of mankind? And what principles apply to the development of self-governing capabilities? How do we distinguish between general principles and the specific processes and structural variables related to the development of democracy in many countries?

Resolving such questions are matters of great importance for all of us. The authors of the chapters in this book address many of the crucial issues related to the unfolding of self-governance capacities in most of the regions of the world including North America, South America, Western Europe, Africa, and in specific countries including Guatemala, Russia, Burma, China, and Japan.

Some readers in today's world might think that the work of a scholar who was writing about a nascent democracy more than 150 years ago would be totally irrelevant to today's events. Unfortunately, some contemporary scholars do read Tocqueville as simply a matter of history. What this book contributes so well is that Tocqueville brought a mode of analysis to his work that foreshadows a great deal of modern democratic theory. The basic analytics of Tocquevillian thought that Craiutu and Gellar lay out in chapters 1 and 3 help us see that relationship. While Tocqueville indeed thought history was important to understand national character and the national institutions at any one point in time, he also stressed the importance of the physical environment in the ways it shaped political, economic, and social structures. Then in addition to history, he was one of the first institutional theorists who stressed understanding laws not simply from the perspective of what was written in a law book but rather the legal structures that affected the incentives citizens and their officials faced. Without understanding the institutions, it is hard to understand whether any system will sustain itself over time or collapse. Knowing a good deal about the existing level of equality or inequality, the kind of religion that people have adopted, and the role of language is also an important lesson that one carries away from the chapters of this book as applied in the analysis of processes all over the world.

Aurelian Craiutu and Sheldon Gellar have brought together a number of thoughtful scholars who illustrate the importance of Tocqueville's work for understanding much of what is going on in the world today. Through the eyes of this distinguished group of scholars, one can see some of the good things that are occurring in Latin America, some of the everyday events and some of the threats. One does not need end up with a sense that democracy will just happen south of the border in Latin America, but the Tocquevillian analytics presented in this book helps the reader see why we should encourage further developments of local-level and regional governments and discourage further efforts to create concentrated hierarchies.

Traveling east to Asia, one can again gain a sense that some villagers in rural parts of China have unknowingly applied Tocqueville's lessons. Tocqueville did not expect that people needed to read his work to apply the lessons of developing democracy from the grass roots. The people in China who are building aspects of contemporary democracy in their country obviously are developing their own strategies and ways of trying to build a democracy from the bottom up (without disturbing those in command too much). Readers of this book will get a better sense of these possibilities in China and some of the deep threads of current developments in Burma. We would not have expected Tocqueville's ideas to be relevant for an understanding of events in Japan, but now we know differently.

Moving to Africa, we also get a better sense of the applicability of Tocquevillian analytics for understanding the rich diversity of contemporary efforts to achieve democracy in Africa. For those of us interested in democracy in the world at large, we all now have a better understanding that looking only at what is going on at the national level hides both the good and the bad that may be the foundation for future developments. Without understanding the foundations, social scientists will not be able to explain why some systems topple and others remain strong even in times of turmoil.

We have gained greatly from participating in the original seminar that led to this book and from reading the final chapters that are in this volume. It is a pleasure to recommend it to other scholars.

Elinor Ostrom and Vincent Ostrom
Workshop in Political Theory and Policy Analysis
Indiana University

Acknowledgments

The publication of this book coincides with the commemoration of 150 years from Tocqueville's death. *Conversations with Tocqueville* was initially inspired by our participation in the Tocqueville panel at the WOW3 conference organized by the Workshop in Political Theory and Policy Analysis in Bloomington in May 2004 and the commemoration of Tocqueville's bicentenary at the same institution in April 2005.

We would like to express our gratitude to all those who accepted our invitation to contribute to this volume. The completion of our project would have not been possible without the generous financial support provided by the Earhart Foundation and Indiana University's Workshop in Political Theory and Policy Analysis, the College Arts & Humanities Institute, the West European Studies, the Department of Political Science, and the Office of International Scholars at Indiana University.

We also want to express our deepest gratitude to Elinor Ostrom and Vincent Ostrom, co-founders of the Workshop and the Tocqueville Endowment for the Study of Human Institutions, who have been among the greatest supporters of our project and were extremely generous in sharing with us their insights and suggestions. Csilla Kajtar served as research assistant for this project and we would like to thank her for her assistance. We would also like to thank Patty Lezotte for her superb editorial assistance and Gayle Higgins, Jacqui Bauer, and Carol Buszkiewicz for their invaluable help at various stages of this project. Many individuals provided useful comments and suggestions on previous drafts of the book. In particular, we would like to thank Cheryl Welch, Jeremy Jennings, Filippo Sabetti, and Barbara Allen, who were extremely generous to share with us their insights on the topics discussed in this book.

During the past three decades, the Workshop in Political Theory and Policy Analysis has been a vital presence on Indiana University's Bloomington campus. It has provided a unique environment for vibrant academic exchanges and created a truly engaging intellectual community that includes many contributors to the present volume. Numerous colleagues, friends, students, and librarians have helped us with their generous assistance. Special thanks are due to Amos Sawyer, Mike McGinnis, Jeffrey Isaac, and Russell Hanson for their comments and suggestions, and to Alin Fumurescu for providing the index to this volume. Finally, we would like to express our thanks to Lexington Books, in particular to Serena Krombach and Joseph Parry, for their encouragement, patience, and faith in our project at the heart of which lie democracy's hopes and prospects in the twenty-first century.

1

Tocqueville and Us

Aurelian Craiutu and Sheldon Gellar

> A world that is totally new demands a new political science.
> —Alexis de Tocqueville[1]

Two centuries after his birth, Alexis de Tocqueville is unanimously recognized as the most important theorist of modern democracy whose ideas on freedom, equality, civil society, despotism, religion, and individualism have an enduring relevance for us today.[2] If a century ago there were no celebrations on either side of the Atlantic to mark Tocqueville's centennial in 1905, the situation was entirely different in 2005, when Tocqueville's bicentennial was celebrated in the United States, Italy, Belgium, Germany, Poland, Canada, Argentina, and Japan. Since 2000, four new English translations of *Democracy in America* have appeared;[3] a fifth one, the critical edition translated by James T. Schleifer and edited by Eduardo Nolla, will be published by Liberty Fund in 2009. A new translation by Alan S. Kahan of the two volumes of Tocqueville's *The Old Regime and the Revolution* was also published by the University of Chicago Press in 1998 and 2001. Moreover, a significant number of new interpretations of Tocqueville's works have appeared in both French and English, shedding fresh light on lesser-known facets of Tocqueville's persona: the philosopher, the moralist, the writer, the defender of the French colonization of Algeria.

The diversity of viewpoints expressed by these diverse interpretations demonstrates that the greatness of Tocqueville does not lie in any single doctrine that he espoused but rather in the ambivalent and often critical lenses through which he analyzed the multiple facets of democracy. Historians, political scientists, sociologists, and anthropologists have acknowledged his original contribution to their disciplines and the current relevance of his ideas on freedom, equality, civil society, religion, political culture, individualism, democracy, and despotism. Scholars have mined Tocqueville's extensive work on America, France, England, and other Western European countries and more recently have explored his writings on Algeria and India. Contemporary thinkers on both the left and the right have claimed Tocqueville as one of their own, admiring him either for his insightful views on democratic citizenship and the art of association, or for his passionate defense of decentralization and self-government and his skepticism toward big government. Last but not least, numerous U.S. presidents and politicians from Dwight Eisenhower and Ronald Reagan to Bill Clinton and George W. Bush have often quoted Tocqueville in their speeches.

The current fascination with Tocqueville's writings goes beyond the fashionable trends of the moment. What makes Tocqueville's case unique, arguably more so than any other modern thinker including Rousseau, Mill, and Marx, is that many ideas of *Democracy in America* appeal even to his skeptical readers who do not always agree with his conclusions and methodological assumptions and are anxious to move beyond conventional readings of his works.[4] This is hardly surprising since there are "many Tocquevilles"[5] speaking various languages and addressing various constituencies, left and right. The Frenchman has become, so to speak, the "unsurpassable horizon" of our times, and his ideas offer an indispensable starting point for anyone interested in assessing the prospects for democracy today. We enjoy conversing with Tocqueville because his work "seems to retain a greater measure of normative and exploratory power—and intellectual provocation—than that of many other nineteenth-century thinkers."[6]

That Tocqueville achieved his highly ambitious goals was confirmed by no one else than John Stuart Mill, who praised Tocqueville in unambiguous terms. "You have accomplished a great achievement," Mill wrote to Tocqueville in 1840:

> You have changed the face of political philosophy, you have carried on the discussions respecting the tendencies of modern society . . . into a region of height and of depth, which no one before you had entered, and all previous argumentation and speculation in such matters appears but a child's play now.[7]

The Frenchman was "the first anthropologist of modern equality"[8] and his writings addressed important topics such as civil society, pluralism, religion, participatory democracy, the democratic mind, and the limits of affluence. Today we feel the need to converse with Tocqueville's "complex mixed messages of dire warning and hopeful counsel"[9] because his ideas stimulate our reflection on contemporary political dilemmas even when we might find his unconventional form of liberalism puzzling.[10] At the same time, Tocqueville's particular combination of historical, philosophical, and sociological investigations provides us with a set of prescient psychological insights into the democratic mind and teaches us important lessons about how to moderate and educate democracy.

As Serge Audier and Jean-Louis Benoît reminded us, American interpretations of Tocqueville have differed from the French ones in several important regards.[11] Tocqueville's French interpreters analyzed his works within the framework of a critique of modernity and tended to underestimate the role of local associations and the importance of religion in Tocqueville's works. In turn, the Americans focused on Tocqueville's views on citizenship, religion, decentralization, and self-government. It is not a mere coincidence that in the United States the debate on civil associations has overlapped with the revival of interest in Tocqueville's writing, particularly *Democracy in America,* in which he praised the Americans' propensity to form civil and political associations. Tocqueville regarded these associations as laboratories of democracy that teach citizens the art of being free and give them the opportunity to pursue their own interests in concert with others.

An interesting case in point is offered by the neo-Tocquevillian school in the United States that has often presented the Frenchman as a precursor of communitarianism inviting us to rethink the ethic of individualistic achievement and self-fulfillment and the unrivalled predominance of the language of individualism and individual rights in the contemporary American society. The very diversity of this school mirrors the complexity of Tocqueville's own thought that has sometimes been taken as an inspiration for moving beyond a simple deontological form of liberalism and a rigid understanding of individual rights. Beginning with Tocqueville's *Democracy in America*, it has been customary to regard the United States as unusually "civic" in comparison to other states. Its high degree of civicness has traditionally been attributed to the high density of networks of civic and social engagement.[12] Nonetheless, a growing number of scholars from Francis Fukuyama and Michael Sandel to Robert N. Bellah and Robert Putnam have lately challenged the traditional optimism regarding the vibrancy of civil society in America and raised serious doubts about the long-term prospects for democracy there. The signs of civil decline and political apathy range from increasingly lower voter turnout to declining participation in town meetings, Parent-Teacher Associations (PTAs), trade unions, and bowling leagues. Although religious groups, charitable institutions, and churches continue to retain significant influence in contemporary American societies, the traditional communities that made up American civil society at mid-twentieth century, from families and neighborhoods to workplaces, have been under constant assault.[13]

In *Bowling Alone: The Collapse and Revival of American Community*, a book inspired by Tocqueville's ideas on civil society and associational life, Robert Putnam interpreted the diminished civic engagement and lower social connectedness as the outcome of a host of social, cultural, and technological factors that have radically altered community life in late twentieth-century America. "By almost every measure," Putnam argued,

> Americans' direct engagement in politics and government has fallen steadily and sharply over the last generation, despite the fact that average levels of education—the best individual-level predictor of political participation—have risen sharply throughout this period. Every year over the last decade or two, millions more have withdrawn from the affairs of their communities.[14]

Putnam argued that the fast pace of economic growth and the major technological changes in the past few decades have had a complex impact on civil society broadly construed that led, among other things, to a decline of civic engagement in America, depleted social capital, moral relativism, asocial individualism, increasing privatism, and civic apathy. Long gone are the famous temperance societies that impressed Tocqueville, who was struck by the fact that responsible adults pledged to use the force of association to resist one of the most intimate urges of each human being. While many civil associations foster character traits needed for the proper functioning of democratic regimes such as independence of spirit, general tolerance for pluralism and respect for diversity, the membership in many associations today is mostly nominal, the payment of membership dues being often the only sign of participation in these associations.

Both Putnam's and Bellah's solutions for revitalizing associational life and overcoming the shortcomings of individualism have a distinctive Tocquevillian ring demonstrating that Tocqueville's thought has been well assimilated in its coherent totality, including the issue of religion, by American scholars who have used Tocqueville's themes as background for their own reflections on civil society and social capital. As Don Eberly remarked a few years ago, "in Tocqueville, we find an uncanny foretelling of the American cultural and social debate at the turn of the twenty-first century. Without a vibrant and functioning civil realm, he held that the state would emerge to fill the vacuum, producing . . . a gentle despotism."[15] More so than any other political thinker, Tocqueville grasped the seminal role that civil and political associations play in the framework of modern society and understood that in order to remain civilized, modern democratic regimes must constantly cultivate and promote the art and freedom of association.

Yet, it would be a mistake to think of Tocqueville as an infallible guide or prophet. As contemporary historians of American democracy suggested, his understanding of American politics was far from perfect.[16] Among other things, Tocqueville misunderstood the role played by political parties and had little to say about key institutions such as the Congress or the Supreme Court. As Cheryl Welch pointed out, when confronted with the legacy of slavery and mismanagement in the colonies, Tocqueville unexpectedly regarded administrative centralization (which he had previously considered as a significant threat to freedom) as a possible solution.[17] Tocqueville's belief that ex-slaves could be convinced that their interest lay in temporary subjection to the bureaucrats in Paris, and that the French state would protect them from social oppression can hardly be reconciled with his deep skepticism about the neutrality, competence, and benevolence of the French state.

Yet in many ways, as Keith Baker argued, the study of Tocqueville's blind spots might be as instructive for his interpreters as focusing on his most perceptive theoretical insights. For example, in his analysis of the Old Regime, Tocqueville downplayed the extent and various forms of political contestation before the Revolution of 1789. Baker attributes this curious oversight in part to the fact that Tocqueville was not entirely convinced of the sincerity of the *parlements'* commitment to the principle of equality and liberty. Instead, Baker argued, Tocqueville "found the *parlementaires* a particularly egregious example of the transformation of the nobility into a self-interested caste seeking to restrict their membership to a small, closed aristocracy."[18]

For all these blind spots and contradictions, Tocqueville was in many ways far ahead of his time in elaborating an eclectic but coherent interdisciplinary methodology to study the movement of societies from aristocratic to democratic orders. He successfully integrated lessons learned from his experience as a practicing politician with philosophical reflection and empirical political, cultural, social, and economic analysis. He also made extensive use of archival materials, fieldwork, and interviews. Not surprisingly, the Tocquevillian renaissance that we have witnessed during the past two decades or so has a lot to do with democracy's triumph across the globe. As the editors of the tenth anniversary issue of the *Journal of Democracy* (dedicated entirely to the author of *Democracy in America*) acknowledged, the democratic revolution about which Tocqueville wrote has spread far beyond the United States and Europe to every corner of the globe.[19] Tocqueville's merit is to have identified with his characteristic subtlety not only the key features of this democratic revolution (that Marx, for example, failed to understand) but also the main dilemmas of democracy, a regime that, in his view, had to be purified of its potentially destructive elements. Tocqueville felt himself called to provide the guidelines of a new political science for a new world. He believed that the task of modern legislators is "to educate democracy—if possible, to revive its beliefs; to purify its mores; to regulate its impulses; to substitute, little by little, knowledge of affairs for inexperience and understanding of true interests for blind instincts."[20]

The Nature of the Book

These words written almost two centuries ago remain highly relevant to our present concerns. One of the assumptions undergirding all the texts published in this volume is that Tocqueville's new science of politics—what we call "Tocquevillian analytics"—offers a coherent framework, concepts, and tools for studying the processes of democratization and the state of democracy, not only in North America and Western Europe, but also in Asia, Africa, and Latin America. The questions and issues that Tocqueville raised in exploring the roots of democratic revolutions in America and Western Europe are just as pertinent today in understanding the evolution of democracy in the non-Western world as they were two centuries ago. He correctly identified the equality of conditions as the core element of all democratic societies, pointed to excessive centralization and the undermining of local liberties as detrimental to participatory democracy, and asserted that religion would remain an important institution in democratic societies rather than fading into obscurity as Marx believed.

It is important to repeat that our volume does *not* treat Tocqueville as an oracle who was always right in predicting the future. Nor do we want to argue that he urged all nations to imitate the laws and mores of America and those of Western Europe as the only possible (or desirable) path to democracy. To be sure, Tocqueville was no reductionist in politics or history. He constantly resisted the temptation of putting forward simplistic unidimensional theories of social and political change and rejected abstract political models posing as panaceas. As Tocqueville himself acknowledged in an important passage from his *Recollections*, he detested

> those absolute systems, which represent all the events in history as depending upon great first causes linked by the chain of fatality, and that, as it were, suppress men from the history of the human race. They seem narrow under their pretence of broadness, and false beneath their air of mathematical exactness.[21]

Tocqueville understood that many important political events can and should be explained by accidental factors in which chance plays a key role. While heralding democracy as the wave of the future and an improvement on aristocratic societies, Tocqueville also recognized that democracy had its own flaws and vulnerabilities on which he commented both in his published work as well as in the unpublished notes to *Democracy in America*.[22] He also recognized that all societies are diverse and pluralistic in composition, molded by history, the physical environment, culture, and laws, and constantly evolving. As such, Tocqueville added, "antecedent facts, the nature of institutions, the cast of minds and the state of morals are the materials of which are composed those impromptus which astonish and alarm us."[23]

Many of the previous volumes on Tocqueville published in the English-speaking world focused primarily on Tocqueville as theorist of American democracy.[24] In the United States, there is a tendency to focus solely on *Democracy in America* while ignoring the fact that his analyses were not intended mainly for an American audience. Furthermore, when discussing the relevance of Tocqueville's thought, many scholars tend to overlook other important writings such as *The Old Regime and the Revolution*, the *Recollections*, the *Memoir on Pauperism*, and his writings on India and Ireland. There are, of course, a few important exceptions. In a pathbreaking study published in 1968, Seymour Drescher highlighted the importance of the debates on welfare, prison reform, and the abolition of slavery for Tocqueville's thought. He interpreted Tocqueville's views on these topics against the background of the moderate French liberal tradition represented by Victor de Broglie, Charles de Rémusat, Odilon Barrot, and Gustave de Beaumont. In particular, Drescher pointed out that "Tocqueville's slavery articles strike one as the most assured of his reformist work. . . . They were less indecisive than his works on poverty and less defensive than those on prison reform."[25]

The essays collected in this volume seek to render justice to the complexity of Tocqueville's thought as a social scientist, concerned with identifying independent variables that allow us to explain phenomena such as revolutions, class conflict, associational life, and the prerequisites of successful democratic transitions. Addressed to a wider audience than Tocqueville scholars, our book moves *beyond* a North American and Eurocentric perspective. It demonstrates how the tools used by Tocqueville in his study of the democratic revolution in the United States and Europe can also be effectively updated and applied to understanding the ongoing global democratic revolution taking place all over the world in the twenty-first century. As such, the essays in this volume reflect a collaborative effort between Tocqueville specialists and social scientists applying diverse aspects of "Tocquevillian analytics" to the study of regional trends and issues in Africa, Latin America, and West Europe and countries like Guatemala, Burma, Japan, China, Russia, and the United States.[26]

The main idea of the book—updating Tocqueville in a dialogue with scholars from around the world—has its roots in the Workshop in Political Theory and Policy Analysis at Indiana University, Bloomington, co-founded by Elinor and Vincent Ostrom in 1973. Tocqueville's legacy has been a major component of the Workshop's quest to understand the nature and constitution of order in human societies since its inception.[27] A great admirer of Tocqueville's new science of politics, Vincent Ostrom has coined the term "Tocquevillian analytics" to describe Tocqueville's methodology and has inspired a wide range of visiting scholars and associates of the Workshop to apply some elements of Tocquevillian analytics in conducting their research. Most of the essays included in this volume have been contributed by scholars presently or formerly associated with the Workshop at Indiana University, Bloomington. They reflect the interdisciplinary and innovative research sponsored by the Workshop over the past three and a half decades. The diverse case studies presented in this book should garner wide-ranging interest among political theorists, sociologists, and area studies specialists.

Although all the authors in this volume organize their contributions around Tocquevillian themes and concepts,[28] they do not necessarily agree or support all of Tocqueville's conclusions, predictions, and normative prescriptions. The diversity of methodological and ideological perspectives offered in this volume speaks for itself and reflects our commitment to engage in an open-ended conversation with Tocqueville. It is also an upshot of our belief that democracy is above all an open-ended process that requires, in the spirit of Tocqueville, a flexible conceptual framework that mirrors the ever-changing constellation of economic, political, social, and cultural factors at work in modern society. In making this point, we do not want to give the impression that we are unaware of the fact that Tocqueville's method and conceptual framework had its own conceptual ambiguities. The latter are discussed at length in Aurelian Craiutu's essay in this volume. In turn, Barbara Allen disputes Tocqueville's overly pessimistic predictions concerning the evolution of race relations in the United States, while Tun Myint's essay on Burma demonstrates that Christianity is not the only religion whose principles support equality. In spite of their diversity, the essays collected in this volume share the belief that it is important to engage in a conversation with Tocqueville in order to reflect on various aspects of our contemporary democratic society.

The Structure of the Book

Conversations with Tocqueville is divided into two parts. The first part illuminates the basic components of Tocquevillian analytics and its potential as a tool for comparative analysis. As such, it provides a portrait of Tocqueville as an innovative social scientist and affirms the centrality of Tocqueville's concept of popular sovereignty as crucial to the survival of democratic republics. The second part of the book uses Tocquevillian analytics as a framework for studying different aspects affecting democracy in North America, Latin America, Europe, Africa, and Asia.

We begin with Vincent Ostrom's essay because his own work on American democracy and federalism has emerged from a deep admiration for Tocqueville's writings and has inspired many of the collaborators to this volume. Originally given as an official speech to commemorate the award of the John Gaus Prize by the American Political Science Association, it should be read primarily as an example of the insight that an appreciation of Tocquevillian analytics and the wisdom of the Founding Fathers might bring. Vincent Ostrom asserts that the analysis offered in *The Federalist* and *Democracy in America* presumes a much more enlightened and active citizenry in the sphere of civil society than simply relying on national-level officials and centralized bureaucracy to govern nation-states. Tocqueville's concept of popular sovereignty implies self-government and citizen participation in governance at all levels of government. Ostrom examines Tocqueville's response to Hamilton's query as to whether societies are capable of establishing good government through reflection and choice rather than by accident and force. In the final section, Vincent Ostrom argues that the concept of sovereign nation-states is a fiction that provides justification for rulers to exercise command and control over others as subjects rather than citizens.

Sheldon Gellar's essay provides a checklist of the diverse components that together comprise the heart of Tocquevillian analytics and argues that these could be applied more systematically to the study of non-Western societies. Gellar also points to Tocqueville's skills as a comparative analyst and his interest in non-Western societies and religions. Tocqueville's broader and more complex concept of democracy is presented as a more reliable guide to understanding the processes of democratization than the narrower and often ahistorical concept of democracy stressing the primacy of multiparty competition and national elections as the hallmark of democratic systems favored by national policymakers.

Aurelian Craiutu's chapter examines what kind of social scientist was Tocqueville and defends him against critics of his methodology who claim that Tocqueville was a superficial social scientist who reasoned a priori and chose to observe only what he wanted to see. By exploring Tocqueville's meticulous empirical research methods in *The Old Regime and the Revolution* and his lesser-known economic writings, Craiutu shows that Tocqueville did not ignore economic "facts," as some of his critics alleged. Nor was Tocqueville insensitive to the plight of the poor. Although Tocqueville was critical of socialism and criticized the state's attempt to control economic life, he did not believe that democracy and free markets are inextricably intertwined. Nor did he downplay the high social costs of industrial capitalism as it emerged in Great Britain. In Craiutu's view, the diverse research methods Tocqueville used in writing his last book clearly demonstrate the seriousness with which he sought to understand the complexity of modern democratic society and to formulate a "new science of politics for a new world."

Part II applies what we call "Tocquevillian analytics" to democratic processes all over the world. Barbara Allen's essay turns to Tocqueville's discussion of the three races in the last chapter of volume one of *Democracy in America* in order to explore the evolution of race relations in the United States. Tocqueville understood that the effects of the democratic revolution would not be universally felt by all social groups in America because ideologies based on race and biological determinism perpetuated inequalities. Allen contrasts Tocqueville's pessimistic expectations for African-Americans with Dr. Martin Luther King Jr.'s conception of a "beloved community" based on racial equality and liberty that would bring blacks and whites together. Allen argues that Tocqueville underestimated the importance of dissent and contestation, the institutional means of changes offered by a compound republic, and the political capacity of free black people to contest racial discrimination. She argues that Tocqueville was largely unaware of the institutions created by free blacks that eventually became the backbone of the modern civil rights movement. According to Allen, the unfolding saga of the civil rights movement offers critical insight into and possibly a correction of Tocqueville's ideas on race and equality.

In his contribution to this volume, Charles Reilly invites us to imagine what Tocqueville would say about Guatemala today and offers a Tocquevillian assessment of a country in which peace-building and development issues continue to overshadow democracy. Reilly notes that Guatemala suffers from many of the problems noted by Tocqueville in his visit to Ireland in 1835—extreme poverty, large landholders forcing peasants off the land, religious tensions, and conspicuous inequality. In his essay, Reilly also explores the legal institutions, inheritance laws, and property arrangements that have buttressed economic elite interests and the central state and hindered the development of democracy in Guatemala. On the other hand, Reilly asserts that Tocqueville might have been favorably impressed by the renaissance of Mayan culture following centuries of repression, the proliferation of non-governmental organizations (NGOs) and other civil society organizations, and the vibrancy of religion and religious institutions involved in peace-making and peace-building.

The essay by Gustavo Gordillo de Anda and Krister Andersson examines recent trends toward the left in Latin America, especially in Mexico, Brazil, Argentina, Venezuela, and Bolivia, as reflected in recent election results. This essay draws on Tocqueville's analysis of the causes of the French Revolution, the dangers of centralization, and the political climate and feuding among political parties of the right and left described in Tocqueville's *Recollections*. The trend toward the left was sparked by the failure of neoliberal policies to reduce inequality in the 1990s. Popular discontent with inequality has enabled populist leaders in several Latin American countries to take power through the ballot box. However, the gains made by populist political leaders do not necessarily translate into greater gains for democracy since populist leaders, once in power, find it difficult to control corruption and in the worst of cases seek to strengthen their own power and that of the central state and reduce the autonomy of social movements and networks, thus creating the conditions for democratic despotism. The two authors address the current debate on populism in Latin America and the extent to which populism can pose a threat to democracy when a large percentage of the people tied to old political cul-

tural norms are willing to accept authoritarian regimes as the price to pay
for policies aimed at reducing social and economic inequality or continue
to maintain highly centralized states and political parties.

Frederic Fransen offers a Tocquevillian analysis of democracy in Western Europe by taking into account the interrelation among cultural, institutional, and environmental factors. Fransen argues that Tocqueville well
understood the dangers of democracy in Europe, and accurately predicted
the collapse of free government there (France in 1851, Italy in 1925–1926,
or Germany in 1933). Fransen claims that Western Europeans have chosen
not to adopt Tocqueville's various remedies for the preservation of healthy
liberty under conditions of rising equality. By examining key Tocquevillian
themes such as political and economic centralization, bureaucracy, local
liberty, associational life, and religion, Fransen takes issues with the Euro
optimists who believe that Western Europe has learned to prevent democracy from declining into despotism and that liberty will reign unchallenged
into the distant future. Europe, Fransen warns, has opted for a different
treatment, principled on something quite in contrast to Tocqueville's prescriptions, placing a heavy emphasis on "solidarity," equality, centralization, and homogenization. He suggests that the sharp increase in Europe's
Muslim population coupled with the rise of Islamic extremist groups may
undermine European commitment to multiculturalism and civil liberties.

In his essay, Peter Rutland offers a Tocquevillian assessment of democracy in post-communist Russia that draws inspiration from both *Democracy
in America* and *The Old Regime and the Revolution*. Despite the emergence
of some democratic institutions, Rutland points out that authoritarian
trends have prevailed, with Freedom House downgrading Russia in 2004
to the "unfree" category. Political scientists have been divided over how to
explain this failure and Rutland turns to Tocqueville for help in order to
decipher the enigmatic nature of Russia's elusive democracy. Rutland argues
that the geopolitical and geographical attributes of Russia are distinctive
and, along with centralization and resentment at the loss of international
status, they tend to play against democratic development in the short and
medium term. Rutland also points out that religion matters to democratic
consolidation and can have an important influence in this regard. Drawing
on Tocqueville's reminder that religion must be at the center of our analysis,
Rutland notes that Russian democracy has been built on the deeply secular
society of Soviet Russia. He also questions the potential of the Orthodox
Church in promoting democratic development in the years to come.

James Wunsch builds upon the core elements of Tocqueville's analytical
framework and insights concerning the relationships between centraliza-

tion and local liberties in describing the nature of local government and the causes underlying the general ineffectiveness of local government in post-colonial sub-Saharan Africa. He traces the failure of centralized colonial governments to establish autonomous local government institutions and analyzes the extent to which the deterioration of ecological and economic conditions (the physical environment) in postcolonial Africa led Africans to pursue survival strategies that reinforced their basic lack of trust in formal central and local-level government institutions. Wunsch concludes by presenting short case studies in three countries (Chad, Uganda, and Ghana) where contextual conditions and decentralization reforms created a more favorable environment for more effective local government. Paradoxically, the collapse of central government in Chad permitted local communities to set up their own autonomous community school systems while in Uganda, the most effective of the five forms of local government established by the central government were those found at the grassroots level. Wunsch's case studies indicate that Tocqueville's analytical framework is a powerful tool for understanding and evaluating the state of local governance institutions.

Tun Myint's essay challenges the commonly held view that Asian societies are inherently hierarchical and asserts that traditional Buddhist principles provide the foundation for creating the conditions of equality similar to those described by Tocqueville in *Democracy in America*. A native of Burma, Myint demonstrates how the Buddhist theory of emptiness affirms that the very existence of the individual is not inherent but based on interdependence with other individuals and it sanctifies associational life as the basis of individual existence. Buddhist principles affirming the essential equality of all human beings and the obligation to treat all human beings with respect favor the emergence of democratic associational life. Myint also draws interesting parallels between Tocqueville's concept of self-interest rightly understood and the concept of karma that motivates individuals to follow Buddhist principles in their own self-interest since violation of these norms will lead to negative consequences. As a former participant in the 1988 movement to overthrow Burma's military regime, Myint argues that one of the major weaknesses of the 1988 Democracy Movement was its greater emphasis on Free Burma and individual liberty rather than the equality of conditions that caused many Burmese to regard it as a Western-inspired movement rather than one rooted in Burmese society. He suggests that the Democracy Movement in Burma pay more attention to evoking Buddhist principles concerning the equality of conditions and the functions and obligations of government and rulers as a means of winning greater popular support and undermining the legitimacy of the military regime in power.

Following Tocqueville, who believed that administrative centralization is the major enemy of local liberty and democracy, Jianxun Wang argues that administrative centralization remains the key obstacle to democracy in China. His essay provides a historical account of political changes since the last period of imperial Chinese rule and the movement toward greater administrative centralization under the nationalist and communist regimes. He demonstrates how centralization led to a sharp decline in local government resources and how the emergence of communist party-state rule undermined civil society. Wang sees democracy as being gradually built from the bottom up in China through local initiatives and reforms. In many rural areas, peasants have taken greater control over formal local government institutions previously dominated by communist party cadres and obtained a greater voice in allocating land and land-use planning. In the urban areas, encouraging signs can be seen in the proliferation of NGOs, civil society associations, blogger networks, and homeowners' associations. Wang sees these groups as schools for democracy and the foundation for a democratic China in the future.

The last chapter of the book, written by Reiji Matsumoto, a distinguished Japanese Tocqueville scholar, discusses both Japan's reception of Tocqueville as well as Tocqueville's relevance to contemporary Japanese democracy. Matsumoto shows that Tocqueville's ideas found a warm reception in Japan where political philosophers took a strong interest in his work. By focusing on key Tocquevillian themes such as equality, egalitarianism, democracy, and centralization, Matsumoto argues that Tocqueville's analysis of democracy and democratization is relevant to Japan, because modern Japanese society is a democratic society and the progress of equality represents an essential feature of the history of modern Japan. Professor Matsumoto also touches upon the historical transition of family from the aristocratic to the democratic type, and finally, discusses the Meiji Revolution as a democratic revolution and explores briefly its resemblance to the French Revolution.

* * *

Conversations with Tocqueville can be read as a chronicle of the various ways in which different forms of democracy continue to shape the world's social and political landscape at the beginning of the twenty-first century. The democratic revolution that Tocqueville described so well in his writings has finally spread beyond the borders of the Old and the New World;

more countries are free today, at least on paper, than ever before in human history. Nonetheless, while liberal democracy has—hopefully—become the unsurpassable horizon of our age, in many parts of the world democratic institutions are dysfunctional and fail to deliver the services that citizens expect from them. Their shortcomings pave the way for populist leaders who might shrewdly exploit people's fears and hopes. There is no better guide than Tocqueville to remind us not only that the apprenticeship of liberty is always difficult but also that a democratic republic can be a wonderful thing if, as Benjamin Franklin so nicely put it, we can keep it alive.

Notes

1. *Democracy in America*, trans. Arthur Goldhammer (New York: The Library of America, 2004), 7.

2. The list with some of the most important new interpretations of Tocqueville published in the last few years includes: Lucien Jaume, *Tocqueville: Les sources aristocratiques de la liberté* (Paris: Fayard, 2008); Jean-Louis Benoît, *Tocqueville moraliste* (Paris: Honoré Champion, 2004); Laurence Guellec, *Tocqueville et les langages de la démocratie* (Paris: Honoré Champion, 2004); Serge Audier, *Tocqueville retrouvé: Genèse et enjeux du renouveau tocquevillien français* (Paris: EHESS/Vrin, 2004); Agnès Antoine, *L'impensé de la démocratie: Tocqueville, la citoyenneté, et la religion* (Paris: Fayard, 2003); Michael Drolet, *Tocqueville, Democracy, and Social Reform* (New York: Palgrave, 2003); Robert T. Gannett, *Tocqueville Unveiled: The Historian and His Sources for the Old Regime and the Revolution* (Chicago: University of Chicago Press, 2003); Sheldon Wolin, *Tocqueville between Two Worlds: The Making of a Political and Theoretical Life* (Princeton, NJ: Princeton University Press, 2001); Cheryl Welch, *De Tocqueville* (Oxford: Oxford University Press, 2001); Pierre Manent, "Tocqueville philosophe politique," *Commentaire*, no. 107 (Autumn 2004): 581–87; Aurelian Craiutu and Jeremy Jennings, "The Third Democracy: Tocqueville's Views of America after 1840," *American Political Science Review* 98, no. 3 (2004): 391–404; *The Cambridge Companion to Tocqueville*, ed. Cheryl B. Welch (Cambridge: Cambridge University Press, 2006); Alexis de Tocqueville (1805–1859): A Special Bicentennial Issue, *The Tocqueville Review/La Revue Tocqueville* 27, no. 2 (2006); and *The Tocqueville Reader*, ed. Oliver Zunz and Alan S. Kahan (Oxford: Blackwell, 2002).

3. These translations belong to Harvey Mansfield and Debra Winthrop (University of Chicago, 2001), Gerald Bevan (Penguin, 2003), Stephen Grant (Hackett, 2000), and Arthur Goldhammer (Library of America, 2004).

4. See Jennifer Pitts's introduction to Tocqueville, *Writings on Empire and Slavery*, trans. and ed. Jennifer Pitts (Baltimore, MD: Johns Hopkins University Press, 2000); Melvin Richter, "Tocqueville on Algeria," *The Review of Politics* 25,

no. 3 (1963): 362–98; and Roger Boesche, "The Dark Side of Tocqueville: On War and Empire," *The Review of Politics* 67, no. 4 (2005): 737–52.

5. Robert Nisbet, "Many Tocquevilles," *The American Scholar* (Winter 1976–1977): 65.

6. Welch, *De Tocqueville*, 1.

7. Letter of J. S. Mill (May 11, 1840) in Alexis de Tocqueville, *Œuvres Complètes, VI: 1. Correspondance anglaise. Correspondance d'Alexis de Tocqueville avec Henry Reeve et John Stuart Mill*, ed. J. P. Mayer and Gustave Rudler (Paris: Gallimard, 1954), 328.

8. Welch, *De Tocqueville*, 50.

9. Welch, *De Tocqueville*, 217.

10. This is the title of Roger Boesche's book, *The Strange Liberalism of Alexis de Tocqueville* (Ithaca, NY: Cornell University Press, 1987).

11. See Jean-Louis Benoît, "Reading Tocqueville: Diachrony, Synchrony, and New Perspectives," and Serge Audier, "The Return of Tocqueville in Contemporary Political Thought," in *Reading Tocqueville: From Oracle to Actor*, ed. Raf Geenens and Annelien De Dijn (Houndmills, Basingstoke: Palgrave Macmillan, 2007), 52–70, 71–89.

12. The relationship between social trust and effective civil and political institutions is a complex one that goes beyond the narrow scope of this introduction. It can be argued that a certain degree of trust is needed first in order to form civil networks and associations; at the same time, it is equally possible to claim that a vibrant associational life promotes and enhances civic trust.

13. On this issue, see Robert Putnam, *Making Democracy Work: Civic Traditions in Modern Italy* (Princeton, NJ: Princeton University Press, 1993); Putnam, *Bowling Alone: The Collapse and Revival of American Community* (New York: Simon & Schuster, 2001); Francis Fukuyama, *Trust: The Social Virtues and the Creation of Prosperity* (New York: Free Press, 1995), 269–323; Robert N. Bellah et al., *Habits of the Heart: Individualism and Commitment in American Life* (New York: Harper & Row, 1985), 250–96; Adam B. Seligman, *The Idea of Civil Society* (Princeton, NJ: Princeton University Press, 1995); and William A. Schambra, "The Progressive Assault of Civil Community," in *The Essential Civil Society Reader: The Classic Essays*, ed. Don E. Eberly (Lanham, MD: Rowman & Littlefield, 2000), 317–51. For an excellent overview of the literature on Tocqueville and civil society, see Stefan-Ludwig Hoffman, "Civil Society and Democracy in Nineteenth Century Europe: Entanglements, Variations, Conflicts" (Discussion Paper SP IV 2005–405, Wissenschaftszentrum Berlin für Sozialforschung [WZB], 2005).

14. Robert Putnam, "Bowling Alone: America's Declining Social Capital," *Journal of Democracy* 6, no. 1 (1995): 68. Also see Putnam, "The Strange Disappearance of Civic America," *American Prospect* 24 (1996): 34–48; and Putnam, *Making Democracy Work*.

15. Don E. Eberly, "The Meaning, Origins, and Applications of Civil Society," in *The Essential Civil Society Reader*, 27.

16. See Holly Brewer, "Tocqueville as Historian of the Struggle between Democracy and Aristocracy in America," and Oliver Zunz, "*De la démocratie en Amérique*: Tocqueville lu par les Américans du XIXe siècle," in Alexis de Tocqueville (1805–1859): A Special Bicentennial Issue, *The Tocqueville Review/La Revue Tocqueville* 27, no. 2 (2006): 381–402, 425–60. Also see Lynn L. Marshall and Seymour Drescher, "American Historians and Tocqueville's Democracy," *Journal of American History* 55, no. 3 (1968): 512–32; Sean Wilentz, "Many Democracies: On Tocqueville and Jacksonian America," in *Reconsidering Tocqueville's Democracy in America*, ed. Abraham S. Eisenstadt (New Brunswick, NJ: Rutgers University Press, 1988), 207–28.

17. Cheryl Welch, "Creating *Concitoyens*: Tocqueville on the Legacy of Slavery," in *Reading Tocqueville: From Oracle to Actor*, 47.

18. Keith M. Baker, "Tocqueville's Blind Spot? Political Contestation under the Old Regime," in Alexis de Tocqueville (1805–1859): A Special Bicentennial Issue, *The Tocqueville Review/La Revue Tocqueville* 27, no. 2 (2006): 270.

19. "Introduction," *Journal of Democracy* 11, no. 1 (2000): 6.

20. Alexis de Tocqueville, *Democracy in America*, trans. Arthur Goldhammer (New York: The Library of America, 2004), 7.

21. Alexis de Tocqueville, *Recollections*, ed. J. P. Mayer, trans. A. Teixeira de Mattos (New York: Meridian Books, 1959), 64.

22. A short fragment (rarely quoted and never published by Tocqueville) that can be found among the notes for *Democracy in America* reveals Tocqueville's state of mind when contemplating the irresistible progress of democracy: "Democracy! Don't you notice that these are the waters of the deluge? Don't you see them advancing by a slow and irresistible effort? . . . If you retreat, the flow continues its march. If you run away, it flows behind you. . . . Instead of seeking to erect powerless dikes, let us try rather to build the sacred ark which must carry the humankind on this shoreless ocean" (Tocqueville, *Democracy in America*, ed. Eduardo Nolla, [Paris: Vrin, 1990], I, 7, fn. r). Also see the slightly different version of Tocqueville's note in *Œuvres*, II, ed. Jean-Claude Lamberti and James T. Schleifer (Paris: Gallimard, Bibliothèque de la Pléiade, 1992), 937–38.

23. Tocqueville, *Recollections*, 64.

24. See, for example, the recently published *The Cambridge Companion to Tocqueville* and the previously mentioned issue of the *Journal of Democracy* 11, no. 1 (January 2000) dedicated to Tocqueville. Also see Audier, *Tocqueville retrouvé*.

25. Seymour Drescher, *Dilemmas of Democracy: Tocqueville and Modernization* (Pittsburgh, PA: University of Pittsburgh Press, 1968), 189. Also see the excellent collection, *Tocqueville and Beaumont on Social Reform*, trans. and ed. Seymour Drescher (New York: Harper, 1968).

26. Due to various constraints, we have not been able to include, as we initially hoped, a chapter applying Tocquevillian analytics to contemporary Middle Eastern societies. The interested reader is referred to Sheldon Gellar's *Democracy in*

Senegal: Tocquevillian Analytics in Africa (New York: Palgrave Macmillan, 2003), which applies Tocqueville's ideas to a country in which Islam is a major presence.

27. The Workshop's elaboration of its Institutional Analysis and Development (IAD) framework reflects a major effort to construct a methodology based on developing and updating Tocqueville's approach to the study of human societies. The Workshop's IAD framework, however, goes beyond Tocqueville in incorporating a wide range of tools, methods, and disciplines not known to Tocqueville, for example, game theory, evolutionary biology, public choice, and so forth. For a sampling of the breadth and depth of the Workshop's methodological pluralism, see Vincent Ostrom, David Feeny, and Hartmut Picht, eds., *Rethinking Institutional Analysis and Development: Issues, Alternatives, and Choices* (San Francisco, CA: ICS Press, 1993) and the three volumes edited by Michael D. McGinnis containing collections of essays written by Workshop associates: *Polycentric Games and Institutions: Readings from the Workshop in Political Theory and Policy Analysis* (Ann Arbor: University of Michigan Press, 2000); *Polycentric Governance and Development: Readings from the Workshop in Political Theory and Policy Analysis* (Ann Arbor: University of Michigan Press, 1999); and *Polycentricity and Local Public Economies: Readings from the Workshop in Political Theory and Policy Analysis* (Ann Arbor: University of Michigan Press, 1999). Also see Elinor Ostrom, *Governing the Commons: The Evolution of Institutions for Collective Action* (New York: Cambridge University Press, 1990); and *Understanding Institutional Diversity* (Princeton, NJ: Princeton University Press, 2005).

28. For a survey of current debates on Tocqueville, see Cheryl Welch, "Introduction: Tocqueville in the Twenty-First Century," in *The Cambridge Companion to Tocqueville*, 1–20. A few important aspects of Tocqueville's work are not treated in our book since they are beyond the scope of the present volume: Tocqueville's writing style, his views on gender, and his political career. The last issue deserves a special note here. From an early age on, Tocqueville entertained great political ambitions and dreamt of playing an important role on the political scene of his country. As Robert T. Gannett reminded us, there were quite a few interesting shifts in Tocqueville's political and rhetorical strategies. For more information, see Gannett, "Tocqueville and the Politics of Suffrage," in Alexis de Tocqueville (1805–1859): A Special Bicentennial Issue, *The Tocqueville Review/La Revue Tocqueville* 27, no. 2 (2006): 209–26. Gannett explains these changes in light of Tocqueville's fiercely independent spirit and his prudential calculations of what he believed best for France at each given moment in time. In 1842 and 1847, Tocqueville was inclined to view universal suffrage as a threat to democracy and voted against lowering the electoral requirements for suffrage. In 1848, he changed his mind and endorsed universal suffrage as being compatible with democracy.

Ostrom =

Democratic peace thesis is to facile: even w/ a democracy, liberal
One can still run into wars
— Simply voting is not enough.
→ French states after every revolution
French state — all went to war

2

Citizen-Sovereigns: The Implications of Hamilton's Query and Tocqueville's Conjecture about the Democratic Revolution

Vincent Ostrom

(sovereignty of people / citizen)
Sovereignty, as opposed to unitary sovereign nation states

only if people are truly sovereign in their localities, would they have opportunity to deliberate and develop the habit and the capability of reflection and political choice

Let it [*Democracy in America*] be read over again and there will be found on every page a solemn warning that [as] society changes its forms, humanity its condition, . . . new destinies are impending.

[T]he principles on which the American constitutions [N. B. plural] rest, those principles of order, of the balance of powers, of true liberty, of deep and sincere respect for right, are indispensable to all republics; they ought to be common to all; and it may be said beforehand that wherever they are not found, the republic will soon have ceased to exist.

—Alexis de Tocqueville[1]

Political experience → only then could they hope to maintain

The essays written by Alexander Hamilton, James Madison, and John Jay in support of the *Constitution of the United States* posed a query that is fundamental to a democratic system of governance. Alexis de Tocqueville, some forty years later, pursued the implications of Hamilton's query for the sovereignty of people in a democratic society rather than presuming states to be sovereign. In this chapter, I pursue the implications of Hamilton's query and Tocqueville's vision of a democratic revolution for what is implied about citizens who are sovereign. This is the essential core of Tocqueville's *Democracy in America*.

clear-headed thinking along clean, in the midst of crises, they are presented w/ bombast
rhetoric for military adventures.

But the improvement in political experience and deliberative capability is an ongoing process.
Only then maintain people
Could they hope to

19

Hamilton's Query

In the opening paragraph of the first essay in *The Federalist*, Hamilton posed the question of "whether societies of men are really capable or not of establishing good government from reflection and choice, or whether they are forever destined to depend for their political constitutions on accident and force."[2] This is a fundamental question about the constitution of order in human societies, the place of constitutional choice in creating "good" government, and the place of citizens in the conduct of democratic systems of governance.

Addressing the people of New York to secure the ratification of *The Constitution of the United States of America*, Hamilton, Madison, and Jay, using the name *Publius*, engaged in a diagnostic assessment of the failure of the *Articles of Confederation* and an extended analysis of the basic provisions of the newly drafted constitution of the United States. Both constitutional documents had been drafted in response to the Declaration of Independence, which asserted that ". . . it is the Right of the People . . . to institute new Government, laying its foundation on such principles and organizing its powers in such form, as to them shall seem most likely to effect their Safety and Happiness." The aggregate constitutional order included the constitution of the United States, along with the constitutions of the several states comprising the United States and the systems of governance within each state. Authorities pertaining to legislative, executive, and judicial functions were assigned limited powers. Limits on the general authority of the federal government were adopted in the first ten amendments prior to their ratification by all of the states.

Limits on the authority of government and the diverse instrumentalities of governance created opportunities for contestation in diverse arenas evoking an open public realm for the enlightenment of citizens and the practice of citizenship in the proper exercise of governmental authority. What was meant by "good" in referring to good government had earlier been addressed by Adam Smith and David Hume during the British constitutional era of the seventeenth and eighteenth centuries. Smith, in *The Theory of Moral Sentiments*, identified sympathy as the sentiment that enabled human beings to establish the grounds for reflection and moral judgment.[3] Hume indicated that such patterns of reflection and moral judgment enabled human beings to recognize and designate values that might apply to the creation of order in human societies.[4] This intellectual tradition is consistent with the basic moral and ontological teachings of Moses of Sinai, Jesus of Nazareth, Muhammad of Mecca, and Confucius of China among others. The principle of "*do onto others as you would have others do onto you*" is grounded in sympathy and is the key to normative thinking and moral judgment. These are essential teachings for the enlightenment of democratic citizens.

These cognitive capabilities that might accrue as human cultural achievements are required to confront a Faustian bargain that the enforcement of rule-ordered relationships requires recourse to force and the exercise of coercive capabilities—instruments of evil. Police and military components in human societies can be used by some to gain advantages and profits from opportunities for repression and corruption that pervade rule-ordered relationships.

Hamilton's query was concerned with how reflection and choice might override accident and force in the constitution of human societies. His diagnostic assessment of the failure of confederation identified individuals as being the responsible actors rather than collectivities as such. The problem of inquiry in democratic societies must extend to the enlightenment of the person of citizens as they engage in diverse processes of constitutional, collective, and operational choice. Voting in elections is not an adequate basis for the operation of democratic societies. The analysis offered in *The Federalist* presumes a much more enlightened and active citizenry in the constitution of civil society and in the conduct of governing arrangements than simply relying on officials to govern nation-states. Their analysis was one of artisans creating artifacts for the governing arrangement that became the United States of America. What might be called *public administration* is the organization and conduct of enterprises to render public services to communities of people.

Tocqueville's Democratic Revolution

Alexis de Tocqueville, a citizen of France, whose family had endured the tragedies evoked by the French Revolution, turned with his colleague Gustave de Beaumont to the United States of America to inquire about their system of governance some four to five decades after the inquiries presented in *The Federalist*. His two-volume work was addressed to his fellow citizens of France. He later undertook a similar inquiry about France. The first volume in a projected two-volume work was published as *The Old Regime and the Revolution*.[5] His analyses were assessments of human achievements and failures in light of efforts to transform societies.[6]

Tocqueville engaged in his inquiries in light of a more general set of conjectures about "a great democratic revolution" occurring among mankind. He viewed that revolution as having endured over some seven hundred years in Europe marked by strong aspirations for equality against the prior traditions of aristocracy and servitude built into the structure of property rights, law, social order, and defense capabilities.

Tocqueville admitted to "a kind of religious awe" in observing a movement that could not be stopped but required a reawakening of religious beliefs, enhanced standards of moral judgment, of statecraft, and of knowledge about time and place exigencies in which people live their lives. His concluding sentence amid these conjectures asserted that "A new science of politics is needed for a new world."[7]

In conceptualizing the aggregate system of order in democracy in America, Tocqueville advanced the concept of the principle of the sovereignty of the people. In commenting on the application of that concept to democracy in America, Tocqueville asserted:

> [T]here society governs itself for itself. . . . All power centers in its bosom, and scarcely an individual is to be met with who would venture to conceive or, still less, to express the idea of seeking it elsewhere. The nation participates in the making of its laws by the choice of its legislators, and in the execution of them by the choice of the agents of the executive government; it may almost be said to govern itself, so feeble and so restricted is the share left to the administration, so little do the authorities forget their popular origin and the power from which they emanate. The people reign in the American political world as the Deity does in the universe.[8]

It is easy to dismiss Tocqueville's use of language as political rhetoric. It might also be seen as a response to Hamilton's query applied to many different efforts to create good government from reflection and choice that might apply to each state, to governments within each state, and to diverse patterns of association that are constitutive of society. Among alternatives to a concept of the sovereignty of the people might be the sovereignty of states in a world of nation-states or other concepts that societies of people might use to create systems of governance.

The Challenge of Machine Politics and Boss Rule

Nearly four decades after Tocqueville and Beaumont's visit to America, a judicial decision known as Dillon's Rule asserted the doctrine of legislative supremacy to the effect that municipal corporations were the creatures of state legislative authority.[9] Legislatures enacted individually specified municipal charters, including the creation of charter obligations to construct facilities for private endeavors with the municipality and its residents assuming the obligation for funding these efforts. Such opportunities led to bosses slating candidates gaining control over legislative, executive, and judicial authorities, electing U.S. senators who formed a club of bosses and gained dominance over state, federal, and local governments. Ostrogorski's *Democracy and the Organization of Political Parties* demonstrates how machine politics and boss rule came to prevail and usurp the authority of citizens in the United States.[10]

In response, newspapers with reform agendas, city clubs, civic associations, and public fora began to explore reform agendas through constitutional methods to alter arrangements for the exercise of state and local governments. Typical provisions adopted in revised state constitutions placed limits on state legislatures confining their authority to the enactment of general legislation, denying authority to create public debt without approval of the electorate in referenda, authorizing municipalities to create charter commissions to establish home-rule charters subject to popular referenda, and enabling citizens to amend constitutions and charters by popular initiatives or referenda following the example of Switzerland. Similar provisions allowed for the recall of public officials during their terms of office. Such efforts became the focus of a Progressive Reform movement that achieved reform efforts among state and local governments throughout the United States. A new system of primary elections was created so that the candidates for public offices were nominated through public electoral arrangements rather than by party bosses.

Through these efforts of constitutional revision, Tocqueville's concept of the sovereignty of the people was reestablished in American democracy through the Progressive Reform movement by the second decade of the twentieth century. Machine politics and boss rule no longer prevailed through the revised structure of what might be called democracy in America.

National Governments and World Affairs

In the closing decades of the nineteenth century, a war with Spain and an increasing preoccupation with world affairs were accompanied by an intellectual persuasion, perhaps best articulated by Woodrow Wilson. The essays written in *The Federalist* were addressed by Wilson as "literary theory" that failed to come to terms with political realities. Reality, Wilson believed, required "a [single] centre of power."[11] Wilson's *Congressional Government* saw the Congress as that center of power, but in the preface to the fifteenth printing [dated 15 August 1900], Wilson indicated that "the new leadership of the Executive" may "put this whole volume hopelessly out of date."[12] That leadership took its place among the victorious powers in two world wars in the first half of the twentieth century. National governments in sovereign nation-states yielded monumental disasters in world affairs.

Leading European nation-states had created worldwide empires during the sixteenth, seventeenth, and eighteenth centuries. Revolutionary movements following the example of the United States of America came to prevail in the nineteenth century leaving Latin America with numerous sovereign nation-states subject to coups d'état, military governments, and violent revolutionary struggles. Accident and force came to prevail among nation-states claiming sovereign authority to exercise rulership prerogatives within its territorial domain.

The end of European empires in Africa after the Second World War was succeeded by autonomous nation-states that also became the object of coups d'état, military dictatorships, and adventurous warlords and their combatants who pillaged and plundered the numerous African peoples in sub-Saharan Africa. Peoples in diverse language communities and ways of life in Africa were ignored in the quest for "democracy" among sovereign nation-states in their conduct of world affairs.

Two great proletarian revolutions in the Russian and Chinese empires, which called for the liberation of the workers of the world, were also treated as sovereign nation-states in a world of nation-states. The promise of liberation from *capitalism* and the organization of collective enterprises in what was called *socialism* resulted in monumental disasters of starvation amid mass movements, imprisonment, and death in forced labor camps as dictatorships of the proletariat prevailed in the Soviet Union and the People's Republic of China.

The dominance of Faustian bargains through recourse to accident and force meant that societies of men created monumental disasters rather than reflection and choice. Erroneous diagnostic assessment can create serious illusions that turn into disasters of monumental proportions. The doctrine of sovereign nation-states with a single supreme authority does not facilitate reflection and choice in human affairs.

The Intellectual Challenge of Today and Tomorrow

After nearly a thousand years in what Tocqueville referred to as "a great democratic revolution going on among us," we need to confront Hamilton's query of whether societies of men are really capable or not of establishing good government by reflection and choice or whether they are forever destined to depend for their political constitutions on accident and force. World wars and other monumental disasters need to be subject to diagnostic assessments and the exploration of alternative possibilities.

In the concluding section of the second volume of *Democracy in America*, Tocqueville makes this following observation: "I am of the opinion that, in the democratic ages which are opening upon us, individual independence and local liberties will ever be the products of art (i.e., artisanship); that centralization will be the natural government."[13] Enlightened citizens are needed to craft systems of governance that take account of multiple communities of relationships.

The enactment of treaties by European nation-states to create first the European Community and later the European Union has brought an enduring peace since the Second World War as diverse authorities have pursued discussions and deliberations about problems faced in common by the peoples of Europe. The drafting of a constitution, including much of what represented a code of laws, has received a negative response in recent referenda. Processes of reflection and choice call for further reflections to capture the aspirations of Europeans in light of deepening inquiries about the meaning of European civilization. Harold Berman in *Law and Revolution* identifies the formation of the Western legal tradition with the papal dictate of Pope Gregory VII in 1075 establishing the autonomy of the Church from secular authority.[14] The contestation over the meaning of law and the codification of law among Europeans contributed to the creation of free cities with their own self-governing charters, the establishment of guilds of skilled artisans working with one another across diverse language communities, the conduct of open markets throughout Europe, the emergence of merchant law, and the creation of enlightened codes of law. These developments were accompanied by the transformation of the Holy Roman Empire into a European confederation. How these endeavors contribute to what it means to engage in covenants of a constitutional character needs to become a part of the continuing reflections among Europeans and other democratic peoples in the next millennium.

The confederate-like structure of the Holy Roman Empire was subject to some of the weaknesses identified in Hamilton's and Madison's diagnoses of the failure of American confederation. The Napoleonic conquests, marking the end of the Holy Roman Empire, failed to undertake diagnostic assessments and to engage in deliberative efforts to establish good government from reflection and choice.

Rather than sovereign nation-states and associations of nation-states as created in the League of Nations and the United Nations, we need to give serious attention to Tocqueville's concept of the principle of the sovereignty of the people reinforced by the assessments of Hamilton and Madison about the essential place of individual responsibility in the exercise of the prerogatives of persons and citizens. Fictions created by the association of individuals are helpful only in light of shared understandings and complementarities of actions amid continuing reflection and choice. These fictions, as such, do not engage in reflection and choice. Fictions are ways of creating concepts about social realities, not reality as such. The mutual understandings grounded in language yield misunderstandings unless they come back to the place of individual persons and citizens engaged in reflection, choice, and the presence of activities grounded in mutually understood patterns of artisanship.

If we rely upon the inquiries and teachings of Hamilton and Madison in *The Federalist* and of Tocqueville in *Democracy in America*, life in civil society is constituted by how individuals as persons and citizens relate to one another in multitudes of shared communities of understanding in the pursuit of innumerable opportunities. Among these innumerable opportunities are values that we characterize as learning, enlightenment, and scholarship.

Citizens in self-governing democracies are the ones who recognize problems and potentials among communities of people in contrast to persons in sovereign nation-states who run the risk of individuals in command of instruments of force exercising coups d'état to establish military dictatorships and presume to exercise supreme authority. This awareness turns to discussions about the nature of the situation and of the communities of people who share these problems and potentials. Some may have special advantage and ignore impending difficulties. Proceedings in equity jurisprudence may need to be undertaken to determine the scope of the problem and what might be a workable and equitable resolution in establishing a public entity capable of coping with the problem. Both preliminary inquiries and proceedings to create an appropriate public entity and negotiate working arrangements with existing public entities are aspects of public entrepreneurship to establish an appropriate public enterprise to operate in a public service economy in a self-governing society.

Monitoring performance occurs in the way that problems and potential are realized among those who share in the open public realm of a republican character, the scrutiny of public auditors, and the inquiry of grand jurors concerned with the discharge of public trust/ All such forms of entrepreneurship, performance of services, and open public scrutiny are features of public administration that might more appropriately be identified as democratic administration. Fragmentation of authority and overlapping jurisdictions are essential attributes of democratic administration, but their republican character—openness—enhances complementary performance.

If constitutions enunciate rules of fair games, they can evoke widespread support approaching unanimity. Reoccurring processes for selecting personnel to exercise public authority, levying taxes, allocating funds, and creating specific endeavors and obligation can involve less demanding rules for taking collective decisions given effective rules of constitutional law.

Constitutions, statutory enactments, regulations, contractual undertakings, and shared communities of understanding all bear upon processes included in the principle of the sovereignty of the people. The field of law, the study of jurisprudence, and the exercise of proceedings in equity jurisprudence are essential features of what might be called *entrepreneurship* in the creation and conduct of working public enterprises.

Many of the essential goods of life in advanced societies are shared in common by communities of people living in diverse ecological settings. Sharing in common requires the exercise of some governmental prerogatives identified with public enterprises in contrast to private enterprises. Individual endeavors and private enterprises depend upon complementary public endeavors in the ecological exigencies in which people live their lives. Public entrepreneurship adhering to the principles of the sovereignty of people requires attention to the complementarities of diverse exigencies rather than the command and control from a single center in sovereign nation-states. Intellectual competence and collegiality replace the prerogatives of command and control. By implication, Tocqueville's "new science of politics for a new age" requires a reawakening of sympathetic religious beliefs, enhanced standards of moral judgment, and diverse patterns of governance, historical traditions, and ecological exigencies. Given the great ecological diversity in which people live their lives, civic enlightenment requires citizens to achieve sufficient intellectual competence to draw upon the competence of others to take advantage of a variety of opportunities that are available as citizens acquire knowledgeable grounds to work with colleagues in self-governing societies.

When citizens are sovereign, political scientists confront the task of civic education reaching toward knowledgeable enlightenment and working collegiality in shared communities of sympathy and understanding. This is our intellectual challenge in political science as we extend patterns of association and political authority from the local to the global in the next millennium. What we call *public administration* has become *public entrepreneurship*. Recourse to covenants of mutual understanding in constituting enduring collective endeavors capable of achieving complementary working relationships is the way of constituting federal systems of governance that reach out to larger communities of relationships. A world of sovereign peoples will be vastly different than a world of sovereign, mutually exclusive, nation-states.

We who identify ourselves as political scientists are also required to recognize that other disciplines in the social sciences and humanities are necessary complements of what is manifest in human societies. As Harold Lasswell and Abraham Kaplan have indicated, ". . . all of the social sciences have an identical subject matter, but they adopt toward this subject matter varying observational standpoints (frames of reference) leading to different sets of problems."[15]

The exercise of reflection and choice, both in constituting societies and in gaining enlightenment about self-governing potentials, draws upon and contributes to the emergence of human civilization. Lasswell and Kaplan's identical subject matter of the social sciences becomes Tocqueville's concern about feelings, sentiments, mores, ideas, movements, and laws among self-governing peoples, and Hamilton's concern for good government by reflection and choice in contrast to accident and force.

The concept of sovereign nation-states in a world of mutually exclusive nation-states is a fiction that justifies who is entitled to exercise command and control over others in which individuals as persons become subjects rather than citizens. It is always individuals in human societies who think, act, and achieve whatever it is that humans are able to accomplish. Life is a drama conducted on a stage of rule-ordered relationships.

We have much to learn and to extend our understanding of what it means to become citizen-sovereigns in the "great democratic revolution . . . going on among us." But, citizen-sovereigns run the risk of failure when acting on erroneous concepts, grand illusions, and lack of comprehension. Critical scrutiny is necessary to reflection and choice.[16] A new political science has an essential place for the lives of citizen-sovereigns in a new age.

Notes

This chapter is a revised version of Vincent Ostrom, "Citizen-Sovereigns: The Source of Contestability, the Rule of Law, and the Conduct of Public Entrepreneurship," *PS: Political Science & Politics* 39, no. 1 (January 2006): 13–17. Reprinted with the permission of Cambridge University Press.

1. Alexis de Tocqueville, *Democracy in America*, 2 vols., ed. Phillips Bradley (New York: Alfred A. Knopf, [1835–1840] 1945), 1: xix, xxi.

2. Alexander Hamilton, John Jay, and James Madison, *The Federalist*, ed. Edward M. Earle (New York: Modern Library, [1788] n.d.), 3.

3. Adam Smith, *The Theory of Moral Sentiments* (Indianapolis, IN: Liberty, [1759] n.d.).

4. David Hume, *Hume's Moral and Political Philosophy*, ed. Henry D. Aiken (New York: Hafner, 1948).

5. Alexis de Tocqueville, *The Old Regime and the [French] Revolution*, trans. Stuart Gilbert (Garden City, NY: Doubleday, Anchor Books, [1856] 1955).

6. See Barbara Allen, *Tocqueville, Covenant, and the Democratic Revolution: Harmonizing Earth with Heaven* (Lanham, MD: Lexington Books, 2005); Sheldon Gellar, *Democracy in Senegal: Tocquevillian Analytics in Africa* (New York: Palgrave Macmillan, 2005); Alexander Obolonsky, *The Drama of Russian Political History: System against Individuality* (College Station: Texas A&M University Press, 2003); Amos Sawyer, *Beyond Plunder: Toward Democratic Governance in Liberia* (Boulder, CO: Lynne Rienner, 2005); and Sujai Shivakumar, *The Constitution of Development: Crafting Capabilities for Self-Governance* (New York: Palgrave Macmillan, 2005).

7. Tocqueville, *Democracy in America*, 1: 7.

8. Tocqueville, *Democracy in America*, 1: 57–58.

9. John C. Peppin, "Municipal Home Rule in California," *California Law Review* 30, no. 1 (November 1941): 1–45. Peppin gives an extensive account of "the principle of legislative supremacy" as an opportunity for delivering the government of cities and other local subdivisions into the hands of political spoilsmen in the state legislature.

10. Moisei Ostrogorski, *Democracy and the Organization of Political Parties*, 2 vols., edited and abridged by S. M. Lipset (Garden City, NY: Doubleday, Anchor Books, [1902] 1964).

11. Woodrow Wilson, *Congressional Government: A Study in American Politics* (New York: Meridian, [1885] 1956), 30.

12. Wilson, *Congressional Government*, 23.

13. Tocqueville, *Democracy in America*, 2: 296.

14. Harold Berman, *Law and Revolution: The Formation of the Western Legal Tradition* (Cambridge, MA: Harvard University Press, 1983).

15. Harold Lasswell and Abraham Kaplan, *Power and Society: A Framework for Political Inquiry* (New Haven, CT: Yale University Press, 1950), 215.

16. Jared Diamond, *Collapse: How Societies Choose to Fail or Succeed* (New York: Viking Press, 2005); Jane Jacobs, *Dark Age Ahead* (Toronto: Vintage Canada, 2004).

PART I

Tocquevillian Analytics

3

Tocquevillian Analytics and the Global Democratic Revolution

Sheldon Gellar

Most social scientists regard Tocqueville as a brilliant commentator on American political institutions and culture who captured the essence of American democracy. Others who know his writings on France, England, Ireland, Germany, and Switzerland appreciate his interdisciplinary talents in history, sociology, comparative politics, and normative political theory. They see *Democracy in America* as an effort to understand the processes of democratization and its future in the Western world. Although social scientists and democratic theorists often refer to Tocqueville's work in their analyses of American and European societies, they rarely apply his methodology and insights to the development of democracy elsewhere.[1]

The Democratic Revolution evoked by Tocqueville in *Democracy in America* has spread beyond the borders of North America and Western Europe and is evolving into a Global Democratic Revolution. This chapter argues that Tocquevillian analytics, as reflected in his multilayered concept of democracy, specific modes of analysis, and the issues and concerns he raised, is particularly relevant today for understanding the movement toward democracy in Eastern Europe and the developing world as well as the current state of democracy in the United States and Western Europe.[2] The central questions raised by Tocqueville in his studies of America, France, and other European countries are just as crucial for understanding the course of the Global Democratic Revolution taking place in Latin America, Africa, Asia, and the Middle East. How does the weight of the past, that is, what Tocqueville called the "point of departure," affect the evolution of new political institutions and political behavior? What are the

33

relationships between social equality, freedom, and democracy? To what extent does centralization destroy the capacity for local initiative and self-governance? What conditions are needed to nurture the flourishing of self-governing communities? What safeguards are needed to preserve freedom and to prevent democracies from regressing into dictatorships?

Tocqueville's questions and methodology can help us understand how and why the modern Democratic Revolution that began with the American and French Revolutions is now spreading all over the world and confirms that democracy is not just for Western nations or dependent upon westernization. His approach also helps explain why democracy has had many problems in taking hold in many parts of the world and why democracy there will not be carbon-copy replicas of Western-style democracies. Tocquevillian analytics also helps explain why and how democratic gains can be reversed under certain conditions, and liberty extinguished.

Tocqueville's Definitions and Concepts of Democracy

Tocqueville himself never provided a precise and consistent definition of democracy.[3] Its meaning depended upon the context in which he wrote. Tocqueville made distinctions between democracy as a type of society and democracy as a type of political system. As a society, democracy was based on the principle of equality; as a political system, democracy was based on the principles of popular sovereignty. The ideal democracy also required liberty. Democracy without liberty led to tyranny.

Like the liberal French *Doctrinaires* who influenced his thinking, Tocqueville often employed the term "democracy" when discussing the leveling equalitarian tendencies in society.[4] Tocqueville used democracy to refer to equality of social conditions when analyzing the social state of societies undergoing the transition from aristocratic to democratic political orders. Democracy did not mean a society where all men were necessarily equal in power and wealth but a society where there were no more castes, fixed classes, privileges, and special and exclusive rights based on birth as was the case in aristocratic societies.[5]

Tocqueville also referred to democracy as a political system based on popular sovereignty.[6] Equality was a prerequisite for popular sovereignty. Social equality implied the capacity of all individuals regardless of birth to participate in public affairs and logically led to demands for popular sovereignty. Universal suffrage enabled all to vote and affirmed their right to choose their lawmakers and have a voice in making the law. For

Tocqueville, democracy as a political system was not an end in itself but a necessary condition and instrument for promoting self-governing communities and the active participation of citizens in the management of public affairs.

Although Tocqueville saw democracy as desirable and inevitable, he had no illusions that democracy would necessarily lead to an ideal society and political system. Social equality and popular sovereignty could lead to democratic despotism when the people accepted excessive concentration of power in the hands of a single person, political institution, bureaucratic administration, or when the "tyranny of the majority" discarded the rights of the minority.[7]

Equality, popular sovereignty, and despotism could easily coexist since equality of conditions was likely to atomize society, weaken social solidarity, and leave individuals dependent upon a highly centralized state. Moreover, popular sovereignty and universal suffrage provided no guarantees that the people would not elect a despot. Even worse, elections and plebiscites could be used to legitimize the authority of despots. For Tocqueville, democratic despotism had the nefarious effects of fostering the destruction of solidarity among individuals, a decline in national morality, materialism, and widespread corruption.

In Tocqueville's hierarchy of values, liberty/freedom took precedence over equality and was the antidote to despotism.[8] Individual political and civil liberties, religious freedom, the freedom to form autonomous voluntary associations, and the rights of communities to run their own affairs were all critical elements of viable democratic societies and bulwarks against tyranny. These traits ensured the constitution of liberal democracies. Their absence would lead to democratic despotism or what is now called illiberal democracies.[9]

When Tocqueville wrote *Democracy in America*, America was the only modern democracy in the world. Since then, democracy has been consolidated throughout Europe and much of the Western world and spread to the non-Western world. In *The Third Wave: Democratization in the Late Twentieth Century*, which appeared 150 years after the publication of the second volume of *Democracy in America* in 1840, Samuel P. Huntington credited Tocqueville for having predicted the global trend toward democracy as it began.[10]

While Huntington and Tocqueville both maintained that democracy was the wave of the future and vulnerable to setbacks and reversals, especially in countries where democracy and democratic mores had not been firmly entrenched, they presented different definitions and approaches toward the study of democracy. With his emphasis on liberty, equality, popular sovereignty, and self-governance as the foundations of democracy, Tocqueville offered a broader vision of democracy than Huntington, Schumpeter, and other contemporary analysts who see democracy as based primarily and more narrowly on universal suffrage, periodic elections, and multiparty competition.[11] Following Schumpeter, Huntington defined political systems as democratic "to the extent that its most powerful decision-makers are selected through fair, honest, and periodic elections in which candidates freely compete for votes and in which virtually all the adult population is eligible to vote."[12]

Though Tocqueville and Huntington both regarded popular sovereignty as expressed through universal suffrage to be an essential feature of democratic regimes, they differed sharply as to what that meant and how it was to be applied. For Huntington, popular sovereignty gave the people the right to choose and oust rulers through the ballot box and operated primarily at the *national* level when citizens elected *national* political elites to govern them. The national elites chosen by the electorate then used the state apparatus to rule over the people in the name of the people.

Tocqueville visualized popular sovereignty quite differently. He saw popular sovereignty as sovereignty directly exercised by and with the people through their participation in politics and self-governing institutions at all levels of society, not just in national elections.[13] Tocqueville observed that in America the body of the people themselves made the laws or chose duly elected representatives to act in their name under their close and immediate supervision. In America, the people governed themselves.[14]

Tocqueville also had a radically different conception of the state and the role of the state in a democratic order[15] than Huntington, who accepted the Hobbesian concept of the state that gave the state a monopoly over political authority and unlimited and indivisible authority over those living in a given territory, that is, the nation-state. Tocqueville rejected the idea that political authority needed to be monopolized by the state. For Tocqueville, such concentration of power was detrimental to the new democratic order and could easily lead to tyranny.

Following in the Hobbesian tradition, Huntington saw politics as unrelenting competition and advocated a strong state to ensure order and political stability. Weak central governments were bad governments. Hence, whatever strengthened central government institutions was good for the country and the public interest.[16] Huntington argued that democracy, especially in the developing nations, had to be built from the top down by national elites in charge of a strong state that could preserve order and effectively deal with "primordial" claims.

In his *Democracy in America*, Tocqueville used the American example to demonstrate that a decentralized form of the state was possible in a democratic order.[17] In America, Tocqueville discovered that the absence of administrative centralization and the existence of multiple and diffuse sources of political authority permitted citizens to participate directly in the management of public affairs to solve their problems.

The kind of ideal democracy envisioned by Tocqueville promoted self-government and the active participation of citizens in local government. People learned how to be self-governing within the framework of family, neighborhood, village, and other community-based institutions. For Tocqueville, these institutions needed to enjoy a certain degree of autonomy from the state in order to flourish. Free self-governing institutions and associations provided a bulwark against state tyranny. Huntington, on the other hand, regarded subnational group identities and communities based on religion, ethnicity, and kinship as potential dangers to political stability and obstacles to political modernization.

Huntington justified using a minimal and procedural definition of democracy based on free, fair, and open elections because it made it easier to classify political systems. Asserting that broader normative definitions of democracy may muddy the waters, he dismissed them out of hand:

> To some people . . . 'true democracy' means *liberté, égalité, fraternité*, effective citizen control over policy, responsible government, honesty and openness in politics, informed and rational deliberation, equal participation and power and various other civic virtues. These are, for the most part, good things and people can, if they wish, define democracy in these terms. Doing so, however, raises all the problems that come up with the definitions of democracy by source or by purpose. Fuzzy norms do not yield good analysis. Elections open free and fair are the essence of democracy, the inescapable sine qua non.[18]

Unlike Tocqueville, Huntington had little to say about equality in discussing democracy.[19] His analysis was elite-centered and focused on how elites come to power and maintain it. Huntington defines democracy primarily as a political system that gives the people a voice in the circulation of elites rather than a mechanism for promoting self-governance and preserving liberty. His emphasis on the primacy of centralized political institutions and national elites in politics also leaves little room for the people to manage their own affairs.

For Tocqueville, the "democratic revolution" marked the transformation of aristocratic orders based on birth and privilege into societies where political, social, and legal equality prevailed. Tocqueville regarded human equality as both a fact and article of faith that implied that all human beings had the capacity for self-government regardless of their social status at birth.

Tocqueville insisted on liberty as essential to an authentic democracy and the most important safeguard against tyranny. For Tocqueville, the remedy to the flaws of democracy was more liberty rather than more order. In a vibrant democracy, individuals would use their liberties to form associations to solve their common problems, establish a free press to debate public policy, and defend the prerogatives of local government vis-à-vis the state.

As we shall see, Tocquevillian analytics requires going well beyond Huntington's top-down approach to the analysis of democratization processes focusing on national elites, central government, elections, and the nation-state. Tocquevillian analytics looks at history, the physical environment, institutions and mores of diverse societies, their capacity for self-governance, and the extent to which they have made the transition from aristocratic to democratic political orders.

Brilliantly applied in *Democracy in America, The Old Regime and the Revolution*, and other works, Tocquevillian analytics provides a more powerful and comprehensive tool for understanding the processes of democratization and constitution of order in postcolonial and postcommunist societies than the concepts used by Huntington and others like him pursuing similar lines of analysis.

Two Models of Democracy: America and France

Tocqueville presented two contrasting models of democracy: one based on the American experience, the other on the French experience.[20] Unlike France, which had reverted to despotism and monarchy after the French Revolution, America had remained politically stable, prosperous, and free since the establishment of the Republic. Tocqueville wanted to know why. Although writing about America, he was addressing his fellow Frenchmen. He wanted them to absorb the lessons to be learned from the American experience.

Tocqueville saw America as a democratic self-governing society built from the bottom up rather than a state-governed society built from the top down as was the case in France.[21] The absence of a centralized form of administration in America and the manner in which Americans participated and succeeded in managing their own affairs contrasted with the loss of local initiatives and liberties that he found in France's highly centralized political system both before and after the French Revolution. In America, political and economic power was dispersed throughout the country. In France, political and economic power was concentrated in Paris.

The American model stressed freedom for the individual and autonomy for local communities and associations. The French model stressed the need for a strong unitary system of government and was wary of autonomous intermediary institutions or corporate bodies standing between the individual and the state. The American model accepted diversity and granted local, state, and federal government broad powers in their respective jurisdictions and voluntary associations freedom to pursue their own affairs with little government intervention. Unlike the American federal system, the French model based on a unitary state encouraged a uniformity of rules and laws that failed to consider local and regional differences, traditions, and environmental conditions and sought to highly regulate associational life.

Under the French model, popular sovereignty was incarnated in the central government that alone had the authority to speak in the name of the people. In the American model, popular sovereignty was exercised at all levels of government by the people through their participation in public affairs.

Most American social scientists are more familiar with *Democracy in America* than they are with *The Old Regime and the Revolution, Recollections,* and other works of Tocqueville. The American model places more emphasis on freedom of religion, association, and expression; local government; elected judges; and the absence of aristocratic class structures and centralized administration as contributing factors to the establishment and consolidation of liberal democracy. In contrast with his work on America, Tocqueville's writings on France focus more on the obstacles to liberal democracy such as a highly centralized administration, state tutelage over local government and associational life, restrictions on associational life and freedom of the press, the people's lack of experience and commitment to freedom, and the harm done by a privileged aristocracy under the *Ancien Régime* and a predatory middle class using its control over the state to enrich themselves under the July Monarchy.

Tocquevillian analytics relies as much on the insights, concepts, and methodology used by Tocqueville to study France and other Western European countries as those found in *Democracy in America*. In fact, most of the political and social orders in Latin America, Africa, the Middle East, and Asia, whether colonized or not, were closer to and had more in common with Tocqueville's France than with America.

While stressing the exceptionalism of the American experience with its relatively egalitarian social structures and absence of aristocratic traditions, Tocqueville was, of course, aware that his analysis of America's egalitarian social structures applied only to white America. In a long discourse on America's three races, he deplored the institution of slavery and racism and predicted the demise of the Native Americans.[22] Although an enthusiastic advocate of the principles underlying the American political system, he was highly critical of the rampant materialism throughout the society and evoked the danger of a new industrial aristocracy based on concentration of wealth.[23] He took an even more critical view of America in the 1840s and 1850s.[24]

Though Tocqueville saw America as the vanguard of democracy and predicted that Europe was moving toward democracy, he argued that France should not slavishly copy America's institutions. Tocqueville insisted that democratic regimes in France and elsewhere in Europe would not become exact replicas of American democracy because of significant historical, political, social, religious, cultural, and ecological differences. The same point is, of course, equally valid for the evolution of democracy outside of America and Western Europe.

Tocqueville's Comparative Historical Perspective

Although a political treatise on America, *Democracy in America* also reflected a strong historical comparative perspective with its descriptions of the development of institutions and mores in colonial America, the evolution of social equality over the centuries in France, and its frequent references to and comparisons with France.

Tocqueville asserted that the point of departure for understanding the factors affecting the transformation of contemporary societies began with a look at their origins:

> If we could go right back to the elements of societies and examine the very first records of histories, I have no doubt that we should there find

the first cause of their prejudices, habits, domineering passions and all that comes to be called the national character. We should there be able to discover the explanation of customs which now seem contrary to the prevailing norms, or laws which seem opposed to recognized principles, and of incoherent opinions still found here and there in society that hang like broken chains still occasionally dangling from the ceiling of an old building but carrying nothing.[25]

Tocqueville was particularly concerned with tracing the transition from aristocratic to democratic orders, that is, the march toward equality, the conditions leading to and supportive of liberal democracies, and the impact of state centralization on local liberties and initiative. Tocqueville realized that societies did not undergo massive political and social changes overnight. Tocqueville knew better than to start his study of democracy in America with the American Revolution. He went back to the beginning of European colonization of North America. To understand the march toward democracy in France, he did not begin with the period immediately leading up to the French Revolution. He went back seven hundred years in French history and traced the decline of the noble and the rise of the commoner.

Tocqueville's frequent references to differences between America and France in a book that was addressed primarily to Frenchmen followed his precept that "the mind becomes clear only by comparison."[26] As Raymond Aron pointed out, Tocqueville was a comparative sociologist par excellence in comparing types of societies belonging to the same species and identifying and comparing characteristics of modern democratic societies.[27] For example, Tocqueville compared the relative openness and adaptability of the aristocracy in England with the oppressive and predatory nature of the aristocracy in Ireland and differences in status, mores, and economic conditions of the peasantry and working classes in England, France, and Ireland.[28]

He also sought to examine and to understand the relationships between religion, politics, and social structures in different settings. He looked at the impact of religious institutions on society, noting that the established Anglican church in England was losing its popularity because it was aligned with privilege, that the Catholic Church had been discredited in France because of its alliance with the *ancien régime*, and that in Ireland, the Catholic Church retained the loyalty of the peasantry because its priests remained close to the people and shared their poverty.

Tocqueville did more than read political theories, academic books, histories, articles, memoirs, and travel accounts to learn about the different societies he was analyzing. He also did interviews and fieldwork when he could and spent some time traveling in most of the countries—America, England, Ireland, Switzerland, and Algeria—that he wrote about at any length. After making extensive notes for a proposed book on India, he decided to cancel the project after realizing that he would be unable to travel to that country.[29]

In his day, Tocqueville did not have much to say about the future of democracy in the non-Western world. With democracy not yet established in Europe, one could not expect Tocqueville to discuss the future of democracy in the non-Western world. However, when he did look at areas like Algeria and India that had come under European rule, Tocqueville demonstrated a keen interest in their political institutions, social structures, and religious beliefs and in the administrative institutions that enabled France and England to govern their colonies.

Like most nineteenth-century European thinkers, Tocqueville asserted that European civilization was more advanced than indigenous civilizations in the Americas, Africa, and Asia. However, as a believer in human equality, he did not accept that the peoples of these areas were innately inferior to Europeans. His justification for France's colonization of Algeria was based more on the need to provide the French with a project that would turn their attention away from the materialism that was rampant in France and to prevent England from extending its colonial empire to North Africa than to bring civilization and progress to backward peoples, which was the general rationale underlying European colonialism.[30]

To better understand Algeria and its people, Tocqueville visited Algeria twice in the 1840s and studied the history, customs, and mores of its Kabyle and Arab populations, differences in political and social organization, and how these differences might affect their relationships with the French.[31] Today, it would be difficult to defend Tocqueville's embrace of the French conquest and colonization of Algeria, which was characterized by campaigns of massive brutality, terror, and destruction of its indigenous Muslim populations. Although a supporter of colonization, Tocqueville himself was prophetic in seeing the outcome of a colonial system based on oppression and suppression as eventually leading to a bitter struggle between the French and the indigenous Algerian populations.[32]

An ardent abolitionist, Tocqueville called for ending slavery in Senegal and in France's West Indian colonies. As a deputy, he headed a committee looking into the abolition of slavery and wrote a report comparing French and British plans to end slavery.[33] Tocqueville knew about Liberia, which had been established in 1820 by the American Colonization Society that had sent groups of freed American slaves to settle there.[34] He noted with some irony that the former black slaves had learned to be free in America where they had been slaves and had succeeded in transplanting America's free institutions (e.g., representative government, the legal system, Christian churches, and newspapers) to Africa.

Tocqueville was puzzled by the ease with which England was able to conquer and rule the vast Indian subcontinent with its population of one hundred million people with only a few thousand troops, while France had met great resistance in its efforts to conquer Algeria.[35] Tocqueville found his answer in India's Hindu beliefs, caste system, and the absence of centralized administration. The tolerance and passivity of Hindu religion coupled with the absence of a strong central government explained India's vulnerability and limited resistance to foreign conquest. The collapse of central government in India was not accompanied by a similar collapse of local government that remained dominated by the upper castes under a wide variety of foreign rulers.

Tocqueville looked at religion from a comparative perspective. His experiences in America reinforced his belief that the spirit of religion and religious values reinforced democratic politics and that Christianity had done much to spread the idea of equality by preaching the inherent equality of all before God. On the other hand, looking at the Ottoman Caliphate in his time, he had little confidence in Islam's potential for fostering social equality and democracy. He asserted that Islam was doomed to decline in a democratic era because it was too detailed in its prescriptions and rules that required enforcement by a theocratic state.[36]

While Marx and later modernization theorists saw religion as fading in importance with the advance of science, political democracy, and economic development, Tocqueville saw religious faith as an inherent part of human nature. Religion would survive in democratic times because religious beliefs were deeply rooted in the heart of man, especially the common man.

Unlike his contemporary Karl Marx, who used the term "feudal" rather than "aristocratic" to describe preindustrial societies, advocated the smashing of feudal structures, values, customs, and religion, and stressed class conflict as the motor of change, Tocqueville sought a peaceful and orderly transition from aristocratic to democratic societies, eschewed class conflict, and did not regard all institutions and values in non-Western societies as backward and to be swept away.[37]

Tocqueville used examples drawn from all parts of the world to make his points. For example, he noted that Mexico's efforts to copy the Ameri-

can federal system were doomed to fail because of differences in sociological conditions and political traditions[38] and that imperial China in his
day was almost an ideal type of extreme centralization that explained that
country's lack of dynamism.[39] He also saw the rise of Russia as another
potential great power but operating under very different political principles from those prevailing in America.[40]

Components of Tocquevillian Analytics

In *Democracy in America*, Tocqueville identified mores (manners and customs, habits of the heart and mind); laws (institutional arrangements); and
environmental factors (geography, topography, climate) as the three main
factors shaping American democracy. The interrelationships between culture, institutional arrangements, and environmental factors constitute the
heart of Tocquevillian analytics as a methodology. However, Tocquevillian analytics also subsumes and highlights other concepts and variables
based on his analyses of France, England, Ireland, and other European
countries.

The following components can be regarded as a checklist of elements
for conducting a comprehensive Tocquevillian analysis:[41]

1. *The impact of the physical environment in shaping political, economic,
and social structures and relationships.*[42] Tocqueville was acutely aware of the
importance of physical environment in shaping the organization of societies. America's abundant natural resources and the availability of land facilitated the development of equalitarian social structures and a high degree of
mobility. The physical environment also had a major impact in shaping the
development of political institutions and relationships. In Africa, the flat
savannah country facilitated transportation and trade in the West Sudan,
the rise of large-scale empires, and the spread of Islam, while societies in
the dense tropical forest zones where communication was more difficult
generally were more egalitarian, smaller in size, and more self-sufficient.
Climate and topography have affected the organization of societies all over
the world. High mountains, for example, have provided some protection
against foreign conquest from Switzerland to Afghanistan.

2. *The importance of history in shaping national character and institutions.*[43] To understand a society's character, Tocqueville argued that one
needed to go back to its origins. Because Tocqueville did not concentrate
only on looking at national elites and national-level institutions, he was
able to see the great variety of institutions and mores within countries and

their evolution. Tocqueville did not see history as deterministic. Although influenced by history, individuals, peoples, and nations had choices in determining their historical paths. In Asia, history provides clues concerning the origins of cultural differences between China, Korea, and Japan. In Africa, precolonial history, political institutions, and social structures still affect African attitudes toward government and other ethnic groups and communities and institutional arrangements in the postcolonial era. Differences in colonial regimes (e.g., French, British, Belgian, Spanish, German, Portuguese, and Dutch) and the degree of colonial oppression and repression of indigenous institutions have played an important role in shaping national political institutions and attitudes of Asians, Latin Americans, and Africans toward government after independence. It would be difficult to understand contemporary postcolonial societies without having some knowledge and understanding of the precolonial mores of their indigenous populations, colonial class and state structures, and the evolution of religious institutions. It would also be difficult to fully understand societies in postcommunist countries without going back to the precommunist period.

3. *The importance of laws, especially property rights and inheritance laws in shaping political, economic, and social structures.* Tocqueville noted that the aristocratic order in Europe was based on land and property rights. Property-rights systems in America favored more egalitarian distribution of land than the primogeniture system prevailing in Europe. The *latifundia* system introduced under Spanish colonial rule still remains one of the main obstacles to democratization in Latin America in countries like Guatemala. During the nineteenth century, a "latifundia" system dominated by English aristocrats forced Irish peasants off the land and led to mass starvation and mass emigration of landless peasants to America. Historically, laws defining slaves as property of their owners held back the development of democracy in much of the world. Property rights and inheritance laws still hold women back in many societies.

Social-Cultural Components

1. *The degree of social equality in society and the extent to which there is movement toward greater equality.* Tocquevillian analytics examines the state of social equality within a given society and its influence on political institutions, behavior, and mores. Tocqueville was particularly interested in tracing the transformation of aristocratic societies into egalitarian soci-

eties. Although Tocqueville generally used national societies as the unit of analysis, he also looked at regional and local differences concerning the state of equality within larger national societies. The non-Western world had a wide range of societies ranging from highly egalitarian to highly aristocratic societies. Caste and slavery were important elements in many parts of the world. Different types of colonial regimes affected the relative degree of equality, some weakening and some strengthening precolonial forms of inequality. Colonial regimes also introduced new forms of inequality based on racial criteria and the creation of a new political elite based on knowledge of the language and institutions of the colonizer. The degree of democratization is limited in societies where caste, slavery, and gender inequality are present or prevalent. In India, Mahatma Gandhi fought the caste system and championed the rights of the Untouchables, thus contributing to the advance of democracy in that country. Hitler's racist ideology, which excluded Jews as human beings, regarded Slavs as destined to serve the Aryans and non-Aryans as inferior, provided the foundations for one of history's most autocratic regimes.

2. *The importance of mores, customs, and values (culture) in shaping political institutions and political behavior.*[44] Tocqueville was acutely aware of the importance of moral values and norms determining social status and people's behavior toward each other in society. Mores, customs, and norms vary widely throughout the world, affecting attitudes toward authority, strangers, gender, and different age groups in society. Traditional concepts such as caste, honor, loyalty, justice, clientship, and hospitality continue to affect political behavior and expectations concerning political institutions and other groups and communities. In many parts of the non-Western world, deference to elders and those in authority remains an important value.

3. *The central role of religion and religious institutions in shaping political attitudes, institutions, and relationships.* Tocqueville saw Christianity as a belief system proclaiming the equality of man before God and supportive of egalitarian trends. In America, religion reinforced democratic principles; in France, the prerevolutionary Catholic Church, by aligning itself with the old regime, set off a reaction against the church during the French Revolution. Today, most African societies remain profoundly religious. Different forms of traditional religions, Islam, and Christianity continue to deeply affect the values and behavior of Africans. Tocquevillian analytics distinguishes between the spirit of religion and religion as an institution. The Spirit of Religion refers to religious values like human equality, tolerance, quest for peace or their polar opposite, the elect as belonging to the only true religion, intolerance of other religions, and the obligation

to impose one's religion on others by proselytizing or forced conversion. Religion as an institution refers to concrete organizations like the Catholic Church, which has its own rules for membership, governance, and participation. Unlike Marxists and modernization theorists, Tocqueville did not see religion as the opium of the masses or atavistic and destined to decline with the spread of a scientific worldview. Although the influence of religion in Europe has been declining since the French Revolution, religion still plays a major role in the United States, Latin America, the Middle East, and Asia.

4. *The crucial role of language as an instrument for promoting mutual understanding and group identity.* Tocqueville was highly sensitive to the importance of language in defining group identity. He described how English became the dominant language in America and contributed to forming a distinctly American identity among different nationalities. He also pointed to differences in the use of language in aristocratic and egalitarian societies. Language forms one of the most important foundations of group identity. Ethnic identity was usually based on the speaking of a particular language. Because of the presence of hundreds of different languages in Africa, many Africans were multilingual and often used a common lingua franca to communicate with strangers. Under colonial rule, Western education and mastery of the language of the colonizer gave individuals in Africa, Asia, and the Middle East higher political and social status. With the spread of Islam, literacy in Arabic also became an important component of group identity for Muslims throughout the world.

Political Components

1. *The importance of popular sovereignty and constitutional choice in the design of political institutions and the extent to which rules and laws after being prescribed are invoked, applied, and enforced.* Tocqueville maintained that popular sovereignty and the ability of people to make their own laws through constitutional choice were key elements in modern political systems. Tocqueville's notion of popular sovereignty focused on self-governance and participation of the people in managing public affairs rather than state sovereignty exercised by elected national elites ruling in the name of the people. He also noted that formal rules providing for democratic institutions and liberties would not necessarily be applied by rulers nor invoked by people in societies without liberal democratic traditions. Some precolonial societies in the non-Western world exercised a

certain degree of constitutional choice in organizing their political orders. In Africa, for example, these political orders were based on custom or charters elaborated by representatives of different groups in society. Under colonialism, colonized societies lacked the freedom to establish their own political order. At independence, many leaders adopted liberal Western constitutions based on European models without consulting the people. After independence, one-party states, military regimes, and personal dictatorships violated political and civil rights guaranteed by their country's constitution and gave their people little say in making the laws and rules governing their lives.

2. *The identification of the concentration of power in centralized governments and bureaucracies as restricting freedom and initiative and leading to despotism and dependency.* Tocqueville regarded concentration of power in the hands of a single person, political institution, or bureaucracy as an obstacle to liberal democracy. Many precolonial African societies in Africa lived under highly centralized monarchies, particularly during the heyday of the slave trade. Colonial regimes throughout the world established highly centralized autocratic state structures. The indigenous inheritance elites who took power after independence often maintained or reinforced these state institutions. Concentration of power and overcentralization has subverted democracy in Latin America, many of the newly independent nations, and more recently in postcommunist societies. Recent efforts by the Bush administration to concentrate more power in the hands of the president are perceived by some observers as constituting a threat to American democracy.

3. *The importance of local liberties and the constitution of self-governing communities as vital to democracy.* Tocqueville asserted that local liberties gave communities the right to manage their own affairs and reinforced their taste for liberty. In highly centralized regimes, decentralization provided a vehicle for local communities to take more initiative and have a greater voice in public affairs. Many societies in precolonial Africa were self-governing communities that fiercely defended their independence. The imposition of colonial rule was often accompanied by the demise of local liberties. During decolonization and after independence, political elites placed more emphasis on gaining control of national-level institutions rather than seeking to reestablish local liberties and decentralized democratic governance. However, local liberties did not necessarily ensure more democratic norms of governance. Localities dominated by aristocratic elites, rural notables, and warlords also could demand and fight for local liberties from central government without establishing democratic institutions. In Asia, local war-

lords historically sought greater freedom from centralizing states, while in India the upper castes dominated local government.

4. *The crucial role of political and civil liberties, especially freedom of association and the press as bulwarks against tyranny.* Tocqueville believed that freedom of association and freedom of the press were more important than holding free and periodic elections in preserving freedom and protecting minorities against the tyranny of the majority. He also believed that the "art of association" was the key to creating stable, self-governing communities in the democratic era. Most colonial regimes sharply restricted freedom of association, freedom of the press, and civil liberties. In many colonies, indigenous populations were subject to forced labor, forbidden to organize political parties and trade unions, or to publish independent newspapers. In much of the developing world, military regimes and one-party states restricted political and civil rights and placed local government and civil, economic, and cultural associations under the tutelage of the state or the dominant party. Wherever allowed, freedom of association and the press permitted people to organize and criticize the governments and enabled them to put pressure for greater democratization. For example, the Solidarity Movement, spearheaded by an autonomous trade union in postwar Communist Poland, led the drive toward democratization in that country.

5. *An empirical approach to the study of societies that rejected the application of abstract political theories and philosophies.* Tocqueville attacked the eighteenth-century *philosophes* and revolutionaries for creating "an imaginary ideal society in which all was simple, uniform, coherent, equitable and rational."[45] He recognized that the best of societies has its flaws and weaknesses. Tocqueville did not believe that any one model of democracy could be applied universally and made it clear that the triumph of democracy would depend upon the application of principles rather than the export of models of democracy. While he proclaimed that America was the most advanced of democracies, Tocqueville insisted that the American model with its federal institutions could not be easily adopted in Europe.

Tocqueville respected the great diversity of humanity and the need for different societies to find viable institutions that incorporated old and new mores, values, and customs in such a way as to make the best of what he considered the universal movement toward democracy. Tocqueville was far from being a determinist. As he acknowledged in his *Recollections*:

When I see the modern world in greater detail, when I consider the prodigious diversity found there, not just in the laws but in the principles of the laws and the different forms that property has taken. . . . I am tempted to the belief that what are called necessary institutions are only institutions to which one is accustomed, and that in matters of social constitution the field of possibilities is much wider than people living within each society imagine.[46]

Tocqueville's words remind us that throughout the world, the face and pace of democracy will vary as different societies experiment with mixes of old and new political institutions that reflect diverse traditions, value systems, and physical environments.

Although more demanding than most approaches to the study of democracy in the non-Western world, Tocquevillian analytics provides a more accurate and comprehensive portrait of societies undergoing processes of democratization and the state of societies with long democratic traditions than more narrow approaches to the study of democracy focused primarily on elections, multiparty competition, and national elites.

Notes

1. For some of the rare examples of scholars systematically using Tocqueville to understand democracy in the non-Western world, see Vincent Ostrom, *The Meaning of Democracy and the Vulnerability of Democracies: A Response to Tocqueville's Challenge* (Ann Arbor: University of Michigan Press, 1997); Carlos A. Forment, *Democracy in Latin America, 1760–1900* (Chicago: University of Chicago Press, 2003); Sombat Chantornvong, "Tocqueville's *Democracy in America* and the Third World," in *Rethinking Institutional Analysis and Development: Issues, Alternatives, and Choices*, ed. Vincent Ostrom, David Feeny, and Hartmut Picht (San Francisco, CA: ICS Press, 1988), 69–99; and Sheldon Gellar, *Democracy in Senegal: Tocquevillian Analytics in Africa* (New York: Palgrave Macmillan, 2005).

2. The term "Tocquevillian analytics" was first coined by Vincent Ostrom, who saw Tocqueville as a political theorist using an insightful configurative analytical approach to understand and explain how democracy in America evolved and operated by examining its constitutive components and how these shaped democracy. See *The Meaning of American Federalism: Constituting a Self-Governing Society* (San Francisco, CA: ICS Press, 1994), 11–20; and *Meaning of Democracy*, 12–18. While interest in Tocqueville revived in the United States during the 1950s and 1960s among political theorists of democracy, comparative politics as a subdiscipline of political science showed little interest in Tocqueville's comparative methodology. For example, an often-cited review of developments in and contributions to comparative politics methodology during this era failed to mention Tocqueville. See Ralph Braibanti, "Comparative Political Analytics Reconsidered,"

Journal of Politics 30, no. 1 (1968): 25–65. Even today, most American political scientists consider Tocqueville primarily as a political philosopher or theorist of American democracy.

3. For a detailed discussion of how Tocqueville wrestled with the fact that he could not come up with a clear-cut definition of democracy, see James T. Schleifer, *The Making of Tocqueville's Democracy in America*, 2nd ed. (Indianapolis, IN: Liberty Fund, 2000), 325–39.

4. For the influence of the French *Doctrinaires* led by Guizot, Royer-Collard, and other French liberal thinkers of the 1820s on Tocqueville, see Larry Siedentop, *Tocqueville* (Oxford: Oxford University Press, 1994), 20–40; and Aurelian Craiutu, *Liberalism Under Siege: The Political Thought of the French Doctrinaires* (Lanham, MD: Lexington Books, 2003), 87–122.

5. Alexis de Tocqueville, *Democracy in America* (New York: Harper & Row, 1988), 335–36.

6. Tocqueville, *Democracy in America*, 58–60.

7. Tocqueville's awareness of the vulnerability of democracies to the threat of democratic despotism and the "tyranny of the majority" is treated in great detail in Ostrom, *Meaning of Democracy*.

8. Tocqueville's superb foreword to *The Old Regime and the Revolution* provides a passionate defense of freedom as a supreme value. Freedom and liberty have different meanings and connotations in English. Freedom is often described as "liberation from slavery or restraint from the power of another," while liberty is defined as "the power to do as one pleases" or "freedom from arbitrary or despotic control." The French term *liberté* embraces both meanings depending on the context in which it is used. See *Merriam-Webster's Collegiate Dictionary*, 10th ed. (Springfield, MA: Merriam-Webster Inc., 1993), 446, 670.

9. In recent years, scholars have described countries that have held free and fair elections but where civil rights and other basic freedoms have been sharply restricted as illiberal democracies. For example, see Fareed Zakaria, "The Rise of Illiberal Democracy," *Foreign Affairs* 76, no. 6 (1997): 181–95.

10. Samuel Huntington, *The Third Wave: Democratization in the Late Twentieth Century* (Norman: University of Oklahoma Press, 1990), 17.

11. See, for example, Joseph A. Schumpeter, *Capitalism, Socialism, and Democracy* (New York: Harper, 1950); and Robert A. Dahl, *Polyarchy: Participation and Opposition* (New Haven, CT: Yale University Press, 1971). Policymakers, especially in the United States, have placed great emphasis on elections as the essence of democracy despite the fact that free elections have often put dictators in power or consolidated their regimes from Louis Napoleon to Robert Mugabe.

12. Huntington, *The Third Wave*, 17.

13. Tocqueville, *Democracy in America*, 58–60.

14. Tocqueville, *Democracy in America*, 60.

15. For a discussion of Tocqueville's overturning of the prevalent European idea of the state and sovereignty, see Siedentop, *Tocqueville*, 41–43.

16. Samuel Huntington, *Political Order in Changing Societies* (New Haven, CT: Yale University Press, 1968), 26.

17. For a sharp denunciation of the authoritarian European state tradition and a vigorous defense of Tocqueville's approach affirming the importance of decentralized politics and local self-government in fostering freedom, see Michael Hereth, *Alexis de Tocqueville: Threats to Freedom in Democracy* (Durham, NC: Duke University Press, 1986), 39–44.

18. Huntington, *Third Wave*, 9.

19. For example, there are no entries for equality in the index of *The Third Wave*.

20. For a systematic attempt to analyze Tocqueville's comparisons between American and French democracy, see Jean-Claude Lamberti, *Tocqueville et les deux démocraties* (Paris: Presses Universitaires de France, 1983).

21. Siedentop, *Tocqueville*, 43.

22. See Tocqueville, *Democracy in America*, 316–407, for an insightful analysis of slavery, race relations, and the plight of the Native American.

23. Tocqueville, *Democracy in America*, 555–58.

24. See, for example, Alexis de Tocqueville, *Tocqueville on America after 1840: Letters and Other Writings*, trans. and ed. Aurelian Craiutu and Jeremy Jennings (Cambridge, England: Cambridge University Press, 2009); also Aurelian Craiutu and Jeremy Jennings, "The Third *Democracy*: Tocqueville's Views of America after 1840," *American Political Science Review* 98, no. 3 (2004): 391–404.

25. Tocqueville, *Democracy in America*, 26.

26. Cited by Schleifer, *Making of Tocqueville's Democracy in America*, 129.

27. Raymond Aron, *Main Currents in Sociological Thought*, vol. I (New York: Basic Books, 1965), 184–85.

28. Alexis de Tocqueville, *Journeys to England and Ireland*, ed. J. P. Mayer (New Haven, CT: Yale University Press, 1958).

29. Siedentop, *Tocqueville*, 107.

30. Critics have sharply criticized Tocqueville for supporting French colonialism and domination as contradicting his commitment to freedom and democracy. See, for example, Hereth, *Alexis de Tocqueville*, 145–71; and Cheryl B. Welch, "Colonial Violence and the Rhetoric of Evasion: Tocqueville on Algeria," *Political Theory* 31, no. 2 (2003): 235–64.

31. Tocqueville wrote extensively on Algeria. For a collection of some of his writings on Algeria, see *De la Colonie en Algérie*, ed. Tzevetan Todorov (Paris: Gallimard, 1968); and *Œuvres*, vol. I, ed. André Jardin (Paris: Bibliothèque de la Pléiade, Gallimard, 1991), 658–951.

32. His critique of French policy following the conquest of Algeria in 1830 had much in common with flaws in American policy in Iraq following the defeat of Saddam Hussein in 2003. In Algeria, the French totally destroyed the administrative and military infrastructure of the Ottomans who previously ruled the country, adapted a hostile policy toward Islamic religious leaders opposing the conquest, and

wreaked massive destruction on the civilian population in pacifying the country. The result was a religious uprising that took more than two decades to put down. In Iraq, the disbanding of Saddam's army, dismantling of his administrative structure, hostility to Shiite religious leaders sympathetic to Iran, and massive destruction wreaked on the civilian population also sparked an insurgency led primarily but not exclusively by radical religious leaders opposing the occupation.

33. Tocqueville's "Rapport fait au nom de la Commission chargée d'éxaminer la proposition de M. de Tracy, relative aux esclaves des colonies" (July 1839) in *OC*, III: 1, 41–78. An English version of Tocqueville's report of July 23, 1839, was translated by Jared Sparks's wife as *Report Made to the Chamber of Deputies on the Abolition of Slavery in the French Colonies by Alexis de Tocqueville* (Boston, 1840). For a revised version of the 1840 original English translation, see *Tocqueville and Beaumont on Social Reform*, trans. and ed. Seymour Drescher (New York: Harper, 1968), 98–136. Also see Alexis de Tocqueville, *Report Made to the Chamber of Deputies on the Abolition of Slavery in the French Colonies, July 23, 1839* (Westport, CT: Negro Universities Press, 1970).

34. Tocqueville, *Democracy in America*, 359.

35. For an analysis of Tocqueville's interest in India, see Siedentop, *Tocqueville*, 106–11; and Tocqueville, *Œuvres*, vol. I, 960–1080 (for Tocqueville's writings on India).

36. Tocqueville, *Democracy in America*, 445. Tocqueville failed to see that Islam, like Christianity, preached the inherent equality of humanity in general and that of the community of believers in particular and was not necessarily an obstacle to democracy. For example, see Gellar, *Democracy in Senegal*, 108–23. Tun Myint's chapter in this volume also highlights the equalitarian elements in Buddhist teachings as providing a foundation for democracy in Burma.

37. For an excellent collection of Marx's writing on colonialism and Third-World societies in the nineteenth century, see Shlomo Avineri, ed., *Karl Marx on Colonization and Modernization* (New York: Doubleday Anchor, 1969).

38. Tocqueville, *Democracy in America*, 165.

39. Tocqueville, *Democracy in America*, 91.

40. Tocqueville, *Democracy in America*, 412–13.

41. The original checklist that was developed as a guide for applying Tocquevillian analytics to the study of democracy in a single African country concentrated primarily on using African examples (Gellar, *Democracy in Senegal*, 6–10). However, the list of components can also be used to study the processes and state of democratization in any contemporary society.

42. Tocqueville, *Democracy in America*, 23–30. Tocqueville used the term "physical configuration" to refer to the physical environment and how it shaped people's thinking and attitudes.

43. Tocqueville began his study of *Democracy in America* with an analysis of its history. Although not an historian, Tocqueville looked to history to provide the background for understanding the causes of such phenomena as the evolution of

democracy and the French Revolution. Tocqueville stressed the need to understand what he called the "point of departure" of a nation in order to appreciate its political institutions and social conditions.

44. In writing *Democracy in America*, Tocqueville struggled with determining which factor most affected the maintenance of America's democratic institutions. In the end, he pointed to *moeurs* as the most significant factor explaining the success of American democracy. The term embraced American values, morality, ideas, attitudes, and customs. As James Schleifer (*Making of Tocqueville's Democracy in America*, 58–61) demonstrated, Tocqueville went to great length to incorporate political culture into his analyses.

45. Tocqueville, *Old Regime*, 146–47. Tocqueville complained that the French men of letters who shaped the national temperament and outlook on life were able to do so because the French had little training in politics.

46. Alexis de Tocqueville, *Recollections*, ed. J. P. Mayer, trans. A. Teixeira de Mattos (New York: Meridian Books, 1959), 81.

4

What Kind of Social Scientist Was Tocqueville?

Aurelian Craiutu

> They absolutely want to make me a party man and I am not that in the least; or rather I have only one passion, the love of liberty and human dignity.
> —Alexis de Tocqueville to Henry Reeve, 1837[1]

In spite of his current popularity among historians, sociologists, and political scientists, Alexis de Tocqueville remains a notoriously difficult subject for his interpreters and a surprisingly elusive target for his critics. To consider him as a prophet would be as great a mistake as pretending that he should have entirely shared our contemporary lenses and biases. In the past years, Tocqueville's method as a social scientist and observer of American democracy has been the object of both admiration and criticism among historians and political scientists such as James T. Schleifer, Rogers M. Smith, Sheldon Wolin, and Gary Wills.[2] The forthcoming publication of the English translation of Eduardo Nolla's updated critical edition of *Democracy in America* will reveal the laboratory from which Tocqueville's masterpiece emerged and will shed fresh light on his method of inquiry and writing style. By presenting an extensive selection of early outlines, drafts, marginalia, unpublished fragments, and other materials relating to the writing of Tocqueville's book, the English translation of the Nolla edition, along with excerpts from Tocqueville's travel notebooks, will allow English-speaking readers to familiarize themselves with the ways in which Tocqueville's ideas developed and went through a long process of rewriting.

A proper assessment of Tocqueville's methodology is hardly possible without first achieving a proper grasp of the particular problems from which he started. Otherwise, we are bound to misread and ultimately misunderstand Tocqueville's political message and, more importantly, we might fail to adequately recognize the outstanding quality and unique nature of his thought.[3]

Tocqueville's Critics

In two important articles published almost four decades ago, Melvin Richter criticized Tocqueville for being imprecise in his use of concepts and insufficiently technical in his study of democracy. Compared to Montesquieu's allegedly scientific approach to politics, Tocqueville appeared to Richter as a less sophisticated social thinker lacking the philosophical depth of Pascal or Rousseau.[4] More recently, Sheldon Wolin's *Tocqueville between Two Worlds*, while stopping short of accusing Tocqueville of distorting the true image of American democracy, has invited us to reassess the strengths and weaknesses of Tocqueville's methodology. Wolin approached Tocqueville from a different (post-modern) perspective by bringing to light and emphasizing the *philosophical* aspects of Tocqueville's works. For Wolin, Tocqueville's method lacks scientific rigor because it resembles the approach of a traveler who ascends to the top of the hill (heights being a metaphor for loftiness of purpose) and looks down into the valley in order to acquire a panoramic view of the world. According to Wolin, "the ascent of Tocqueville's *theoros* is an escape from details in order to achieve a panoramic vision."[5] Tocqueville suppressed some "mundane" facts (administration, party politics) in order to be able to "see" more clearly the general contours of American society.[6] Even when Tocqueville claimed to look for and concentrate on facts, Wolin added, the latter were primarily "the means of *displaying* theoretical meaning rather than serving primarily as supporting proof for theoretical statements."[7]

Other interpreters of Tocqueville also expressed doubts regarding the accuracy of his method of inquiry and theoretical conclusions. Some have gone so far as to suggest that Tocqueville got America wrong because he worked with a flawed method that made him perceive only what suited his ideological biases and intellectual inclinations. For these interpreters, Tocqueville's conclusions were a strange concoction of mostly unwarranted generalizations and impressionistic observations based on a priori ideas that he brought with him from France. Hence, the final portrait that we get from Tocqueville's writings must arguably be taken with a grain of salt since it might tell us more about his own inclinations than about the new world that he set out to describe to his fellow countrymen.

This last point loomed large in Gary Wills's article, "Did Tocqueville 'Get' America?" (2004), claiming that Tocqueville's considerable popularity is in large part derived not from the soundness of the "Tocquevillian analytics"[8] but from the convenient support that his ideas lend to all political groups, regardless of their ideology. Tocqueville's conclusions can be easily detached from the larger context to which they belong in order to make them palatable to the dominant ideology of the moment. "Conservatives," writes Wills, "find in him a proleptic attack on the welfare state, a defense of states' rights, and the insistence on democracy's need of a supporting religion. Liberals find in him the praise of equality as the essence of democracy and the central role he gives to courts of law."[9]

Wills's main charge is that Tocqueville did not get America right because he was simply "uninterested in the material bases of American life"[10] and willingly ignored important details about American capitalism, manufactures, banking, or technology that should have captured his attention when writing volume one of *Democracy*. In Wills's view, Tocqueville's method displays a disquieting scarcity of examples and contains dubious generalizations that gloss over the facts. As such, Tocqueville created his own stylized America that was considerably different from the one that existed in reality two centuries ago.[11] After condemning "the shallow empirical basis of [Tocqueville's] study" and the fact that "he showed little interest in what ordinary people were doing at their work or in their homes,"[12] Wills went on to add "what Tocqueville did not see is often more interesting than what he did. . . . Most of his opinions were formed at his first encounters with an idea and they were rarely altered afterwards."[13] He criticized the Frenchman's propensity to form instant judgments and suggested that in many respects, the author of *Democracy* reached his conclusions about America mainly "because of prejudices he brought with him from France."[14] Not surprisingly, in Wills's opinion, Tocqueville did not offer an objective account of what he saw in America, since his main audience was a French one that he sought to "inoculate" against democracy's dangers.

Finally, Wills's profound dissatisfaction with Tocqueville's methodology led him to argue that "the taste for the grand simplification is apparent in all of Tocqueville's work,"[15] including *The Old Regime and the Revolution*. Even in his last book, Wills opined, Tocqueville continued to show "no interest in the material bases of a national culture" and used the same aphoristic and almost oracular style that one can find in his earlier work. As such, Wills concluded, Tocqueville's analysis remained superficial and vague, and his political conclusions should never be considered without a great deal of skepticism.

"A New Science of Politics"?

Was Tocqueville a superficial social scientist who reasoned a priori rather than from facts and worked with a shallow empirical basis by choosing to observe only what he wanted to see? These important questions call for a longer study than I can offer in these pages. While it is not my intention to provide a point-by-point rebuttal of Wills's claims,[16] I am interested here in asking more broadly what kind of social scientist was Tocqueville and what we should learn from his eclectic method. To this effect, I shall first make a few general observations about Tocqueville's methodology before focusing on his research and writing method used in *The Old Regime and the Revolution*. The last section is devoted to examining Tocqueville's economic ideas and interest in political economy that, according to some critics, constitute the weakest part of his work.

I should like to stress from the outset that Tocqueville brought about a new way of analyzing social and political phenomena, one that went far *beyond* the methods used by his contemporaries. This point was duly recognized early on by an astute reader of *Democracy in America* such as John Stuart Mill, who famously claimed that the Frenchman put forward an approach to the study of democracy that was "the true Baconian and Newtonian method applied to society."[17] Tocqueville never believed that there are any axiomatic truths in political science and vehemently opposed rigid deterministic theories of political and social development. As both Pierre Manent and Laurence Guellec remarked, Tocqueville's sociology was incomparably "more political" than that of both Marx and Comte. He had a strong passion for political action—"I have always placed action above everything else,"[18] he once confessed to his friend, Louis de Kergorlay—and entertained the dream of playing an important role in the politics of his country. Tocqueville's works must therefore be seen as belonging to a larger French tradition of political engagement and political rhetoric in which the writer enters into a subtle and complex pedagogical relationship with his audience seeking to convince and inspire his readers to political action.[19]

Not surprisingly, Tocqueville's approach was never axiomatic or overly systematic, as some of his interpreters (such as Jon Elster) claimed.[20] Sometimes, as James Schleifer noted, Tocqueville sought to carry his readers along by the sheer force of logic, while at other times he relied on carefully chosen metaphors and examples, parallel structures and contrasting pairs, in order to make his points more persuasively.[21] The merits of all these strategies were evaluated by Tocqueville in his unpublished notes that constitute a fascinating dialogue with himself as well as with his closest friends and readers (his father and brother, Gustave de Beaumont, and Louis de Kergorlay). In these notes full of queries that reveal a less moderate and guarded thinker endowed with an uncommon degree of self-awareness, Tocqueville drafts a clear writing strategy, summarizes his findings, and pays great attention to refining his writing style. To this effect, he painstakingly weighs his choices of words and spends a lot of time reflecting upon the definitions of key concepts. He also muses about the reception of his ideas and takes into account the critical observations made by his closest friends.

Tocqueville's notorious tendency of deducing a broad philosophical picture from a narrow set of specific facts must be related to another striking feature of his method and writing style: the complex contrast and harmony between his quest for general laws and universal causes on the one hand, and the immersion in particular facts and historical contingencies on the other hand.[22] Not surprisingly, Tocqueville's general laws and predictions have a good deal of flexibility. As Tocqueville's subtle discussion of the roots of democratic institutions in America demonstrates, he constantly sought to adjust his own methodology to the ever-changing contours of political reality. In so doing, he displayed a sharp awareness of being a conceptual and methodological innovator who managed to bridge the gap between formal and interpretative approaches or between micro and macro levels of analyses.[23]

The scientific nature of Tocqueville's method has been emphasized by Raymond Boudon, who argued that Tocqueville had "an explicative and not interpretative conception of social-historical phenomena," because he aimed at providing a scientific explanation rather than a literary interpretation of facts.[24] According to Boudon, Tocqueville understood that the goal of explanation can be achieved only if one takes into account concrete facts and starts from solid foundations—in this case, methodological individualism. In the second volume of *Democracy* and *The Old Regime*, the general views that Tocqueville put forward were based on various types of analysis of "exact facts" that were the outcome of comparisons of concrete data rather than being deduced from abstract concepts.

While there is some truth to the claim that Tocqueville's comparative approach was limited by the fact that it was often invoked mostly in reference to France, the breadth of his comparative perspective cannot—and may not—be overlooked. For, as Seymour Drescher observed, "Tocqueville's perspective ranged far beyond places that he actually visited or intensively studied"[25] and benefited immensely from his intellectual restlessness. Tocqueville took a strong interest not only in classical settings such as England, Germany, and Switzerland, but also in more exotic lands such as the United States, Canada, Algeria, and even India. Far from "imagining" these countries, he carefully and painstakingly studied their mores and social conditions before drawing his own set of political conclusions or recommendations.

Tocqueville's own method combined in an original way explanation and interpretation, descriptive and normative analysis by using a mixture of quasi-formal methods and a very effective research strategy that should be evident to anyone who has carefully studied the writing process of *Democracy in America* and *The Old Regime and the Revolution*. As both Saguiv Hadari and Raymond Boudon pointed out,[26] in his last book Tocqueville carefully traced macro-social effects to the rational motivations and choices of individuals and groups placed in specific economic, political, and social contexts. According to Hadari, "when reaching for an explanation of phenomena involving complex social interactions, Tocqueville repeatedly devised an abstract model detailing the appropriate rational behaviors of the actors involved and deducing the results, often unintended, of their combination."[27]

Yet, Tocqueville confronts us with an interesting paradox upon which it is worth reflecting for a moment. While he may have been a modern social scientist *avant la lettre*, as Boudon and Hadari would have it, his belief in the possibility of a comprehensive (hard) science of society must be taken with a grain of salt. Tocqueville was notorious for avoiding unidimensional definitions of key concepts such as democracy.[28] More than half a century ago, George Wilson Pierson addressed the issue of Tocqueville's allegedly "inexact and confusing use of the word *démocratie*" and claimed that this was an "unconscious lack of precision"[29] on the part of the French author. In *Democracy in America*, the term "democracy" refers primarily to *civil* equality of conditions but it also designates, among other things, political self-government, an inescapable worldwide phenomenon, an anthropological fact, and the government by the people. Nonetheless, it would be unfair to accuse Tocqueville of working with a misleading notion of democracy. The conceptual ambiguity surrounding the term "democracy" should be viewed in a more positive light, as a token of Tocqueville's intention to offer a broader definition of democracy as a multifaceted social, anthropological, and political phenomenon. Furthermore, as Pierre Manent pointed out, Tocqueville established a close relationship between the nature of democracy and the dispositions of the democratic soul, a modern variation on the old Platonic analogy between the order of the city and the order of the human soul.[30]

The plural definitions of democracy in Tocqueville's work should not obscure the fact that one of his greatest merits is to have emphasized the importance of studying the *social* condition of a democratic regime. Democracy, claimed Tocqueville, brings about a new social condition and a new type of society whereas the sovereignty of the people is primarily to be seen as a political concept signifying a new form of government.[31] This approach constitutes a significant departure from our present understanding of democracy that tends to concentrate primarily on *political* democracy equated with the sovereignty of people, universal suffrage, elections, and majority rule.

Furthermore, as a perceptive reader of Montesquieu, Tocqueville was aware that no explanation of social and political phenomena could be adequate without paying due consideration to the "spirit" of society as a whole.[32] Tocqueville's sociological and psychological insights allowed him to grasp the essential facts of American society that he interpreted by using an original conceptual framework not devoid of strong normative connotations. In spite of his commitment to studying the "facts," he also had a passion for philosophical speculation that often allowed him to soar above the realm of facts. This original blend of subjectivism and objectivism can be found at the heart of his new political science suitable to a democratic world.

The best expression of Tocqueville's views on this important topic is an important (and often overlooked) speech that he gave in Paris in April 1852. Addressing the members of the Academy of Moral and Political Science, Tocqueville drew a seminal distinction between the *art* of government and the *science* of government, and insisted on the *scientific* nature of his approach to the study of politics. He went as far as to claim that he did not doubt the scientific character of moral sciences. Because the art of government closely follows the ever-changing flux of political phenomena, it varies according to the diversity of events and seeks to meet the ephemeral needs of changing political circumstances.[33] The true science of government, argued Tocqueville, differs from the art of government in many important ways. It covers the immense space between philosophy, sociology, and law and accounts for the natural rights that belong to individuals, the laws appropriate to different societies, and the virtues and limitations of various forms of government. It is grounded in "the nature of man, his interests, faculties, and needs and teaches what are the laws most appropriate to the general and permanent condition of man."[34] As such, it does not reduce politics to a mere question of arithmetic or logic nor does it attempt to build an imaginary society in which everything is simple, orderly, uniform, and in accord with reason. The science of government, concluded Tocqueville, is a powerful science that forms around each society an intellectual atmosphere in which everyone breathes and from which both citizens and their representatives derive their principles of behavior.

If Tocqueville's new "science" was idiosyncratic, it was not—and did not pretend to be—value-neutral, *wertfrei*. While in his correspondence with his friends,[35] he occasionally liked to compare himself to an impartial observer standing between two worlds and casting a neutral look on both of them, in reality Tocqueville had strong preferences and tastes. His moving apology of political freedom in volume one of *The Old Regime* is an eloquent case in point. It represents one of the most inspiring hymns to liberty ever written and is worthy of the pen of the best French moralist.[36]

Furthermore, Tocqueville's new science of politics aspired to avoid the twin pitfalls of both "political impressionism" and historical determinism threatening to rob individual human beings of their freedom and dignity. Tocqueville's well-known opposition to determinism came to light in many of his writings, from *Recollections* to the correspondence with Arthur de Gobineau. Tocqueville's rejection of determinism in history stemmed from his belief that in order to adequately explain social and political phenomena a flexible theoretical approach is required, one that resists the temptation of deducing rigid causal forces and explanations showing little or no respect to human beings as independent political actors. A historical probabilist at heart, Tocqueville vigorously opposed what he called "the literary spirit" in politics and criticized in unambiguous terms the "literary" style of politics of his predecessors (and contemporaries), who looked for what was ingenuous and new rather than what was appropriate to their particular situation. Taking the political game as a play, they paid special attention to "good acting and fine speaking without reference to the play's result" and preferred to judge "by impressions rather than reasons."[37] Tocqueville was categorically opposed to this type of political argument and engagement, as he made it clear in *The Old Regime and the Revolution*, a book on which I focus in the next section.

Writing *The Old Regime and the Revolution*

It is time to explore in further detail Tocqueville's use of sources and writing method in *The Old Regime and the Revolution*, which is arguably the best example of the sophistication and complexity of his overall methodological approach. In many ways, *The Old Regime* was a surprising book, above all for Tocqueville himself, who spent a lot of energy and time—almost six years—writing and reflecting on it. The conclusions of the book that was finally published in 1856 were significantly different from the initial assumptions that had prompted Tocqueville to begin his investigation of the origins of the Revolution six years earlier. This surprisingly long process of maturation allows us to better appreciate and understand Tocqueville's sophisticated method and writing style. Our reexamination of the writing process of *The Old Regime and the Revolution* should therefore serve as a cautionary note to those scholars who criticize Tocqueville for his allegedly impressionistic style and sloppy method.

More austere in composition and less philosophical than *Democracy in America*, Tocqueville's *The Old Regime and the Revolution* has never been a best-seller in America.[38] Historians who tend to concentrate on history-making events are likely to be taken aback by the message of Tocqueville's book that downplays the originality and achievements of the Revolution by arguing that the real "revolution" had, in fact, occurred long before 1789. Not surprisingly, until recently the archives of *The Old Regime and the Revolution* have not been studied as closely as those of *Democracy in America*. The result is that few readers of Tocqueville's last book have been able to fully comprehend the subtle and complex architecture of his analysis of the Old Regime and to properly appreciate the research method used by Tocqueville and the richness of his historical sources.

A former student of the late François Furet, Robert T. Gannett, has given us a superb and learned book that achieves, *mutatis mutandis*, what James T. Schleifer's classic *The Making of Tocqueville's Democracy in America* accomplished three decades ago for Tocqueville's other earlier masterpiece. Gannett obtained permission to consult Tocqueville's family archives, which turned out to be a true goldmine. They revealed that Tocqueville wrote not one but several "books" about the Old Regime and the French Revolution. They were very different in focus, scope, and method, and their differences tell us a lot about Tocqueville's shifting ideas and interests from 1850, when Tocqueville began thinking about the book's outline, to 1856, when volume one was finally published. With the skill of a competent and passionate detective fascinated by his subject, Gannett lifts for his readers the veil of secrecy imposed by Tocqueville himself. Thus, we learn that the Frenchman chose *not* to reveal many of his sources for volume one of *The Old Regime and the Revolution*, hiding from the readers' eyes its complex architecture and making it almost impossible to guess the impressive research and careful reflection required by the writing of the book.

Any attentive reader of *The Old Regime and the Revolution* will note that Tocqueville did not reason a priori and did not ignore economic facts. He carefully crafted the form and substance of his book in response not only to his findings in the archives at Tours and the Hôtel de Ville in Paris but also to the theses advanced by some of his prominent contemporaries with whose works he was entirely familiar. As already mentioned, the assumptions from which Tocqueville started differed from the conclusions he reached at the end of his archival research. Tracing this intellectual journey allows us to shed fresh light on what kind of social scientist Tocqueville was and what type of research was required for the completion of his book.

The writing of volume one of *The Old Regime and the Revolution* took a surprisingly long time, either six years or twenty years, depending on whether or not we take into account his important essay composed in 1836 comparing England and France (volume two was never completed). From 1850 onward, Tocqueville was stricken with recurring and painful stomach and lung ailments and also had to overcome many doubts regarding his subject, method, scope, and genre. In spite of all these challenges, he traveled between different places—archives in Tours, Normandy, and Paris—to gather historical data and reevaluate his findings. Tocqueville's many writing blocks—there were four such writing blocks in 1852, 1853, 1856, and 1858, as his correspondence shows—forced him to reassess at regular intervals the focus and method suitable to his historical investigation.

As Robert Gannett pointed out, there are approximately 3,700 pages of archival notes preserved in Tocqueville's archives. They allow us to catch a glimpse into his readings and extensive preparatory notes that provided him with an immense arsenal of ideas and data. Tocqueville wrote detailed endnotes that contain his famous "hic" observations and passionate rejoinders, ranging from single words to full pages of commentary demonstrating his varying levels of engagement with his texts, sources, and authors. Tocqueville was heavily influenced not only by Burke's *Reflections* but also by the ideas of other authors such as Louis-Antoine Macarel, Antoine Dareste de la Chavanne, Benjamin Constant, and Prosper de Barante, who are not usually listed among his sources (they do not appear, for example, on the index of Richard Herr's older book on the same subject, *Tocqueville and the Old Regime*).

The first sketch of *The Old Regime and the Revolution* appears in Tocqueville's letter to his old friend, Louis de Kergorlay, written on December 15, 1850, from Sorrento, Italy. In this letter, Tocqueville expressed his preference for a philosophical history seeking to unearth the hidden causes of events beneath the visible surface of history. At the same time, it is important to remember that Tocqueville's interest in history was always accompanied by the strong interest he took in the politics of his day. This explains why the historical book he wanted to write purported to offer "an ensemble of reflections and insights on the current time, . . . the cause, the character, the significance of the great events that formed the principal links in the chain of our time."[39]

This ambitious goal indicates the extent to which Tocqueville followed in the footsteps of two prominent predecessors, Madame de Staël and François Guizot, whose *Considerations on the Principal Events of the French Revolution* (1817-1818)[40] and *History of Civilization in Europe* and *History of Civilization in France* (1828-1829)[41] masterfully blended the analysis of historical facts with philosophical history. Moreover, there was something else that Tocqueville shared with his famous forerunners: his ambition to influence the course of political events. Most of the historical writings published during the Bourbon Restoration displayed an unusual degree of political partisanship, as historians sought to use the lessons of the past in order to justify their own political agenda. Those who *wrote* history during this time often tried to *make* history as well. It is not a mere coincidence that Staël's *Considerations* came to be seen as the Bible of all French liberals and Guizot's lectures on the history of civilization in Europe and France inspired an entire new generation of young French intellectuals.[42] Even if Tocqueville was not able to "make" history in the 1850s during the Second Empire, he hoped at least that his book would have an awakening influence on his countrymen and would inspire them to fight for liberty.

In January 1852, when Tocqueville set out to write his new book, the outline of the volume had surprisingly little to do with the Revolution per se. This detail can be explained by the fact that at the heart of Tocqueville's original project lay a genuine political concern. He was intrigued by his country's oscillation between despotism and liberty and sought to explain this tendency by concentrating on the figure of Napoléon Bonaparte whose gradual rise to power he wanted to account for. In order to achieve his purpose, Tocqueville soon realized that he had to understand and describe first the society that emerged out of the Revolution. He started with the Directory and carefully read and annotated Lafayette's memoirs as well as Constant's writings from 1796 and 1797 (*On the Force of the Current Gov-*

ernment and *On Political Reactions*). Preoccupied with finding the proper balance of facts and judgments, Tocqueville resorted to a subtle combination of sociological investigations and a psychological analysis of revolutionary actors and phenomena. He also planned to consult witnesses of that period and was intent on reading numerous printed documents and memoirs of the Revolution.

Seeking to understand the direction of public opinion during the Directory, Tocqueville eventually realized that all the aforementioned sources were only of limited help in unveiling the spirit of a bygone age. That is why in 1852 he decided to shift his research focus from printed memoirs to original sources in the archives; consequently, he devoted the next four years to completing this arduous task. It was during his solitary work in the archives at Tours that the famous thesis of the continuity between the Revolution and the Old Regime came to Tocqueville's mind for the first time. While this idea emerged rather late in the conception of the book, its impact on its overall vision was fundamental. What was initially meant to be a history of the Revolution and the First Empire slowly became a historical account of the Old Regime. Tocqueville grasped that the administrative regime of the Consulate and Empire was not a creation *ex nihilo* but a mere restoration of some of the institutions of the Old Regime. It was at this point in time that Tocqueville realized that in order to understand the rise of Napoléon, he had to dig deeper into the history of the Old Regime where he could discover the real roots of the French malaise.

As Gannett showed, this pathbreaking shift in Tocqueville's method and emphasis occurred in August 1853 when he decided to write a full-length book on the period *preceding* the Revolution. It was this change that gave Tocqueville the proper historical perspective that other interpreters of 1789, including Burke, one of Tocqueville's main interlocutors in *The Old Regime and the Revolution*, lacked, in spite of their political acumen. Yet, Tocqueville's change of direction did not help him overcome his famous writing blocks that had a deeper cause. Far from being the mere expression of a temporary lack of inspiration, Tocqueville's writing blocks stemmed, to quote Gannett again, from "a contradiction at the heart of his historical vision, as he struggled to reconcile his view of the Revolution's continuity, seen in its administrative structures, and its radical ideological transformation."[43]

Anyone who follows Tocqueville's work in the archives at Tours will be impressed by his research skills and method. The work in the archives allowed Tocqueville to comprehend the evolution of feudal rights and the growth of administrative centralization during the Old Regime. He was a remarkably gifted social historian who did not shy away from research-ing a wide array of resources including journals, histories, memoirs, dip-lomatic papers, letters, and unpublished manuscripts. His capacity for archival research was certainly impressive, equaled only by his well-known penchant for theoretical generalizations. Tocqueville was able to delve into huge collections of documents, sometimes poorly organized, and to extract from them the essential information he needed for his study. He consulted a huge mass of documents of various weight and substance in order to gain knowledge of specific historical facts. Last but not least, Tocqueville had the luck of being assisted at Tours by a competent director of the collec-tions, Charles de Grandmaison, with whom he spent half an hour every time he arrived at the archives in order to go over his materials and assess their significance.

The sheer difficulty and magnitude of Tocqueville's task must also be duly acknowledged. For example, when exploring the issue of the land own-ership of the peasantry in order to assess the remains of feudalism in 1789 (one of the most heavily documented chapters in his book), Tocqueville used a remarkably diverse array of legislative acts, record of properties from 1790, a count of property holders in 1852, and demographical data documenting the population growth between 1788 and 1852.[44] Thus, he eventually arrived at a somewhat counterintuitive conclusion, one of those Gallic paradoxes deplored by Gary Wills and others, namely that the peas-ants' feudal hatred paradoxically increased with the lessening of their feu-dal obligations.[45]

By carefully studying the archives, and most notably the correspon-dence of the *intendants*, Tocqueville also came to understand the causes of the growth of administrative centralization in France, one of his enduring obsessions. He first grasped that the absenteeism of the nobles had made possible the growth of royal power and then he moved on to examine how local administrators treated ordinary citizens. Subsequently, he sought to determine the practical effects of those practices as well as the customs and expectations they engendered.[46] At Tours, Tocqueville carefully studied the complex overlapping and competing jurisdictional claims in order to understand the growth of administrative centralization. It was during his study of the *intendants'* correspondence and the pre-Revolutionary admin-istrative law and practice in the archives at Tours and Paris that Tocqueville discovered how the royal administrative machine grew unopposed at the expense of local government and liberties. The continual and minute inter-vention of the administrative power within the judicial sphere particu-larly caught his attention because it stifled local initiatives and freedoms, destroyed intermediary powers, and in the end strengthened royal tutelage. Tocqueville correctly perceived that this pattern of development had created an arbitrary regime, powerful and feeble at the same time, and incapable of reforming itself. It was this peculiar combination of absolute power and administrative weakness that finally paved the way for the Revolution of 1789 and the ensuing violent overthrow of the Bourbon monarchy.

In this regard, Tocqueville's notes on Turgot's administrative reforms are of special interest (they were translated into English only in 2001).[47] In commenting on Turgot, Tocqueville drew an impressive list of shortcomings of the administration of the Old Regime. "The reformer Turgot," Tocqueville wrote, "is at the same time very much a centralizer. Not only does he not decrease government paternalism, he increases it while improving it."[48] Turgot's reforms did not lower the crushing weight of taxation, nor were they successful in establishing effective municipal governments. Interested in the actual administration of the countryside, Tocqueville carefully studied the duties and powers of the local administrators, the poor condition of the lower classes, and the role of the *parlements*. Noting the almost unlimited power of the intendants, Tocqueville wrote in his notes: "The idea of having the governed participate in government and to use them for this purpose is an idea seemingly absent from Turgot's head."[49] Reviewing the functions of local governments according to Turgot, Tocqueville pointed out the lack of self-government with regard to important tasks such as the administration of common property or schools. Turgot's plan for urban municipalities, Tocqueville noted, had "no representative body properly speaking."[50] After reviewing Turgot's reforms, Tocqueville commented on the political inexperience of the French nation as follows:

> What is confounding . . . is that [Turgot] thinks he is making an administrative reform chiefly destined to facilitate the reform of taxation and its proper division, and that he does not recognize that he is starting an immense political revolution which changes the state's constitution from top to bottom.[51]

No interpreter of Tocqueville's works may ignore the creative use he made of the famous *cahiers des doléances*[52] that helped him follow the course of public opinion before 1789 and "eavesdrop" on the ideas, habits, and mores of that time. Tocqueville was entirely familiar with Proudhomme's 1789 *Résumé général, ou Extrait des cahiers* in which he observed the divisions between the nobles and the Third Estate prior to 1789. It is surprising to notice how much attention Tocqueville paid to *economic* and *social* factors—something that both Wills and Wolin claimed Tocqueville consistently failed to do—and how little he was initially preoccupied, as the book outline written in June 1853 demonstrates, with the role of ideas in general. Tocqueville examined the factors of economic change and recognized the significance of the division of labor in modern French society.

It is equally important to explore the intense intellectual dialogue that Tocqueville had with many authors while writing *The Old Regime and the Revolution*. As Robert Gannett demonstrated,[53] Tocqueville found in Dareste's essay on the Old Regime (1843) the main source of instruction regarding feudal rights. He made extensive use of Dareste's feudal sources and vocabulary to reach a different conclusion. While the latter emphasized the solidarity among the classes of the Old Regime, Tocqueville saw mostly isolation, distrust, and polarization. His famous concept of "collective individualism" described this situation and accounted for the irresistible trend toward administrative centralization. The absenteeism of the nobles was a key factor in the growth of central power and stifled the development of local liberties. Thus, Tocqueville understood early on that there had been, in fact, *two* revolutions in France prior to 1789 that reinforced each other. The first one made the French peasant a freeholder of property, while the second one released him from the government of his absentee feudal lords. Tocqueville also made creative use of the ideas of lesser-known historians and economists, such as Macarel and Le Trosne, whose conclusions he criticized and rejected.

Tocqueville's most important interlocutor was undoubtedly Edmund Burke, whose texts were seminal for the Frenchman at a crucial point in writing *The Old Regime and the Revolution*. Tocqueville came to know Burke rather late in his career, after having read Charles de Rémusat's two long essays on Burke published in *Revue des Deux Mondes* in 1853. Tocqueville regarded Burke as his primary interlocutor in the book and made a highly efficient use of his ideas. Tocqueville went straight to the core of Burke's thought on the Revolution and, as Gannett showed,[54] adapted them to his own rhetorical purposes. Tocqueville believed that Burke lacked a proper historical perspective and was misguided by the events he closely witnessed in 1789, thus missing what was most important in the Revolution. He did not realize that the Revolution was not a mere French accident and that its fundamental objective was the pursuit of equality (of conditions), which could not have been stopped by any legislator. Burke, Tocqueville argued, also poorly understood the causes of the fall of the Old Regime and failed to grasp the extent to which French monarchs had contributed to the death of local liberties and the growth of administrative centralization. That is

why, in Tocqueville's opinion, the revolutionaries did not commit the great
crimes that Burke attributed to them; in reality, "they had only dismem-
bered corpses."[55] Overall, Tocqueville's treatment of the *Reflections on the
Revolution in France* downplayed the broad areas of congruence between
their ideas. By overstating the continuity between pre-revolutionary and
revolutionary France, Tocqueville ended up understating the break introduced by the Revolution, a point forcefully made by Burke.

To conclude, Tocqueville's investigation of the Old Regime was a mas-
terful blend of archival research, historical, sociological, political, and philosophical analysis that sought to retrace the loss of local liberties and the
growth of centralization in France. Tocqueville regarded his book as providing the essential catalyst for the revival of liberty in France and hoped
that by illuminating the causes of the fall of the Old Regime he would be
able to contribute to the rejuvenation of political liberty under the Second
Empire. "Certain nations," he wrote in a memorable passage from Book
III of volume one of *The Old Regime and the Revolution*, "pursue freedom
obstinately through all kinds of perils and miseries. . . . Others tire of liberty in the midst of their prosperity. . . . What do they lack to make them
free? What? The very desire to be so. Do not ask me to analyze this sublime
desire, it must be felt."[56] It was this very sublime yet mysterious taste for
freedom—the freedom to be able "to speak, act, breathe without constraint,
under the government of God and the laws alone"[57]—that Tocqueville tried
to awaken in the heart of the French living under the despotic regime of
Napoléon III. By stressing the continuity between the Old Regime and the
Revolution, he also invited his contemporaries to espouse a more balanced
view of the Revolution and to refrain from exaggerating its achievements
and failures.

Not surprisingly, as we have already seen, Tocqueville had a hard time
finishing the book. Precisely because he immersed himself in a huge mass
of documents and was far from relying on a priori judgments (as Wills
claimed), Tocqueville found it difficult to sort them out and extract from
the data the essential information he needed. To his wife, Mary Motley, he
once confessed: "Unfortunately, I still don't find any ideas to illuminate my
path. . . . Lost amidst an ocean of papers whose banks I cannot see, . . . what
is most difficult is conceiving clearly what it consists of and understanding
it."[58] It is no accident that at some point, he deliberately refrained from relying on his voluminous notes and focused instead on extracting the essential
information and ideas. In this respect, he was neither an impressionistic
painter uninterested in facts nor a thinker striving to find meaning in accidental outcomes and events, but a methodologically sophisticated thinker

who cared about ideas as much as about facts and was intent on producing an accurate, elegant, and inspiring book.

Tocqueville's Views on Economy and Social Reform

It is time to turn our attention to examining Tocqueville's economic views, a subject that has often been neglected or misunderstood by many of his commentators. Some of them went so far as to claim that he did not ultimately grasp the full consequences of the Industrial Revolution and had a weak understanding of economics, weaker than Marx's. Others compared Tocqueville unfavorably to Michel Chevalier, whose *Lettres sur l'Amérique du Nord* (1836) offered a detailed analysis of the effects of the Industrial Revolution in nineteenth-century America. We should be grateful then to Michael Drolet, author of *Tocqueville, Democracy, and Social Reform* (2003), for having reminded us that although Tocqueville was not a political economist, he devoted considerable time to reading the works of important economists such as Jean-Baptiste Say, Duchâtel, and Villeneuve-Bargemont.[59] As Tocqueville's reading notes (published in volume XVI of his *Complete Works*) attest, he carefully read Duchâtel's articles on Malthus published in *Le Globe* as well as Say's *Complete Course in Political Economy*, which he used as a guide for exploring the influence of commerce on modern society.

That Tocqueville spent so much time reading J. B. Say might come as a surprise to those critics who accused Tocqueville for having no interest at all in economics. By departing from the physiocrats, Say argued that industry rather than agriculture was the source of revenue and contended that the working of land and commerce were to be regarded as forms of industrial activity. The economic and political implications of Say's classification did not escape Tocqueville's attention. By challenging the primary role of agriculture and the power of landed aristocracy, Say's ideas amounted to an indirect argument against primogeniture and in support of equality. As Drolet pointed out, the fact "that Tocqueville would later emphasize the beneficial consequences the absence of primogeniture had for the equality of conditions in *Democracy in America* is indicative of Say's influence."[60] Tocqueville's *Democracy* vicariously endorsed a new liberal political economy that reflected the growth of industry and challenged the preeminence of large landed interests.

The last chapter (21) of volume two, part two of *Democracy in America* clearly shows, *pace* Wills and other critics, that Tocqueville was well aware of the reciprocal influence between democracy and industry and predicted the appearance of a "manufacturing aristocracy" *sui generis*, which he considered as "one of the hardest that has appeared on earth."[61] Tocqueville also followed in Say's footsteps in stressing the relationship between self-interest and self-government in an egalitarian society. As Drolet remarked, "Tocqueville's description of American democracy resembled uncannily Say's description of the market economy in the *Cours complet*. America embodied the spirit of commerce and industry, it permeated the whole society and marked the entire population."[62]

It is worth pointing out that Tocqueville eventually came to advocate a more traditional economic doctrine, rooted in the belief that small- and medium-scale agriculture rather than industry should have priority in the use of a nation's resources. He became interested in a larger debate about the nature of political economy, a science that the author of *Democracy in America* regarded as intrinsically linked to morals and politics. Unlike Say and Duchâtel, Tocqueville did not believe that morality, political economy, and politics could—or ought to—be separated from each other. Nor did he share Say's conviction that the natural sciences could serve as a model for social and historical studies. Finally, Tocqueville realized that Say's political economy, which ascribed such an important role to self-interest and individual calculating rationality, ended up legitimizing an unfettered pursuit of financial and material interests that Tocqueville, the aristocrat, scorned. He feared that industry, the engine of democracy, might become the driving force of a new social order based solely on acquisitiveness and greed.

Because it turned a blind eye to the loftier aspirations of the human soul, the new science of economics espoused by Say could hardly satisfy the longing of an aristocratic and restless mind such as Tocqueville who feared that an all-consuming passion for wealth and industry would pose a considerable threat to liberty and greatness.[63] In Tocqueville's opinion, Say, who believed that economies follow certain natural laws *sui generis*, adopted a simplistic approach when arguing that industry and material prosperity were alone capable of guaranteeing liberty. While admitting the existence of a strong relationship between prosperity and liberty, Tocqueville oscillated between understanding liberty as independent of commerce (industry) and conceiving of liberty as an upshot of commerce (industry). He never shied away from affirming his unconditional belief in the priority of *liberty* over any other principle; on his view, it is liberty that leads to prosperity rather than the other way around.[64] As Michael Drolet remarked, in his economic writings Tocqueville attempted to formulate a way in which liberty and commerce formed a virtuous and reinforcing relationship. . . . But he also believed, like Rousseau, liberty to be a value independent of market society. He frequently understood liberty in the same spiritual terms Rousseau reserved for virtue. . . . By thinking of liberty as a supreme moral value Tocqueville endowed it with an evaluative potential that was missing from the works of liberals like Smith or Say.[65]

This proves to be one of the most original and innovative aspects of Tocqueville's thought that accounts in part for his unconventional liberalism.

That Tocqueville was deeply influenced by Christian political economy will come as a surprise to those interpreters who claimed that he was not interested in economic theories at all. As Michael Drolet demonstrated, Tocqueville's thinking on economic and social issues was strongly influenced by Villeneuve-Bargemont's book *Christian Political Economy*, which he read in the autumn of 1834. Anchored in an older Catholic tradition, Villeneuve-Bargemont's ideas strengthened Tocqueville's belief that economics and politics must be properly combined with moral and religious considerations. By stressing the potentially nefarious consequences of the unregulated pursuit of wealth in a market society, Villeneuve-Bargemont's book exercised a salutary influence on Tocqueville's unconventional liberalism, reinforcing his skepticism toward materialism and the market's sometimes corrosive effects on individuals and society. Perhaps even more importantly, Villeneuve-Bargemont's ideas prompted Tocqueville to take a strong interest in social charity and pauperism. True to his methodological commitments, Tocqueville decided to analyze pauperism not as an isolated phenomenon but within the larger context of the development of democracy and in relation to social justice and political stability.

In so doing, he started from the following paradox. As civilization develops, social classes become more refined while the poor find themselves regressing, as it were, into a new form of "barbarism." In attempting to account for this apparent paradox, Tocqueville resorted to the ideas of Malthus, who helped him understand better the close relation between combating poverty and crime. Tocqueville, who took a strong interest in penitentiary reform, focused on the relation between the rise of industry, the growth of the working-class population, and crime. By studying the writings of Malthus and Say, he sought to understand how economic crises generate a rise in unemployment which, in turn, contributes to an increase in crime and poverty.

Tocqueville's first report on pauperism (he authored two such reports) was modeled on his previous report on prisons.[66] He distinguished between two kinds of welfare—private and public—and noticed that pauperism had grown more rapidly in England than in any country. His visits to England and Ireland were catalysts for his thinking on the issues of political economy, poverty, and the role of local government and local aristocracy. Tocqueville understood the importance of free trade in promoting economic growth in modern society, but warned at the same time that one of the outcomes of free trade is more poverty for a significant number of individuals left behind. Tocqueville proceeded then to highlight the economic causes of pauperism and boldly concluded that accepting the principle of a legal right to welfare was the main cause of the growth of pauperism in England: "Any measure that establishes legal charity on a permanent basis and gives it an administrative form thereby creates an idle and lazy class, living at the expense of the industrial and working class. . . . Such a law is a bad seed planted in the legal structure."[67] In England, Tocqueville noted, the legal right to welfare robbed the poor of their liberty by forcing them to remain within their own parishes. Moreover, the principle of a legal right to welfare made it in practice impossible to distinguish between the undeserving and the deserving poor. This was no minor issue for Tocqueville, who believed that rights ought to be wedded to responsibilities. Unfortunately, he warned his readers, a legal right to welfare ignores this point and paradoxically ends by fostering greater class conflict, thus breaking down the bonds of community.

For Tocqueville, the only reasonable solution was the creation of private charities harmoniously and effectively linking private and local initiatives. He accepted, however, that during serious economic crises it was legitimate for the state to give emergency funds. Tocqueville emphasized the importance of creating an economy whose main branches (agriculture, trade, and industry) worked harmoniously together to reduce the impact of severe economic crises. In an unpublished text entitled "A Fragment for a Social Policy" (written around 1847), Tocqueville listed a few necessary elements for a reasonable and effective social policy meant to improve the living conditions of the poor. The list included a general reduction of public charges (taxes), the establishment of a few institutions such as saving banks, credit agencies, free schools, laws limiting the work hours, and hospices.[68] Tocqueville also stressed the role of civil associations and widespread property ownership that, in his view, could help lessen dependency and reduce poverty in the long run. Workers, Tocqueville thought, must be given the feeling for and the habits of property and should also be encouraged to build up capital funds that could be invested.

To this effect, Tocqueville proposed the creation of independent saving banks whose effectiveness, he opined, could be enhanced if they were linked to *monts-de-piété*.[69] In his *Letter on Pauperism in Normandy*, Tocqueville went on to discuss in detail various practical ways of combating poverty and advocated the creation of local associations that could provide for mutual assistance and effectively eradicate vagrancy and beggary. In all of his proposals, Tocqueville focused on the relationship between taxation, welfare, and social responsibility and sought to reform the whole system of taxation in such a way as to diminish the burdens on the poor by raising the contributions of the rich. He envisaged increasing the number of saving banks, pawn shops, mutual aid societies, and charitable workshops, and endorsed the creation of hospices, *bureaux de bienfaisance*, welfare payments, free schools, and laws restricting working hours.[70]

Tocqueville also took a strong interest in the fate of abandoned children, an issue that in his view was inseparable from poverty and crime. He wrote four such reports for the general departmental council of La Manche between 1843 and 1846. The reports examined the issue of whether it was the responsibility of central government and local authorities or that of wet-nurses and adoptive parents to provide foundlings with clothing, and also examined whether it was fair for young single mothers to be entitled to a legal right to welfare. In exploring this issue, Tocqueville expressed again his opposition to the limitless expansion of welfare and argued against the practice of the *tour* that allowed families to abandon unwanted offspring. Tocqueville's opposition stemmed from his belief that a different approach was needed to properly solve the issue of abandoned children (he would eventually endorse the creation of local admission offices).

* * *

To conclude, a cursory examination of Tocqueville's method in *The Old Regime and the Revolution* and his lesser-known economic writings shows that he did not ignore the economic facts and theories of his time, as some of his critics alleged. Nor was Tocqueville insensitive to the plight of the poor and the fate of the working classes, in spite of his visceral opposition to socialism, so obvious in his *Recollections* and parliamentary speeches. Tocqueville's drafts and notes for both *Democracy in America* and *The Old Regime and the Revolution,* along with his often-ignored travel notes in America (translated as *Journey to America*),[71] are indispensable sources for anyone wanting to familiarize oneself with Tocqueville's laboratory. These documents show that he chose to leave out a significant amount of information not because he ignored facts or was not interested in them, but because he made a number of conscious choices in light of his rhetorical strategies and intellectual inclinations.[72]

One can hardly overstate the exquisite quality of Tocqueville's writing style that never fails to impress even his most skeptical readers. Tocqueville is regarded today as a first-rate writer and moralist in the best French classical tradition and his fascinating correspondence ranks among the best epistolary exchanges of the nineteenth century, a period that excelled at the art of letter writing.[73] As his private letters and notes show, Tocqueville believed that the style and form of his writings were as important as his ideas and drafted many pages and notes before settling on a definitive version. One of Tocqueville's recent translators, Arthur Goldhammer, described him as a genuine architect of language who "sought to create a harmonious edifice, a structure in which each part was carefully proportioned and subordinated to a conception of the whole."[74] Those who claim that *Democracy in America*, for example, "is badly structured and often incoherent"[75] only prove that they are incapable of appreciating the subtle beauty of Tocqueville's classic style. By reexamining his notes and drafts for both *Democracy in America* and *The Old Regime and the Revolution*, we stand to gain a new appreciation for the seriousness with which Tocqueville sought to understand the complexity of modern democratic society and attempted to formulate a new science of politics for a new world.

Notes

A previous version of this chapter was presented at the WOW3 conference, Workshop in Political Theory and Policy Analysis, Indiana University, May 2004. The present chapter also draws on my review essay of Robert T. Gannett's *Tocqueville Unveiled* and Michael Drolet's *Tocqueville, Democracy, and Social Reform*, which appeared in *History of Political Thought* 26, no. 1 (Spring 2005): 181–86. Published by permission of Imprint Academic. Special thanks to Sheldon Gellar and Jeremy Jennings for their comments on previous drafts of this text.

1. Alexis de Tocqueville, *Selected Letters on Politics and Society*, ed. Roger Boesche, trans. Roger Boesche and James Toupin (Berkeley: University of California Press, 1985), 115.

2. James T. Schleifer, *The Making of Tocqueville's Democracy in America*, 2nd rev. ed. (Indianapolis, IN: Liberty Fund, 2000); Schleifer, "Tocqueville's Journey Revisited: What Was Striking and New in America," in Alexis de Toc-

queville (1805–1859): A Special Bicentennial Issue, *The Tocqueville Review/La Revue Tocqueville* 27, no. 2 (2006): 403–24; Sheldon Wolin, *Tocqueville between Two Worlds: The Making of a Political and Theoretical Life* (Princeton, NJ: Princeton University Press, 2001); Rogers M. Smith, "Beyond Tocqueville, Myrdal, and Hartz: The Multiple Traditions in America," *American Political Science Review* 87, no. 3 (1993): 549–66; and Gary Wills, "Did Tocqueville 'Get' America?," *New York Review of Books* 51, no. 7 (April 29, 2004): 52–56.

3. No one understood better this point than the late François Furet, whose writings on Tocqueville and the French Revolution are indispensable to all Tocquevillian scholars. See Furet, *Interpreting the French Revolution* (New York: Cambridge University Press, 1981), and his essay "The Intellectual Origins of Tocqueville's Thought," *The Tocqueville Revue/La Revue Tocqueville* 7 (1985–1986): 117–27.

4. Melvin Richter, "Tocqueville's Contributions to the Theory of Revolution," in *Revolution*, ed. Carl J. Friedrich (New York: Atherton Press, 1966), 73–121; and Richter, "The Uses of Theory: Tocqueville's Adaptation of Montesquieu," in *Essays in Theory and History*, ed. Melvin Richter (Cambridge, MA: Harvard University Press, 1970), 74–102.

5. Wolin, *Tocqueville between Two Worlds*, 140.

6. Wolin, *Tocqueville between Two Worlds*, 141–43. I commented on Wolin's book in my review published in *The Review of Politics* 64, no. 2 (2002): 537–40.

7. Wolin, *Tocqueville between Two Worlds*, 143.

8. For more information, see chapter 3 in this volume by Sheldon Gellar.

9. Wills, "Did Tocqueville 'Get' America?," 55.

10. Wills, "Did Tocqueville 'Get' America?," 52.

11. "Tocqueville reasoned a priori rather than from the facts he found in America. He 'divines' America—or 'intuits' it" (Wills, "Did Tocqueville 'Get' America?"), 52.

12. Wills, "Did Tocqueville 'Get' America?," 52.

13. Wills, "Did Tocqueville 'Get' America?," 53.

14. Wills, "Did Tocqueville 'Get' America?," 54.

15. Wills, "Did Tocqueville 'Get' America?," 55.

16. The two classical accounts are those of George Wilson Pierson, *Tocqueville and Beaumont in America*, 2nd ed. (Baltimore, MD: Johns Hopkins University Press, 1996); and Schleifer, *Making of Tocqueville's Democracy in America*.

17. Mill as quoted in Saguiv A. Hadari, *Theory in Practice: Tocqueville's New Science of Politics* (Stanford, CA: Stanford University Press, 1988), 43.

18. Letter of October 4, 1837, in Alexis de Tocqueville, *Œuvres Complètes, XIII:1. Correspondance avec Louis de Kergorlay*, ed. Jean-Alain Lesourd (Paris: Gallimard, 1977), 47.

19. Pierre Manent, "Tocqueville, Political Philosopher," in *The Cambridge Companion to Tocqueville*, ed. Cheryl B. Welch (Cambridge: Cambridge University Press, 2006), 111; Laurence Guellec, "Tocqueville and Political Rhetoric," in

Cambridge Companion to Tocqueville, 170. Also see Eduardo Nolla's introductory study in Tocqueville, *Democracy in America*, vol. I, ed. Eduardo Nolla (Paris: Vrin, 1990).

20. See, for example, the following claim made by Jon Elster: "The main flaw in Tocqueville's analysis is that it is sometimes too systematic. Oscillating between intentional and functional explanation, he strives to find meaning in what were more plausibly accidental or incidental outcomes of political struggles" ("Tocqueville on 1789," in *Cambridge Companion to Tocqueville*, 64).

21. James T. Schleifer, "Tocqueville's *Democracy in America* Reconsidered," in *Cambridge Companion to Tocqueville*, 122–24.

22. Hadari, *Theory in Practice*, 6. Here is a revealing confession of Tocqueville, taken from a letter he sent to Gustave de Beaumont on July 8, 1838: "Le chapitre que j'écris en ce moment a pour object d'examiner quelle influence exercent les idées et les sentiments démocratiques sur le gouvernement. J'ai commencé, m'appuyant sur tout l'édifice de mon livre, *par établir théoriquement* que les idées et les sentiments des peoples démocratiques les faisaient tendre naturellement, et à moins qu'ils ne se retiennent, vers la concentration de tous les pouvoirs dans les mains de l'autorité centrale et nationale. . . . Maintenant, *je veux prouver par les faits actuels que j'ai raison. J'ai déjà beaucoup de faits généraux* (car je ne puis employer que ceux-là), *mais j'en voudrais advantage.* … C'est assurément un *grand tableau* et un *grand sujet*" (*Œuvres Complètes*, VIII:1. *Correspondance d'Alexis de Tocqueville et de Gustave de Beaumont*, ed. André Jardin [Paris: Gallimard, 1967], 311; emphasis added).

23. See Raymond Boudon, "L'exigence de Tocqueville: la 'science politique nouvelle,'" in *The Tocqueville Review/La Revue Tocqueville* 27, no. 2 (2006): 13–34.

24. Boudon, "L'exigence de Tocqueville," 20.

25. Seymour Drescher, "Tocqueville's Comparative Perspectives," in *Cambridge Companion to Tocqueville*, 21–48.

26. See Hadari, *Theory in Practice*, chap. 3; and Raymond Boudon, *The Unintended Consequences of Human Action* (New York: St. Martin's Press, 1982). Schleifer also comments on Tocqueville's method in "Tocqueville's *Democracy in America* Reconsidered," 122–30.

27. Hadari, *Theory in Practice*, 42.

28. For an informed analysis on this topic that also compares Tocqueville's ideas with those of his contemporaries, see Lucien Jaume, *Tocqueville: Les sources aristocratiques de la liberté* (Paris: Fayard, 2008), 28–35.

29. See Pierson, *Tocqueville and Beaumont in America*, 158–59.

30. Manent, "Tocqueville, Political Philosopher," 114–15. For more details, see chap. 19, "Some Meanings of *Démocratie*," in Schleifer, *Making of Tocqueville's Democracy in America*, 325–39.

31. For more details, see Jean-Claude Lamberti, *Tocqueville et les deux démocraties* (Paris: PUF, 1983), 33.

32. On Tocqueville's hermeneutics, see Hadari, *Theory in Practice*, 89–90.

33. Tocqueville, *Œuvres Complètes, XVI: Mélanges*, ed. Françoise Mélonio (Paris: Gallimard, 1989), 230.

34. Tocqueville, *Œuvres Complètes, XVI*, 230; also see 231–32.

35. See, for example, Tocqueville's important letter to Eugène Stoffels, October 5, 1836, in Tocqueville, *Selected Letters on Politics and Society*, 112–15.

36. It can be found in chapter 11, book 2, of volume one of *The Old Regime and the Revolution*.

37. Alexis de Tocqueville, *Recollections* (London: MacDonald, 1970), 67.

38. It is a pity that the recent translation (by Alan S. Kahan) of volume two of *The Old Regime and the Revolution*, including Tocqueville's notes, has passed largely unnoticed among political theorists in the Anglo-American world.

39. The letter is quoted in Gannett, *Tocqueville Unveiled*, 29.

40. In her widely acclaimed book, Madame de Staël claimed that far from being fortuitous, the fall of the Old Regime in 1789 was in fact inevitable, the outcome of a long historical evolution that could not have been blocked by the efforts of a few individuals. It was in this regard that Staël's analysis anticipated Tocqueville's meticulously researched diagnosis of the internal crisis of the Old Regime. By focusing on the lack of public spirit and the absence of a genuine constitution prior to 1789, she demonstrated how the Revolution was an irreversible phenomenon that arose in response to the deep structural problems of the Old Regime in France. For a new edition of Madame de Staël's book, see *Considerations on the Principal Events of the French Revolution*, ed. Aurelian Craiutu (Indianapolis, IN: Liberty Fund, 2008).

41. For a recent edition, see François Guizot, *History of Civilization in Europe*, ed. Larry Siedentop, trans. W. Hazlitt (London: Penguin, 1997).

42. I commented on this issue in Aurelian Craiutu, *Liberalism under Siege: The Political Thought of the French Doctrinaires* (Lanham, MD: Lexington Books, 2003), 19–85.

43. Gannett, *Tocqueville Unveiled*, 39

44. For more details, see Gannett, *Tocqueville Unveiled*, 43–45.

45. On this issue, also see Harvey Mitchell, *Individual Choice and the Structures of History: Alexis de Tocqueville as Historian Reappraised* (New York: Cambridge University Press, 1996). For a new translation, see Tocqueville, *The Old Regime and the Revolution*, vol. I, trans. Alan S. Kahan (Chicago: University of Chicago Press, 1998).

46. Gannett, *Tocqueville Unveiled*, 83–87.

47. Tocqueville, *The Old Regime and the Revolution*, vol. II, trans. Alan S. Kahan (Chicago: University of Chicago Press, 2001), 1–52.

48. Tocqueville, *Old Regime*, 303.

49. Tocqueville, *Old Regime*, 326.

50. Tocqueville, *Old Regime*, 339.

51. Tocqueville, *Old Regime*, 341.

52. Tocqueville, *Old Regime*, 352–63.

53. Gannett, *Tocqueville Unveiled*, 50–51.

54. Gannett, *Tocqueville Unveiled*, 76.

55. Quoted in Gannett, *Tocqueville Unveiled*, 75.

56. Tocqueville, *Old Regime*, vol. I, 217.

57. Tocqueville, *Old Regime*, vol. I, 217.

58. Tocqueville, *Old Regime*, vol. II, 10–11.

59. It is the incontestable merit of Seymour Drescher, Eric Keslassy, Jean-Louis Benoît, Michael Drolet, and Matthew Mancini to have called our attention to the richness of this aspect of Tocqueville's thought. In the Anglo-American academic world, Drescher's excellent anthology, *Tocqueville and Beaumont on Social Reform*, trans. and ed. Seymour Drescher (New York: Harper, 1968) and his pathbreaking study, *Dilemmas of Democracy: Tocqueville and Modernization* (Pittsburgh: University of Pittsburgh Press, 1968) deserve special mention. In *Alexis de Tocqueville* (Woodbridge, CT: Twayne Publishers, 1994), Matthew Mancini argued that Tocqueville was familiar with the economic theories of his time and used them to advance his arguments in favor of welfare reform and emancipation. Eric Keslassy's *Libéralisme de Tocqueville à l'épreuve du pauperisme* (Paris: l'Harmattan, 2000) and Michael Drolet's *Tocqueville, Democracy, and Social Reform* (Houndmills, Basingstoke: Palgrave, 2003) offer rich interpretations of Tocqueville's economic views against the background of nineteenth-century debates in political economy. I also recommend the anthology Alexis de Tocqueville, *Textes économiques: Anthologie critique*, eds. Jean-Louis Benoît and Eric Keslassy (Paris: Pocket-Agora, 2005).

60. Drolet, *Tocqueville, Democracy, and Social Reform*, 41.

61. Tocqueville, *Democracy in America*, trans. Harvey C. Mansfield and Delba Winthrop (Chicago: University of Chicago Press, 2000), 532.

62. Drolet, *Tocqueville, Democracy, and Social Reform*, 65.

63. See Aurelian Craiutu, "Tocqueville's Paradoxical Moderation," *The Review of Politics* 67, no. 4 (2005): 599–629.

64. While emphasizing the importance of mores and customs, Tocqueville was also prepared to affirm liberty as *independent* of its association with manners, customs, modes of thought, and laws.

65. Drolet, *Tocqueville, Democracy, and Social Reform*, 70, 71.

66. See Alexis de Tocqueville, *Memoir on Pauperism* (Chicago: Ivan R. Dee, 1997); and Alexis de Tocqueville and Gustave de Beaumont, *On the Penitentiary System in the United States and Its Application in France* (Carbondale: Southern Illinois University Press, 1964).

67. Tocqueville, *Memoir on Pauperism*, 58.

68. Alexis de Tocqueville, *Œuvres Complètes, III:2. Écrits et discours politiques*, ed. André Jardin (Paris: Gallimard, 1985), 743.

69. For more details, see Drolet, *Tocqueville, Democracy, and Social Reform*, 153–60.

70. Tocqueville, *Œuvres Complètes, XVI: Mélanges* (Paris: Gallimard, 1989), 158–61.

71. Alexis de Tocqueville, *Journey to America*, ed. J. P. Mayer, trans. George Lawrence (New Haven, CT: Yale University Press, 1962).

72. Schleifer, "Tocqueville's *Democracy in America* Reconsidered," 132.

73. For an outstanding collection, see Alexis de Tocqueville, *Lettres choisies. Souvenirs*, ed. Françoise Mélonio and Laurence Guellec (Paris: Gallimard, 2003).

74. Arthur Goldhammer, "Translator's Note," in Alexis de Tocqueville, *Democracy in America* (New York: The Library of America, 2004), 873.

75. This claim was made by Jon Ester, "Tocqueville on 1789," 64. Elster's new book, *Alexis de Tocqueville: The First Social Scientist*, will be published by Cambridge University Press in 2009.

PART II

Tocquevillian Analytics and the Contemporary World

5

Racial Equality and Social Equality: Understanding Tocqueville's Democratic Revolution and the American Civil Rights Movement, 1954–1970

Barbara Allen

In 1831, Alexis de Tocqueville embarked on a journey to North America, escaping, for a time, the cycle of political revolution and reaction that had jolted his native France since 1789. American democracy offered many surprises, including the astonishing diversity of peoples that seemed to have been woven into a single social fabric. "Imagine a society formed of all the people of the nations of the world: English, French, Germans," Tocqueville wrote immediately after arriving in New York City.[1] By his time's standards, the scene was remarkable. A glimpse of New York prompted a novel, if now familiar, hypothesis that interest in a democratic age could prove an antidote to ancient divisions and animosities.

In *Democracy in America*, Tocqueville presented an analytical foundation for these conjectures along with details about the institutional and ideational sources of Americans' particular expression of such possibilities. Federal institutions and the *foederal* or covenantal theology that, in part, inspired the particular frame of limited, distributed, shared constitutional authority of the United States, figure prominently in his observations and deductions. Informants like Jared Sparks stressed the significance of the New England town, while interviews with other notables emphasized church and civil covenants, charters, and compacts that lay a foundation for New England governance.[2] Yet, some features of American democracy conformed neither to Tocqueville's general portrait of the democratic

potential nor to the mental stance of a covenanting culture. Racial antipa-
thy produced by slavery in the United States limited the reach of democratic transformations. The relations and institutions of the "slave states,"
Tocqueville assured his readers, however, were "American," not "democratic." Leaving the systematic analysis of race slavery to the conclusion of
his initial (and, at its time of publication, the only envisioned) volume on
the lessons and future of American democracy, Tocqueville offered a dismal prognosis for American federalism and race relations.

Tocqueville's assessment of "race" and democracy in the United States
raises several theoretical puzzles: How compelling are the ideas and actions
spurring the democratic revolution? How might experience inform social
learning and, in turn, move a polity toward the political and social integration of distinct peoples? Additional questions emerge as we attempt
to generalize from Tocqueville's analysis: How are a people's beliefs about
the cause and nature of existence connected to the structure of its society? How does culture influence the political capacities of a people—or
a person? Tocqueville's conjectures about American race relations also
present an opportunity to look more closely at his analytical methods and
conclusions.[3]

Much in Tocqueville's analysis rings true, even at the beginning of a
new millennium. Race slavery in the American south, he argued, created a
social structure and political environment ultimately at odds with republican institutions. Constitutional compromises perpetuating slavocracy
would jeopardize civil society north and south for generations, Tocqueville
predicted, as "Anglo-Americans," united in the shared economic interests of
both regions, maintained the social practices—if not legal institutions—of
race dominance and segregation. Still, other aspects of Tocqueville's prognosis seem unduly pessimistic, viewed from a vantage now approaching
nearly two centuries since he observed the American case. Undoubtedly,
he underestimated the capacities of African Americans, as slaves and free
persons, and perhaps underrated the durability of the Union and adaptability of American federalism.

How did Tocqueville's analytical method enable accurate predictions?
What sources of error led to mistaken judgments? Is it possible to use his
analytical approach to "correct" miscalculations made in the nineteenth
century? These are some of the methodological questions that the present
chapter addresses along with the theoretical puzzles raised by Tocqueville's
analysis of "race" and its implications for the democratic revolution. To
begin, we must examine Tocqueville's understanding of "race" and its
meaning in the new age of social equality.

Race and Political Inquiry in an Age of Equality

While Tocqueville observed the diversity of peoples forming an American political culture, the foundation for "scientific" investigations of "racial" differences was being cemented in European and American intellectual circles. Theories of British and German naturalists, American physicians and paleontologists, Swiss zoologists, and French anthropologists would soon inaugurate new scientific disciplines and spark scientific and social movements in eugenics based on new classifications of *homo sapiens*.[4] Advancing beyond taxonomy by the mid-nineteenth century, statistical studies claimed to correlate such indicators of type as average head size with the social traits, talent, and intellectual capacities of various racial categories. Such widely cited methods of classification meshed with ideology in Old and New World politics. In antebellum America, the science of "race" denoted an infraspecies division below the taxonomic rank pertaining to all human beings. In Europe, similar developments linking "race" to shared history helped legitimate political consolidations, building nation-states premised on affinities that demanded a unitary religion, language, culture, and "people." Although Tocqueville rejected social theories based on racial determinism, he used the terminology of "race" in comparing the social and political development of specific cultural groups. The scientific study of "race" represented the conjunction of two seemingly contrary intellectual tendencies of the democratic age: a penchant for excessive generalization, coupled with a drive for increasingly finer differentiation. The former evinced a philosophical urge to grasp the "whole of humanity," while the latter emerged from a psychological desire to stand apart from the democratic mass, an aim readily accomplished by classification denoting antithesis as well as difference.

In the nineteenth century, historians and pioneers in the sciences of society expressed this democratic intellectual orientation in grand theory, often claiming universality for their models of the human being and the citizen. Tocqueville challenged the new orthodoxy of his generation's social engineers who seemed to believe

> that there is only one rational way for men to govern themselves; that this way is rationally clear to everyone; that the same institutions are equally applicable everywhere to all peoples; that everything which is not this rational government . . . should be destroyed and replaced by this ideal which first the French, [and then] the entire human species must end up adopting.[5]

The nineteenth-century American's tendency "to withdraw narrowly into himself and claim to judge the world from there" underscored the second characteristic of the democratic philosophic method. The extremes of excessive generalization among democratic historians and students of the nascent social sciences and the self-referential "empiricism" of the democratic psyche paradoxically generated little creative or innovative thinking. Instead, Tocqueville observed, reason cowered and voices of genuine inquiry silenced themselves in the face of a new intellectual authority, the "social power," public opinion.[6] On the subject of "race," commonly received opinion often consisted of persistent prejudices that could survive and subvert legislative reform.

Tocqueville contrasted the democratic amalgam of excessive generalization and particularistic reasoning with the intellectual traditions of an aristocratic age, which he likewise rejected. In *The Old Regime and the Revolution*, Edmund Burke played the foil opposite the role of scientists of society, representing a type of historiography that imprisoned human will in a deterministic natural order of rank and role. Tocqueville sought a middle way between traditionalist and rationalist extremes, which, as he pointed out, alike rendered liberty and self-government irrelevant, as nature, in the former philosophic approach, and the unyielding logic of egoistic choice, in the latter view, similarly determined the destinies of persons and peoples.[7] Within the broad structure of history, Tocqueville explained, the particularities of culture and the specific responses of individuals, as well as happenstance, brought short-term variations in the democratic social condition and influenced the trajectory of long-term historical development. In Tocqueville's terms, historical structure, culture, language, social conditions, and "accidental" circumstances traced a "fatal circle" around each individual and people, but within the vast limits of its circumference humanity was free. The implications were as important for the analyst to grasp as it was for the democratic citizen. Those who thought that "peoples are never masters of themselves . . . and that they necessarily obey I do not know which insurmountable and unintelligent force born of previous events, the race, the soil, or the climate" were doomed, or doomed those whom they studied, to servitude.[8]

Analysts of social phenomenon must view choice, the interpretation of its meaning and consequences, within the structure of history, which is itself a category of interpretation bearing a culture's ontology and epistemology. The democratic social condition, similarly, must be understood in terms of the *longue durée*, a greater trajectory of causation from which universal trends appeared to emerge.[9] A given historical moment was dependent on paths whose origins might be intuited but never certainly known. Such patterns of history, even those discerned by the most careful human observer, must always be viewed as conjectures and constructions of the human intellect.[10] Tocqueville offered his readers several pathways of cause and conjectures about the points of departure for the peoples of North America.

Although he consistently rejected biological inheritance, among other "unintelligent forces," as a factor influencing American intellectual and institutional development, Tocqueville had initially included "race" and environmental features such as soil and climate as plausible explanations of the character of American democracy.[11] He eventually combined such features as the physical environment, historical events, and political geography with other "circumstances" (les circonstances) signifying the "point of departure" for a people. Mores, "the whole moral and intellectual state of a people," added another causal category to Tocqueville's explanation.[12] Laws and, more generally, authoritative institutions, including the governing framework, completed his portrait of the "general causes tending to maintain a democratic republic in the United States."[13] Nevertheless, "race" continued to offer a certain explanation, if only as a placeholder for cultural inheritances that influenced mores and laws.

Social Inheritance and Political Capacity

Intellectual habits cultivated through generations, not a deterministic biological inheritance, explained the diverse institutional development of societies. Historical "accidents" including conquest might change the trajectory of a people's development; more often, subtle changes in law or belief set institutions on a new course. Tocqueville noted the exogenous sources of ideational and institutional transformation, distinguishing these from the tensions that might exist among the principal features guiding a people's way of life. The broadest structure of cause, the democratic revolution (or in another epoch, the mentalité and principles of the reigning social state), not only drew from but also assisted such endogenous sources of change. Institutional developments facilitating trade among distinct communities had often placed a commercial ethos in tension with other social principles and values. As peoples "saw, listened, and borrowed," their mores and laws might change in a common direction that seemed universally favorable to the democratic social condition. Yet, antecedent "facts" unique to a given polity continued to yield variation in the responses to even the most uni-

versal trends. Although Tocqueville, like many of his contemporaries, used
the term "race" to signify such mediating social inheritances, he generally offered the broader idea of national character to account for diverse
responses to the democratic social state.

National character could prove a considerable constraint on transculturation: "If nature has not given each people an *indelible* national character
one must at least admit that physical and political causes have made a people's spirit adopt habits which are very difficult to eradicate, even though it
is no longer subject to the influence of any of those causes."[14] Tocqueville
sketched several illustrations of the idea, including notes explaining why
the German character might lend itself to colonial enterprises, but not necessarily to self-government.

German immigrants in America, he reflected, formed small rural
enclaves, keeping "intact the spirit and ways of their fatherland" by isolat-
ing themselves from the challenges and opportunities of the democratic
age.[15] German towns in western Pennsylvania enjoyed local liberty but
they reproduced a political culture whose custodial orientation to authority suppressed individual enterprise and liberty. Tocqueville characterized the culture as "immobile," concluding that "the German limits his
desires to bettering his position and that of his family little by little . . . he
sticks to his domestic hearth, encloses his happiness within his horizon
and shows no curiosity to know what there is beyond his last furrow."[16]
Tocqueville encountered expressions of nativism and prejudice aimed at
German immigrants in his American encounters, but these do not seem
to be the source of his thinking on the matter.[17] Instead, he hypothesized
that the imposition of Roman law on the societies of continental Europe
had for centuries linked a repressive public criminal code to a liberal code
of rights; the result, he argued, was equality in servitude and nationalistic
pride.[18] These observations, most of which never found their way systematically into published work, cast Tocqueville's better-known hypotheses
linking foundational beliefs and institutional development in a new light.
A thorough understanding of a people's religious belief remains a keystone
in Tocquevillian analytics, but the crucial variable—religion—also had a
history shaped by antecedent circumstances.

Habits of heart and mind, Tocqueville argued throughout his writings,
developed in accordance with the most fundamental presuppositions a
people held about the cause and nature of existence. No ideas, Tocqueville
contended, were more important in the development of political concepts
than a people's understanding of the relationship between God and human-

ity and the resulting idea of right relations among human beings.[19] "Next to every religion," he also observed, "is a political opinion that is joined to it by affinity."[20] Christianity, he contended, showed a particular affinity for the tenets of democratic equality.[21] Nevertheless, the moral and ethical ideals he associated alike with Christian teachings and the democratic age—the moral equality of persons—could inform various political and social constructions of equality. In Tocqueville's analysis of Pennsylvania Germans, continental Europeans, and Roman law, national character emerges from a legal culture that in turn mediated the ever-evolving affinity of religious and political ideas.

Likewise, Tocqueville's depiction of German village life suggests great variation in the expressions given to the ubiquitous human capacity for self-organization in which local liberty and the resulting daily opportunity to confront shared problems seemed to suffice to produce the foundations of republican government. Pennsylvania Germans seem to have little in common with the archetype of civic-minded citizens depicted in Tocqueville's New England town. The contrast seems to suggest that a society that "acts by itself on itself" may fail to produce a lasting political body with sufficient cohesion to maintain its way of life or build a democratic republic.[22] In a continental republic whose territory offered a vast expanse for continued settlement, the democratic social condition could indeed promote insularity instead of cultural exchange. Although Tocqueville famously cautioned against the rise of powerful cultural and political centers as harmful to the voluntaristic spirit of republican government, a republican political culture required more than bucolic simplicity. Cities attracting a diverse population seemed better suited to permit "interest" to dissolve the barriers raised by "national character" and religious sources of contesting beliefs. In *Democracy in America*, the assimilation of a minority population of American Catholics to the majority Protestant culture illustrated the conjecture.

Interest, "Circumstances," and Political Integration

Tocqueville portrayed American Catholics as unquestioning believers who could nonetheless engage effectively in a civil society emphasizing secular political judgment and action. Using Irish Catholic immigrants as an example, he suggested that such a people might maintain conservative political views but would nonetheless support democracy because, being poor, "they need all citizens to govern in order to come to government themselves," and being a minority, "they need all rights to be respected to be assured of the free exercise of theirs."[23] "Interest" again emerged as a motivating force, along with other elements of this minority's self-understanding enabling priest and congregants to respect principles of republican government and "democratic instincts that are not contrary" to faith.[24]

Catholics and Protestants alike explained that an allegiance to the Roman Church posed no problem to the self-governing polities of the United States. From a Boston Protestant he heard: "We are not afraid of Catholicism in the United States because we are sure that with us it will be so modified that it will have no influence on our political approach." Catholics seemed to corroborate the general notion that the democratic social state had a greater effect on American Catholicism than the Roman Church.[25] Tocqueville also learned that the American Church contended with little hierarchy in the selection of priests since the United States was considered primarily to be a missionary field for the "conversion of a pagan country." As had been the case with local liberty in civil orders left to themselves in colonial times, priests and congregants in the United States formed societies characterized by a significant degree of self-government, but geography also had inhibited any effort to isolate their parishes from the majority culture. In such circumstances, Catholic institutions had emerged as the premier sites of secular education, socially integrating Protestant sects in their spiritually informed, yet, secular mission.[26] Toleration, assimilation, and a potentially powerful indirect role for religion had become possible for a religious culture that many Europeans rejected as unalterably opposed to the idea of liberty.[27]

A second example of political and social integration may be culled from Tocqueville's description of New England's seventeenth-century covenanters. Tocqueville portrayed the colonies of Massachusetts Bay and Connecticut as essentially homogeneous on many of the main cultural features of language and history. Their startling capacity to engage political differences productively and innovate institutionally depended, he maintained, on their ability to shield their religious doctrine from dissent. Yet, on the dimension of existence of most importance to these peoples—religious doctrine—and their attitude toward dissent, he surely overstated the case. The Connecticut colony that Tocqueville discussed formed as a result of religious differences with Massachusetts Bay. Despite doctrinal disputes, the resulting civil and church polities united themselves in federated associations as they continued their inquiries into matters of faith.

Dissenters in colonial New England may be more accurately described as distinguishing between the foundations constituting their common existence and "things indifferent," as they would classify a variety of possible expressions of common belief. The constitutional foundation of town covenants and church order were frequently opened, or "invented," to public appraisal and amendment. After all, the *foederal* (taking the Latin, *foedus* for covenant) theologians of New England divined their system of interlocking covenants as a result of "lifting the veil" and responding to the core doctrine of Calvinism, predestination.[28] As Unitarian minister William Ellery Channing had explained to Tocqueville, the leading lights of New England continued to press beyond "the first innovator" (John Calvin) as "human reason progress[ed] to greater perfection" in the nineteenth century.[29] Covenantal practices brought order to individual and collective inquiry in the seventeenth century, permitting experience to inform invention in faith as well as in politics. Federated church polities could become "orderly knit together" without requiring absolute conformity; civil federations followed the same form, uniting colony-wide governments and intercolonial associations.[30] With this "correction" of Tocqueville's discussion of the New England "point of departure," we can see in American *foederalism* and the resulting federal constitutional form, an institutional basis enabling the political integration of diverse peoples.

Tocqueville told his readers that the institutional and intellectual culture of New England permeated the union, its frontier settlements, and the established communities of new states like Ohio.[31] It was a claim made by several of his American informants that he seemed only to question in regard to the "other branch of the Anglo family" inhabiting the "slave states." Perhaps covenant-informed political institutions and highly participatory civil society would enable peoples of distinct "national character" to develop shared standards of value from pursuing shared interests in the context of local liberty and individual self-reliance; perhaps in Ohio even "the German" would adopt an "American" understanding of authority. Such possibilities conform to the general arc of Tocqueville's assessment of democracy's power to stimulate transculturation in the direction of a dominant culture whose institutions and mores encouraged an enlightened understanding of "interest." When it came to the two branches of the Anglo-American family divided by race slavery, however, the common ground of "interest" was often less apparent. When these regions' interests did coincide, moreover, the resulting union often failed to serve the cause of African American liberty.

"Race" Prejudice and the Barriers to Political Capacity and Integration

However possible it might have become to integrate the various waves of European immigrants into American politics, the circumstances of race slavery presented a much greater challenge. Of the three races of North America, Tocqueville observed:

> The men spread over [the American continent] do not form, as in Europe, so many offshoots of the same family. From the first one finds in them three naturally distinct, and, I could almost say, inimical races. Education, law, origin, and even the external form of their features have raised an almost insurmountable barrier between them; fortune has gathered them on the same soil, but it has mixed them without being able to intermingle them, and each pursues its destiny separately.[32]

Where physical difference had become a mark associated with bondage, the stigma of servitude extended the barrier between races indefinitely through generations.[33]

Race and Race Slavery

Tocqueville had little firsthand knowledge of the lives of people living in the culture of slavocracy. His description of American slavery drew heavily on interviews with notables including, in New England, former president John Quincy Adams, as well as lawyers and planters throughout the American south. Tocqueville learned that law prohibited the intimate association of whites and blacks where slavery had been abolished. Custom, he heard in the north, raised barriers to shared commercial interests as well as friendships between Americans and the "foreign race." Tocqueville heard that the "badge of inferiority" associating servitude with color prohibited political and social integration alike. Free blacks could be enfranchised in the north, but violent reprisals awaited them at the polls. The prejudices hindering social relations would resist all efforts to produce legal equality; segregation would likely follow emancipation. Prejudice increased with abolition and "nowhere is it shown to be so intolerant as in those states where servitude has always been unknown."[34] Abolition, he concluded, would not emancipate America from its destructive racial consciousness.

Tocqueville incorporated all of these observations into *Democracy in America*, but he returned to his general thesis of experience, cultural learning, and "character" to explain the temperament and political capacities of "slave" and "master," according to typologies referring to incentive structures, social learning, and consequent mores and *mentalité* necessitated by the system. In the exceptionally vicious system of American race slavery, the characters of master and slave alike were debased.[35] The psychology and political economy of slavery incapacitated both slave and master from the standpoint of republican citizenship. The southern slavocracy created a perverse aristocracy, twisting expressions of honor, virtue, and courage in this caricature of the bond between master and servant. The master was indolent, arrogant, and cruel; his plantation family was parasitic. Race prejudice "vilified work" by an ethos of entitlement that, over generations, wrapped the master class in a mythology of "scientific" theories of race.[36]

In the violence that created the slave, "oppression with one blow [took] from the descendents of the Africans almost all the privileges of humanity!" In the United States, the "Negro," Tocqueville said, "has lost the memory of his country; . . . the language of his fathers; . . . their religion and their mores." In no longer belonging to Africa, "he has however acquired no right to the goods of Europe; but has stopped between two societies, sold by one and repudiated by the other. . . . The Negro has no family; he cannot see in woman anything but the passing companion of his pleasures, and his sons, by being born, are his equals."[37] By utterly denying human agency, theories of biological determinism renounced the philosophical rationale for republican government along with the idea of human liberty. By destroying conceptions of person, life, and value, along with language, memory, and hope, habits of the heart learned in slavery eliminated all possibility for human society.[38] Tocqueville developed broader political implications from his conjectures about roles and relationships developed under slavery.

Abolition and emancipation alone would not surmount the barriers of color prejudice or rectify the effects of involuntary servitude in America's particularly vicious system of human bondage. To the extent that slavery had robbed the slave of political rationality, forbearance, and prudence, emancipation freed the slave of one bond, but did not convey the virtues required for self-government. To become "free" was not necessarily to enter into society. Liberty in the absence of self-control might even be a destructive force, Tocqueville argued. A free person who cannot employ human capacities for reflection and choice would be mastered by a variety of transient desires, and the ungovernable self would be vulnerable to the dominion of others.[39] No person in the south was so poor not to own slaves, Tocqueville contended; at the very least, no southern white could fail to conceive the possibility of mastery.

From infancy, "the American of the South finds himself invested with a sort of domestic dictatorship;" along with the mentality of domination he develops a passion for hunting and war, directing his energy toward violent exercise, blood sport, and adventure.[40] Such a "race" would not voluntarily renounce their positions or their justifying ideologies, and would be likely to use lessons learned from the hunt, familiarity with arms, any other necessary means to subvert any policy so aimed.[41] As the traveler proceeded more deeply into the south, it became more difficult to see how to abolish slavery advantageously.[42] The dilemma encouraged political paralysis, allowing prevailing interests to ease moral pressure on all entangled in slavocracy for the sake of preserving political unions, if not the institutions of race slavery.

Federal Institutions and Race Slavery

Although Americans in the south, Tocqueville noted, seldom spoke publicly of slavery and the developing constitutional crisis, northerners worried over little else; as Tocqueville noted, northern commercial interests were not necessarily at odds with the institution. In many cases, shipping, export, and financial interest benefited from southern slavocracy.[43] As long as interests united the regions, according to one line of reasoning Tocqueville advanced about the future of the "American Union," fundamental differences might be set aside. Before taking up the consequences of shared interests in this case, we must take a closer look at Tocqueville's understanding of the Union.

In the first part of *Democracy in America*, Tocqueville had explained the importance of appreciating the historical development of municipal institutions and, especially, the "spirit of the township" to understanding American federalism. Wise delegates tasked with amending the Articles of Confederation (1777) had drafted the U.S. Constitution (1789) framing the institutions of a Federal government that would articulate its laws directly to the citizens of the states, without usurping the authority of the state governments in their proper spheres. Tocqueville described their work as attempting to move beyond a confederal league without centralizing authority in a national government. He pointed to numerous ways in which the state constitutions completed the Federal constitution, including state authority to establish the qualifications of electors for federal officers. He cited possibilities for increasing Federal authority, particularly through a Federal judiciary whose rulings potentially touched the lives of all inhabitants of the nation. The U.S. Supreme Court, through its authority to interpret the Federal constitution as well as rule on disputes between citizens of different states and contests between states, could expand or contract the "sovereignty of the Union."[44] This jurisdictional advantage gave the Federal government a preponderant power, regardless of the relative balance of authority announced by any of its courts' particular decisions. Tocqueville familiarized himself with *The Federalist*, James Kent's *Commentaries on American Law*, and other examinations of the compound republic formed by the "limited constitutions" emphasizing concurrent and shared authority of state and Federal governments. Ideas attributed to Alexander Hamilton and James Madison appear throughout his analysis, which accurately concludes that "the Union has, not states, but plain citizens, for those governed. . . . Past federal governments were faced with peoples, that of the Union has individuals."[45] As Hamilton had advocated in *Federalist* nos. 15 and 23, the Union must transcend its prior incarnation as a confederation formed by a compact among states. Treated as "corporate bodies," the state governments had proven impossible to restrain, providing too few safeguards against abuses of power and, in that way, failing to conform to the spirit and practice of republican government.

In his concluding evaluation of the system, Tocqueville returned to this central idea, but characterized the Union as a compact among states. In "dividing sovereignty," the Federal government "assures the independence and greatness of the nation, things that do not immediately touch particular persons," while the states "maintain freedom, regulates rights, guarantees the fortunes, secures the life, the whole future of each citizen."[46] Perhaps the actual circumstances of slavery and observation of the tariff dispute occasioning threats of "interposition" and "nullification" led him to accentuate the powers of the states and adopt language and theory used by the U.S. Senator from South Carolina, John C. Calhoun.[47] Tocqueville understood that the doctrine of nullification "in principle destroys the federal bond and in fact brings back the anarchy from which the Constitution of 1789 had delivered the Americans." Nevertheless, he underscored the institutional weaknesses of the Union as it confronted each state's constitutional "right to fix the civil and political capacity of citizens, to regulate the relations of men among themselves," and to render justice according to its people's shared idea of right. Sentiments favoring the more distant and, for many, merely abstract notion of the Union could not match the attachments formed by daily experience in the organic communities of the states.[48]

Yet, there was another understanding of which he might have become aware. During Congressional debates over Missouri leading to the Great Compromise (1818–1819), House member Timothy Fuller of Massachusetts told the Federal legislature that "the Declaration of Independence . . . defines the principle on which our National and State Constitutions are all professedly founded . . . that all men are created equal."[49] Vermont antislavery Republican Charles Rich described the Declaration as "that great *national covenant*" from which the constitutional frame followed.[50] President Abraham Lincoln offered metaphor and theory building on these ideas. The "principle that clears the *path* for all—gives *hope* to all" and that could not be obtained without "the *Constitution* and the *Union*" is "Liberty to all." A fortunate "*expression* of that principle" is found in "our Declaration of Independence," which elevated the struggle against an oppressive British government to "something better than a mere change of masters." By asserting "that *principle*, at that time" the cause took on a different meaning: "Which was the 'apple of gold' to us. The *Union*, and the *Constitution*, are the silver picture, subsequently framed around it. The picture was made, not to *conceal*, or *destroy* the apple; but to *adorn*, and *preserve* it. The *picture* was made *for* the apple—*not* the apple for the picture."[51]

On such readings, the Declaration of Independence functioned as a part of the nation's fundamental law, stating and defining a people's highest principles for which the U.S. Constitution laid out an appropriate government frame. As such, the Declaration can be read as a covenant preceding a "due form of government" expressed in Constitution and Union.[52] Or, to use Lincoln's imagery, the signers of the Declaration covenanted to uphold spirit and letter of a transcendent principle, "human liberty," the precious object "entwining itself more closely to the human heart" now found within the setting or frame of Constitution and Union.

The Declaration of Independence does not figure in Tocqueville's analysis (nor is it indexed in translations of his field notes), although he attended an Independence Day celebration in Albany, New York, where copies were printed on press carried by one of the parade floats for distribution to the crowd and the document took pride of place at a public reading in a local church shortly thereafter. He noted that it was "a truly admirable piece" that evoked real sentiments from its reader and audience, but was primarily interested in the Americans' use of a church for its civil celebration.[53] Tocqueville's study, of course, predates Lincoln's rhetoric of Americans as an "almost chosen people" and covenantal framing of the

Declaration. Nevertheless, these ideas had been in the American mind for several decades. Perhaps Tocqueville failed to note carefully the attachment to the Union such ideas mirrored—and the theory that constitutional assurances of republican governments for the people of the states provided a legal basis for maintaining the Union by force, if necessary. The sentiment made the Union a good not easily disposed, even for the moral cause of abolition; sentiment and constitutional theory made it possible to raise state and Union forces.

Even so, Tocqueville's main conclusions resonate: citizens of every state feared federal encroachment on local powers more than any other "evil"; their culture of self-reliance could constrict their scope of their concern; commerce makes peoples neighbors; and, north and south, neighbors had interests in common and, often, a shared understanding of race prejudice.[54]

The impetus for constitutional change—the political will of the people—remained far from obvious long after Tocqueville departed the New World. The delegates to the 1787 Convention drafted a frame of government that failed to address the authority of persons, a problem that was only partially addressed by a proposed Bill of Rights limiting the authority of Congress in some areas of individual liberty.[55] The formula apportioning delegates to the House of Representatives by "adding to the whole number of free persons . . . three fifths of all other persons"—slaves—(Article I, Section 2) represented a compromise deeply at odds with the aim of guaranteeing "a republican form of government" to every state (Article IV, Section 4). Although anti-slavery legislators argued from 1818 onward that the U.S. Constitution had only permitted slavery to persist as a local institution and had not established a national institution or right, Tocqueville perhaps saw the flaws in American law and opinion more clearly.

Tocqueville's Expectations for the "Races" and for American Federalism

The Thirteenth, Fourteenth, and Fifteenth (Civil War) Amendments to the U.S. Constitution abolished slavery, established national citizenship, and ensured due process and equal protection of the laws to the citizens of the United States, and prohibited a state or the Federal government from denying the franchise on the basis of race, color, or previous condition of servitude. Yet, even these changes in fundamental law did not unequivocally answer Tocqueville's basic concerns about the foundations of the

republican project. The constitutional theories asserted to prohibit slavery in new states and organized territories or to support the movement of
Union troops against the states in succession, arguments used to permit
emancipation through executive order rather than an act of Congress—
however convincing (and there is ample legal reasoning and evidence in
their support)—could not resolve the constitutional impasse.[56]

Constitutional settlement came largely by coercion of arms. Although
the Thirteenth Amendment gained the necessary support of three-fourths
of the states for ratification within a year, several states of the former Confederacy withheld their consent; Mississippi failed to ratify until 1995.
Ratification of the Fourteenth Amendment, which was mandatory for the
former states of the Confederacy to be readmitted to the Union, took two
years to accomplish. Ratification of the Fifteenth Amendment faced similar resistance. State laws creating "Black Codes" and a host of voting tests
designed to deny African Americans the franchise despite these constitutional protections undercut the substance of these changes to fundamental law.[57] Federal marshals, who had been sent to the southern states in
order to enforce the law, faced guerilla warfare, engaging individuals who,
as Tocqueville had described, were skilled in the hunt, experienced in combat, and trained from infancy to stand as domestic dictators. After federal marshals were recalled in the political compromises of 1875, African
Americans faced several more generations of terrorist lynching, burning,
and bombing.[58]

Federal lawmaking and judicial decisions during the period of reconstruction also tell a dismal story. Civil Rights Acts passed by Congress in
1866 and 1875 to prohibit discrimination in public accommodations were
struck down by Supreme Court decisions that limited the application of
the Civil War Amendments to enterprises owned or leased by the state
or municipal governments. Constitutional objections to the racial segregation brought about by the Black Codes were crushed in 1896 with the
U.S. Supreme Court "separate but equal" doctrine announced in *Plessy v.
Ferguson* (1896). According to the Court, "the enforced separation of the
races . . . neither abridges the privileges or immunities of the colored man,
deprives him of his property without the due process of law, nor denies him
the equal protection of the laws."[59] Progressive Era reforms segregated the
Federal Civil Service by Executive Order of President Woodrow Wilson
in 1913. Legislation passed in southern (as well as in some middle western, eastern, and western) states in response to the *Plessy* ruling brought
about a system of racial apartheid and ideology that influences American
politics to the present day.[60] By most measures, the era of Reconstruction

and twentieth-century legislative reform lived up to Tocqueville's predictions. Shared interests united the distinct cultures of southern and northern Anglo-Americans in shared understandings about race.

Taking only this perspective, however, it is difficult to account for developments leading to the *Brown* (1954, 1955) decisions, which lay *Plessy* to rest, or the modern civil rights movement (1945–1975), which fundamentally altered American race ideologies. We can sketch a Tocquevillian approach to understanding these changes by pulling forward another thread from his discussion of public opinion and legislative change. In his concluding chapter on race and the Union, Tocqueville focused our attention on the power of majority opinion (or, more broadly, the "social power" with its attendant customs and mores) to determine the parameters of law and the pressures of the democratic social condition that encouraged the homogenization of opinions and enhanced the social power. But that was not the whole story. In considering avenues of change in race ideology and its institutional manifestations, Tocqueville might have returned to his discussion of dissent and the possibility for a persuasive minority view to influence the public mind. These ideas are taken up briefly in his discussion of voluntary associations, particularly political meetings calling for public discussion of the tariff question.

The political yet nongovernmental conventions on tariffs and trade, which he observed in Philadelphia, served as a model of the dissenting tradition and its potential.[61] As his American hosts explained, "the object of the Convention is not to act, but to persuade; it represents an opinion, an interest, and does not set out to represent the nation which is there, all complete, in Congress." A convention served as an additional deliberative body, which, in contrast with the Congress, "starts from the assumption that it does not represent the majority, but wishes to act on public opinion and change the persuasion of the majority." The public nature of discourse in the nongovernmental assembly was its most important quality; organs of publicity—a free press—as well as rights of assembly and petition were vital to republican government. Newspapers alone could not perform the same function as a public discussion in convention, Tocqueville was told; only in public speech could a minority assert a moral presence more powerful than its numbers.[62] Tocqueville might have called upon these views to analyze continuing legislative debate on slavery, abolitionist writings and meetings, and the dissent in Supreme Court decisions. Such dissent played a critical role in public discourses throughout the eras of reconstruction and progressive reform. In *Brown*, for example, we find the voice of Justice John Marshall Harlan whose dissent in *Plessy* eventually offered a basis for ruling against segregation. Dissent became increasingly mainstream in the influential journalism and literature of three generations of "New South" writers whose work drew white northern and southern allies into mid-twentieth-century civil rights activism.

Tocqueville underestimated the importance of dissent and contestation as well as the institutional means of change offered by a compound republic—ideas whose effects he observed but failed to apply to the problem of race ideology. His portrayal of the political capacities of the slave and free African Americans proved inadequate for a different reason. Here, his speculations suffered from their extreme reliance on a static, highly stylized portrayal of roles and resulting inexorable logic of incentive and behavior. In this instance, Tocqueville may be criticized for offering an almost deterministic logic, much like the physiocrats' uninformed appraisals of the French peasantry that he so thoroughly condemned. Perhaps there was little opportunity for him to make observations to test his initial conjectures. Undoubtedly, it is fairer for his twentieth-century readers to view his discussions of "the slave" and "the master" as simply offering hypotheses, since there is no indication that his American interlocutors offered to take him to the gatherings of free blacks in institutions of their own creation such as the African Methodist Episcopal (AME) churches. That institution, which was founded in 1787 and formally organized in 1816, offered an example of a self-organizing, politically skilled community in impressively large congregations to be seen in Boston, Baltimore, or Philadelphia. If Tocqueville had visited such organizations, he would have observed a people deeply involved in the art and science of association, exercising capacities for financial management, engaging in profound theological and philosophical inquiries, and leading dignified lives in community.[63]

At the end of the nineteenth century, AME Bishop Daniel Payne (1811–1893) described the political consequences of such an organization, drawing on the writings of AME founders, Philadelphia minister and former slave Richard Allen (1760–1831) and Baltimore minister and missionary to Liberia, Daniel Coker (1780–1846), who responded to segregationist policies in the Methodist Episcopal (ME) churches in their communities in a manner that profoundly changed the civil as well as spiritual estates of their congregants:

> Under the control of the M.E. Church . . . the colored man was a mere hearer. We were dependent upon them [i.e., white leaders] for government. Although the colored members of the M.E. Church always supported to their utmost ability the institutions [of the Church] . . . because

their white brethren were so vastly in the majority, that support which was so cheerfully and cordially given could not be felt. . . . For the last seventy years . . . [the AME Church] has been governing itself and supporting itself. . . . Being compelled to teach others, its ministry has been constrained to teach itself. . . . It has forced them to implore and explore earth and heaven. . . . Compelled to govern others, its ministry has been constrained to read and investigate church history for models of government . . . to discriminate between laws which were just . . . and unjust. . . . Compelled to support their own institutions our members have learned to economize and forecast as they never could or would, had they remained in connection with their white brethren. . . . Lastly: The separation of our Church from the M.E. Church . . . has been beneficial to the man of color by giving him an independence of character. . . . Independent thought . . . has resulted in independent action; this independent action has resulted in the extension of our ecclesiastical organization over nearly all of the States and also into Canada . . . and this independent hierarchy has made us feel and recognize our individuality and our heaven-created manhood.[64]

Payne's observations of the AME founding suggest possibilities for transcending a culture of bondage through an act of separation. There were other examples of such political artisanship within Tocqueville's reach. He noted, for example, the American Missionary Society project of relocating former slaves on the West African coast:

In 1820, the society . . . succeeded in founding a settlement in Africa . . . to which it gave the name *Liberia*. The latest news was announcing that two thousand five hundred Negroes were already gathered at this point. Transported to their former\native country, blacks have introduced American institutions to it. Liberia has a representative system, Negro jurors, Negro magistrates, Negro priests; one sees churches and newspapers there, and, by a singular reversal of the vicissitudes of this world, it is forbidden to whites to settle within its precincts. There for sure is a strange play of fortune! Two centuries have passed since the day when the inhabitants of Europe undertook to remove the Negroes from their families and their country to transport them to the shores of North America. Today one encounters the European busy with carrying the descendants of those same Negroes across the Atlantic Ocean again so as to carry them back to the soil from which he had formerly dragged away their fathers. Barbarians have drawn the enlightenment of civilization from the midst of servitude and learned in slavery the art of being free.

Until our day, Africa was closed to the arts and sciences of whites. The enlightenment of Europe, brought in by Africans, will perhaps spread there. There is, therefore, a beautiful and great idea in the founding of Liberia; but this idea, which can become so fruitful for the Old World, is sterile for the New.[65]

In offering this sketch, Tocqueville's focus remained on the impossibility of ensuring liberty for persons of African descent in America and the irony, in his view, of discovering "the enlightenment of Europe" in slavery; unnoticed is the potentially greater irony that enlightenment demanded a project of colonial imposition. Also set aside were the central discoveries that persons brutalized by race slavery could transcend that circumstance, exhibiting a significant example of political capacity and skill specific to republican government. Although such abilities were also being exercised in the United States in 1851, Tocqueville paid much greater attention to the inability of the white majority to change its ideas and institutions. He had little doubt that, given the means, the Anglo Americans would isolate themselves along racial lines; as he noted, although "a man places himself outside the prejudices of religion, country, race . . . a whole people cannot thus put itself in a way above itself."[66] Greater attention to the possible institutional development of African Americans in the segregated north of the early nineteenth century, coupled with a somewhat different slant on the dissent tradition—and its institutional instantiation—might have foretold of a different outcome for the American races.

Despite the constitutionally sanctioned injustices that characterized the century following the Civil War, the struggle for political equality brought forth vital African American financial and educational institutions, valiant leadership, and an unquenchable desire for citizenship. In the African American churches that fostered the modern civil rights movement, this quest for inclusion was often interpreted as spiritual destiny to cleanse the soul of the United States by making its government live up to the principles of liberty and equality enshrined in the Declaration of Independence. The Alabama Penny Savings and Loan Company, an African American bank founded by Reverend William R. Pettiford in 1890 (which, as one of the few financial institutions in the state to weather the 1893 panic and depression, was incorporated in a special legislative act), promoted African American homeownership through painstakingly planned real-estate investments. The founding of other financial institutions (including the Peoples Investment and Banking Company and the Prudential Savings Bank, the Atlanta Life Insurance Company and Booker T. Washington

Life Insurance Company) by African American ministers, physicians, and educators add to a picture of capacity and possibility.[67] Educational institutions—like Tuskegee Institute and other historically black colleges and secondary schools staffed by social entrepreneurs who had earned degrees at northern colleges such as Oberlin, which recruited African American students as part of their abolitionist mission—taught the next generation of African American leaders in the segregated cities of the South. African American newspapers—along with local and national business, trade, cultural, and civil associations—completed the picture of parallel institutions in southern as well as northern urban African American communities. When, in 1955, Dr. Martin Luther King Jr. joined other civil rights leaders to call upon the municipal government of Montgomery, Alabama—and soon the nation—to return to the principle of human equality and right found in the Declaration of Independence, he stood on the foundation of African American institutions that had been more than a century in the making. These institutions, as he, like Lincoln, made clear, found the source of their power in principles that were entwined; yet, at the same time, they transcended the U.S. Constitution and the government it framed.[68]

Tocquevillian Analytics and Tocqueville's Expectations of American Race Relations

Photographs and television news footage of the 1963 confrontation of non-violent civil rights protestors with dogs and water canons wielded by police in Birmingham, Alabama, tell a story of intransigent local authorities in defiance of Federal desegregation orders. Similarly, images of the phalanx of U.S. Army personnel (the 101st Airborne) who were required to escort nine African American students to classes at Central High School in Little Rock, Arkansas, depict the heroic attempt to enforce the U.S. Supreme Court school desegregation ruling in the face of violent state and local resistance.

The conventional wisdom taken from such visual references has been that the more centralized the national power, the more swiftly justice might have been served; if state and local governments had been collapsed into a uniform national political authority, justice and civil rights would have triumphed more quickly. Tocqueville had similarly offered this assessment, suggesting that it would take a "despot coming to intermingle the Americans and their former slaves under the same yoke."[69] Yet, even the brief overview of constitutional development offered here should raise doubts about such interpretations.

The protracted struggle to abolish slavery and secure political equality and civil rights for African Americans, if anything, demonstrates the depth of prejudice in all arenas of governance throughout the United States. In the language of Tocqueville, it seems that in the period immediately following the civil war, the democratic social power, public opinion, did not hold that the preservation of the Union or the abolition of slavery necessitated the political integration of African Americans; nor did the majority power or its representatives appear to understand legal segregation and the accompanying terrorism necessary to maintain racial codes to form the foundation of a new form of race-based servitude. It is unclear how a greater concentration of administrative or government authority in a national government would have improved the cause of civil rights under such circumstances.

Yet, by supplying multiple forums for individual legal tests of state, local, and federal statutes, the principles of a compound republic expressed in the design of the federal judiciary also enabled voluntary associations such as the National Association for the Advancement of Colored People (founded in 1909) to whittle away at segregation laws and the mentality that protected them, despite the "empire of opinion." Without an institutional framework that encourages inquiry and contestation, majorities can exercise unlimited power in legislation and administration as well as silence dissent. As Tocqueville perceived, the democratic credo—that the majority is always right—can make thinking and rising above prejudice very difficult. As King understood, however, cultural change may occur one heart at a time. Institutions developing from a *foederal* tradition and experience not only offered a public space for dissent but also concurrent arenas of contestation, negotiation, and change.[70]

From the Montgomery Bus Boycott (1954–1955) to Albany, Georgia (1961) and Birmingham, Alabama (1963), local leaders lay the foundations of what would become a regional protest of student-led sit-ins, marches led by clergy, and boycotts carried out by entire communities.[71] Without the civil, political, and commercial voluntary associations, which Tocqueville recognized as a consequence of the political culture fostered by the institutional framework of American federalism, it is difficult to imagine how African Americans would have mounted the many local campaigns that eventually brought new civil rights legislation.

Tocqueville's nineteenth-century analysis continues to illuminate many facets of race relations today with hypotheses that transcend the American case. Nevertheless, he undervalued the theory and practical design of a compound republic and underestimated the capacities of African Americans to prevail and transcend the heinous institution of race slavery. In *Democ-*

racy in America, the analysis of race and race slavery suggested a significant qualification to Tocqueville's primary hypothesis—that the social condition of equality "modifies whatever it does not create" in the array of laws, mores, and culture defining a people. Nevertheless, as we have seen, interest in the age of equality may unify cultures—in injurious compromises, such as those permitting race slavery and segregation. Within racially segregated communities, the equality hypothesis has also played an important role, enabling for better and worse, many of the consequences of middle-class society—its individualism, myopic interest, and excessive materialism—that Tocqueville's readers also encountered. The liberal ideal of liberty and right, as Tocqueville made clear, is never the exclusive goal of a democratic people. Interests that may today unite peoples across the boundaries raised in an earlier age by race, religion, and ethnicity must be informed by a larger conception of human connectedness, liberty, and right.

These were the ideals of King and his contemporaries—as well as their forebears. The activism of African Americans—which called for American law, including constitutional interpretations, to live up to the principles of equality, liberty, and justice made plain in the Declaration of Independence—gives a vivid example of the requirements of citizenship in a self-governing democracy. The design of a limited constitutional authority is premised on the expectation that citizens will undertake the necessary inquiry into the justness of law and law enforcement. Tocqueville's predictions linking the drive for equality to the increasing centralization and concentration of authority raise questions about the sustainability of such local arenas of choice and action enabling such inquiries. My analysis suggests that Tocqueville looked at the question of racial integration at too grand a scale in 1831; we may today find ourselves responding similarly with overly general models and expectations. The history of race relations in the United States suggests a much greater role for the quotidian in our analyses, especially local arenas of civil society. The proposition in a compound republic is not "either/or"; rather, it is by observing the strength of relationships among the various arenas of experience, rule making, and implementation that we must proceed. At its core, such an approach is indeed Tocquevillian.

Notes

1. Tocqueville's letter to Ernest de Chabrol (June 9, 1831) in Alexis de Tocqueville, *Selected Letters on Politics and Society*, ed. Roger Boesche, trans. James Toupin and Roger Boesche (Berkeley: University of California Press, 1985), 38.

2. Barbara Allen, *Tocqueville, Covenant, and the Democratic Revolution: Harmonizing Earth with Heaven* (Lanham, MD: Lexington Books, 2005).

3. In this analysis, I focus on Tocqueville's discussion of race slavery in the American case. For an analysis of his views on colonialism and, particularly the record of Anglo American and Amerindian relations, see Allen, *Tocqueville, Covenant,* 231–33, 252–58; and Allen, "Alexis de Tocqueville and the Universal 'Democratic Revolution:' Liberty, Equality—and Empire?" (paper presented at the annual conference of the American Political Science Association, Philadelphia, PA, August 2006), http://64.112.226.77/one/apsa/apsa06/index.php?cmd=apsa06.

4. In addition to the writings of Tocqueville's frequent correspondent on the subject, Arthur de Gobineau (1816–1882), see for example works by Samuel Morton (1799–1851), Louis Agassiz (1807–1873), Alexis Carrel (1873–1944), Georges Vacher Lapouge (1854–1936), as well as popularizations of Charles Darwin's *On the Origins of Species by Means of Natural Selection, or the Preservation of Favoured Races in the Struggle for Life* (1856). Darwin's brief allusion to human evolution ("light will be thrown on the origin of man and his history") notwithstanding, works applying various understandings of evolution to hereditary improvement in humans (eugenics) along with adaptations of these ideas in fields such as sociology and economics inaugurated a new paradigm based largely on an analogy drawn between biology and sociology.

5. Alexis de Tocqueville, *The Old Regime and the Revolution,* ed. and intro. François Furet and Françoise Mélonio, trans. Alan S. Kahan (Chicago: University of Chicago Press, 2001), II: 86.

6. Tocqueville, *Democracy in America,* trans. Harvey C. Mansfield and Delba Winthrop (Chicago: University of Chicago Press, [1835–1840] 2000), 236, 246–47, 403–4. See also Allen, *Tocqueville, Covenant,* 166–82.

7. See James Ceaser, *Liberal Democracy and Political Science* (Baltimore, MD: Johns Hopkins University Press, 1990); Allen, *Tocqueville, Covenant,* 262–65.

8. Tocqueville, *Democracy in America,* 676.

9. Lectures of François Guizot that Tocqueville attended before traveling to America may have inspired some of these ideas. See Aurelian Craiutu, "Tocqueville and the Political Thought of the French Doctrinaires (Guizot, Royer-Collard, Rémusat)," *History of Political Thought* 20, no. 3 (1999): 456–94.

10. Tocqueville, *Democracy in America,* 411, 28–31; see also Harvey Mitchell, *Individual Choice and the Structures of History: Alexis de Tocqueville as Historian Reappraised* (New York: Cambridge University Press, 1996).

11. See James Schleifer, *The Making of Tocqueville's 'Democracy in America',* 2nd ed. (Indianapolis, IN: Liberty Fund, 2000), 78–79. In letters responding to the doctrines of race determinism of his former protégé, Arthur Gobineau, Tocqueville denounced such theories, citing the pernicious effects of using race, a spurious biological classification, in social science. See *Œuvres Complètes, IX. Correspondence d'Alexis de Tocqueville et d'Arthur de Gobineau,* ed. M. Degros (Paris:

Gallimard, 1959), 203; and *Alexis de Tocqueville on Democracy, Revolution and Society*, trans. and ed. John Stone and Stephen Mennell (Chicago: University of Chicago Press, 1980), 320–22.

12. Tocqueville, *Democracy in America*, 275.

13. Tocqueville, *Democracy in America*, 264–65.

14. Alexis de Tocqueville, *Journey to America*, ed. J. P. Mayer, trans. George Lawrence (New York: Anchor Doubleday, 1971), 162.

15. Tocqueville, *Journey to America*, 162.

16. Tocqueville, *Journey to America*, 162–63. In private correspondence, Tocqueville more directly expressed his misgivings about German immigration, which he feared would bring political ideas and mores deeply at odds with republican government. See Tocqueville's letter to Gustave de Beaumont (August 6, 1854) in Tocqueville, *Selected Letters*, 308–9. Tocqueville continued to harbor these misgivings as he undertook his final work on European revolutions. The Germans' excessive deference to authority, he hypothesized, would assist absolutism in the democratic revolution sweeping across the European continent. In the New World, the same orientation would facilitate social isolation and collective individualism, a habitual narrow-mindedness he had identified in the caste-like social divisions of prerevolutionary France. The insularity and entropy resulting from this mental stance, Tocqueville suggested, had facilitated legalized terror and, in the bourgeois democracy of his time, encouraged the development of mild despotism of a tutelary state. For more details, see Tocqueville, *Old Regime*, I: 162–63.

17. Francis Lieber was among Tocqueville's respondents who commented on the German character, explaining that political unification of his native country would require "subjugation by an iron yoke" (apud Tocqueville, *Journey to America*, 44). Tocqueville's critical appraisals of character extended to other cultural groups. In a short essay offering "Some Ideas about What Prevents the French from Having Good Colonies," he explained that French political culture joined the worst aspects of adventurers and domesticity. As a result, the French citizen could seldom be motivated to venture beyond the "snug" comforts of his birthplace; yet, once transplanted to another land, he developed an "insatiable need for action, for violent emotions, for vicissitudes and dangers." See Alexis de Tocqueville, *Writings on Empire and Slavery*, trans. Jennifer Pitts (Baltimore, MD: Johns Hopkins University Press, 2000), 2. The investment necessary to create lasting relations and institutions rarely emerged in French colonies, causing the central Parisian administration to take control of the narrowest local concerns even as impulsive adventurers recklessly advanced (Tocqueville, *Writings on Empire and Slavery*, 1–4).

18. Françoise Mélonio, *Tocqueville and the French*, trans. Beth G. Raps (Charlottesville: University Press of Virginia 1998), 91–93; Tocqueville, *Old Regime*, II: 247–50, 279–82; and Tocqueville's letter to Gustave de Beaumont (May 18, 1849) in Tocqueville, *Selected Letters*, 230–32.

19. Tocqueville, *Democracy in America*, 417.

20. Tocqueville, *Democracy in America*, 275.

21. The basic tenets of the Christian faith, he said, uniquely offered such ideas as the moral equality of persons and universally called to salvation individuals who would abide by articles of faith that could be rendered so general as to influence politics only indirectly as a salutary moral constraint. By eliminating the numerous laws regulating daily existence in the "ancient" world, the Christian gospels opened new vistas of institutional innovation and political experimentation. Christian doctrine, he further explained, elevated the milder virtues of mercy and compassion above such imperatives as retribution, and in this way also contributed an ontology consistent with (even constitutive of) democratic notions of equality, liberty, and justice. In contrast, Tocqueville pronounced various faiths and beliefs other than Christianity inadequate or antagonistic to democratic progress. Their primary flaws included: a lack of universality that limited its moral imperatives to a community, class, or caste, and, among the religions envisioning a universal call, the excessive regulation of daily life in ritual, form, and law. A religion whose tenets applied only to a particular people or applied differentially to immutable classes or castes could support the ideas of neither equality nor consent. Belief that infelicitously mingled faith with temporal rewards and punishments risked cyclical extremes of quiet abandonment and horrific zeal. Tocqueville based his negative assessment of Judaism, Hinduism, and Islam (among other systems of belief) as allies to democratic liberty on conventional misunderstandings of many aspects of these religions. Nevertheless, the features that he believed opposed and those he supposed to comport with democratic ideals form two instructive lists. In many cases, ideas projected as at odds with democratic political cultures had their counterparts in the tenets of various Christian sects. Calvinist determinism offers one example of a Christian doctrine, which he rejected as incompatible with the mores of a democratic age. Monotheism and a doctrine of the immortality of the soul represented the general ideas at the core of a democratic faith. The supposition of a unitary order of reality—a *uni*-verse—encouraged by monotheism advanced a rule of law as a crucial counter to arbitrary force. Yet, to the ideal of a purposeful order of existence must be added hope. A belief in the immortality of the soul played such a role; democratic times also brought further qualifications of this idea, however. In an age of equality, faith must not diminish care for the present world even as it raised the sights of the believer beyond temporal existence. Indifference to worldly authority—as an article of faith or as a capitulation to fate—made a people vulnerable to conquest and force. Suppositions linking faith and response must place some degree of responsibility for personal destinies within human reach; mindfulness in worldly relations might even incorporate a healthy dose of self-interest into the order of transcendence. All manner of deterministic philosophies and theologies eliminated such possibilities, Tocqueville argued. Religions that limited the necessary relationship between Creator and creature to an elect segment of humanity thereby similarly limited the diffusion of political ideals related to such capacities for reason, justice, and consent. The universality of the salvation religions advanced the ideals of equality, but additional concerns

arose in the fine line such faiths might draw between the proselytism and persecution of those who failed to embrace an opportunity open to all. Nothing was foreordained about how a universal call to relationship with God might translate into the moral and, subsequent, political equality of the faithful and nonbeliever alike. Too much zeal for too many restrictions could turn belief into a violent opponent of democracy; indifference to faith and dependence on individual efforts to grasp the unfathomable through reason alone rendered belief inert and unable to elevate the democratic soul above the hubris of power and selfish excess. The balance between secular and ecclesiastical orders proved challenging for even the Christian polities whose adherence to "general ideas" turned much more on cultural specificities than Tocqueville initially indicated. For more details, see Allen, *Tocqueville, Covenant, and the Democratic Revolution*.

22. Tocqueville, *Journey to America*, 54–55. Indeed, Tocqueville's conjectures raise doubts about the capacities of some self-governing groups to establish communities that are able to resist aggressive cultural—or military—incursions. I examine Tocqueville's fear that a society "where no government is to be found"— that is, a polity oriented to voluntarism and collective problem solving through laudatory municipal institutions—could not take a sufficiently strong stance on the stage of international relations in Allen, "Alexis de Tocqueville and the Universal 'Democratic Revolution.'" His views raise important questions about his orientation to the state and understanding of American federalism. For a discussion of his views about the ethical obligations of democratic states to participate as "great powers" in international relations, see David Clinton, *Tocqueville, Lieber, and Bagehot: Liberalism Confronts the World* (New York: Palgrave Macmillan, 2003).

23. Tocqueville, *Democracy in America*, 275–76.

24. Tocqueville, *Democracy in America*, 423–24.

25. Tocqueville's Protestant hosts voiced their satisfaction with the arrangement of church and civil orders with more sanguinity than their Catholic counterparts. As one interlocutor put it, in America, where all seemed to agree that the separation of ecclesiastical and civil authority benefited religion, it was possible to "forget the Church without being hostile to it" (Tocqueville, *Journey to America*, 15).

26. Tocqueville, *Journey to America*, 48, 71–72. In Maryland, where English Catholics had made "tremendous political progress," Tocqueville was told that prominent Catholic educational institutions had become the leading choice among all sects. Catholic universities made no effort to convert Protestant students, he was assured; it was not only unthinkable to try to turn children against the religion of their parents but unnecessary. A Catholic education for young women, who were thought particularly receptive to the faith, could bring conversions through a betrothal to a Protestant studying at a coeducational institution (Tocqueville, *Journey to America*, 69, 73).

27. Tocqueville, *Democracy in America*, 280–83.

28. New England covenanters arrived at an innovative doctrine of saintly election through a prior covenant mediated by Christ, whose resulting observable commitment to an upright life could be taken as a response sign of grace. This innovation enabled a "national" or community-wide covenant with God to form a Church polity. These innovations, Anne Hutchinson and her followers reasonably argued in one of the most serious disputes of the colony, would seem to take Massachusetts Bay back to the heresy of "works righteousness" against which Calvin fought. Whatever its theological status, federal theology's theory of internal and external covenants offered a more workable basis for communal life than the doctrine that Hutchinson summarized succinctly as "the saint does best who endeavors least." David D. Hall, ed. *The Antinomian Controversy, 1636–1638: A Documentary History* (Middletown, CT: Wesleyan University Press, 1968), 231. It was a doctrine of determinism that Tocqueville similarly recognized as antithetical to political liberty.

29. Tocqueville, *Journey to America*, 52–54.

30. Allen, *Tocqueville, Covenant, and the Democratic Revolution*, 56–65.

31. Tocqueville, *Democracy in America*, 29, 76, 379.

32. Tocqueville, *Democracy in America*, 303.

33. Tocqueville, *Democracy in America*, 327, 342.

34. Tocqueville, *Journey to America*, 36, 48, 50, 65, 156, 232–33; *Democracy in America*, 329.

35. Tocqueville, *Democracy in America*, 327, 329, 335, 342–43, 361.

36. Tocqueville, *Democracy in America*, 331–35.

37. Tocqueville, *Democracy in America*, 304.

38. Tocqueville, *Democracy in America*; and *Alexis de Tocqueville on Democracy*, 320–1; *OC* IX: 203.

39. Tocqueville, *Democracy in America*, 304–5.

40. Tocqueville, *Democracy in America*, 333, 360.

41. Tocqueville, *Democracy in America*, 345–47.

42. Tocqueville, *Democracy in America*, 337.

43. Tocqueville, *Democracy in America*, 344; *Journey to America*, 232–33.

44. Tocqueville, *Democracy in America*, 137.

45. Tocqueville, *Democracy in America*, 148.

46. Tocqueville, *Democracy in America*, 351.

47. Tocqueville, *Democracy in America*, 182–83, 372–75; John C. Calhoun, *Union and Liberty: The Political Philosophy of John C. Calhoun*, ed. Ross M. Lence (Indianapolis, IN: Liberty Fund, 1992), 565–69; and Allen, *Tocqueville, Covenant, and the Democratic Revolution*, 249–52.

48. Tocqueville, *Democracy in America*, 155, 351–52, 375.

49. See Sean Wilentz, "Jeffersonian Democracy and the Origins of Political Antislavery in the United States: The Missouri Crisis Revisited," *Journal of the Historical Society* 4, no. 3 (2004): 375–401; the cited fragment is on p. 395. Also see *Acts of Congress* (*AC*) 15th Congress 2nd sess. 1180.

50. *AC* 16th Congress 2nd sess. 1395.

51. Abraham Lincoln, "Fragment on the Constitution and the Union," in Roy P. Basler, ed. *Collected Works of Abraham Lincoln* 4 (1953): 168–69. Proverbs 25:11 gives "a word fitly spoken is like an apple of gold in pictures [settings] of silver."

52. Daniel J. Elazar, *The Covenant Tradition in Politics*, vol. 3 (New Brunswick, NJ: Transaction Publishers, 1998), 48–71.

53. Pierson, *Tocqueville in America*, 180–81.

54. Tocqueville, *Democracy in America*, 329, 343, 355–57, 366, 368–69, 577.

55. Barbara Allen and Vincent Ostrom, "Constitutional Choice and Constitutional Development," in Vincent Ostrom, *The Political Theory of a Compound Republic*, 3rd ed. (Lanham, MD: Lexington Books, 2008), 133–79.

56. Most constitutional inquiries asked whether the extension of slavery into the organized territories or new states could be prohibited. Abolitionists generally found little constitutional support for ending slavery in the south, a circumstance that led William Lloyd Garrison to call America's fundamental law a "covenant with death and agreement of hell." (The analogy refers to Isaiah's [28: 14–18] condemnation of Israel's civil leaders who had forsaken their promises to do justice and righteousness.) Various "nonextension" arguments were advanced. Arguing from a natural rights perspective, the Free Soil party advocated the "freedom national" doctrine, maintaining that if the federal government could not abolish slavery, it could similarly not establish it. Many simultaneously argued that the Declaration of Independence preceded the U.S. Constitution in time and essential principle, requiring an adjustment of constitutional interpretation to fit the principle of natural equality. Theories also turned to the Northwest Ordinance (1787), an agreement accepted by southern as well as northern states that prohibited slavery in the developing Northwest Territories.

57. Theodore B. Wilson, *The Black Codes of the South* (Birmingham: University of Alabama Press, 1965).

58. For example, on Easter Sunday 1873, more than one hundred African American men seeking to exercise their right to vote were gunned down in Grant Parish, Louisiana. In Lexington, Kentucky, as in many other southern places, a poll tax was used to deny the vote to an otherwise qualified African American. The U.S. Supreme Court decisions in the legal cases that resulted, United States v. Reese 92 U.S.214 (1875) and United States v. Cruikshank 92 U.S. 542 (1875), effectively denied an enforceable Federal guarantee for the right to vote that would not be rectified until the Voting Rights Act of 1965 (42 U.S. sec. 2 1965). See Robert M. Goldman, *Reconstruction and Black Suffrage: Losing the Vote in Reese and Cruikshank* (Lawrence: University Press of Kansas, 2001). Following the Civil War, the battle for civil rights continued as a prolonged, unequal struggle carried out under adverse circumstances and plagued by gross injustices.

59. See *Slaughterhouse Cases*, 83 U.S. 36 (1873); *The Civil Rights Cases*, 109 U.S. 3 (1883); *Civil Rights Act* 14 Stat. 27 (1866) and 43 Stat. 235 (1875); and *Plessy v. Ferguson*, 163 U.S. 537 (1896), quoted at 27–28.

60. See Barbara Allen, "Martin Luther King's Civil Disobedience and the American Covenant Tradition," *Publius: The Journal of Federalism* 30, no. 4 (2000): 71–113; and Allen and Ostrom, "Constitutional Choice and Constitutional Development." By the middle of the twentieth century, when the *Brown* (*Brown v. Board of Education of Topeka*, 348 U.S. 886 (1954); *Brown v. Board of Education*, 347 U.S. 483 (1954); *Brown v. Board of Education*, 349 U.S. 294 (1955)) decisions proclaimed the inherent inequality of segregated facilities, the list of segregated facilities not only included the infamous water fountains, lunch counters, and public transportation services that were ubiquitous throughout the South but also separate books for listing the telephone numbers of African Americans and whites in Oklahoma, separate elevators in Georgia, and separate storage facilities for the schoolbooks of African American children in North Carolina and Florida. See Wilson, *Black Codes of the South*; and C. Vann Woodward, *The Strange Career of Jim Crow* (New York: Oxford University Press, 1974). Local governments in New Jersey, Pennsylvania, Ohio, and Illinois were permitted to continue de facto school segregation although those states had outlawed the practice. In Indiana, according to an 1877 law, African American children were allowed to attend white schools if a town did not construct segregated facilities; state law permitted local school districts to engage in the practice of school segregation until 1949.

61. Tocqueville, *Democracy in America*, 180–85.

62. Tocqueville, *Journey to America*, 222–3. The ideas quoted are those of Tocqueville's interlocutor, Charles Jared Ingersoll, the son of Connecticut representative to the 1787 Philadelphia Convention, Jared Ingersoll and a Federalist candidate for vice president of the United States in 1812.

63. Richard Allen, "Richard Allen Describes the Founding of the African Methodist Episcopal Church," in *Black Nationalism in America*, ed. John H. Bracey Jr., August Meier, and Elliot Rudwick (Indianapolis, IN: Bobbs-Merrill, 1970), 4–10.

64. Daniel A. Payne, "Bishop Daniel A. Payne Reviews the Contributions of the Negro Church," in *Black Nationalism in America*, 11–13.

65. Tocqueville, *Democracy in America*, 344–45.

66. Tocqueville, *Democracy in America*, 342.

67. Lynne B. Feldman, *A Sense of Place: Birmingham's Black Middle-Class Community, 1890–1930* (Tuscaloosa: University of Alabama Press, 1999); C. A. Spencer, "Benevolent Black Societies and the Development of Black Insurance Companies in Nineteenth-Century Alabama," *Phylon* 46 (1985) 251–61; and Walter B. Weare, *Black Business in the New South: A Social History of the North Carolina Mutual Life Insurance Company* (Urbana: University of Illinois Press, 1973).

68. Allen, "Martin Luther King's Civil Disobedience," 71–113.

69. Tocqueville, *Democracy in America*, 342.

70. Allen, "Martin Luther King's Civil Disobedience," 71–113.

71. Glenn T. Eskew, *But for Birmingham: The Local and National Movements in the Civil Rights Struggle* (Chapel Hill: University of North Carolina Press, 1997); Andrew M. Manis, *A Fire You Can't Put Out: The Civil Rights Life of Birming-*

ham's Reverend Fred Shuttlesworth (Tuscaloosa: University of Alabama Press, 1999); Michael Chalfen, "Reverend Samuel B. Wells and Black Protest in Albany, 1945–1965," *Journal of Southwest Georgia History* 9 (1994): 37–64; and William G. Anderson, "Reflections on the Origins of the Albany Movement," *Journal of Southwest Georgia History* 9 (1994): 1–14.

6

Democracy? In Guatemala?

Charles A. Reilly

"Bienvenido Don Tocqueville"

Were Tocqueville to visit post-colonial, post-independence, post-Cold War, post-conflict Guatemala, and were he to talk to a broad, multilevel sampling of its people, I suspect he would recall his 1835 visit to pre-famine Ireland rather than to America. But Guatemala would intrigue him. Like in Ireland, I suspect he would ask more questions than offer theories. Like elsewhere in Latin America, he would find a western nation with an indigenous near majority. He would quickly perceive the country lacks the homogenized baseline of other democratizing societies. He would regret how rife with violence is this "postconflict" society. My essay will examine the light his questioning might shed on a country where peace-building and development issues continue to overshadow democracy.

Despite or because of his noble lineage, Tocqueville would marvel at the gross inequality of this society (among the most inequitable in Latin America, which region is itself the most inequitable in the world). Recalling the divide-and-conquer politics of French kings, he would perceive the rigidity of class divisions, the fault lines between indigenous and *mestizo*, the Babel of twenty-four Mayan languages butting up against Spanish, and now English. He would probably require some tutoring to understand the global economic model visited on Guatemala, the weight of structural adjustment and implications of the Central American Free Trade Agreement (CAFTA). He would be cautioned on prudence, to avoid comments like in Ireland when he advocated "the necessity for radical redistribution of wealth" due to "the drastic way in which landed property is not divided

117

up."[1] Many Guatemalans have been killed for less drastic observations. While perhaps predisposed to welcome economic and political constraints on this nation state, on further examination, he would see how little the economy has done for popular sovereignty. Then he would look further back in history.

He would review the precolonial Mayan experience, their tall temples and cities larger than many then in Spain, and trace the centralizing Spanish colonial legacy, the development of a plantation export economy with elites controlling most of the arable land and squeezing indigenous peoples on to near vertical subsistence plots on mountain slopes. He would trace the successive agricultural export cycles—cotton, sugar cane, coffee—followed by drastic land clearing to add yet more cattle to the world market. Strong economic elites (an aristocracy?) have long bent weak governments in preferred directions (right up to the twenty-first century). He would observe the laws and coercion that delivered an indigenous labor supply for this plantation economy and be struck by similarities to the Irish pre-famine tenant farmer regime. There, the fault line fell between Catholic and Protestant. Here the gap lies between *mestizo* and Mayan. Equality is definitely not in the cards.

He would recognize, though not praise the legal institutions, inheritance laws, and property arrangements that have buttressed economic elite interests and the central state ever since the colony. Property was concentrated in the hands of relatively few *ladinos*, with continually shrinking small holdings for the indigenous majority. Civilian governments seldom alternated in presidential elections during the nineteenth and much of the twentieth century—the long-term military strongman was usually the norm. Nearly a decade ago, after peace accords were signed, the U.S. and European governments promoted local government, but self-governance is a long way off. The 2003 and 2007 presidential elections were encouraging, but for Tocqueville, like for many Guatemalans, elections do not equal democracy. Many vote with their feet. First political repression, then poverty, has led 10 to 15 percent of the population (between 1 and 1.5 million) to emigrate north—and their remittances of more than $2.5 billion in 2006 exceeded the combined direct private investment, foreign aid, and international bank lending to the country. For too many migrants, the Arizona desert crossing today replicates Irish coffin ships of the nineteenth century.

Tocqueville's *Journey to Ireland* and *Democracy in America* have something in common with the Mayan foundational holy book *Popol Vuh*—deep respect for equality. As Tocqueville wrote: "Among the laws that rule human societies there is one that seems more precise and clear than all the others. If men are to remain civilized or to become so, the art of associating together must grow and improve *in the same ratio* in which the equality of conditions is increased."[2] The Mayans summarized the same point crisply: "let no-one be left behind." Yet, Guatemala's inequality is worsening, association has been equated for a long time with subversion, and opportunity decreases for those at the bottom of the social pyramid. Tocqueville also admired the simultaneous growth of equality and association among New England yeoman. He would find more parallels to 1835 Ireland than to New England—extreme poverty, landholding patterns, social cleavage, religious tensions, and conspicuous inequity. He called Ireland "two nations entirely distinct on the same soil. The one rich, civilized, happy; the other poor, half savage, and overwhelmed. . . ."[3]

Tocqueville asked some challenging questions of an Irishman in 1835. They would be usefully put to Guatemalans 174 years later.

> Tocqueville: (Of its 5 million population) "How many individuals do you estimate are unemployed in Ireland although they are willing to work?"
> William Murphy (a wealthy Catholic): "Two million."
> Tocqueville: "What do you think can be done?"
> Murphy: "I suppose, but this is only an opinion on my part, if one could settle a portion of the poor population of Ireland on land not yet cultivated but farmable, this would be a great help."
> Tocqueville "Is there much uncultivated but farmable land?"
> Murphy: "Yes."
> Tocqueville: "But is it owned by somebody"?
> Murphy: "Yes, it forms part of vast properties which were formerly acquired for nothing by rich individuals."[4]

Concurrence: Ireland 1835 and Guatemala 2008

When I first read his *Journey to Ireland*, I was struck by parallels to contemporary Guatemala. Emmet Larkin alerted me to three basic themes that had taken root in his (Tocqueville's) mind since his arrival in Ireland. The first was the extraordinary poverty of the Irish people. The second was their enduring and implacable hatred for the Irish aristocracy, and the third was their deep and touching attachment to the church of their fathers.[5] I was intrigued, but frustrated that Tocqueville never completed his work on Ireland—we have only his field notes and letters. He deferred to his friend Gustave de Beaumont who wanted to write on the island they had traveled together. So we have his questions, we feel his passion, we know the inquiry. We can imagine what his thick description might have been, and I like the liberty to fill blanks and connect dots while spanning centuries and continents.

For many years, I have been a participant observer of the painfully slow unfolding of democracy in Guatemala. Military dictators came and went; a brief democratic interlude in the 1950s was interrupted with the help of American intervention in 1954. Then came prolonged civil war dating from 1963 that caused nearly 250,000 deaths, a peace agreement signed in 1996, and a decade of struggle since to invent, or to import, a "*mestizo*" version of (electoral) democracy. Tocqueville is an obligatory reference point for any student of this part of the world.

While some may impugn revisiting classical authors for *answers* to contemporary questions, I make no apology for replicating classical *questions*, especially if they spring from an inquirer like Tocqueville. He was an educator as well as an analyst, a moralist as well as a comparativist, a unique French blend of Socrates and Paulo Freire. He reflected Socrates's method of persistent questioning to elicit hidden truths. His social commitments anticipated the problem-posing educational methodology of Paulo Freire, the Brazilian educator whose approach to literacy training influenced Latin America including Guatemala, Africa, Europe, even Harvard. Freire's educational methodology of "*conscientization*" created space for the experience and creativity of adult learners.[6] His critical approach did not sit well with military authoritarian governments camouflaged in anticommunism throughout Central and South America. I appreciate Tocqueville's comparative approach and that he, like Socrates and Freire, practiced normatively driven social inquiry. All three sought to improve the conditions of life of a specific human population, were inductively grounded in real-world problems, and thoroughly critical or evaluative.

Tocqueville's analytic approach, as illustrated by *Democracy in America* and *The Old Regime and the Revolution*, sought alternative routes from aristocratic to democratic governments that might avoid the bloodshed of revolution or "despotism of the majority." His visit to Ireland for a few weeks in 1835 came between completing volumes one and two of *Democracy in America*. Based on his travels and comparisons, he insisted that maxims and rules do not have identical outcomes when applied in different institutional settings and contexts. Historical specificity is of seminal importance and customs do matter. As two recent commentators put it, customs and *moeurs* refer "not only to manners properly so called—that is, to what might be termed the 'habits of the heart'—but to the various notions and opinions current among men and to the mass of ideas which constitute their character of mind."[7]

Tocqueville was forthright, whether in his questions or in his conclusions. "Is the poverty of pre-famine Ireland the result of unjust English policies or the moral and/or biological inferiority of the Irish?"[8] was a typical blunt inquiry. Others were more subtle, more hypothetical. "Aristocracy can be one of the best or one of the worst forms of government that exist in the world."[9] Having contrasted the English and Irish versions as prototypes of good and bad aristocracy, Tocqueville argued that they "have the same origin and manners and almost the same laws."[10] And he went on to add: "However, embedded in different societies, one gives the English one of the world's best, the other, the Irish, one of the world's 'most detestable' governments. England enjoys the benefits of aristocratic freedom while Ireland suffers the evils of extreme aristocratic tyranny."[11]

His sketchy notes and letters from *Journey to Ireland* offer a Tocquevillian springboard for examining contemporary Guatemala and its search for democracy and development after decades of conflict. Ireland in the nineteenth century and Guatemala in the twenty-first century both grappled with inequitable land tenure systems, the demise of subsistence agriculture, rapid urbanization, and grinding poverty. In both settings, emigration would offer sometimes illusory hope. Tocqueville would today be surprised at the Celtic tiger's leap to affluence, though he would likely still question its poverty midst plenty and the as yet unresolved Northern Irish "troubles." He had traveled to England to understand the changes driven by English industrialization, its new industrial aristocracy, and a labor force that included many Irish immigrants. He was repelled by his visit to Manchester, where workers were trapped "between poverty and death."[12] "In Manchester," he added, "competition with workers from Ireland lowered the wages of English workers to almost the same low level as that of the Irish."[13] Tocqueville observed the emergence of an industrial working class, noting that such shocking disparities cannot for too long exist in one society without producing a deep malaise.

Tocqueville was a traveling inquirer, a moralist, and an analyst. He employed comparison and history to achieve a degree of critical distance. He traveled in America to find answers that might be applied in France, while constructing a "new science of politics" through theory in practice. He went to Ireland to learn more about the prospects for democracy in England. Ireland was also a laboratory for testing his hunches on religion and politics. The visit confirmed his admiration for the arrangement in America that was buffered structurally, but not "customarily," by separation of church and

state. He often suggested that the Irish clergy might accept subsidy or payments from the English crown—a proposal they roundly rejected. He saw
the hypocrisy of the Irish Emancipation of 1829, which appeared to grant
liberal opportunities to the Irish Catholic "colonists" when the economic
and educational structure was thoroughly stacked against most of them. He
expressed surprise at the large numbers of absentee Protestant landlords,
and the taxes levied on Catholics to support Church of Ireland pastors with
their tiny flocks. He marveled at the structures of inheritance, at the huge
landholdings, at the system of tenancy in Ireland. He was astounded at the
poverty and probed for possible solutions of the tiny rented plots contrasted
with huge plantations and large, uncultivated properties. He looked into
possible replication of the "peasant proprietary" approach to land redistribution after the French Revolution. His bottom line conclusion: "If you want
to know what can be done by the spirit of conquest and religious hatred
combined with the abuses of aristocracy, but without any of its advantages,
go to Ireland."[14] His letters show him appalled by what he saw in Ireland, as,
I submit, he would be in Guatemala today.

Like Ireland then and now, Guatemala is a deeply divided society, but
not entirely for the same reasons. Hardly an old aristocracy like France, nor
a young yeoman's nation like America, today's Guatemala would intrigue
Tocqueville. Its thirty-six-year civil war did little to encourage association, and a decade of peace has brought scant movement toward greater
equality. In fact, many leaders of student, labor, and human rights organizations, even catechists and cooperative members and their associations,
were viewed as subversive and persecuted. Despite remarkable economic
growth, the distribution of wealth has been minimal. Neither America nor
France of the nineteenth century much resembled Guatemala now, but
contemporary Guatemala does share all too much of the poverty, social
and religious division, educational deficit, and governmental centralization
observed by Tocqueville in Ireland years ago. Granted, nineteenth-century
answers do not fit twenty-first-century problems—but the questions, at
least, travel well over time and space.

Tocqueville would approach Guatemala, as he did Ireland, with a bunch
of questions, a comparative scholar's "survey instrument" culled from his
earlier reflections on France, America, and England. Together, they inform
the so-called "Tocquevillian Analytics," a concept formulated by Sheldon
Gellar and Aurelian Craiutu in part I of this volume that provides a broad
framework for Tocquevillian comparative analysis. Here, however, I shall
stick closer to his social inquiry guided by specific questions and observations from his Irish journey.

Tocqueville was a normative inquirer, problem poser, educator, and passionate but fallible espouser of values. He was a methodical (if not methodologically correct) political anthropologist and political theorist (well before either label or discipline had been invented). I like his questions, his probing, the way he pursued key issues. Tocqueville, like Freire, would not be hamstrung by the cult of neutrality[15] and would disregard the artificial divorce between descriptive and normative analysis. As Saguiv Hadari remarked, "the normative stand is not added at the end of the writing. . . . It informs the quest and its findings, the questions posed and the answers—preferably new questions—reached."[16]

The contextual, social, cultural, and political components that characterize the analytic do help unveil Irish (and Guatemalan) reality, although I regret Tocqueville's all too brief exploration of the economic underpinnings of democracy. While welcoming his celebration of citizen sovereignty and warnings of state despotism, I regret that he did not give greater attention to markets. His encounter with extreme Irish poverty was perceptive and compassionate, his condemnation clarion clear, but was accompanied by too little analysis of the economic roots that concentrated economic and political power in few elites.

Tocqueville sought to evoke from his interviewees their interpretation of politics, society, and culture. His sampling in Ireland was narrow and selective—only men, mostly clergy (Protestant and Catholic), and local judges or justices of the peace. His survey strategy would not pass muster with Gallup. Implicit was his broader analytic framework, but here I will follow his inquiry, his probes about religion, education, law and institutions, decentralized power, his undisguised emotional commitments, and his effort to maintain critical distance through comparison even as he observed the particular case.

Tocqueville's First Impressions

"*You cannot imagine what a complexity of miseries five centuries of oppression, civil disorders, and religious hostility have piled up on these poor people*," Tocqueville wrote to his father from Ireland.[17] Poverty loomed large in his observations and letters written from Ireland. They might have been written from Guatemala today. "The particular misfortune of this country has been to fall into the hands of an upper class who are different from the masses in race, in custom, and in religion and who nevertheless are invested with sovereign power, which they exercise under cover c the all powerful protection of England."[18] During his Guatemala visit, he would be alert to class differences and religious tensions, I suspect, and of course, England would be displaced by the United States as "the all powerful protector." He would be unable to ignore the dilemmas of *minifundia* or small holdings. Whether in France, America, Ireland, or now Guatemala, the division of land into small properties was fundamental to Tocqueville's definition of democracy. He would recall his and Beaumont's recommendations in Ireland for a "peasant proprietary" reform, modeled after the French revolution's land distribution, but would probably find this (or any other) approach to land reform rejected out of hand in Guatemala.

Like nineteenth-century Ireland, Tocqueville would learn that twenty-first-century Guatemala is a beautiful country with a deeply divided society. The fault line separating Mayan and *mestizo* spans centuries, with frequent prejudice—judgments of "moral or biological inferiority" toward the indigenous majority. Mayan and other indigenous peoples inhabited the region for a millennium before the Spanish conquest, while *mestizos* or *ladinos* trace their origins through intermarriage from the Spanish colonial period and subsequent immigrants. The Mayan indigenous civilizations covered large swaths of what is now Central America and Mexico, reaching a classical period nearly six centuries before the first Spanish appeared in the early 1500s when Mayan nobility had assumed civil, military, and religious leadership. Vestiges of a more egalitarian culture persist in "customary" legal and political "councils" and religious "cofradias" or brotherhoods. The indigenous population was quickly subjugated and Guatemala became one of the key centers of the Spanish colonial rule, its university one of the first three in the Americas.

Guatemala's topography is punctuated by tall volcanoes, high mountain ranges, and fertile tropical plains along both Atlantic and Pacific coastlines. Especially in the late nineteenth and twentieth century, there was progressive concentration of property ownership on the fertile coasts in large plantations, replicated with the advent of coffee production on the hillsides. Over successive generations, small landholdings, often perched on steeply pitched mountains and volcanoes, were subdivided into plots so small they can no longer support family subsistence. Until the civil war, ˙ndigenous peoples have mainly populated the highlands. They identified ˙ particular municipality and its hinterland (like the county in the ˙tes) rather than the nation. Twenty-four Mayan languages are ˙riers to integration. Despite efforts to maintain Mayan cus-˙xpression, and extended family ties, indigenous cultures with their traditional markers of language and colorful woven garb slowly yield to Western dress and Spanish. Less changed is the sometimes unconscious racism of many Ladinos toward the Indian.

While the country shows slow but small positive growth rates, Guatemala is far from competitive in the global marketplace. Assembly plants have multiplied and some industrial jobs have been created, but protectionist agricultural policies in the United States and Europe mean that sugar or fruit do not get through not so "free trade" filters, while North American corn and wheat can overwhelm local markets. Foreign investment continues low and the economy relies heavily on tourism and remittances, with elites ever poised to pull their capital at the first threat of instability. Concentration of wealth continues the most imbalanced in the Americas, tied with Brazil. Guatemala's social policy is retrograde, its education and health services rank well below regional standards. Entrenched social divisions are the rule between ladino, indigenous Maya, and Afro-Caribbean slave descendants, the Garifuna and the Xenka. Today, like in nineteenth-century Ireland, it is intergenerational transfer of poverty, violence, and insecurity that have driven rural/urban and international migration to unprecedented levels.

Convulsive Politics

Independence led to a brief experiment with a Central American federation in the nineteenth century, then a return to what have been dubbed as "nonviable nation states." As in much of Latin America, Guatemalan military dictators and caudillos ruled for much of the past two centuries. There were alternating disputes between liberals and conservatives, military and civilians, and then Guatemala became a Cold-War pawn. If not quite a "colonial" relationship, there could be little doubt that by the twentieth century, the United States would continue its role of overseer, if not intervener, in its smaller neighbors to the south. Democracy seems conditional, depending on "acceptable" outcomes. Tocqueville would regret that two democratically elected presidents, who launched a peaceful "Revolution of October" in the 1950s, then attempted land reform by expropriating and reimbursing unused plantation land of Guatemalans and the United Fruit Company. This provoked a United States CIA-supported invasion and imposition of a string of military presidents. Democratic elections were not a United States priority during the Cold War—support for Latin American militaries was.

Frustration with chronic underdevelopment and blocked social change led a group of junior officers (ironically, several of their leaders trained in U.S. military bases) to become a small guerrilla force in the early 1960s, hopeful of replicating the Cuban revolution. There was occasional urban violence but the rebels were swiftly neutralized in the eastern part of the country. Sporadic warfare shifted to the North and West, squeezing mostly indigenous populations between two armies, followed in the 1980s by severe repression with many civilian casualties. Atrocities, most of them by the security forces, left nearly a quarter of a million dead. So fierce was the repression, and strong the reaction of U.S. public opinion, that the U.S. Congress suspended some of its military assistance.

Three recent democratic elections (1999, 2003, and 2007) have interrupted patterns of military dictatorships. Political parties are still weak and personalistic. Democracy's roots are shallow. The one constant among these elites is their conviction that the state should remain weak. Private police services illustrate the distrust and antigovernment posture of the wealthy. Organized violence, criminal infiltration of police forces, and drug trafficking heighten citizen insecurity. Poorly served by its political and economic elites, torn by thirty-six years of fratricidal war, plagued by inequitable distribution of wealth, Guatemala's populace is still quite undecided on the relative benefits of democracy or authoritarian rule.

Traveling in Guatemala, Tocqueville would observe the poverty in urban slums and countryside and ask how it compares to other twenty-first-century places. He would learn that the UNDP Human Development Report for 2005 placed Guatemala in 117th place, the lowest-ranking country in Central and South America, with its income levels now lower than in 1980.[19] Equality, or progress toward equality, is hardly "providential" in either nineteenth-century Ireland or twenty-first-century Guatemala. Among the legacies of its thirty-six-year civil war, violence pervades Guatemalan cities and countryside. Citizen insecurity is shared by rich and poor in Guatemala, but only the wealthy can live behind walls topped with razor wire and omnipresent armed guards.

He would learn that economic elites adopted the rhetoric of economic liberalization and accused the government constantly of corruption (as though there were no private sector accomplices). Legacies of racial dis-
'mination, enmity from the "internal conflict," fragmentation, and atom-
' meant that organized civil society, represented by NGOs, church
'ayan organizations, and sometimes by a national civil society
'\. though indispensable for social services, have been unable
,stently so as to effectively influence government or mar-

ket actors, although the assembly did successfully block an attempted *coup d'état* by civilian president, Vinicio Cerezo,when he tried to shut down the Congress and Judiciary.

Tocqueville would have to inquire about the economic development models for the country. First came centuries of agro-export from a plantation economy. Next was a weak effort at import substitution through protected, often monopolistic industries, followed by a market-driven "free trade" approach combined with austerity and state-shrinking. This neoliberal recipe (Joseph Stiglitz, a former World Bank economist calls it "economic fundamentalism") prevailed as the Peace Accords were signed in 1996. In recent years, absolute and relative poverty have grown. Job opportunities are limited or low-paying. Assembly plants or *maquiladoras* offer improvements on the nineteenth-century working conditions Tocqueville saw in Birmingham or Manchester, but he would learn how rapidly the owners can pack up and move elsewhere when wage demands increase. Hence, Guatemala's lead export is now its people, emigrants whose remittances bring new capital to the grassroots. Social reconstruction after prolonged civil war will require much more time and greater investment.

From War to Peace Accords

As the 1980s ended, it was clear that the Guatemalan military would not definitively root out the *guerrilla*, nor did the isolated guerillas have any chance to take power. Scattered military actions and persistent sabotage of the physical infrastructure led economic elites to welcome a cease-fire and search for peace. Guatemalans had reached "ripeness," or what can be called a mutually hurting stalemate after thirty-six years. The road to a peace agreement was initiated after unofficial dialogues between military, guerrillas, and politicians with international interlocutors as well as the Catholic Saint Egidio peace-building community. It was sustained by local mediators like Bishop Quesada Toruño and international observers who helped build trust or *confianza* among the military and guerrilla leadership. It required time, spanning the administration of four democratically elected Guatemalan presidents. The United Nations was incorporated into the process and would figure significantly in the implementation phase.

Tocqueville would quickly recognize that the list of accords agreed to in Guatemala was very ambitious, ranging from items clearly linked to the cessation of hostilities (ceasefire, demobilization of combatants, repatriation of exiles), others linked to the causes of the conflict (land distribution, racism, civil and military relations, for example), and still others relating to concrete public and private policy questions (like multilingual education, decentralization, and so forth). Expectations were high that, with peace, all good things would follow, not just for the elites, but for everyone. But in many ways, Guatemala looks all too much like Ireland in 1835.

Peace will have to be built, not just on the accords that serve more as North Star than road map, but on the hard lessons learned during implementation. Absolute and relative poverty has grown. Violence and corruption have increased, quite overwhelming sometimes complicit police and the justice institutions like those that Tocqueville studied in Ireland. He would see that the land ownership issues that dominated the history of the country still do, even as (for him) novelties like information technology, competition, job creation, environmental degradation, and water scarcity add contemporary challenges. To build peace, Guatemalans will have to develop consensus mechanisms for redistribution to reduce inequity in the country, and they will have to build political institutions to process conflicts and channel social demands. Tocqueville would have a lot of questions and much to learn, but he would be an apt consultant.

Like in Ireland, he would insist on interviewing middle-range actors who link political and economic elites with the people. There are several arenas and institutions that always interested Tocqueville, settings where bridge-builders from civil society have been deeply engaged, including educators, religious leaders, and local government officials. Tocqueville would find important parallels between nineteenth-century Ireland and twenty-first-century Guatemala in religion, governance, and education.

Religious Pluralism and Civil Society

Religion was important to Tocqueville the political observer, even if problematic as a believer. On his arrival in the United States, the religious aspect of the country was the first thing that struck his attention. In his visit to Ireland, he focused on religion, even though his expressed purpose was to examine the functioning of the *assize*, or circuit courts. He questioned and probed as to what should be the relationship between church and state. He did not disguise his low esteem for the Church of Ireland clergy and the unjust tax structure levied on poor Irish Catholics that maintained the official Protestant church. He was, on the other hand, impressed with the close ties between the Roman Catholic clergy and their people, while wary of the political influence of the bishops, "as much the heads of a party as the representatives of the church."[20] His sense of humor was well-tuned to the Irish. After an interview with Bishop Kinsley of Kilkenny, Tocqueville wrote:

> Msgr. is a very likeable man, very spiritual, perspicacious, having enough sense to be impartial (as far as an Irishman can be) and finding pleasure in showing it. . . . I believe that he is very sincere in wishing that the church should not be part of the state, but I wonder if he does not think, at bottom, that the state would do well enough as part of the church. These are nuances. I am perhaps mistaken.[21]

Tocqueville, I suspect, would be critical of the blending of "cross and sword" by the colonial Catholic Church in Guatemala, curious about Guatemalan independence struggles and nineteenth-century liberal checks on church hegemony, but genuinely appreciative, as in Ireland, of the Catholic clergy's identification with the poor. He would have been a frank admirer of Bartolome de Las Casas and his noble experiment to exclude Spanish occupation troops from the Vera Paz or "true peace" region of Guatemala in the 1540s, so that he might invite Indians to become Christians without threat of forced conversion.[22] He would have endorsed Las Casas's adamant argument with the Spanish crown and theologians in favor of the rights of indigenous peoples, and I believe he would have had high regard for the peace-building role of religions in the twentieth century, just as he did the nineteenth-century Irish clergy's commitment to education.

Tocqueville would find that Guatemalan Christian and Mayan believers, unlike the Irish, get along quite well. They have come a long way from Catholic hegemony through uncomfortable coexistence to growing collaboration in peace-building, poverty alleviation, and seeking equitable development during the past two decades. The Catholic Church plays a major role in providing social services, education, and healthcare that, especially in rural regions, would be otherwise lacking. Evangelical churches grew rapidly over several recent decades, especially in the cities, forging close community cohesion, and offering social services and sometimes, political involvement. Especially at the "high church" level of Catholic hierarchy and Evangelical confederation, collaboration is frequent. Mayan priests and religious practices have positively reinforced the identity of a people who had routinely experienced discrimination. The top three presidential candidates in the 2003 election included a Catholic (Oscar Berger), an Evangelical pastor and retired general, Efrain Rios Montt, and Alvaro Colom Argueta, probably the only Guatemalan Ladino who has been inducted into the Mayan shaman priesthood by an association of Mayan priests. Their religion was not a major issue in the campaign.

Tocqueville would soon learn that Catholics, evangelicals, and Mayan religions were all differently affected by the civil war. The Guatemalan Catholic church had two major challenges between 1960 and 1990: how to respond to increasing repression as well as how to deal with growing numbers of evangelical church adherents. The three visits of Pope John Paul II sought to slow this evangelical church growth as well as plead for serving the poor, repudiate repression, and reinforce his notion of centralized hierarchy in Rome. While evangelical churches grew in numbers, the Catholic Church adapted to their stimulus with its own expressions of reform such as church-based communities and charismatic revival. Religious competition has been good for Guatemalan Catholicism.

The church in Guatemala has zig-zagged from strong anticommunism in the mid-twentieth century to a "preferential option for the poor," driven by repression and by shifts in its theology, world view, and social practice during the war. Its religious personnel greatly resemble the nineteenth-century Irish clergy visited by Tocqueville. For the military and many Guatemalan economic elites, these changes linked the church to the left. Repression targeted the church, high and low, hierarchy and laity, to a degree seldom before seen in the region, or in Guatemala's own conflictive history. Thirteen priests, two bishops, a number of religious women, and hundreds of lay catechists were assassinated. Yet, Catholicism is far from monolithic in Guatemala. There are important conservative religious and lay organizations like Opus Dei and the Legionnaires of Christ far more identified with the wealthy than opting for the poor.[23]

Besides the emergence of Evangelical churches during the final decades of the twentieth century, long invisible Mayan religious practice resurfaced in the public square. A radical departure in Guatemala, many public, including state events now begin with Mayan priests celebrating rituals, lighting multicolored candles at the four cardinal points, and chanting invocations to "Ajau," the Creator manifest in nature. The lyric poetry and humor of Maya Quiche poet Humberto Ak'abal, steeped in respect for religiosity and tradition, has achieved national and international recognition.[24] A sometimes romanticized interpretation of Mayan respect for nature is contrasted with the ravages of modern commercial culture and its destruction of the environment. Mayan shrines and the deep interpenetration of Mayan-Christian beliefs have been finally recognized and welcomed. A new generation of Mayan teachers and intellectuals exudes self-confidence and embodies social change. The "mores" have perdured.

Options for the Poor and Peace-Building

Intense religious social activism during the 1950s and 1960s met repression throughout the civil conflict, especially during Guatemala's "holocaust" period (1978–1983), when nearly 200,000 were killed under Generals Lucas Garcia and Rios Montt. Bishop Juan Gerardi had helped the Catholic hierarchy find its voice for social justice throughout the war. Tocqueville would have admired him. The bishop led the church's human rights defense and pastoral support, culminating in a report entitled *Guatemala: Nunca Mas* (*Never Again*). The "Recovery of Historic Memory Project" (REMHI) presented the findings of the Catholic Church's study of atrocities. The military response to this effort at truth and reconciliation was the murder of Bishop Gerardi by soldiers in April 1998, two days after its publication. He became one of the high visibility "symbolic victims" associated with the war and the peace process.

Well beyond peaceful coexistence, the Guatemalan churches have jointly created space for dialogue and building a more vibrant civil society by helping expand notions of civic responsibility and social service. Many NGOs or civil society organizations (CSOs), such as cooperatives, human rights groups, or neighborhood associations, sprang from Christian as well as Mayan religious origins. Tocqueville would note that besides health, education, and community-development activities, Guatemalan CSOs were acquiring a more political dimension. In 2003, representatives of all but one of twenty-two political parties have been meeting in a "Permanent Forum," a very novel "space" for learning and discussion. Using the peace accords as a starting point, the forum discussed what should be the ongoing role of the Guatemalan state and agreed on a "shared national agenda" to increase internal democracy of civil society organizations and political parties. This agenda included the restoration of the 2000 fiscal pact to finance and institutionalize the peace accords and to strengthen the congressional and executive branch along with human rights offices. Groundswell from civil society for significant change in public education led the forum to endorse civil society's "National Campaign for Educational Reform." It lobbied for increases in the education budget to 4 percent of GDP immediately, with a middle-term goal of 7 percent.[25]

Religion was the hinge of Irish social conflict before and since the nineteenth century. "Is the religious dissension (conflict) so great as to be harmful to social relations?" Tocqueville asked in 1835 and the reply was: "The Catholics and Protestants avoid seeing and speaking to each other."[26] Guatemala almost two centuries later is different. Tocqueville would indeed recognize that churches there, beyond conflict or peaceful coexistence, have jointly created space for dialogue, democracy, and for building a more civil society. Hundreds of civil society organizations trace their origins and continuing support to Christian as well as Mayan religions. They have helped expand notions of civic responsibility, grown more involved in poverty alleviation and the promotion of equality—though the majority of the population is still far from the "providential" reality that Tocqueville admired elsewhere.

What of Governance? Local Government, Administration, and Justice

"*Is it true that the people have not the least confidence in justice?*" Tocqueville asked a priest. "*Not the least. The poor believe themselves in some way outside the law.*"[27] Tocqueville's memory of the French Revolution was vivid. In a conversation with a Dublin lawyer about growing violence and crime in Ireland, he asked: Q. "Do you think that a temporary dictatorship exercised in a firm and enlightened manner like that of Bonaparte after the *18 Brumaire* would be the only way of saving Ireland? A. I think so. But England herself is unsteady," replied the lawyer.[28]

Tocqueville visited America some sixty years after its revolution. He was ever conscious of the outcomes of the French Revolution. Given the poverty and injustice he witnessed in Ireland, he was fearful of revolution there. But he would learn that Guatemala has suffered a surfeit of Bonapartes, then a failed revolution, and painful peace process. I am convinced he would once again focus on associational life and local governance as an antidote to authoritarian schemes, and be encouraged by the emergence since the war of a more vibrant civil society.

Tocqueville's visit to Ireland was planned around visits to observe the functioning of the "*assize*"—a periodic session of superior English courts for civil and criminal cases held in rural counties. His interest in the *assize* was prompted by his doubts about the effectiveness of centralized government and especially bureaucratic institutions administered by local elites for the English crown.[29] He probed attitudes toward the administration of justice and heard that for the Irish peasantry, and many of the priests identified with them, justice was simply not available through the local system. In fact, he was told that "in Ireland, nearly all justice is extra-legal."[30] He interviewed local business and religious leaders, many of whom insisted "that the aristocracy has governed the country very badly."[31] Tocqueville's traveling companion Gustave de Beaumont published his work on Ireland in 1839, several years after their trip together. Larkin suggests that his study may be taken as a reliable surrogate for Tocqueville's views on Ireland. "What Ireland needs," Beaumont wrote, "is a strong administration, superior to parties, in the shade of which the middle classes might grow, develop and educate themselves, while the aristocracy would crumble and their remnants disappear."[32] Both Frenchmen had some ambivalence about the best way for Ireland, and England, to move beyond "obsolete aristocracy" and yet both were committed to "the general theory of association" and democracy. Learning the history of military dictators and their abuses should dissuade them from seriously proposing an *18 Brumaire* approach in Guatemala. Tocqueville would recognize its de facto aristocratic setting despite formally democratic institutions, just as he did in Ireland. But he would also bring to Central America his impressions of associational life and local government in North America, and grapple with a context long inimical to citizen organization, let alone citizen sovereignty. Guatemala has not yet arrived at his ideal as described in the following statement:

> So one may think of political associations as great free schools to which all citizens come to be taught the general theory of association: how to maintain order among large numbers of individuals, what procedures bring agreement, how to submit one's will to others, how to make one's particular exertions subordinate to common action.[33]

Guatemala has had its heavy history of firm but unenlightened strong men, paramilitary organizations, lynchings, and vigilante justice. Frustration with policing has led many citizens to take justice into their own hands, just as military governments for many years used clandestine organizations (often made up of soldiers or police forces) for extrajudicial killings, social cleansing of delinquents, and disappearances of activists, union and community organizers, and opposition leaders. Tocqueville would find it ironic to learn that nineteenth-century Irish rebels who refused to pay tithes were called "white boys," while twentieth-century Guatemala had its paramilitary organizations and hit men financed by the right called the *mano blanco* or white hand. Today, criminal violence and gangs of all colors are endemic. Citizen insecurity is the norm in Guatemala, but state violence, repression, or "state terrorism" has backfired over and over. Security and human rights must come together. Rather than resort to the hard-line *18th Brumaire* response, Tocqueville should interview Guatemalan citizen advocates like Rigoberta Menchu, Helen Mack, and Frank La Rue who, after many years of persecution, advised the administrations of Presidents Oscar Berger and now Colom Argueta on how to join human rights to justice.

Municipal Governance

As Sheldon Gellar has noted, the exercise of citizen sovereignty requires freedom of association and an end to state tutelage over associational life.[34] The pivotal institution between the state and civil society for working out citizen sovereignty is local government. While the Guatemalan Peace Accords represented a pact of elites, democratic governance in Guatemala, the efficacy of the peace accords, and citizen sovereignty will have to be proven ultimately at the local level by local "associations." Guatemala has twenty-one departments with appointed governors and 331 municipalities that elect their officials. The Constitution of 1985 recognized municipal autonomy (always a relative concept) and designated a fixed portion (first 8 percent, then 10 percent) of national income to the municipalities for improving core support and local service delivery. While financial transfers from central government to local governments date back to 1985, the latter still depend heavily on the center.

Tocqueville saw clearly how historical legacies shape the present. He would not be surprised to see in Guatemala the ebb and flow of ancient communal expressions reappearing centuries later. For example, communal property survives and forms of indigenous governance (the "auxiliary mayor" position in local government), suppressed or eclipsed during authoritarian and military regimes, have made a comeback, as have Mayan cultural and religious expressions. Tocqueville would not be prepared for the shifting from communal to national and now even international identity, even by people who speak twenty-four different languages.

Were Tocqueville to visit Guatemala, he would have to take into account the post-conflict impacts on society, on governance, and on the prospects for democratization.

> Tocquevillian analytics makes a distinction between 'local liberties' which refers to the desire and ability of local communities to manage their own affairs and decentralization, which transfers powers previously exercised by the state to formal local government units, which may themselves have been created by the state.[35]

The Guatemalan municipality blends both. Despite rhetorical "autonomy," the municipality has been long dependent on "transferred power" and financing from the central government. Today, there is growing pressure for greater "self-management" and the desire to exercise local liberties. Tocqueville and his message would be warmly welcomed by the mayors, especially their national association.

A National Association of Mayors (ANAM), sometimes co-opted, has begun to serve as a more effective instrument seeking stronger local government. Tocqueville would learn that citizen involvement and control has been enhanced now that they can organize and elect municipal officials through local civic committees. He would most likely approve this innovation that encourages more direct political participation unencumbered by unresponsive national political parties (which had seldom impressed him elsewhere). The civic committees have been particularly effective in indigenous communities consistently excluded by parties, and today, 131 municipalities have elected indigenous mayors. Although the municipality is a key arena for democracy and peace-building, it remains a weak institution like the exercise of rights and responsibilities of citizenship.

There is great need for training in administrative and technical skills for mayors, whether former guerrillas, soldiers, or traditional elites. Ideological labels lose their edge in the boondocks, where local-level politicians know they have to deliver on a daily basis, and they are learning that all "deliveries" should be transparent. Tocqueville, Popol Vuh, Boss Daley, Tip O'Neill, or Rigoberto Quemé (twice the indigenous mayor of Quetzaltenango, Guatemala's second largest city) all would agree that all politics, like development, democracy, and peace-building, is ultimately local. As Tocqueville memorably put it, "the strength of free peoples resides in the local community. Local institutions are to liberty what primary schools are to science; they put it within the people's reach . . . and accustom them to make use of it."[36]

In Guatemala, the authoritarian approach had been tried often and found wanting. In Ireland, an interview with several priests underlined the futility of fear and their hope in education. Tocqueville and Beaumont asked the priests in the impoverished northwest of Ireland about the patience of peasants when confronted with starvation and indifferent landlords. Tocqueville commented: "That shows admirable virtue." Reply:

> You must not have any illusions, sirs. Religion doubtlessly accounts for much of this patience; but fear counts for even more. This unfortunate population has been so long the butt for so cruel a tyranny. It has been so

decimated by the gibbet and transportation that all energy has finally left them. They submit themselves to death rather than resist. There is not a population on the continent that in the face of such miseries would not have its *three days* (*uprising*). And I confess that if I were in their position, and if I were not restrained by the strongest religious passions, I would indeed have difficulty in not revolting against this tyranny and unresponsive aristocracy.[37]

Tocqueville reflected later: "It was evident that these men, if they were not encouraging the people to revolt, would not be in the least sorry if they did revolt and their indignation against the upper classes was lively and deep."[38] The priest added with a note of hope: "The only effectual way to raise up again the demoralized spirits of these unfortunates is to educate them with open hands. Consequently, that is what we have undertaken, and we are doing it with all our might. You will see our schools tomorrow."[39] And he did.

Education: "An Act of Hope"

If Tocqueville would be inclined to examine the "mores," ideas, and habits of heart and how those habits are formed in Guatemala, he would be challenged by its complex, multicultural society. He would probably recall his assessment of America's treatment of Indians, and then its slave populations. With the exception of relationships between whites and blacks or Indians in the United States, compared to England, France, and the United States, Ireland was unique in its degree of cleavage, a cleavage produced by the superimposition of extreme class polarization on religion and national differences.[40] Guatemala might well trump those cleavages, based on its long-term class and ethnic differences.

Tocqueville was distressed by the educational levels of the Irish but hopeful at the efforts being made there. In contemporary Guatemala, like many observers, he would be disappointed and would probably pose many questions. He would be flattered to hear a prominent Guatemalan citizen quote his words in the year 2000:

> Peace is a dynamic process—no ready-made package but a work-in-progress requiring constant communication. It means education, an act of hope in personal and social perfectibility. . . . The peace accords gave us new paradigms, including those grounded in tolerance, pluralism and equity which lead to mutual respect with no exclusions.

Education makes it possible that such values be realized in our country among our people.[41]

Scholars note that Tocqueville used the term "mores" to refer to "the whole moral and intellectual state of a people."[42] At its core, mores refers to morals, and most especially, to ideas. Tocqueville attributed to education a key role in holding in check selfishness and maintaining public order, civic virtue, and human perfectibility. He had a deep and long-standing interest in the evolution of educational institutions.

Tocqueville would have noted that three of the Guatemalan Peace Accords of 1996 directly address education. It was seen as a necessity for achieving a multiethnic, multicultural, and multilingual society. How can government and society and the market ensure the quantity and quality of education required first for improved equity, increased civility, and meeting the requirements of a competitive, globalized economy?

Tocqueville would ask if Guatemalans can educate their people for citizenship and for jobs so as to compete in this global activity. Not now. Not while, as in the past decade, of every ten students who entered Guatemalan schools, 42 percent failed the first grade (primarily due to lack of bilingual teachers) and fewer than three reached the sixth grade (many need to work). Only one in ten students completes secondary, and only one in one hundred graduates from university. In pre-primary and primary public education in 2002, there were 20,339 rural and urban primary schools, led by 80,000 teachers, teaching 2,339,953 students. The National Teachers' Assembly estimates that another 100,000 children receive no primary schooling for lack of schools and a shortage of approximately 7,000 teachers.[43] Given the inadequacies of public schools, middle and upper classes opt for private education at all levels whenever possible. They are indifferent to public education and reluctant to add tax payments to their already heavy investment in private education.

Deficits also appear on the qualitative side of education. Overcrowded classrooms and poorly prepared, undermotivated, underpaid teachers lead to unproductive classes and ill-instructed children. Passive pedagogy, authoritarian lectures, memorized answers, lack of books and teaching materials, absence of reinforcement at home, or alternative places for reading and studying outside of the classroom yield at best, low-quality students, more frequently, early dropouts. Tocqueville might, however, detect some pressure for change. In 2002, seventy-four civil society organizations launched a national campaign for education, lobbying for an increase to the Education Ministry's budget. An educational reform initiative was

launched in 2001 based on proposals of the 1998 Peace Accords and recommendations of the Commission for Educational Reform. There has been
slow improvement in literacy levels in the country. Teachers' grievances
must also be dealt with. Their organizations focus heavily on contract, salary, and benefit issues. Teachers went on strike and shut down schools for
seven weeks during 2003. The Minister of Education has endorsed proposals from civil society organizations for continued increases in the budget
for education, which has been increased during the current administration
by 15 percent annually.[44]

With twenty-three recognized languages and dialects, the challenge of
multilingual education is enormous. Long-standing agendas of racial bias
must be addressed through combined economic, legal, moral, and educational approaches that can make educational opportunity for all a reality—
not a rhetorical flourish. A major shift in attitudes will have to occur at the
local level, school by school, and district by district. Without investment in
human capital, there is no prospect for social capital formation. And without better education at all levels, there can be little hope for a skilled labor
force, an enlightened electorate, or the development of citizen sovereignty.
Like other post-conflict societies, the *real* history of cycles of violence and
its dead ends should replace romantic narratives of the past and militarized
civic celebrations.

Tocqueville described a village in 1835 Ireland that resembles hundreds
of villages in 2006 Guatemala. The priest shows him a tiny schoolhouse
with thirty kids squeezed into it. "Forty years ago, Sir, a Catholic who dared
to give instruction to these poor children was severely punished. And they
complain that the Catholic population is still half barbarous. . . . Education
is a vital need for Ireland." Then Tocqueville asked: "Why was that group of
peasants gathered at the door of the school"? Reply: "The men whom you
saw are poor laborers, who come at the end of their day's work and they
gather at the door of the school so that the teacher, after he has finished his
lessons, can read the paper aloud to them."[45] Might the Irish poor of 1835
have had greater educational opportunity than many Guatemalans today?

Poverty, Equity, Migration, and Remittances

In his notes on Ireland, Tocqueville asked: "*Is the poverty of pre-famine Ireland the result of unjust English* (neoliberal) *policies or the moral or biological inferiority of the Irish?*"[46] He knew how to frame a provocative, leading
question as he began his inquiry in Ireland. He was no stranger to major

shifts in political economy brought by industrialization such as he witnessed in Birmingham and Manchester, England, and the beginnings of urbanization in America. His original inquiry in Ireland and my hypothetical exploration of contemporary Guatemala would require of Tocqueville (and of us, neo-Tocquevillians) far greater attention to political economy, to examination of persistent, concentrated wealth, and power by elites that undermine citizen sovereignty.

In Guatemala, Tocqueville would get many responses to the paraphrased question above and would have to look at multiple levels of causality, including not just a divided society, not just a nearby empire, but also a global economy. He would have to engage twenty-first-century debates about neoliberal rules governing world and local markets and the mobility of labor. As Terry Lynn Karl wrote:

> Had he lived today, Tocqueville would probably not have been a neo-liberal. He could hardly have embraced an approach that privileges efficiency and the creation of wealth over its distribution; he was far too concerned with the 'providential fact' of social equality and its implications for democracy. For Tocqueville, the 'general equality of condition' that so struck him during his stay in the U.S. was the basic building block for political democracy.[47]

He would perhaps recognize that to escape underdevelopment today requires efforts deprived of the strategies and tools that advanced countries had used, like protection for native industries, major investment in human and social capital through public education and social services, and a muscular if not flabby state. Tocqueville would not find growing equality in Guatemala, or many other Latin American countries, and would likely explain poverty from the "unjust policy" rather than "racial inferiority" side of the argument. He would see neoliberal strategies of economic development as a sure recipe for ongoing exclusion of the poor, that is, of most people in poor countries. Indeed, he would probably express alarm at the distributional trends, not just of Guatemala and elsewhere in the global South, but even of "providentially-blessed," one-time egalitarian America. He would note a trend toward permanent underclasses, with social policy (public and private) short on education and health services. He would find societies growing increasingly accustomed to 70 or 80 percent of their population, stuck on the margins.

Would Alexis be surprised at the twenty-first-century aspirations of many Guatemalans? Three blocks from my home in Southern California live a dozen or so Guatemalan Indian day laborers who, driven by economic constraints, tolerate precarious undocumented life in the United States. Without hope for eventual U.S. citizenship, neither can they gamble on incipient "citizen sovereignty" that is obscured by acute poverty at home back in the highlands of Guatemala. Tocqueville would criticize Guatemala's pathology of inequality and appalling distributional patterns and he would be most concerned about their impact on democracy. Available evidence confirms Tocqueville's belief that "nations are less disposed to make revolutions in proportion as personal property is augmented and distributed among them."[48] In other words, the degree of equality, rather than the level of economic development, may be the best indicator of political stability in democracies. Simply put, democracies with severe income inequality are unstable.

But Tocqueville would seek other views. Some would be more pragmatic. Moises Naim, the Venezuelan-born editor of *Foreign Policy* (and arguably a pragmatic neo-Tocquevillian), asks why scholars and development experts worry more about equality today than in the past, even though it may not everywhere be worsening. (He would have to agree that it is worsening in Guatemala.) Rather than excessive hand-wringing on the issue, Naim advocates measures to improve education, health, housing, and so forth, which are corrective of both poverty and inequality. Tocqueville would engage the debate, and he would likely resonate with Naim's anti-poverty recommendations for the future that do not count primarily on cures from the state:

> Yes, inequality is morally repugnant and politically corrosive. But it is also stubbornly immune to direct government interventions. The world has a long history of failed attempts at fighting inequality, including changing the tax system, labor market interventions, reform of property rights, massive subsidies, protection from foreign competition, and price controls: the list is endless. Nothing has worked. Countries that are unequal have stayed unequal (or gotten worse). . . . What to do then? The best tools to achieve a long-term, sustained decline in inequality are the same as those that are now widely accepted as the best available levers to lift people out of poverty. Provide access to better education and health care, clean water, justice, steady jobs, housing and credit. The recipe is well known, even boring.[49]

Agnosticism about remedies for inequality and certainty about cures for poverty would bring Tocqueville, and the rest of us, back to the importance of associational life, markets with economic growth and distribution that multiplies consumers, and a limited but strong role for the state. All three—state, market, and civil society—must combine to form human and social capital. Meanwhile, as debates drag on, 10 to 15 percent of Guatemala's population have assessed their global opportunity structures and migrated to the United States (just as many did in pre- and post-famine Ireland). During the past half decade, they have sent increasing amounts in remittances back to their families, occasionally collective remittances sent for community projects. The volume of remittances since 2003 has exceeded $2 billion per year, topping $4 billion in 2006—an amount that exceeds all direct private investment, bilateral and multilateral foreign aid, and loans by development banks combined. Tocqueville noted the tragic situation of Irish immigrants in English cities during his century. Were he to visit Guatemala today, he would probably explore the impact of their financial remittances on poverty, development, and democracy.

Pending Questions

Were Tocqueville, analyst, moralist, inquirer, to once again visit the Americas, North and Central, I think he would be disappointed in both. As Larkin put it, "the problem . . . that apparently haunted Tocqueville the most, from the beginning to the end of the Irish journey, was not how political power was to be safely redistributed in Ireland, but rather what was to be done about the all pervasive problem of poverty."[50] Tocqueville would be haunted by the same problem in Guatemala and in the United States.

Would he find hope for democracy in Guatemala? He would perceive how cold and hot wars dramatically undermined its associational life. He would see little movement toward equity and probably question an economy that yields so much for so few. Nevertheless, Tocqueville would be impressed by the plethora of NGOs and civil society organizations that have sprung up since the peace accords ended the thirty-six-year civil war. He might even celebrate the Mayan renaissance following centuries of repression and delight in Humberto Ak'abal's lyric poetry. He would look for and be pleased to find a positive role of religion, with many church leaders, including traditional Mayan priests involved in the process of negotiation, peace agreement, and peace-building. He would likely question both historical and contemporary involvement of clergy in public life as he did in Ireland. He would explore the hopeful, but somewhat artificial grafts intended to bring democratic governance to life in the 330 municipalities of the country. He might even adopt terms like "human" and "social capital" as he recognizes the need for education and enhanced opportunity for the Guatemalan population. He would have to grapple with an economy that tends toward more rather than less inequality.

He challenged rigid, unresponsive aristocracies as dangerous political anachronisms. He questioned remnants of the old regimes and *nouveaux riches* who would keep most wealth and power for themselves. He would question contemporary political and economic elites in Guatemala about why associational life and equity, peace-building, and development continue to elude their country. Perhaps Tocqueville and latter-day Tocquevillians who pose Socratic questions over time and space can stir change, not just thoughtful replies.

Notes

1. Cited by Emmet Larkin in *Tocqueville's Journey in Ireland* (Washington, DC: Catholic University of America Press, 1990), 144.

2. Alexis de Tocqueville, *Democracy in America* (New York: Harper & Row, 1988), 517.

3. Cited by Larkin, *Tocqueville's Journey in Ireland*, 8.

4. Cited by Larkin, *Tocqueville's Journey in Ireland*, 22.

5. Cited by Larkin, *Tocqueville's Journey in Ireland*, 7.

6. For example, see Paulo Friere, *Pedagogy of the Oppressed* (New York: Herder and Herder, 1970).

7. Enrique Krauze and Theresa Sheridan, "Mores and Democracy," *Journal of Democracy* 11, no. 1 (2000): 20.

8. Cited by Larkin, *Tocqueville's Journey in Ireland*, 9.

9. Alexis de Tocqueville, *Journeys to England and Ireland*, ed. J. P. Mayer, trans. George Laurence (New York: Doubleday, 1968), 149.

10. Tocqueville, *Journeys to England and Ireland*, 151.

11. Cited by Whitney Pope, *Tocqueville: His Social and Political Theory* (Beverly Hills, CA: Sage, 1986), 59.

12. Tocqueville, *Journeys to Ireland and England*, 92–98.

13. Cited by Pope, *Tocqueville*, 89.

14. Cited by Pope, *Tocqueville*, 58.

15. On this topic, see Charles Taylor, "Neutrality in Political Science," in *Philosophy, Politics, and Society*, ed. Peter Laslett and W. G. Runciman (Oxford: Basil Blackwell, 1967), 48.

16. Saguiv Hadari, *Theory in Practice: Tocqueville's New Science of Politics* (Stanford, CA: Stanford University Press), 148.

17. Cited by Larkin, *Tocqueville's Journey in Ireland*, 8.

18. Cited by Larkin, *Tocqueville's Journey in Ireland*, 8.

19. United Nations Development Program, *Human Development Report 2005* (New York: United Nations Development Program, 2006).

20. Cited by Larkin, *Tocqueville's Journey in Ireland*, 46.

21. Cited by Larkin, *Tocqueville's Journey in Ireland*, 61–62.

22. Gustavo Guttiérez, *Bartoleme de las Casas* (Maryknoll, NY: Orbis Press, 1993), 289.

23. See Ricardo Bendaña Perdomo, *La Iglesia en Guatemala* (Guatemala: Artemis-Edinter, 1996).

24. For example, see Humberto Ak'abal, *Poems I Brought Down from the Mountain* (St. Paul, MN: Nineties Press, 1999).

25. *Prensa Libre*, October 14, 2003.

26. Cited by Larkin, *Tocqueville's Journey in Ireland*, 13.

27. Cited by Larkin, *Tocqueville's Journey in Ireland*, 13.

28. Cited by Larkin, *Tocqueville's Journey in Ireland*, 7.

29. Pope, *Tocqueville*, 55.

30. Cited by Larkin, *Tocqueville's Journey in Ireland*, 21.

31. Cited by Larkin, *Tocqueville's Journey in Ireland*, 49.

32. Cited by Larkin, *Tocqueville's Journey in Ireland*, 145.

33. Cited in Cheryl Welch, *De Tocqueville* (Oxford: Oxford University Press, 2001), 93.

34. Sheldon Gellar, *Democracy in Senegal: Tocquevillian Analytics in Africa* (New York: Palgrave Macmillan, 2005), 180.

35. Gellar, *Democracy in Senegal*, 181.

36. Tocqueville, *Democracy in America*, 63.

37. Cited by Larkin, *Tocqueville's Journey in Ireland*, 135.

38. Cited by Larkin, *Tocqueville's Journey in Ireland*, 135.

39. Cited by Larkin, *Tocqueville's Journey in Ireland*, 135.

40. Pope, *Tocqueville*, 58.

41. Carlos Escobar Armas, *Revista ASIES*, no. 3 (2000), 11.

42. Tocqueville, *Democracy in America*, 287.

43. *Prensa Libre*, January 11, 2003.

44. *Prensa Libre*, July 22, 2005.

45. Cited in Larkin, *Tocqueville's Journey in Ireland*, 119. The village was in Galway, Ireland.

46. Cited in Larkin, *Tocqueville's Journey in Ireland*, 9.

47. Terry Lynn Karl, "Economic Inequality and Democratic Instability," *Journal of Democracy* 11, no. 1 (2000): 149–56.

48. Tocqueville, *Democracy in America*, 254.

49. Moises Naim, "Our Inequality Anxiety," *Foreign Policy* (May/June 2006): 95.

50. Larkin, *Tocqueville's Journey in Ireland*, 144.

7

Grafting the Head of Liberty? Latin America's Move to the Left

Gustavo Gordillo de Anda and Krister Andersson

> Every time that an attempt is made to do away with absolutism the most that could be done has been to graft the head of Liberty onto a servile body.
>
> —Alexis de Tocqueville[1]

Latin American polities—political parties, social movements, or networks—have in recent times moved toward different forms of leftist options, whether in discourse or in policymaking. Although the initial transitions from authoritarian to democratic regimes were coupled by more center-to-right regimes, the present leftist trend should come as no surprise. Democracy was reestablished almost at the same time as the Washington consensus policies were implemented.[2] Almost two decades after these neoliberal policies were launched, their basic promise of increased welfare for all citizens has not been fulfilled.

Although social, economic, and cultural inequalities are deeply rooted in Latin American societies and were already notorious well before the Washington Consensus, it is more or less a generalized impression that these policies have aggravated the old inequalities.[3] Although there is still much debate on their precise impacts on inequality, poverty, and economic growth, what can be said beyond contestation is that strengthening democracy has made social inequalities more apparent, public policy responses more transparent, and hence political representation more accountable. Secondly, expectations concerning high rates of economic growth have not been met in any country in the region, except for Chile.[4] The public's impression of policies largely failing to respond to increasingly visible social inequalities has triggered a shift of political preferences toward the left, which is evidenced by recent election results as well as the general discourse in the political debates throughout the region. The purpose of this chapter is to develop a deeper understanding of the underlying logic and possible consequences of this leftist trend in Latin American politics.

In doing so, we address the current debate on populism and the extent to which it poses a threat to democracy. This debate has been obscured by extreme views that either condemn all forms of policies that seek to confront inequalities or hail such policy efforts blindly. We argue that this debate needs a more nuanced examination of the specific institutional characteristics of what has been coined as populism in contemporary Latin American democracies.

As Alexis de Tocqueville's works remind us, during times of change— even radical ones—there are important strings of continuity that ought to be considered because they are crucial determinants of restorations. The de facto governance structures in modern Latin America are often shaped by traditional relationships between members of the oligarchy rather than by recent political reforms. The political culture and its norms continue to shape interactions in contemporary Latin American politics. Various paths are being pursued to overcome the crises related to governance structures, the vulnerability of governing coalitions, and mechanisms of representation in Latin America. However, success in pursuing these paths requires addressing the major issue of inequality. We discuss the question of how to mitigate inequality, combat discrimination, and ensure scrutiny and accountability of public authorities while consolidating democracy. This takes us back to another of Tocqueville's main concerns. As Vincent Ostrom put it, "Tocqueville's task in *Democracy in America* was to understand the American efforts to organize a republican system of government and to determine whether it offered a promise of maintaining liberty under conditions of equality."[5]

Change with (Subtle) Continuity

While in a different historical context and representing a different level of de jure democracy, the current Latin American context may be consistent with many of the features described by Tocqueville in his search for the causal roots of the French Revolution. We do not imply by using this analogy that Latin America is on the brink of a revolutionary outbreak but rather that fragile democracies still have the imprint of authoritarian regimes and thus restorations are possible. In *The Old Regime and the Revolution*, Alexis de Tocqueville analyzed several factors that determined the French Revolution of 1789: a decadent feudal system; the highly centralized administration based in Paris; and a class structure, with the nobility having no real legitimate political power, but being still attached to its privileges. Since the guidance of public opinion was entirely in the hands of the intellectuals due to the weaknesses of the political parties, Tocqueville pointed out that the directives of the Revolution were expressed through abstract principles that largely overlooked political realities. Moreover, because of the bond between the church and the old institutions, the Revolution adopted an antireligious discourse and promoted secular values. Tocqueville also emphasized on the extinction of political life and public deliberation that fostered in turn low solidarity and division between different classes: "Under the old order the government had long since deprived the Frenchmen of the possibility and even the desire, of coming to each other's aid. . . ."[6]

When glancing at the current political trends in Latin America, some similarities with politics in eighteenth-century France become obvious. But as Tocqueville captured it so well, for France on the eve of the Revolution, the strengths of centralization and executive predominance are also weaknesses for Latin American states.

Truncated Transitions

The political regimes that the recent Latin American democracies inherited—consisting of a divergent mix of formal and informal institutions in which the informal institutions keep adapting and reinventing themselves to capture whatever gains modernization reform brought—carry with them their own decay. The coexistence of many traits of the old authoritarian regimes with new institutional arrangements is a direct consequence of the paths that democratic transitions took. Whether by attrition or negotiated takeover, the crucial trait was that democratic transitions were in fact negotiated between the political elites that survived the authoritarian regimes. In both Brazil and Mexico, key actors from the authoritarian past also played a crucial role in the transition and its aftermaths. In other cases, the political elites linked to the traditional parties that were banned during the authoritarian rule made a comeback. Such is the case in Argentina, Uruguay, Chile, and partly in Peru. In many Central American countries, the initial split among political elites, which contributed to ignite the guerrilla warfare, gave birth to the present party system through peace agreements. In Venezuela, and to a lesser degree in Ecuador and Bolivia, major changes took place as a consequence of the breakup in the political party system. Even in these cases, what is most striking is the very modest intergenerational renewal of political elites.[7]

This characteristic of democratic transitions in Latin America is very consistent with Tocqueville's writings. In fact, the relevance of Tocqueville's *The Old Regime and the Revolution* for the analysis of this contemporary political context in Latin America stems from his emphasis on investigating the continuing thread that runs through the great disruptions brought about by radical changes. This impulse goes well beyond a sophisticated academic exercise as it underlines the ways in which the old regime emerges from the ashes to form a new political order that paradoxically is not radically different. It is actually radically similar. This similarity is based on the fact that administrative centralization was not reversed as the regime changed but was in fact further reinforced. This has been the case in almost all Latin American countries, even in Bolivia, where radical decentralization programs were launched in the mid-1990s but where the reforms included very little devolution of political decision-making autonomy and of economic power. Political and administrative centralization has been a political tool to control regional elites and new economic and political actors. Thus, the possibility of authoritarian restoration, a central theme in Tocqueville's analyses:

> Centralization was built up anew, and in the process all that had once kept it within bounds was carefully eliminated. Thus there arose, within a nation that had but recently laid low its monarchy, a central authority with powers wider, stricter, and more absolute than those which any French King had ever wielded. . . . [when] the ideal of freedom had lost much of its appeal and the nation, at a loss where to turn, began to cast round for a master—under these conditions the stage was set for a return to one-man government.[8]

On the other hand, the political elites—much like the French nobility—defend their privileges but continue to lose their legitimacy as they struggle to maintain their positions vis-à-vis new actors that emerge in the mass media, the business community, and civil society.[9] Much throughout the region, political deliberation has suffered severely because of the public's weakened trust in the institutions of political parties, legislatures, and judiciaries.[10]

Fragmentation and Social Mobilization

The weaknesses of basic forms of social aggregation such as political parties, associations, and unions have prompted to the forefront not only philosophers and intellectuals but what may be referred to as *media ideologues*. In fact, radio and television have filled the void left by weak associational life.[11]

Recent social mobilizations in Latin America, despite their diversity,[12] seem to be driven by relatively similar passions as those referred to by Tocqueville in analyzing the French Revolution. The message of all these mobilizations is clear: Citizens not only demand greater equality of opportunities but they also reject an exclusionary vision of redistributive justice centered on corporatist agreements.[13] They demand participation in the decision-making process and in the implementation of policies. Their unifying principle is the notion of popular sovereignty.

This expanded notion of popular sovereignty combines three core concepts: equality, as the articulating concept of social justice; suffrage, as the articulating concept of democracy; and the concept of autonomy, as the articulating concept of deliberation and self-governance.[14] The discourse on autonomy confronts the fact that corporatist arrangements embedded in societies often impede individuals to attain full citizenship. These mobilizations attempt to change the existing power relationships and to augment the negotiating capabilities of dissatisfied social actors. Frequently, they express symptoms of deeper malaises as the inability of the institutional arrangements to address citizens' concerns.[15]

The rediscovery of civil society in Latin America, as in other relatively young democracies, has revealed several limitations when it comes to its actual role in shaping governance decisions. Although it would be fair to say that many of these shortcomings were evident before, as many of its promoters exaggerated the expected benefits of increased civil society involvement, much like a panacea against bad top-down, centralist government. Specifically, these limitations stem from two factors. First, Latin American societies have been, and continue to be, characterized by large and complex social networks, highly diverse cultural attributes, and the concentration of political and economic power with elite groups situated in narrow, but deep pockets of wealth. That is, political pluralism, with social fragmentation at the bottom, and concentration of power at the top. Second, the antisocial, individualistic, and opportunistic behavior—as exemplified by the culture of impunity and illegality—also shape the behavior of different actors included in what we call civil society.

Unfortunately, what has happened to many recent social mobilizations in Latin America is a rapid escalation of the levels of violence in the confrontations between protesters and law enforcement. The latter has often responded to protests with measures of direct repression or with ad-hoc, short-term solutions, such as the repeated co-optation of leaders. Both types of responses seem to be misguided as they will continue to erode legitimacy of government in fragile democracies, increase the likelihood of institutional breakdown, and prevent effective policy responses to collective dilemmas.[16]

This absence of adequate channels for dealing with social conflicts is symptomatic of the malaise that some Latin American political elites suffer from paltriness and shortsightedness. The long-term social consequence of a vision that ignores the innovative potential of mobilizations or, worse, that resorts to coercive methods is the erosion of governmental legitimacy and authority. This erosion, in turn, reduces the capacity of public programs to reestablish stability and cohesiveness, generating institutional cleavages through which regional oligarchies may capture the decision-making processes. Do such problems exist? To explore answers to that question, we now turn to a discussion of the results of the 2006 presidential elections in Latin America. The results are indicative of shifts in citizens' perceptions with regard to democratic consolidation.

Democracies with Remorse: The 2006 Elections in Latin America

Eleven presidential elections were held in 2006, while in nine countries legislative elections were also held. For the presidential elections, incumbency was victorious in five countries: Brazil, Chile, Colombia, Mexico, and Venezuela. Opposition candidates ended up winning in the other six: Bolivia, Costa Rica, Ecuador, Honduras, Nicaragua, and Peru. Three of the five incumbent winners were consecutive reelections, the fourth was a reelection of a governing coalition in Chile, and the fifth, in Mexico where reelection is forbidden, a candidate from the ruling party won. When evaluating the successes for the opposition, one should consider that in two of the countries there were interim presidents immediately before the elections, making reelection impossible (Bolivia and Ecuador). Also, in Peru, where the opposition won, the coalition of the previous president did not present its own candidate. In Nicaragua, the incumbent government did not manage to maintain its political coalition united. In Costa Rica, corruption scandals shook the government party that had held power during the twelve of the last sixteen years, *Partido Unidad Social Cristiana*.[17]

Our discussion of citizens' perceptions of democracy in Latin America draws on the 2004 UNDP Report and the 2006 Latinobarómetro Report.[18] Although the public perception of electoral fairness is improving, more than 50 percent of the population still believes that elections are not fair. In most countries of the region, the majority of citizens believe that the last national elections held were not fair.

Four out of ten Latin Americans associate democracy with civil liberties and individual freedoms, while only one in ten associates the term with equality and justice. This particular result takes us to a much broader reflection as to why citizens in Latin America tend to identify better with the liberal actor rather than the democratic actor. There is a basic tension between liberalism and democracy in the sense that liberalism deals much more with pluralism, the individual and its differences; whereas democracy addresses the abstract, homogeneous citizen. In a region that is considered the most unequal in the world with enormous gaps in social status, it is understandable that citizens reaffirm their differences rather than their commonalities. This is, indeed, the main challenge to overcome social fragmentation that pervades the fabric of most Latin American societies.[19]

In fact, the vast majority of respondents believe that even if they were born poor they could become rich one day.[20] Nevertheless, only 31 percent believe that there is equal opportunity to lift oneself out of poverty. When looking at all the countries in the region individually, this proportion is less than half for all countries. This is puzzling, but it may be again that the liberal streak plays in the first answer whereas in the second what is being considered is the lack of a level playing field. Or, to put it another way, aspiration guides the first answer and realism the second. This is confirmed when analyzing data on intergenerational social mobility. A Latin American citizen, whose father did not receive more than primary education, has less than a 40 percent chance of surpassing this level of education.

In terms of citizenship intensity,[21] around 19 percent are classified as participative democrats and about the same percentage—22 percent—are participative ambivalent or participating non-democrats. However, 35 percent are nonparticipative, ambivalent, or immobilized non-democrats and 24 percent are nonparticipative democrats. The concept of citizen intensity is derived from Guillermo O'Donnell's low-intensity citizenship term and will be discussed within the context of our discussion on populism in the last section of this essay.

The most interesting group in this classification is the ambivalent group, who support democracy but believe that it is valid to take antidemocratic decisions when running the government if circumstances so demand. They prefer a democratic government but believe that it is more important to develop the country than preserve democracy. More importantly, this group is distinguished by accepting that the president may impose order in times of crisis through force, control of the media, and ignoring the national legislative body and the parties. This almost one-third of the citizenry probably constitute the social base for the so-called populist wave in the recent political scenario.[22]

Within this same perspective on finding in citizens' perceptions an explanation for the leftist surge in Latin America, the 2006 Latinobarómetro Report points to the emergence of a new group of citizens in the region who are described as "civic rebels." An important part of the electorate (14 percent regional average) in many countries considers that the most effective way to act for change is to participate in protest movements. The civic rebels support democracy to a lesser extent (50 percent) than the population at large (59 percent), and are more disapproving of their president in office (44 percent vs. 39 percent).[23]

As the 2006 elections unfolded, different levels of political tensions emerged. The first was related to the deep inequality between oligarchies exercising privileges due to their monopolistic status, especially in the financial, communication, and political spheres, and the "new plebeians," including a growing urban informal working class, evolving also around special privileges such as protection of illegal fringes of economic activity like drug trafficking, smuggling, and illegal reproduction and pirating of musical and film properties. Here we are in the presence of a tension in citizens' expectations with respect to changes in the way their societies are being governed.

The second refers to the relation between governments and de facto power structures based on criminal activities such as drug and human trafficking. This tension is related to the meaning of the concept of public space as a result of the combined effects of citizen insecurity and a perception of inequity in political decisions. There is a general perception that these countries are governed by small oligarchies that work for their own advancement and not for the well-being of the citizens. More than two-thirds of Latin American citizens consider that they are governed by a small number of powerful groups.[24]

The third tension confronts the political party system[25] and its relation with coalitions of citizens demanding administrative efficiency, transparency, and accountability. This tension may evolve into a delegitimation of crucial institutions such as political parties and legislatures. For example, the 2006 Latinobarómetro Report shows that only four out of every ten citizens rate the legislatures as performing well, while only four countries (Dominican Republic, Venezuela, Uruguay, and Colombia) have performance ratings over 50 percent. Only one-third of Latin American citizens consider political parties to perform well, while only 38 percent rate the judiciary as performing well.

Although the outcomes differ substantially, corruption has involved many governments including some leftist governments, as in Argentina with De la Rua's regime or at the end of Lula's first term in Brazil. In Argentina, it led to the demise of a regime with the famous chant of "*Que se vayan todos*" ("Let's get rid of them all") against the political elites. In Brazil, it did not affect the reelection of President Lula but it did impact the structure of the main governmental party, the *Partido dos Trabalhadores* (PT). In fact, most of the leadership had to resign after the corruption scandals known as the "*mensalao.*"[26] More importantly, the electoral base of the PT changed radically from the working class in the south to the northeast poor, mostly underemployed rural and urban dwellers.

The approach and instruments used to implant structural reforms triggered all three tensions to express themselves simultaneously. Crisis in expectations, deterioration of the public space, and delegitimation of basic democratic institutions triggered this penchant toward the Left. But in general, we are speaking of a particular brand of Left. According to the 2006 Latinobarómetro Report, on a scale ranging from 0 (extreme left) to 10 (extreme right), the mean score for the region as a whole was 5.4. No country scored more to the left than Panama, which ended up with a score of 4.6. Only four countries had mean scores that were below 5.0 (Panama, Uruguay, Bolivia, and Chile) and could therefore be classified as leftist concerning their citizens' political orientation. This would indicate that the winning recipe for the leftist parties in many Latin American countries has been the ability to attract votes from the center. The report also indicates that the Right is becoming increasingly unable to attract voters from the center, hence the recent leftist surge in a region with predominantly right-wing individual preferences. Perhaps it would be more accurate to interpret this trend as citizens considering themselves as centrist moving toward the Left in terms of demands and aspirations.

Next, we turn the discussion to a set of underlying forces that have shaped the contemporary political trends in Latin America: the structural reform processes that were implemented during the eighties and nineties.

La Rage de Vouloir Conclure

It is perhaps due to the persistence and resilience of inequality[27] that policies tend to have a differentiated effect on people, communities, regions,
and associations.[28] Many times, the nonintended consequences of policies play an important role. Because of this, the exercise of governmental
power during the past two decades seems to move in two opposite directions. On the one hand, we witness the revamping of practices of enduring patrimonial governance. On the other hand, democratic practices such
as regular and fair elections, accountability mechanisms, and freedom of
speech and association seem to herald the consolidation of democracy. In
its new guise, patrimonial governance is characterized by administrative
centralization coupled with loose clientelist ties at the different echelons of
government, that is, municipal, local, and regional government. Another
main trait is a divided government in the sense that the president has to
govern with a parliament that has no clear majority or a majority from the
opposition parties.[29]

Finally, except for a few countries such as Chile, Uruguay, or Costa
Rica,[30] many political parties resemble electoral machines that command
and control the state apparatus, but seem to have lost touch with citizens
and their forms of associations in society. A divided government and weak
political parties and administrative centralization at the upper echelons
have strongly affected mechanisms of social aggregation in unions and
business and farmer associations. Moreover, this combination has produced a political discourse detached from citizens' concerns and the realities of corruption and mismanagement, thus, nurturing distrust in politics
and cynicism.

In this context, one can better understand the impact of structural
reforms as the transition toward democracy unfolded in the culture and
norms of Latin Americans, and above all in the diverse political agendas
followed by the governments in the region. More than two decades after
these reforms first started,[31] the evidence is clear that these reforms failed
to produce the expected benefits, even for the elite groups that once promoted them.[32]

It is likely that the twenty-five-year period in which structural reforms
have been in effect in Latin America (1982–2007)[33] will pass as one of the
most noticeable failures of modernization policies. There are at least three
lessons that we can draw from the implementation of these policies. The
first has been a frequently traumatic lesson arising from the region's early
processes of structural adjustment, namely, that markets do not work on

their own. Rather, they require public intervention, for example, in the form of property rights and legal regulations. Conversely, the weak development of specific markets or the existence of incomplete markets calls for public interventions, but not necessarily from government institutions.[34]

Second, modernization policies[35] are ineffective and even destructive when they impose homogeneity on an environment characterized by cultural diversity and social plurality. To be effective, modernization reforms need to address the tensions that result from the prevailing social, economic, and political inequalities, but under a political framework that nurtures the exercise of liberty and the spirit of innovation.

The opposition that modernizing reforms now face in many countries may be traced back to the ways in which the initial reforms were implemented and the types of reforms that were selected. In many countries in Latin America, the discrepancies that frequently exist between formal rules and social norms can be explained through an analysis of the governance structure and political culture within which the operational rules must function. Constitutional rules, on the other hand, have experienced shifts in authority toward the executive power and sometimes toward de facto oligarchies when parliaments are weakened as a consequence of the crisis within political party systems and the judicial power does not succeed in gaining social credibility.[36]

To understand the centrality of these lessons, it is helpful to analyze them within a framework that separates the different key phases of the reform process.[37] The first stage of structural adjustment programs (SAPs) aimed at economic stability. Given that there was no automatic mechanism for defining what constituted "right" prices, arbitration was necessary.[38] The essential problem that arbitration sought to resolve had to do with public policy failures, namely, the mechanisms that generate institutional rents.[39] To achieve this, arbitration required ad hoc agreements with the business community; and the encapsulation of public organizations and technocrats in charge of the arbitrage process.[40] The main consequence of this institutional order was that it hollowed out the legal instances empowered by law or by constitutional mandate to accomplish that type of arbitration.

The second phase of the reforms, developed during the latter part of the 1980s and the early 1990s, sought to correct market failures through structural change. Its principal ingredients—trade liberalization, privatization, and deregulation—had a common purpose. The intention was to develop markets that could better deal with information asymmetries such as problems of adverse selection and moral hazard and hence reduce transaction costs. It has been widely documented that in the case of the SAPs in

Russia, as well as in other post-communist countries, correcting the inefficient functioning of the markets required a large set of competent institutions to support the day-to-day operations of the marketplace.[41]

Because of the absence of competitive markets and weak government regulatory functions, informal secondary markets produced their own set of actors, networks, and institutions and spread widely.[42] The substitution of public monopolies for private monopolies was, to a large extent, the result of the prevalence and strength of these secondary markets and their actors.

The initial design of the structural reforms, even when they had strong political implications, suffered from a clear "economistic" bias. We define "economistic" as the explicit or implicit negation of the autonomy of the political sphere in a society.[43] This occurs in societies undergoing reform when policies underestimate the reforms' negative effects on other social actors, especially those disenfranchised by the market economies, as well as on the existing institutional arrangements.[44] Because of the prevalence of these negative effects on the marginalized segments of society and especially on the political elites who lost influence through the reforms, a different incentive structure started to emerge. These incentives, which had been latent and embedded in the traditional political culture even before the reforms started, enhanced opportunities for illegal activities, desertion from previous political agreements, noncompliance with the new rules, and at the margin, increased disloyalty.[45]

The roots of this misjudgment might be traced back to a complex politico-intellectual process that emerged about two decades ago, with different levels of intensity in Latin America, characterized by the common traits of disassociation between political democratization and economic liberalization during modernization reforms. We argue that this mismatch has shaped policy choices regarding structural reforms throughout Latin America and has had an enormous impact on recent political outcomes.

Economic Liberalization and Political Democratization

During this reform era, democratization and economic liberalization were the common points of reference for different political discourses. Hence, it seems appropriate to depict a framework of four approaches to the reformist discourse, each with its own potential coalition.

The first approach galvanized around a central demand to enhance free market reforms. At the same time, it promoted limited political reforms.

This stance invoked an authoritarian implementation of the economic reforms, as was seen in Peru under Fujimori, in Chile under Pinochet, in Argentina under Menem, and in Mexico under Salinas.

The second approach advocated political democratization, while maintaining a traditional role for the interventionist state. This discourse articulated the proposals of reformers who sought modifications in the organizations and procedures related to political representation, but not in the role of the state in economic affairs. Most of the leftist groupings and traditional associations, especially trade unions, assumed this approach initially as a way to confront the economic reformers.

The third approach represents the confluence of two basic social demands—political democratization and economic liberalization—under the premises of a combination of a market economy and democracy. This approach drew together ideas and currents emanating from active participants in civil society and some segments of the traditional political elites. These actors agreed on the need to accompany economic reforms with democratization, but differed in the emphasis placed on each of the two components. Thus, an entire gamut of positions emerged. For members of the business community, its central demand was to continue and deepen economic reforms such as labor and energy reforms. Social movements faced with the most backward forms of state corporatism advocated for basic civil rights. A constellation of organizations and groups that have sprung from the most dynamic, modern fringes of Latin American societies demanded an end to patronage in politics.[46]

Finally, the fourth approach advocated the preservation of the status quo. Simply put, it called for restoration of the corporatist state and its patronage networks.

It has been postulated that both economic and political liberalization have reached a point of no return in Latin America. The 2006 Latinobarómetro Report indicates that an authoritarian comeback is implausible and cites as proof the fourteen presidents who were replaced through popular pressure and not by armed force, before the end of their mandate in the last twenty years. But these new forms of "democratic instability" as the report puts it are also a strong indication of fragile democracies. Paramio considers it a crisis of representation that he defines as a mismatch of the political parties and the governments in which they participated in relation to citizens' expectations. He adds that "it is an adaptive crisis of parties faced with a new economic and social reality as a consequence of the reforms in the nineties and globalization as a context."[47] While emphasizing the importance of political parties for democracy, Tocqueville again reminds us that governments are stronger and more powerful when parties are more permanent and compact.[48]

Certainly, a comeback of the military authoritarian state or the closed import-substitution economies of the fifties and sixties seems implausible. However, an authoritarian restoration would not be an identical image of the past. We will discuss this in the last section of this essay.

It was obvious that in a more transparent political landscape, enlarging the coalition that had initially favored the economic reforms was crucial. This enlargement could only come from the political sphere through reforms that would incorporate previous marginalized or semidisenfranchised actors. The political terrain chosen to operate these reforms was the electoral system. Although some electoral reforms indeed enlarged the possibilities of new actors to participate in elections such as previously barred leftist groups or indigenous communities, the main reforms referred much more to the transparency of the electoral results and to electoral fairness. The *mot d'ordre* of these reforms was counting votes that count. Again, a shortsighted vision failed to understand that although those reforms created a potential ground for enlarged coalitions committed to economic reforms, this outcome was not self-evident.

Coalitions needed to be constructed as a result of a deliberate strategy. The lack of this strategy more than the intrinsic nature of the institution of executive predominance—*presidencialismo*—has deepened fragmentation instead of reinforcing the aggregation function of political parties. Electoral democracy is not congenial to social cohesion when the starting point is a landscape of huge inequalities, a dense network of clientelism and patronage, and enormous distrust in civic participation. Tocqueville once warned that local interests might prevail over the general interest and worried about the potentially demoralizing political effect of this phenomenon.

Ernesto Laclau has argued that Latin America has recently experienced two traumatic and interrelated experiences—military dictatorships and the destruction of economies by "neoliberal" policies that have touched off an institutional crisis due to the incapacity of governments to deal with proliferating social demands expressed through horizontal protest movements that sidestepped the political system.

Even though citizens recognize that important democratic achievements have been accomplished, the Latinobarómetro surveys recorded over the past ten years also reveal a significant dissatisfaction with democracy. The persistence and even deepening of inequalities of income, assets, and access to political decisions and cultural goods have created a climate of pervasive resentment. This resentment in turn is strongly fueled by the privileges of a small but powerful elite that has lost touch with the citizens' demands as parties, unions, and other forms of associations have demonstrated a weak capacity to express the renewed demands of their constituencies. The increasing role of media, the Internet, and mobile phones for a small but influential segment of Latin American societies has exposed in the eyes of probably the small but influential group of participative citizens, privileges and above all impunity. This takes us back to our initial reference on the debate around populism.

Fragmented Identities, Entrenched Oligarchies, and Institutional Weaknesses: To What Democracy are Latin American Countries Heading?

In analyzing the enormous wave of violence that has ravaged Latin America, especially its big cities, Martín Hopenhayn, a Chilean philosopher, proposes the symbol of the specter to decipher the role of the concept of violence in political discourse. We shall use his definition of a specter to unravel the role of populism in the contemporary political narratives in Latin America. Hopenhayn defines a specter as "an intangible that surpasses a phenomenon but based on its specificities impacts perceptions and actions that surround it."[49] He then proceeds in defining a specter's basic traits. First, it operates as a thematic substitute for social conflict. Second, it presents an image that can easily capture the fears and uncertainties that emerge from societies that have strong doses of personal and social insecurities. Third, it operates by stigmatizing specific sectors of population.

Populism as a specter has many things in common with Hopenhayn's analysis. First of all, populism is a specific historical phenomenon both in Latin America or in Russia or in Europe or in the United States. In Latin America, as Schamis puts it,

> Populism as a political actor is history—we should perhaps drop the concept altogether. Once classic import-substituting industrialization ceased to be a feasible strategy—a result of the increasing market integration and financial openness that has come about since the mid-1970s—the economic incentives of the multiclass, urban coalitions that had sustained populism disappeared.[50]

Even major proponents of using populism to discuss contemporary politics in Latin America introduce important caveats. According to Ernesto

Laclau, a leading scholar on Latin American populism, "we are forced to conclude that when we use the term (populism) some actual meaning is presupposed by our linguistic practices, but that such a meaning is not however translatable into any definable sense."[51] Ludolfo Paramio also deals with this issue indecisively. He wrote:

> What is populism? This question has too many answers but for practical reasons we can distinguish between an historical phenomenon—populism in the Thirties and Forties, Vargas in Brazil and Peron in Argentina from a type of political discourse that emerges in different historical moments and is expressed through different economic policies not necessarily distributive or inclusive as the ones implemented during the historical populism.[52]

The ensuing question is why populism has been such a major issue in the recent political debates since it is often based on false historical analogies. We argue that populism has been a thematic substitute for the real issue of increasing social unrest in Latin America triggered by inequality and an ambiguous yet present sense of unfairness in many citizens' minds. Secondly, used as a political tool, it tends to conceal the failures of the structural reforms in terms of delivering wealth to the citizens. It explains the failures as a result of opposition from the special interest groups and asserts the need to persist in the structural reforms albeit implemented in a more thorough manner. Populism as used in massive media campaigns has also galvanized the fears of many low- and middle-income families trapped between the uncertainties of economic vulnerability and social foes related to criminal violence, drugs, and political abuse. It has also been used as a reminder of the fragility of the political regimes by bridging an historical analogy with the periods of high inflation prior to the military regimes. Finally, the concept focuses on the external manifestations of social unrest while avoiding the crucial issue of large-scale inequality. Thus, populism has been used as a deterrent to social reforms in a political discourse organized around fear and alleged menaces.[53]

Nonetheless, the political use of the concept "populism" responds also to the increasing access to power through electoral democracy of different leftist coalitions with different historical trajectories in very different economic, social, and cultural contexts.[54] Leftist regimes as different as the ones led by Lula in Brazil, Bachelet in Chile, and Chavez in Venezuela have one thing in common, that is, their institutional itineraries depend as much from their allies as on the responses from their adversaries. The reaction from the political right and most of the business community, particularly those benefiting the most from the structural reforms, implies a common thread. As Ramirez Gallegos put it:

> The intervention of sectors of the business community and of middle classes in the [failed] *coup d'état* against Chavez, the persistent attack on Lula's government from the mass media consortiums in Brazil or against the candidature of Andrés Manuel López Obrador in México, the fear of middle white classes in Bolivia of the triumph of Evo Morales are but a few of the clear signals of distrust and frequently of the disloyal opposition of the 'winners' from economic liberalization confronted with the possibilities of political change opened by the increased and visible influence.[55]

The institutional arrangements that might have emerged in Venezuela in the absence of the failed coup d'état is a clear example. So are the economic policies implemented in Brazil as a result of an informal agreement with the business community established outside and parallel to the party system and its formal representation with a serious impact on the democratic institutions themselves.[56] Another different example is the renewal of policies in the Bachelet government within the continuity of a sixteen-year-old coalition in power in Chile.[57] These three different trajectories have been strongly influenced by the way rightist coalitions related to the leftist governments. So, in a way, the menace of populism has been used as a deterrent against policies that were deemed to adversely affect the "winners" from the economic reforms. In its extreme version, populism has also been used as a deterrent to any policy that seeks to address seriously the problems of inequality in the region.

Populism is also a political discourse that bridges fragmented identities that have been affected by the implementation of structural reforms. For Laclau, three conditions are required for a populist breakthrough: (1) the polarization of the political discourse—"them" and "us"—, or in typical populist discourse, the oligarchies against the people; (2) the accumulation of unfulfilled demands, a powerful sign of institutional dysfunction; and (3) the existence of "empty signifiers," which means that in order to encompass a great variety of social demands and movements or actors that embody them, the political discourse is extremely simplified to include a much differentiated universe.

Paramio asserts that this form of polarization in attacking the political oligarchies inevitably leads to an attack on the political institutions themselves—beyond the political parties—and to an attempt to create new institutional arrangements tailored to the populist regime needs with very negative and lasting effects for democracy.

Guillermo O'Donnell's concept of "delegative democracy" offers an alternative to the politically manipulated concept of populism. He defines delegative democracy as "a type of democracy which rests on the premise that whoever wins the election for the presidency is entitled to govern as he or she sees fit, constrained only by the hard facts of existing power relations and by a constitutionally limited term of office." And he added that:

> A noninstitutionalized democracy is characterized by the restricted scope, the weakness, and the low density of whatever political institutions it has. Other, nonformalized but strongly operative practices—especially clientelism, patronage, and, indeed, corruption—take the place of the former, jointly with various patterns of highly disaggregated and direct access to the policymaking process.[58]

This also highlights the role that the absence of recognized institutions for conflict management plays in the unfolding of situations that favored the emergence of charismatic leaders and usually led the countries toward different forms of delegative democracy. This absence has affected both economic growth and the kinds of adaptation to economic shocks. Dani Rodrik concludes that

> when institutions of conflict management are sufficiently strong to ensure that ex post distributions follow the 'rule of the law' rather than opportunistic grabs by social groups, neither the severity of the shocks nor the extent of latent social conflicts might play a role in determining the productivity of an economy.[59]

Three Possible Scenarios

As a conclusion, we wish to discuss the implications of our observation in the form of three possible future scenarios. We call our first scenario *managed decadence*. The failure to construct a credible and permanent governing coalition will reinforce trends toward citizens' entrenchment into the private realm rather than increased civic participation. Failing to develop a stable governing coalition might encourage regional or corporatist elites— from local bosses to drug dealers, union leaders, and corporate business—

to entrench themselves in the territories or economic segments that they control. This in turn would weaken the accountability of national governments and further deepen social fragmentation and different forms of de facto secession. Many Andean countries, as well as some countries in Central America, could fall into this scenario.

A second possible scenario would be that of a *conservative restoration*. It may assume either a leftist or a rightist discourse. As Laclau wrote:

> It is enough that the empty popular signifiers keep their radicalism—that is, their ability to divide society into two camps . . . for the political meaning of the whole populist operation to acquire an opposite political sign. The twentieth century provides countless examples of these reversals. In America, the signifiers of popular radicalism, which at the time of the New Deal had a mainly left-wing connotation, are later expropriated by the radical Right, from George Wallace to the 'Moral Majority.'[60]

A leftist restoration would resort to a narrative of political arrangements that prevailed during the import-substitution model years. A rightist restoration might think about the institutions and coalitions that made possible economic reforms during military or authoritarian regimes and evoke the alleged stability and economic progress at that time. Obviously, to have a political model as a guiding principle for action does not mean it is possible to replicate it. However, what left and right restoration has in common is a combination of administrative centralization and restricted democracy. In the context of weak democracies in Eastern Europe, the sociologist Piotr Sztompka[61] reverts to the role that Tocqueville assigned to the habits of the heart and the character of the mind of citizens in reinforcing and strengthening democracies. The argument Sztompka advances is that the whole context of real socialism prevented the emergence of this "civilisational" competence[62] through direct indoctrination and totalitarian control by means of a coercive state apparatus.

Tocqueville asserts that the French Revolution was also the bedrock for an authoritarian restoration even though it had granted freedom and broken social ties among French in the same stroke. It is our contention that when a society has institutions that are incapable of mediating distributive conflicts and there is a simultaneous transition toward democracy and economic globalization, this combination increases the risks for the return of authoritarian regimes because globalization and the deregulation of trade relationships often empower the already strong groups within society—such as export-oriented oligarchies.

The third scenario is what we call democratic *modernization*. To describe this scenario, we resort to Tocqueville's definition of popular sovereignty as the people's right to make laws. In the brief chapter on the sovereignty of the people of America in volume one of *Democracy in America*, Tocqueville presents a classification of countries where states rule over societies and others where powers are shared between the executive power and local self-government. This scenario admits two possible paths that are not necessarily antagonistic. One path implies a clear commitment to democracy in the classic sense with rules to access power based on pluralism and respect for minorities. The outcome would be a package of political reforms oriented toward parliamentarian government, a statute on political parties aimed at strengthening its aggregation role and facilitating political coalitions, and legislation to strengthen transparency and accountability. The second path emphasizes democracy as public deliberation in order to reach basic agreements that allow for the construction of new institutional arrangements based on experimentation and learning for a high-intensity citizenry. Promoters of this path propose a package of political reforms that include diverse forms of direct democracy such as referendums, popular initiative to present laws, greater governance attributes and authority at municipal levels, and equity justice.

Supporters of the first path would certainly feel comfortable with O'Donnell's recent proposition that our definition of democracy needs to transcend the classic definition of "polyarchy," spelled out by Robert Dahl[63] to enlarge citizens' rights, to be able to resolve conflicts through legal prescribed means, and to be "reasonably" effective in the latter purposes. Those that advocate the second path would echo Vincent Ostrom's question: "Can people both individually and collectively maintain basic control over their institutions of government in a way that both allows for the exercise of freedom and imposes limits upon governmental authorities?"[64] This path moves toward a modern definition of citizens' self-government based on a combination of numerous units of government all subject to effective limits in opposition to the idea of a single, ultimate center of authority.

Again, we believe we are witnessing a potential alliance between relevant actors, from the business community to NGOs and social movements, that have been able to converge from time to time in albeit fragile and limited coalitions. This scenario could probably develop in Chile and Uruguay. With a lot more caveats, it could have potential in Brazil, Mexico, and Argentina. In all cases, this kind of alliance depends on a profound reform of both the political party systems, NGOs, and other forms of citizens' associations. It also requires a different perspective to relate with social mobilizations. It seems possible to channel such mobilizations through agreements that allow for experimentation with innovative institutional arrangements potentially mitigating social conflicts. Of course, not all social mobilizations turn into institutional innovation. Some are a result of patronage relations pursuing the capture of institutional rents. There may also be disruptive effects. Nevertheless, we argue that under these circumstances, it is essential to establish a strong relationship between the legal framework and citizens' claims including social mobilizations in order to facilitate a transition between social protest—which in and of itself is spontaneous and sometimes explosive in character—and a broad-based process of collective action that aims to construct new, more legitimate governance institutions. This bridge between legality and social mobilization could facilitate the transformation of protest and conflict into institutional innovation, experimentation, and solutions.[65]

Proponents of both paths agree on the need to reduce inequality, combat all forms of discrimination, establish limits to governments through public scrutiny, and promote counterbalance powers. Sometimes they differ in the timing and the sequencing. Some proponents of the first path distrust the democratic commitment of social movements and citizens' associations and assert that changes should be narrowly limited within formal institutions. Proponents of the second path distrust the democratic commitment of the business community and middle classes and assert that without the ability of citizens to resort to the streets, reforms could be derailed and manipulated by oligarchies.

In sum, there are many threats to democracy in Latin America given its background of vast inequalities, discretionary use of power, corruption, and networks of cronies. We believe that the greatest threat of all is the inability to grasp the exceptional moment in which democratic consolidation and economic modernization appear to coincide in the minds and hearts of many of its citizens.

Notes

We have had the privilege of discussing and receiving relevant comments from Elinor and Vincent Ostrom. Early versions of this chapter were discussed with Armando Razo, Sheldon Gellar, and Frank van Laerhoven at the Workshop in Political Theory and Policy Analysis, Indiana University. Rodrigo Wagner, a doctorate student at Harvard, and Agustín Goenaga from the Instituto Tecnológico de Estudios Sociales de Occidente (ITESO) in Guadalajara, Mexico, provided useful comments and suggestions.

1. Alexis de Tocqueville, *The Old Regime and the French Revolution* (New York: Anchor Books, 1983), 209.

2. For a precise definition of which policies the so-called Washington Consensus encompassed, see John Williamson, ed., *Latin American Adjustment: How Much Happened?* (Washington, DC: Institute for International Economics, 1990).

3. For example, see John Williamson, "Democracy and the Washington Consensus," *World Development* 21, no. 8 (1993): 1329–36; Charles Wyplosz, "Ten Years of Transformation: Macroeconomic Lessons" (paper presented at the Annual World Bank Conference on Development Economics, Washington, DC, April 28–30, 1999); Joseph Stiglitz, "Whither Reform: Ten Years of Transition" (paper presented at the Annual World Bank Conference on Development Economics, Washington, DC, 1999); Stephan Haggard and Robert R. Kaufman, eds., *The Politics of Economic Adjustment* (Princeton, NJ: Princeton University Press, 1992); Moises Naim, "Fads and Fashions in Economic Reforms in Latin America: Washington Consensus or Washington Confusion?" (paper presented at the IMF Conference on Second Generation Reforms, Washington, DC, 1999); and Carlos Salinas de Gortari and Roberto Mangabeira Unger, "The Market Turn without Neoliberalism," *Challenge* (January–February 1999).

4. Nevertheless, since 2004, Latin America has experienced three consecutive years of an economic growth rate above 4 percent, which had not been seen in this region since the seventies.

5. Vincent Ostrom, *The Political Theory of a Compound Republic: Designing the American Experiment*, 3rd ed. (Lanham, MD: Lexington Books, 2008), 138.

6. Tocqueville, *Old Regime*, 206.

7. The minutes of the 1991 Kellogg Institute Conference on Business Elites and Democracy in Latin America, elaborated by Juan J. López, present interesting insights on visions of the business community in Latin America toward the structural reforms and the democratic transitions. Also see John Highley and Richard Gunther, *Elites and Democratic Consolidation in Latin America and Southern Europe: An Overview* (New York: Cambridge University Press), 300–23. For political elites in Mexico, see Peter Smith, *Political Elites in Mexico, 1900–1971* (Madison, WI: Data and Program Library Service [Distributor], 1969), http://www.disc.wisc.edu/mexican_political_elites/index.html (accessed May 25, 2007).

8. Tocqueville, *Old Regime*, 208–9.

9. An interesting revision of different political and social actors can be found in the Inter-American Development Bank report, *The Politics of Policies* (Washington, DC, 2006) (hereafter cited as IADB).

10. Recent surveys conducted by *Latinobarómetro* (Santiago, Chile: Corporación Latinobarómetro, 2006, http://www.latinobarometro.org) and the United Nations Development Program (UNDP), *La democracia en América Latina: hacia una democracia de ciudadanos y ciudadanas* (Buenos Aires: Editoriales Aguilar, Altea, Taurus y Alfaguera, 2004) demonstrate this in a powerful way. We will revert to this point in reviewing the results of these surveys later in the chapter.

11. IADB, part II, 223–24.

12. IADB, 112–16. The report links the rise of "street power" with three types of crises related to the weakness of the state, the weakness of representative democracy, and the weakness of the nation.

13. We follow Ernesto Laclau's use of the concept of "demand": "The word 'demand' is ambiguous in English. On the one hand, it has the meaning of *request* and, on the other, the more active meaning of *imposing* a request—a claim—on somebody else (as in 'demanding an explanation'). In other languages, like Spanish, there are different words for the two meanings. The word corresponding to our second meaning would be '*reivindicación.*'" See Laclau, "Populism: What's in a Name?," in *Populism and the Mirror of Democracy*, ed. Francisco Panizza (London: Verso, 2005), 3.

14. See Gustavo Gordillo, *Reformando a la Revolución Mexicana* (Mexico City: El Nacional, 1990).

15. IADB, 116–19, classifies social movements along two dimensions: the specificity or generality of the issue underlying the social movement—that is, the "breadth" of the movements and the way social movements seek to influence policies by being proactive or by using veto powers and being reactive.

16. Examples of oppressive measures include those imposed in Bolivia by President Sanchez de Losada and in Argentina by President De la Rua. Recent attempts to dampen social protests through co-optation have occurred in Ecuador under Correa and in Nicaragua under Ortega.

17. For details on the elections, see *Latinobarómetro* (Santiago de Chile, 2006).

18. Latinobarómetro is a private, public poll company that since 1995 has presented a yearly report on political opinions and perceptions from citizens in eighteen countries of Latin America. It has conducted almost 200,000 face-to-face interviews and has the most important database on political perceptions in Latin America (see http://www.latinobarometro.org). The 2004 UNDP report is based on a series of surveys conducted with the technical support of Latinobarómetro, direct interviews with leading political and business leaders, and an important number of contributions from leading political scientists from the region. It was coordinated by the former minister of Foreign Affairs from Argentina Dante Caputo. See http://democracia.undp.org/Default.asp?Idioma=2 and also *La democracia en América Latina.*

19. We wish to thank Agustin Goenaga for his suggestion to link this discussion with the theoretical work of both Carl Schmitt and Slavoj Zizek.

20. Latinobarómetro, 2006, 46–47.

21. "Citizen Intensity means the free and active exercise of rights and the fulfilment of duties. . . ." UNDP, 2004, 144–45.

22. UNDP, 2004, 132–40. See also graph 5, p. 133; graph 7, p. 136.

23. The country with the highest percentage of civic rebels is Guatemala with 26 percent, followed by Brazil and Peru with 22 percent, Bolivia with 18 per-

cent, and the Dominican Republic and Paraguay with 17 percent. Also see IADB, 116–17, where the discussion on different institutional crises that trigger mobilizations sheds light on the characteristics of the "civic rebels."

24. Latinobarómetro, 65.

25. See IADB, 31–52.

26. The *mensalao* was a massive and fraudulent operation that siphoned public resources to the pockets of deputies in order to assure their vote for crucial laws and used private companies linked with some of the PT leaders as a way of buying votes in the National Congress. *Mensalao* refers to the tendency for the payoffs to be given in monthly installments.

27. There is an extensive literature on inequality in Latin America. The 2003 World Bank report on inequality in Latin America portrays inequality as extensive, pervasive, and resilient. Also see Leonardo Gasparini et al., *Economic Polarisation in Latin America and the Caribbean: What do Household Surveys Tell Us?* (Buenos Aires: CEDLAS, 2006); Ricardo Haussman and Miguel Szekely, *Inequality and the Family in Latin America* (Washington, DC: IADB, 1999, http://www.iadb.org/oce); Terry Lynn Karl, "The Vicious Circle of Inequality in Latin America" (working paper 177, Juan March Institute, Madrid, 2002); *What Justice? Whose Justice? Fighting for Fairness in Latin America*, ed. Timothy Wickham and Susan Eckstein (Berkeley: University of California Press, 2003); Juan Londoño and Miguel Szekely, *Persistent Poverty and Excess Inequality: Latin America, 1970–1995* (Washington, DC: IADB, 1997); Samuel A. Morley, *The Income Distribution Problem in Latin America* (Chile: ECLAC, 2001); Nancy Birdsall, *Washington Contentious: Economic Policies for Social Equity in Latin America* (Washington, DC: Carnegie Endowment for International Peace and Inter-American Dialogue, 2001); and Ravi Kanbur and Nora Lustig, "Why is Inequality Back on the Agenda?" (paper presented at the annual World Bank Conference on Development Economics, Washington, DC, 1999).

28. This section is an adapted version of Gustavo Gordillo de Anda, *La ansiedad de concluir: le debil institucionalidad en America Latina: El Mercado de Valores* (Mexico City: Nacional Financiera, 1999). The mania for drawing conclusions (*la rage de vouloir conclure*) is a phrase borrowed from the French writer Gustave Flaubert (1863), who claimed that this: "is one of humanity's most dreadful and sterile obsessions. Each religion, and each philosophy, has claimed to have God to itself, to comprehend the infinite and to know the recipe for happiness. What pride and what nothingness!" In *Journeys toward Progress: Studies of Economic Policy-Making in Latin America* (New York: Twentieth Century Fund, 1963), Albert Hirschman adapted this phrase to illustrate the bias of many policymakers in Latin America in presenting panaceas instead of in-depth analysis to confront complexity in developmental dilemmas.

29. See IADB, table 3.1, p. 37. Only Paraguay, Nicaragua, Honduras, and Chile in 2005 does the party or coalition that won the executive branch also have a majority in Congress.

30. However, the very competitive 2006 elections reflected the crisis of the two-party system, due mainly to corruption scandals that had governed Costa Rica for decades.

31. More specifically, these structural reforms refer to a set of policies designed to promote free markets, including trade liberalization, the privatization of state enterprises, the removal of price controls, and the deregulation of financial markets.

32. John Williamson, who coined the term *Washington consensus*, has pleaded to "submit that it is high time to end this debate about the Washington Consensus. If you mean by this term what I intended it to mean, then it is motherhood and apple pie and not worth debating. If you mean what Joe Stiglitz means by it, then hardly anyone who cares about development would want to defend it. In neither case does it merit all the ink that is spilled on the subject or all the foaming at the mouth that it provokes." See Williamson, "Speeches, Testimony, Papers: Did the Washington Consensus Fail?" (outline of speech at the Center for Strategic & International Studies, Washington, DC, November 6, 2002), http://www.iie.com/publications/papers/paper.cfm?researchid=488 (accessed May 25, 2007). We disagree since it is precisely the way these reforms were implemented that helps to shed light on the political consequences we are still witnessing in Latin America.

33. We see the starting point of the structural reforms with the policies introduced by Chile's Pinochet regime in 1982 as a response to the deep economic crisis that the country suffered at that time after almost ten years of dictatorship.

34. Here we are referring to different forms of coprovision and coproduction of public goods and services that imply public interventions but not necessarily from the government alone.

35. Classical modernization theory held that liberal democracy and market economy went hand in hand and that liberal democracy is the outcome of economic development. For example, see Seymour Martin Lipset, *Political Man* (Garden City, NY: Doubleday, 1960).

36. Particular attention must be paid to the basic relation that occurs between the institutional order and norms of behavior, that is, between the form in which authority is distributed and the form in which it is exercised in interactions among different individuals. On what Ronald Oakerson and S. Tjip Walker refer to as *policy regimes*, see "Analyzing Policy Reform and Reforming Policy Analysis: An Institutionalist Approach," in *Policy Studies and Developing Nations: An Institutional and Implementation Focus*, vol. 5, ed. Derek Brinkerhoff (Greenwich, CT: JAI Press, 1997), 33.

37. Moises Naim presents a useful table on the two stages of SAPs at the end of his article, "Fads and Fashion in Economic Reforms: Washington Consensus or Washington Confusion?" (working draft of a paper prepared for the IMF Conference on Second Generation Reforms, Washington, DC, 1999), http://www.imf.org/external/pubs/ft/seminar/1999/reforms/Naim.HTM#I (accessed May 25, 2007).

38. See Rafael Paniagua-Ruiz, *Los componentes centrales de las políticas ligadas al desarrollo rural, la reforma agraria y la lucha contra la pobreza in América Latina y el Caribe* (Rome: FAO, Rural Development Department, 1997).

39. In the literature, the capture of these "institutional rents" is frequently depicted as crony capitalism: "Crony capitalism is usually thought of as a system in which those close to the political authorities who make and enforce policies receive favours that have large economic value. These favours allow politically connected economic agents to earn returns above those that would prevail in an economy in which the factors of production were priced by the market." See Stephen Haber, *Crony Capitalism and Economic Growth* (Palo Alto, CA: Hoover Institution Press, 2002), xii.

40. This "encapsulation" refers to the conviction of the reformers for the need to isolate their policy designers from the influence of particular interest groups, something that history would prove to be wishful thinking.

41. The comments by Joseph Stiglitz seem very pertinent: "China did not follow the dictums of the Washington consensus. It emphasized competition over privatization. . . . We see the track record. It should not be surprising: privatizing a government monopoly is often likely to create a private monopoly with high prices and continued inefficiency. Similarly, one of the objectives of trade liberalization is to enhance competition, but when there is a monopoly importer, tariff revenues may simply be converted to rents accruing to the monopoly importer. The topics that were left out by the Washington consensus are perhaps even more telling: financial markets, competition and regulation, the transfer of technology, the development of institutions—to name but a few whose importance has been increasingly recognized." See Stiglitz, "Distribution, Efficiency and Voice: Designing the Second Generation Reforms" (Conference on Asset Distribution, Poverty, and Economic Growth, Brasilia, Brazil, 1998), 7; and Stiglitz, "More Instruments and Broader Goals: Moving Towards the Past-Washington Consensus" (Wider Annual Lectures 2, Helsinki, 1998).

42. See Alain De Janvry, Gustavo Gordillo, and Elizabeth Sadoulet, *Mexico's Second Agrarian Reform: Household and Community Responses* (San Diego: University of California, Center for U.S.-Mexican Studies, 1997); Stephan Voigt and Daniel Kiwit, "Black Markets, Mafiosa and the Prospects for Economic Development in Russia: Analyzing the Interplay of External and Internal Institutions" (working paper, Max Planck Institute, Jena, Germany, 1995).

43. One of the most paradoxical twists in the dominant approach on structural reforms was the use of one of the weakest ingredients of classic Marxist thought, the alleged correspondence between economic structures and political agents.

44. On the importance of understanding economic change and the impacts on institutions and beliefs, see Douglass North, *Understanding the Process of Economic Change* (Princeton, NJ: Princeton University Press, 2005).

45. The difference between loyal, disloyal, and semi-loyal opposition, according to Juan Linz, has to do with the mediation among opposing parties and the

prevailing political order. A disloyal opposition seeks to transform the political regime, appealing to different rules of the political game because it judges the established rules to be illegitimate. See Linz, *La quiebra de las democracias* (Mexico City: Alianza Editorial Mexicana, 1990), 57–71.

46. Although this position could be found in segments of leftist parties like the PT and the PSDB in Brazil, the PPD in Chile, and PRD in Mexico, this stance was more clearly found in social movements and marginal parties like the *Polo Democrático* in Colombia, the more leftist PSOL which split from the PT in Brazil, and *Alternativa Social Democrata*, a small party led by a coalition of feminists, gays, and environmentalists in Mexico.

47. See Ludolpho Paramio, "La izquierda y el populismo," *Revista Nexos* (2006): 33.

48. Alexis de Tocqueville, *Democracy in America* (New York: Library of America, 2004), 88.

49. Martín Hopenhayn, "Fantasmas de la ciudad: droga y violencia en América Latina," in *América Latina desigual y descentrada* (Buenos Aires: Editorial Norma, 2005), 215–51.

50. Hector Schamis, "Populism, Socialism and Democratic Institutions," *Journal of Democracy* 17, no. 4 (2006): 14.

51. Laclau, "Populism," 1.

52. Paramio, "La izquierda y el populismo," 32.

53. For example, see the political campaigns launched in Mexico against the leftist candidate Lopez Obrador, against Lula in Brazil, against Ollama Humala in Peru, or to Tabare Vasquez in Uruguay. Our point is not only to underscore the similarities in these fear campaigns using the specter of populism but also to show that completely different types of leftist coalitions were all classified as populist.

54. See Guillermo O'Donnell's concept of "delegative democracy," which we discuss later on as a more comprehensive tool to analyze the present situation in Latin America.

55. Franklin Ramirez Gallegos, "Mucho más que dos izquierdas," *Nueva Sociedad* 205 (September–October 2006): 35.

56. One striking example we have already cited is the so-called crisis of the *mensalao* in which the top leadership of the PT was involved.

57. Even the Right most strongly attached to the Pinochet regime has increasingly embraced strong commitments toward democracy. As a result, the first fourteen months of the Bachelet government has been more of a deep-seated struggle within the governing coalition between the old guard and the new generation of politicians and public policy officers that were born or very young during the Pinochet regime.

58. Guillermo O'Donnell, "Delegative Democracy," *Journal of Democracy* 5, no. 1 (1994): 59.

59. Dani Rodrik, "Where Did All the Growth Go? External Shocks, Social Conflict and Growth," *Journal of Economic Growth* 4, no. 4 (1999): 6. In a simi-

lar approach applied to the analysis of historical processes in nineteenth-century Latin America, Adam Przeworski and Carolina Curvale express "that economies grow when political power protects economic power—this is what 'security of property' means—as long as political institutions absorb conflicts and process them according to rules. But unequal political institutions perpetuated economic inequality and generated conflicts—over land (or wages of agricultural workers) and over wages and conditions of work in industry—which were politically destabilizing and economically costly. Hence, while political inequality may be statically efficient, it is dynamically inefficient." "Does Politics Explain the Economic Gap between the United States and Latin America?" (working paper, Department of Politics, New York University, 2005).

60. Laclau, "Populism," 15.

61. We wish to thank Aurelian Craiutu for drawing our attention to this important author.

62. Sztompka draws an analogy from what linguists call "language competence" using the term *civilizational competence* by which he means "a complex set of rules, norms and values, habits and reflexes, codes and matrixes, blueprints and formats the skillful and semi-automatic mastery of which is a prerequisite for participation in modern civilization." "Civilizational Competence: A Prerequisite of Post Communist Transition" (Krakow, Poland: Jagellonian University, Centre for European Studies, 2000), 7.

63. Dahl's two basic components of polyarchy are elections that are reasonably fair and a democratic regime that includes a set of political freedoms, such as freedom of expression, of association, of movement, and access to nonmonopolized information. See Dahl, *Polyarchy: Participation and Opposition* (New Haven, CT: Yale University Press, 1971), 7–8.

64. Ostrom, *Political Theory of a Compound Republic*, 138.

65. In discussing the construction of such bridges, we regard social mobilization as the "means of production of institutions." The process of bridging the gap between formal and informal institutions in the mediation of social conflicts creates the possibilities of "producing" new rules of the game, that is, new institutions. Referring to the importance of bridging institutions in consolidated democracies, O'Donnell notes, "[. . .] in the functioning of contemporary, complex societies, democratic political institutions are a crucial level of mediation and aggregation between, on one side, structural factors and, on the other, not only individuals but also the diverse groupings under which society tends to organize its multiple interests and identities" ("Delegative Democracy," 11).

8

The Peril of Democratic Despotism in West European Egalitarian Democracy

Frederic Fransen

Tocqueville's great work, *Democracy in America*, is premised on a simple idea: that the modern world finds itself in a providential march toward equality. The inevitability of equality was a given for Tocqueville, a dependent variable. Tocqueville's independent variables were liberty and democracy, and Tocqueville greatly feared that in the march of equality, his variables were inversely correlated: as equality led to increasing democracy, liberty would decrease, and that where liberty was strong, democracy would necessarily suffer.

Although Tocqueville's insight was straightforward and might have been presented in a short essay, he instead wrote a big book. The reason he did so is that Tocqueville chose not simply to diagnose the way in which the contagion "equality" infects and cripples the health of a free society but also to propose ways of inoculating against the worst effects of the disease.

Tocqueville's proposed therapy, however, was not a miracle cure but rather a sophisticated, multifaceted, and holistic approach. To preserve my medical analogy, the treatment for equality was not like a polio vaccine that provides lifelong protection but more like the modern response to heart disease in which the physician proposes changes in diet, exercise, and other behavior, as well as prescribes medicines, and in serious cases performs surgery. Moreover, Tocqueville recognized that the particular recommendation for each patient—each society anticipating how to preserve freedom in the face of rising equality—would be different.

In America, Tocqueville not only discovered the disease he had come to identify, he also found a doctor's bag full of medicines, collected by Americans through their long experience with social equality and its political manifestation in democracy. In Tocqueville's analysis, Americans sometimes understood what they were doing, and sometimes were unconscious of it. In some cases, they had developed a powerful theory of how to preserve liberty, but failed in its implementation. In others, they were more successful. Tocqueville's *Democracy in America* and later *The Old Regime and the Revolution*, therefore, are forensic accounts of how equality and democracy came to dominate our political and social views, the risks they pose for liberty, and ways in which those risks can be minimized in the modern world. Despite some appearances to the contrary, his project was less descriptive than prescriptive. He wanted Europe (and America) to be places in which liberty would thrive under the new circumstances brought about by the providential march of equality.

Tocqueville's analytic framework, as a consequence, does not depend on the success or failure of its implementation in America, nor even the historical accuracy of Tocqueville's account of American institutions in the first half of the nineteenth century. Tocqueville saw the rise of equality and its threat to liberty to be universal phenomena. If his analysis was right, then his analytic framework should be useful in analyzing the relation between liberty and equality in other places. Indeed, in a very narrow sense, Tocqueville wrote *Democracy in America* not for Americans but for Europeans as they prepared for the onslaught of equality.[1]

Others have been tasked with applying Tocquevillian analytics to parts of the world outside Tocqueville's own experience, although certainly not outside his area of interest, which was worldwide.[2] My task, by contrast, is to do so with regard to the very audience for which Tocqueville wrote: Western Europeans.

One would be tempted to write that Tocqueville well understood the dangers of democracy in Europe, and accurately predicted the collapse of free government there—whether France in 1851, Italy in 1925–1926, or Germany in 1933. Moreover, one might be tempted to add that Western Europe has now put this danger behind itself—that Western Europe has learned to prevent democracy from declining into despotism—and that liberty will reign unchallenged into the distant future. Indeed, today Western Europeans are tempted to gloat that the real danger of democratic despotism is to be found on the American side of the Atlantic, in the fanatical opinions of a sometimes reactionary, fundamentalist electoral majority, and the "cowboy" politicians they all-too-frequently elect.

It is not the purpose of this chapter, however, to analyze (and criticize) the dominant European interpretation of American democracy, although that would surely be an interesting exercise. Rather, it is to examine Western Europe through Tocquevillian lenses. As outlined by Sheldon Gellar, the overall scheme of such a study should look at the interrelation among cultural, institutional, and environmental factors. With regard to culture, the role of religion in society is one important, if not key, element. Concerns with regard to institutional arrangements should explore questions such as centralization, the degree of local liberty, bureaucratic uniformity, and associational life. Environmental factors should include issues of political as well as physical geography.

Europeans have had the knowledge and ability to adopt Tocquevillian ways and means to the challenges presented to them by the rise of equality and democracy, particularly in the post–World War II era. As this chapter will show, however, Western Europeans have chosen *not* to adopt Tocqueville's various remedies for the preservation of healthy liberty under conditions of rising equality.

This troubling fact can be seen in such issues as political and economic centralization, bureaucracy, local liberty, and associational life including religion. Instead of following Tocqueville's recommendations, I will argue, Europe has opted for a different treatment, principled on something quite in contrast to Tocqueville's prescriptions, placing a heavy emphasis on "solidarity," hyper-equality, centralization, and homogenization.

If my analysis is correct, then Western Europe poses a striking challenge to Tocqueville's normative positions. One of two contradictory conclusions necessarily follows: either freedom can be preserved under conditions radically different than those proposed by Tocqueville; or the long-term future of liberty in Western Europe is grim.

The Influence of Geography on West European Democracy

Geography has played an important role in the development of politics and culture in Europe. First and foremost, unlike America, Europe has only imprecise boundaries and the borders separating western from eastern, central, or southern Europe are cultural rather than geographic. In other words, they are of purely human design. Geographically speaking, Europe is nothing but a peninsula reaching out of the Eurasian landmass, with a group of large islands (Great Britain, Ireland, and Iceland) off the northwest coast. The southeastern quarter of that peninsula is crisscrossed by a series of connecting mountain ranges, making transportation treacherous. The northern third is bounded by frozen seas and the difficult terrain of the

Scandinavian Peninsula. By contrast, the middle third is an extended plain reaching from the Ural Mountains—themselves hardly a barrier—to the Atlantic Ocean. The long southern coast is connected by the easily traveled Mediterranean Sea, and can be seen with the naked eye from Africa as well as the Orient. These northern and southern pathways into Europe have, not surprisingly, been frequently traveled by colonists, settlers, and conquerors, making Europe an extremely dangerous place to live. One author, something of a Tocquevillian himself, described Europe as "Painted in Blood."[3] Europe, by his count, has experienced war one year out of every seven for the past two millennia. For thousands of years, a European of normal life span could expect to see more than one major war fought in his fields or around his village.

Some of these wars have been between civilizations, fought by Greeks and Persians, Germanic tribes and Romans, Christians and Muslims, or most recently, fascist and communist totalitarians and European democracies. Frequently, however, they were akin to civil wars, fought for political reasons or in the name of religion or some other "high" principle, among different groups of the same people, with roughly the same institutions. Sometimes they were both.

The combination of difficult terrain and well-trodden invasion routes has meant that Europe has proven impossible for any one regime to govern for long. Instead, a patchwork of political entities has formed and reformed, sometimes following "natural" borders like the Rhine River or the Alps, and at other times being defined in very different ways. Whenever bigger polities have formed, they have been forced to define an external "other"— often rather vaguely—creating an opportunity for those within to switch allegiances and leave, and more recently for outsiders to claim a right to put themselves under Europe's protective umbrella. That "other" has often been Turks, but it has also included Russians, Slavs, Danes, North Africans, the British, and in recent years Americans.

Geographically, then, Europe has been composed of a fluid and shifting center, often at war with itself, and a periphery, vulnerable to periodic and potentially catastrophic invasions from hostile outsiders. Combined, this double threat has meant that when confronted by a choice, Europeans have usually opted for security over liberty. This is true at both the political and personal levels. In politics, they have been willing to embrace authoritarian regimes that promise security in return for limitations on free expression as well as restrictions on democratic participation.[4] It has also meant that as social equality has advanced, Europeans have been particularly interested in incorporating social security into their institutional forms, often at a cost to individual liberty.

Western European Institutions

In his 2001 book, *Democracy in Europe*, itself an adaptation of the so-called "Tocquevillian Analytics" to the European Community, Larry Siedentop identified four informal conditions Tocqueville considered essential for the success of the American experiment in liberty: local self-government, a common language, an open political class dominated by lawyers, and some shared moral beliefs.[5] Regarding Europe, Siedentop was both cautious and optimistic. He was cautious because he believed Europe had a long way to go before it could institutionalize these conditions in a way that would satisfy Tocqueville's requirements. At the same time, he was optimistic because he believed that the main obstacle to European achievement of these conditions had finally been put to rest, namely, social inequality as it existed under the ancient regime(s).

I will concentrate on the first and last of Siedentop's conditions, not because language is unimportant, but because the only solution to creating a polity with multiple linguistic groups is to create a *lingua franca*, and English now serves that function quite well in Europe. On the question of lawyers, I think this is the weakest part of both Tocqueville and Siedentop's accounts, but to dwell on this would be to distract from what I believe to be the most important challenges facing Western Europe, namely the lack of substantive local government, and the particular aspects of culture around which Europe has unified.

The vision of a unified Europe can be traced back at least into the early Middle Ages and reflects a desire to return to some kind of golden age, as represented by the Roman Empire. Such an impetus probably influenced the rhetoric of Charlemagne's court, and this second Rome continued to inspire post–World War II proponents of European integration such as Jean Monnet, who in 1943, along with others, began describing what would become the European Coal and Steel Community as a "New Lotharingia," named for Charlemagne's middle kingdom.[6]

Such visions have always borne a dual character. On the one hand, its would-be unifiers have imagined Europe as providing a moral compass for the rest of the world, and European unity has implied a missionary task. François Guizot, in *The History of Civilization in Europe*, therefore, sees the

Crusades as the event that brought a common identity to Europeans in the twelfth through the sixteenth centuries.[7] The notion that Europe should unify in order to "civilize" the rest of the world was picked up by a younger contemporary of Guizot, Victor Hugo, who sought to restore France's leading role in the world around this civilizing zeal, France being the embodiment of civilization at the time.

Whatever one thinks today of the idea of imposing one's culture on others, in both cases, and perhaps also among the present motives for European integration, one finds a curious historical pattern: treatises on European unity tend to follow events in which Europe has experienced a military defeat, or at least suffered from a protracted war. The first great treatise on European unity, the Abbé de Saint-Pierre's *Projet pour rendre la paix perpétuelle en Europe* (1713), followed the War of the Spanish Succession. Its object was to propose a union of European states in order to drive the Turks, who had nearly captured Vienna in 1683, from Europe. The next significant treatise on European unity, the Comte de Saint-Simon's *De la Réorganisation de la société européene*, was written in 1814, as The First Empire was crumbling and France was absorbing the fact of the end of its military dominance of Europe (the book appeared in 1817). Victor Hugo first took up the issue of European unity following the defeat of republican government across Europe in 1848, and again with the defeat of France by Prussia in 1871.[8] There was a brief flurry of ideas about European unity after World War I, and again, as already mentioned, in the wake of World War II. In each case, European unity has been presented as a way to spread European culture, while at the same time to turn Europeans' attention away from preparing the next internecine war.

Local Self-Government

Despite almost sixty years of the latest effort at integration, however, the history of Western Europe is still best told in terms of the rise and development of the nation-state. This fact was brought home as recently as 1989, during the revolutions in East Germany and elsewhere. Almost immediately after East German citizens ripped down the wall, discussions of a two-state Germany evaporated, and although they are mostly forgotten today, national fears of a resurgent German Reich were very real in parts of Europe. Despite fifty years of European Integration, Europe has not abandoned national sentiments, and after the end of the Cold War, European unity has sputtered.

As Tocqueville pointed out in the *The Old Regime and the Revolution*, the creation of the nation-state in Europe occurred primarily through the usurpation and suppression of local liberties and the destruction of the independence of the local aristocrats who controlled them.[9] Moreover, these local authorities were not democratic, but formed around local aristocrats.[10] In France, local aristocrats controlled political and judicial offices, which were either inherited or purchased. The German states were even more independent politically, but also subjected to aristocratic control. As a result, there is little native tradition of democratic self-government in Western Europe upon which to draw, were such a thing really desired by Europeans. The great exception, of course, is Switzerland, which began as a union of self-governing states and developed into a federation. Even there, however, there were a variety of forms with greater or lesser democratic content until the homogenization of Switzerland's political organization by Napoleon in 1803.[11]

This is not to say that there are no local groups who would like to increase their independence and authority. On the contrary, although their popularity waxes and wanes, movements for the promotion of regional autonomy exist in most every European country. Prominent movements include the Flemish in Belgium, the Lombards in Italy, and the Catalonians in Spain. There are also many other less successful groups, including the Frisians along the German-Dutch border, Sorbians in Germany, Alsatians in France, and, of course, the Basques on both sides of the France-Spain divide.

Even in their aspirations, however, these groups do not fit Tocqueville's definition of local self-government for two reasons. First, since the groups define themselves in terms of separate peoplehood—whether using ethnicity or something else—they cannot be truly democratic because there will always be some people living within their borders there who do not fit the membership criteria. Their political aspirations are a legacy of the Wilsonian principle of creating ethnically homogeneous nation-states following World War I, a solution that was vigorously applied after World War II. Such homogeneity was believed to be a precondition for democratic self-government, as well as lasting peace. Today, we have declared ethnic cleansing to be a crime against humanity, but we should not forget that it was applied on an unprecedented scale by the Allies following both world wars. By some accounts, during the first few years after World War II, twenty million Europeans were forcibly relocated.[12] But even with such massive relocation, it was not possible to achieve a one-nation, one-state solution for Europe. The persistence of separatist groups is convincing evidence of the impossibility of basing a political order on ethnic homogeneity.

The second reason local self-government cannot be based on regional identity is that the aspirations of at least some of the groups go well beyond local government. Instead, they aspire to real sovereignty. The genius of the American constitution lies in providing a solution for the problem of divided sovereignty—a new kind of federalism—that lasted until 1861 and in a rather weaker form continues today. One of history's greatest friends of liberty, Lord Acton, called federalism the "one immortal tribute of America to political science," and "the true natural check on absolute democracy."[13] In the American understanding, sovereignty was reserved to the states, with control over only certain specified and implied areas transferred to the national government.[14] Although issues of jurisdiction have been present from the start, the boundaries between national and state authority in America have been fairly stable. Moreover, not only do the states maintain independent political authority but they also maintain authority to collect revenue directly and to organize both police and militia forces (in the form of the national guards).

By contrast, Western Europe's operating principle is not federalism but subsidiarity, loosely defined as the principle by which political authority is given to the "appropriate" level of government, with a bias in favor of the lowest possible level. It is noteworthy that the term itself derives from Catholic social thought, and is therefore not really related to complex notions of sovereignty or multiple authorities of last resort, but rather is a default position in favor of the decentralization of administrative responsibility. Sovereignty is ultimately reserved for the highest level of the institutional order. As a result, subsidiarity is very different from federalism as a principle of government. I will elaborate on this issue later.

The rub in any system of multiple authorities, of course, is how to resolve conflicts between them. Without a clear principle, there is a natural tendency for the central authority, or at least its judicial branch, to take on that role. Not surprisingly, centralized arbitrators tend to be biased toward centralization, even in the United States. European central institutions—most prominent in the European Union—are no exception. In fact, from the start, the grand strategy of the European Union's promoters has been premised on a slow accretion of authority to the European institutions, rather than explicit and prior transfers of authority. This is apparent in the original conception of the European Coal and Steel Community, and was stated explicitly in Robert Schuman's announcement of the Schuman Plan on May 9, 1950: "Europe will not be made all at once, or according to a single plan. It will be built through concrete achievements that first create de facto solidarity."[15] One sees evidence of this mind-set in the preambles to many European documents. Note the careful language of the first article of the Single European Act: "The European Communities and European Political Cooperation shall have as their objective to contribute together to making concrete progress towards European unity."[16] Similar statements can be found regarding the failed European Constitution, and in the pronouncements of the European Court.

Taxation

One area where Europe has provided limited tools for local or regional self-government is taxation. Only four of the European Union's members are organized along federal lines, with state governments between national and local authorities: Austria, Belgium, Germany, and Spain. The rest have only central and local governments.[17] Administratively, these four federations delegate responsibility for less government spending than is the case in the United States. With them, an unweighted average of close to 75 percent of taxes are in the form of social security or central government spending, compared to just under 69 percent in the United States. By contrast, in the remainder of the European Union, only 10.7 percent (unweighted average) of government spending is managed by local authorities.[18]

These statistics tell only part of the story, however, because whereas in the United States, state and local authorities have wide discretion to set methods and rates of taxation, in European countries, this is markedly less true. Even in the four federal countries, tax policies are generally set by the central government, and only their administration is carried out at the state or local level. The reason for this is that European taxation is designed, in large part, as a way of redistributing wealth among regions as well as individuals, so it would not serve its purpose if taxes were collected and spent locally. Even where this is the case, local administration is anything but local self-government, because the function of state and local administrators is not to be responsible to the local people, but rather to carry out national policy objectives. Local government has little authority to make policy. Rather, they are simply empowered to manage tasks that in the United States are considered quasi-commercial, and delegated to utilities or even private companies. For instance, under the rubric of the "self-government" responsibilities of local government, a German author proudly states that local governments' "most important self-government tasks" consist of "providing the citizens with water, electricity, district heating, gas, wastewater services and waste removal." In addition, they have responsibility for local zoning.[19] In some American cities, such services are entirely provided by the market, and the need for zoning dispensed with entirely.

The Power of Local Officials

Another area where European countries allow much less local control than America is in law enforcement. Where there are multiple police forces, each one generally has national jurisdiction, sometimes confusingly overlapping and sometimes not. In Italy, for instance, the *Polizio di Stato* work parallel to the *Carabinieri* and the *Guardia di Finanza*, and it is not uncommon to witness jurisdictional disputes between them on the street. The latter two are also organized as military forces. In Sweden and the Netherlands, the police are tied to the national departments of justice. In Germany, the *Länder* each have their own police, alongside the *Bundespolizei*, that patrol transportation centers and border areas. By contrast, the Federal Bureau of Investigation is limited in the United States to the enforcement of federal crimes, and jurisdiction is jealously guarded in other matters. Each state has its own police force, but most law enforcement takes place at the local level.

One very peculiar phenomenon, which especially interested Tocqueville, is the election of a wide range of public officials to carry out non-legislative tasks in America. By my count, the voters in my county directly elect at least twenty local and state officials. Only two of them are elected to perform legislative functions. The rest are elected to perform tasks assigned in Europe to professional state bureaucrats, with guaranteed job tenure.

The most peculiar American elected official, perhaps, is the sheriff. The laws governing sheriffs vary from state to state. In general, however, the sheriff is a law enforcement officer with jurisdiction over a county, or at least its unincorporated areas. In many instances, particularly in rural areas, the sheriff can be the most important elected official in the county. Some of the rules governing sheriffs and their responsibilities can seem quirky. The state of Indiana, for instance, requires the sheriff to feed prisoners in the county jail out of his own salary. To adjust for that, sheriffs in Indiana are among the best-compensated public officials in the state; there are also periodic complaints about the quality of the food.

These minor offices, of course, are what Tocqueville had particularly in mind when he referred to the significance of local self-government.[20]

Subjecting to a vote the choice of coroner or assessor may seem strange to Europeans, but it performs an important function, which is to empower people to see themselves as closely connected to their government, and require that they take responsibility for it. Moreover, it provides a training ground for at least some future politicians so that management skills, rather than political connections, can become an important prerequisite for political office.

What is perhaps most important to note with regard to such offices, including jury duty, something else that fascinated Tocqueville, is that they introduce discretion into what in Europe is thought of as bureaucratic activity. They are an extension of the Common Law into the administrative and judicial functioning of government, and as such allow for circumstantial considerations in the application of justice. Because they give nonprofessional citizens discretion in how to apply the law, they naturally allow for a much wider range of outcomes than is the case in civil law countries with highly professionalized bureaucracies. Another way of saying this is that they institutionalize a much more pluralistic understanding of what constitutes justice. Tocqueville understood that preserving such a pluralistic understanding of justice is essential to the preservation of American liberty, and his great fear was that the logic of majoritarian democracy would eventually homogenize American values, thereby eliminating freedom. In Europe, such uniformity of values would never allow modern liberty to take root.

Although there has been some movement in Europe in the direction of administrative devolution to the local and state level, it has been tepid. Nowhere in Europe, to the best of my knowledge, has a country created any new, nonlegislative elected offices or introduced the jury system into civil (as opposed to criminal) law. Moreover, where administrative decentralization has occurred, it has often been the work of the European Union, rather than of its member-states. One area where this has been applied is through the regional funds of the Union. European regional policy transfers funds from wealthier regions to poorer ones via the European Union. Such patronage generates European loyalties in recipient countries through high visibility projects, and in some instances necessitates the creation of new entities at the regional level, such as the Pomeranian Euroregion, which includes territory in Sweden, Poland, and Germany.

The stated reason for the European Union to conduct a regional policy is to "reduce economic and social disparities," but motives for the European Union's support of regions are complicated. There is good reason to believe that its objective for supporting regions is to weaken the nation-state, rather than strengthen local control. Creating transborder "Euroregions" is one way of doing this. In this way, the European Union is engaged in a subtle form of centralization. The guiding principle in this process is the notion of "subsidiarity."

Subsidiarity, Local Control, and Liberty under the European Union

According to the European Union's glossary of terms, the subsidiarity principle is intended to ensure that decisions are taken as closely as possible to the citizen and that constant checks are made as to whether action at the community level is justified in the light of the possibilities available at the national, regional, or local level. Specifically, it is the principle whereby the Union does not take action (except in the areas that fall within its exclusive competence) unless it is more effective than action taken at the national, regional, or local level.[21] On the surface, this would indicate that the European Union will only be active in areas where there is no alternative, but this is not the case.

The theory of subsidiarity comes from Catholic social teaching, and is designed to assure that only important decisions be brought before the highest authorities of the church. In recent history, various popes have also applied this theory to the relations between secular and religious authorities. This was first implied in the Encyclical of Leo XIII's *Rerum Novarum* (1891). Forty years later, Pope Pius XI explicitly stated:

> Just as it is gravely wrong to take from individuals what they can accomplish by their own initiative and industry and give it to the community, so also it is an injustice and at the same time a grave evil and disturbance of right order to assign to a greater and higher association what lesser and subordinate organizations can do.[22]

This idea was clarified in the 1991 Encyclical of John Paul II, *Centesimus Annus*:

> A community of a higher order should not interfere in the internal life of a community of a lower order, depriving the latter of its functions, but rather should support it in the case of need and help to coordinate its activity with the activities of the rest of society, always with a view to the common good.[23]

The specific context for these encyclicals was to put limits on the notion that the Catholic Church should support the centralization of social support systems—until then largely organized by the churches—under the government in state welfare programs. Subsidiarity is thus an important provision of Catholic doctrine and provides a welcome platform for the church to separate the provision of aid to the poor from a centralizing state authority.

What the Catholic principle of subsidiarity is not, however, is a theory useful in articulating a position of federalism as understood in the United States, whereby sovereignty is lodged with the states, and only partially delegated to the central government. Although the Catholic Church is a far more decentralized organization than one might imagine, at the end of the day it is still unified under a single authority, that of the pope. On the most important questions, the authority of the pope is final, and most significantly, where there are jurisdictional conflicts between different levels of the church hierarchy, it is the higher authority that determines who gets to decide. This is very different from the relation of the states to the federal government in the United States, even after the Civil War and subsequent incorporation under national control of many aspects of sovereignty formerly reserved to the states.

It is important to note, as well, that in the evolution of the use of the concept of subsidiarity within the European Union, there has been a significant shift in the meaning attached to the word. In its original invocation, first articulated in 1975, subsidiarity was cited to assure member-states that the European Community would only seek responsibility for problems that could be solved in no other way, and would be "given responsibility only for those matters which the member states are no longer capable of dealing with efficiently." Thirteen years later, the Single European Act declared that the European Community would apply subsidiarity where it was deemed an outcome to be "better attainable" at the European level.[24] Most recently, according to the proposed European Constitution, under the principle of subsidiarity, in areas that do not fall within its exclusive competence, the Union shall act only if and insofar as the objectives of the proposed action cannot be sufficiently achieved by the Member States, either at central level or at regional and local level, but can rather, by reason of the scale or effects of the proposed action, be better achieved at Union level.[25]

The implication is that the European Union can act wherever it does not believe a member state competent to carry out a certain policy. This principle allows scant room for a state to refuse to carry out a policy, or to implement it differently, when it disagrees with the European Union's decisions. What follows from such logic is a ratcheting effect, in which over time new competencies are added to the European Union, but authority is never shifted downward to lower levels of government. When one adds to this the way in which the European Court of Justice—which should be responsible for resolving jurisdictional disputes—is using its powers of judicial review to add new areas of competency to the European mandate, one finds the European Union engaging in a subtle policy of centralization, using the concept of subsidiarity as an excuse to usurp powers from the states.

What is one to make then, one might ask, of the importance the European Union places on regional and local government? Is this evidence that the European Union takes decentralization seriously? The answer is that the European Union, consciously or unconsciously, has come to recognize that the principle of subsidiarity can be used to create alliances between the European Union and subnational entities in order to strip power from national governments. By promoting and supporting regional and local government, the European Union makes it possible to acquire additional powers from national governments. Moreover, the European Union's regional policy is largely designed to transfer resources from wealthy to poor regions. Thus, the European Union's actions act more to transfer the dependence of regions from the national to the European level, than to empower local government in Europe. It is not surprising that poor regions support the European Union on this matter, nor that wealthy areas that promote regional identity (such as in Lombardy) are often skeptical of the European Union's ultimate willingness to support their desire for increased autonomy.

Liberty, Equality, and Culture in Western Europe

If the political institutions of Europe, including the European Union, are not pursuing lines of development that Tocqueville would have endorsed, then perhaps European culture will act as a barrier to the tyranny that Tocqueville saw threatening liberty in democratic societies. Tocqueville, however, would have been worried by West European culture today. In this section, I would like to look at three issues: religion, "solidarity," and the way in which human rights trump all other considerations in the European consciousness.

Christianity

One of the most interesting and nuanced aspects of Tocqueville's writings is the role religion and religious institutions play in his framework. While the subject of Tocqueville's own religious faith is a matter of some dispute, there is no doubt that he believed churches played an important role in the defense of American liberty. Curiously, in addition to their moral functions, Tocqueville did not see American churches as providing lessons in democratic civic virtue to their members. Rather, he saw them as significant for much the opposite reason. The strength of churches—and in particular the Catholic Church—was in providing examples of well-functioning institutions that do *not* operate according to democratic principles.[26] The hierarchical structure of religion provided for Tocqueville a useful check on the ambitions of democratic institutions and the hubris of those advocates of democracy who believe that all problems can be solved by turning over political institutions to the people. This only can work, however, if churches are strong institutions that exert influence over a significant number of people.

Today, whereas most European churches have preserved a hierarchical structure, they have not continued to thrive in a way that makes their institutional example meaningful. Meanwhile, much of Western Europe has developed an ambivalent relationship to Christianity, and Europe is experiencing a rise in anti-Semitism. When in 2004 the European Union sent forth a new "constitution" for the states to ratify, it described the constitution as "drawing from the cultural, religious, and humanist inheritance" of Europe. When describing Europe's values, the proposed constitution discussed "respect for human dignity, freedom, democracy, equality, the rule of law and respect for human rights," all values of the Enlightenment. It described Europe as holding in common the values of "pluralism, non-discrimination, tolerance, justice, solidarity and equality."[27]

As its critics noted at the time, in a region dominated by the church for more than a millennium, Christianity and even God are conspicuously absent. Cardinal Roberto Tucci was reported to say that leaving God out of the constitution "is an offense to reason, to good sense, and to a good part of Europe's citizens."[28] And Mgr. Peter Erdoe, the Catholic prelate in Hungary, was quoted by Agence Presse France as saying that "without Christianity, the heart of Europe would be missing."[29] The acrimony of this debate may have played an important role in the failure of the constitution to be ratified.

What is ironic is that although this might simply be seen as Europe's desire to remain open to non-Christians (in particular to its rapidly growing Muslim population) at the same time it was failing to acknowledge the role Christianity has played in Western Europe's development, it has repeatedly waffled on Turkey's application for membership in the European Union. Rather than becoming more tolerant, it would seem, post–Christian Europe is becoming more vocal in its desire to suppress religion altogether.

I say post-Christian because despite the preservation of the external signs of religion in Europe—conservative parties still carry the label Christian Democrat and it is hard to miss the plethora of churches in the older parts of every European town—in fact, Christianity is in sharp decline in Western Europe. Church attendance spikes for major holidays such as Christmas, Easter, and rites of passage—christenings, baptisms, weddings, and funerals—but otherwise is low and declining. According to *Eurobarometer* data, whereas only 15 percent of Europeans never went to religious services in 1970, in 2002 close to 27 percent never worshipped. Today, close to 50 percent of Europeans go to church no more than once a year (generally Christmas or Easter). By contrast, only 18 percent of Europeans say they attend services one or more times a week,[30] and only 7 percent of Europeans consider religion among their three most important values.[31]

Of course, religiosity in Europe has had its ups and downs. First the Renaissance, and then the Enlightenment and French Revolution cut heavily into Europe's commitment to religion. Tocqueville believed, however, that European Christianity was on the upswing in the nineteenth century, and on this belief anchored his hope for moderate politics under democracy. The fact that large majorities of Europeans have chosen to abandon Christianity would have greatly troubled Tocqueville and he would have worried about the fate of liberty in Europe as a result.

Solidarity

Europeans value individuality, but not at a cost to social solidarity. This can be seen in a number of ways. Union membership, while on the decline, is still much higher than in the United States. In a 2003 study, labor union density, measured as the percentage of the labor force in unions in a given country, was calculated to be:

- more than 90 percent in Romania;
- 80–89 percent in Belgium, Denmark, Finland, and Sweden;

- 70–79 percent in Italy and Norway;
- 60–69 percent in Cyprus and Malta;
- 50–59 percent in Luxembourg;
- 40–49 percent in Austria and Slovenia;
- 30–39 percent in Hungary, Ireland, and Portugal;
- 20–29 percent in Bulgaria, Germany, Greece, the Netherlands, Slovakia, and the United Kingdom; and
- 10–19 percent in Estonia, Latvia, Poland, and Spain.[32]

By contrast, in 2005 only 12.5 percent of American workers were members of unions. Value priorities follow these indicators. For instance, according to the 2006 *Eurobarometer* survey, 32 percent of Europeans held either "solidarity" or "equality" to be one of their top three personal values, against only 22 percent who listed individual freedom. When put in the context of European Union values, 31 percent placed solidarity or equality among the top three, against only 10 percent who put a priority on individual freedom.[33]

From a Tocquevillian point of view, the problem is that notions of solidarity have a way of feeding into the even bigger problems he worried about, that of factionalism and the tyranny of the majority. According to the same survey, 38 percent of Europeans consider democracy an important European Union value, against only 24 percent who selected the "rule of law." And only 17 percent consider the rule of law to be an important personal value.[34]

One dramatic way in which Europe's preference for solidarity manifests itself is in the frequent strikes that plague Europe. French farmers are often the swiftest group to engage in violent and disruptive strikes, but Airbus workers and French pilots have gone on strike in recent years, and other transportation workers frequently stop work to protest even minor actions. In 1971 in Sweden, even military officers were part of a strike. The point of this is that in Europe, union-enforced "solidarity" trumps individual liberty, often at a significant cost to the rule of law. Support for this attitude is deeply engrained in European culture, and may simply be the modern form of the ancient feudal compact between lords and peasants. We should remember that it was conservatives who introduced the welfare state in Europe in the late nineteenth century, and they structured it so as to preserve the reciprocal obligations of lord and servant, now transformed over to the state. As a result, Europeans have always had a very different understanding of welfare than Americans. In the most telling statistic in this regard, Europeans agreed two to one with the statement that "we need more equality and justice even if this means less freedom for the individual."[35]

It is interesting, however, that Europeans have difficulty accepting the possibility that freedom and equality might be in tension. This is apparent, for instance, in Article II of the failed European Constitution, which is entitled "Freedoms." The first clause embodies a right to "liberty and security," without comment. It goes on to enshrine rights to association, religion, and other familiar freedoms. Soon, however, the freedoms it describes become mixed with entitlements, such as a right to education (Article II–74), right to work (Article II–75), and right to asylum (Article II–78). It goes on to include under the "Freedom" article, rights to dignity for the elderly and for persons with disabilities (Article II–85, 86). I do not want to imply that Europeans should not provide benefits for children, the elderly, handicapped, and foreigners. I only want to point out that the easy mixing of what Isaiah Berlin described as positive and negative liberty[36] is emblematic of the way in which Europeans will limit the negative effects of their preference for solidarity by renaming it a kind of freedom.

Human Dignity

The final area in which Europeans have strayed from Tocquevillian principles is perhaps the most subtle. "Human rights" received the top score (tied with "democracy") on the European Union values chart. It was second only to "peace" in the survey of individual values. Europeans have come to think of themselves as the moral conscience of the world and use the notion of human rights as a way to interfere in the local self-government of each other, and the international community as a whole.

The first title of the proposed Charter of Fundamental Rights of the European Union, following the German Basic Law, concerns human dignity. It states, simply, that "human dignity is inviolable."[37] The German Basic Law places "human dignity" at the top of a hierarchical system of constitutional rights, and presumably this is meant to apply to the European Union's Charter as well. This article has been deemed by German courts to trump all others, and it is not open to amendment by constitutional means. The problem is that the definition of human dignity is open to widely divergent interpretations. In its desire to right the wrongs of the fascist era, Europe has given itself wide latitude to speak on behalf of humanity, often in opposition to more traditional notions of international law and national self-determination.

Public support for this approach is evident in *Eurobarometer* data. More than twice as many Europeans chose "human rights" as "tolerance" among their personal values. Human rights received almost four times as many votes as "respect for other cultures."[38] As French political philosopher Marcel Gauchet pointed out, there are limitations to the possibility of building an entire political culture around the notion of human rights. Indeed, where this is done, he claimed, it is evidence of the weakness of democratic politics.[39]

The ongoing debate over Muslim women's headwear is one example. In 2004, France banned the wearing of outward religious symbols in schools.[40] The main target of this legislation was Muslim women and girls wearing head coverings, but the law was written in a way that would encompass Christian crucifixes and Jewish yarmulkes. In the Netherlands, an effort is currently under way to ban Muslim headscarves, and the issue has become prominent in the United Kingdom, Germany, and elsewhere, including Turkey, which is subject to the European Convention on Human Rights. Increasingly, it would seem, Europe is using laws to enforce its secular, intrusive, cosmopolitan vision on the rest of the world. As Gauchet remarked, human rights as the foundation of politics not only "will not furnish the hoped-for instrument, but they may lead us in the opposite direction."[41]

The Central European institution dedicated to protecting and imposing a unified view of human rights is the Council of Europe and its defining document, the European Convention on Human Rights. This agreement and the court that enforces it have become enmeshed in local practices such as corporal punishment within a family in Britain, quarantining an HIV patient in Sweden, and the status of a communist party in Romania. While it is not the purpose of this essay to examine these claims on the merits, there is reason to believe that it would be fully appropriate to deal with such issues as local matters, not subject to the dictates of an international court.

Finally, the penchant of Europeans to claim universal jurisdiction for their human rights is beginning to cause diplomatic trouble. Starting most famously with the case of a Spanish court trying to extradite Augusto Pinochet out of a British hospital, European judges have used "universal jurisdiction" statutes to claim extradition rights against political figures. Most recently, several members of the Bush Administration have been threatened with indictment in Belgian Courts related to the war in Iraq.[42] Such claims may make it difficult for U.S. officials to travel internationally, including, for instance, to NATO summits, since NATO is headquartered in Belgium.

What is significant about these tendencies in European political culture is that by universalizing European morality and enforcing it with
legal action, Europeans are taking the tools of self-government out of the
hands of ordinary citizens. Self-government, from Tocqueville's point of
view, is something lived and practiced. It requires taking responsibility for
decision-making, and thinking about political issues from the point of view
of someone living in a community, not abstracted into universal terms. Self-
government only exists where local authorities are allowed to make mistakes and are accountable for their mistakes to local people. As Tocqueville
wrote in another context, "The great privilege enjoyed by the Americans
is not only to be more enlightened than other nations but also to have the
chance to make mistakes that can be retrieved."[43] The universal idea of
equality, Tocqueville thought, needed to be tempered by the counterweight
of particularism, manifested in religion and a culture of self-reliance.

Current trends in Europe are undermining the very things Tocqueville
believed essential to the preservation of liberty. In a recent book, *La raison
des nations*, Pierre Manent explicitly tied this to the question of representative government. The poor showing of individual freedom and liberty in
European values demonstrates that what Tocqueville feared may well have
come to pass in Europe. As Manent explained, representative government
requires there be a people to "represent," and that people can only derive
from a nation-state.[44] The implication is that a necessary consequence of
the decline of the nation-state in Europe will be the deterioration of democratic institutions.

Perhaps the most interesting look at cultural values in Europe compared to America comes in the form of the Inglehart-Welzel Cultural Map
of the World from the University of Michigan's *World Values Survey* (see
figure 8.1). This map plots countries on a two-dimensional axis, with the
x-axis measuring people's preference for physical security against personal freedom, and the y-axis measuring their penchant for free thinking
(secular—rational morality) against traditional morality. For Tocqueville,
the preservation of liberty requires moderate religiosity (being slightly on
the traditionalist side of the scale, but not too far), and a strong preference for personal freedom. This is where the United States finds itself, even
today. Western Europe's post–Christian countries, by contrast, find themselves drifting upwards and rightwards. As a result, they run the risk of
becoming immoderate in their pursuit of self-expression and overly rationalist in their outlook.

Among important symptoms of this trend is the demographic collapse
Europe finds itself facing. Free-thinking and self-expression may produce

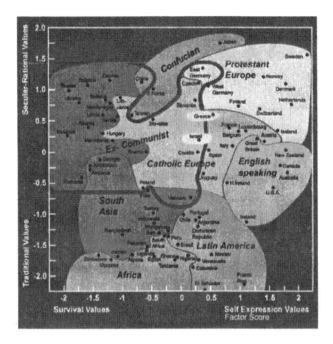

Figure 8.1. Inglehart-Welzel Cultural Map of the World.

Source: http://www.worldvaluessurvey.org

happiness in individuals, but it does not seem to produce many children. Demographers expect more than 27 percent of Western Europe's population to be over age 65 in 2050, supported by a total population that will have returned to 1970s levels.[45] Because Europe's welfare system requires huge intergenerational transfers to the elderly, this is going to place heavy strains on Western Europe's notion of intergenerational solidarity, as well as test its ability to incorporate immigrants into its culture. Already, as the issue of Muslim head coverings shows, Europe is losing its tolerance for immigrants. Something will have to give, and liberty is the likely candidate.

Conclusion

What, then, does Western Europe have to say to Tocqueville's treatment for unchecked equality? Europe has rejected religion, has built ever-more centralized political institutions, and has cultivated a culture built around the unlimited pursuit of self-expression. If Europe can get over the hump of its impending demographic crisis, it might just lead to a new kind of individualist paradise, one hinted at in Marx, where workers put in short work-weeks, spend a few decades engaged in productive work, and then retire to peace, modest prosperity, and Mediterranean vacations. Achieving this is possible, and there might just be a space in which to achieve such a utopia. If this occurs, it would call into question Tocqueville's account of liberty under equality.

Tocqueville, however, would predict quite a different future. Sitting on Europe's doorstep is a time bomb of unprecedented proportions. Europe's abandonment of religion leaves few tools with which to preserve moderation in politics, nor to defend Europeans' individualist cultural values when backed against the wall. Moreover, Europe's neighbors know this. It is doubtful that a clash can be avoided between Muslim countries that cannot support their population, and European ones that cannot replace theirs. Indeed, as the debate over Muslim head coverings shows, the clash between Europe and Islam has already started. To avoid a serious erosion of its own values, Europe will need to discover some way to address issues of cultural assimilation it has never yet mastered, as well as either induce its population to reproduce, or develop a radically new economic and social system built upon a shrinking population. If it does neither of these and the Muslim population within Europe continues to grow, then it will need to rethink, in fundamental ways, its entire social system from schooling to retirement. The Tocquevillian question, of course, is what will happen to liberty as this occurs.

Tocqueville's experience, reflecting on the rise of the first European dictatorship (Napoleon) and his observation of the rise of a second (Napoleon III), would suggest that Europeans can be quick to abandon their liberty when someone promises them security in exchange. Events of the twentieth century have confirmed this on numerous occasions. Tocqueville would predict that in response to serious threats to their way of life, one or more powerful demagogues will arise, promising solutions to Europeans' problems. The rise of anti-democratic parties—of both left and right—is a sign that the European consensus may be breaking down. In Russia, this phenomenon has already occurred and Western Europe is not immune from this either. Europeans can then be expected to abandon their presumptuous attitudes toward human rights, both internal and international. There is some evidence of this already happening. The treatment of Ayaan Hirsi Ali, the Dutch Somali woman and outspoken critic of Islam who was deported rather than protected by the Dutch government, speaks volumes about Europeans' willingness to stand up for their principles when their security is threatened.[46] The timidity of Europe's governments in the Danish cartoon case is more evidence of a lack of will.

Europeans, in recent years, have shown a tendency to temporize rather than face these issues. Their preferences for short-term security and short-term comfort have come to outweigh their willingness to take costly positions. If such a lack of political will persists, it may soon be too late to chart a Tocquevillian course. Both political and personal liberty, Tocqueville would fear, will be among the first casualties.

Notes

1. Alexis de Tocqueville, *Democracy in America*, ed. J. P. Mayer (New York: HarperPerennial, 1969), xiv.

2. Tocqueville, *Democracy in America*, xiv.

3. Stuart Miller, *Painted in Blood: Understanding Europeans* (New York: Athaneum, 1987).

4. Examples of this include not only Hitler and Mussolini but also Napoleon and Napoleon III, Bismarck, and more recently, it helps explain the persistence of the "democratic deficit" in the European Union.

5. Larry Siedentop, *Democracy in Europe* (New York: Columbia University Press, 2001), 10.

6. See Frederic J. Fransen, *The Supranational Politics of Jean Monnet: Ideas and Origins of the European Community* (Westport, CT: Greenwood Press, 2001), 87–114, esp. 89–90.

7. François Guizot, *History of Civilization in Europe* (London: Penguin, 1997), 140–46.

8. On the former, see his "Discours d'ouverture" at the Congrès de la paix à Paris, 1849; on the latter, "Aux Allemandes" and "Pour la guerre dans le présent et pour la paix dans l'avenir," in Victor Hugo, *Politique* (Paris: Robert Laffont, 1985), 299–304, 725–28, 752–56.

9. For Tocqueville's account of aristocratic liberty, see *The Old Regime and the Revolution*, vol. I, trans. Alan S. Kahan (Chicago, IL: University of Chicago Press, 1998), 171–79.

10. There were exceptions, of course, but they go back to the misty forests of Europe's dark ages. In the *Germania*, Tacitus describes the democratic councils of the German tribes who faced off against Rome, and, for instance, in the *Njal Saga*, we see in Iceland examples of local self-government under the rule of law that seem surprising, given the context. These instances are clear exceptions, however, to the general rule.

11. See Denis de Rougemont, *La Suisse ou l'histoire d'un people heureux* (Paris: Hachette, 1965), 105–6.

12. According to the Potsdam Agreement of August 1, 1945: "The Three Governments, having considered the question in all its aspects, recognize that the transfer to Germany of German populations, or elements thereof, remaining in Poland, Czechoslovakia and Hungary, will have to be undertaken."

13. John Emerich Edward Dalberg-Acton, "The Influence of America," in *Selected Writings of Lord Acton*, vol. I, ed. J. Rufus Fears (Indianapolis, IN: Liberty Fund, 1985), 211.

14. According to the Tenth Amendment to the U.S. Constitution: "The powers not delegated to the United States by the Constitution, nor prohibited by it to the States, are reserved to the States respectively, or to the people."

15. "The Schuman Plan Declaration," University of Leiden, History of European Integration Site. http://eu-history.leidenuniv.nl/index.php3?m=&c=29 (accessed August 12, 2008).

16. "Single European Act," *Official Journal of the European Communities*, I: 169/4 (June 29, 1987).

17. It is worth pointing out that Italy has been toying with various regional schemes for several years now.

18. European Commission, "Structures of the Taxation Systems in the European Union 1995–2004," Doc. TAXUD E4/2006/DOC/3201.

19. Dieter Haschke, "Local Government Administration in Germany," in German Law Archive. http://www.iuscomp.org/gla/literature/localgov.htm (accessed August 12, 2008).

20. Tocqueville, *Democracy in America*, 64–66.

21. "Subsidiarity" in Europa Glossary (Brussels: European Commission, 1995–2007).

22. Pius XI, "Quadragesimo Anno," in *Proclaiming Justice and Peace: Papal Documents from Rerum Novarum through Centesimus Annus*, ed. Michael Walsh and Brian Davis (Mystic, CT: Twenty-Third Publications, 1991), 62.

23. John Paul II, "Centesimus Annus," in Walsh and Davis, *Proclaiming Justice and Peace*, 470.

24. For a brief summary of this evolution, see the entry for "subsidiarity" at Euroknow.org. http://www.euro-know.org/dictionary/s.html (accessed August 12, 2008).

25. Article 1–11.

26. Tocqueville, *Democracy in America*, 287–89.

27. "Treaty Establishing a Constitution for Europe," *Official Journal of the European Union* 17 (December 16, 2004), C310.

28. Quoted in Thomas Dixon, "Ignoring God in the Constitution," *Christianity Today*, July 1, 2003.

29. See "Do God and Christianity Have a Place in the European Union Constitution?" Ontario Consultants on Religious Toleration. http://www.religioustolerance.org/const_eu.htm (accessed August 12, 2008).

30. Evi Scholz and Hermann Schmitt, *The Mannheim Eurobarometer Trend File: 1970–1999* (computer file and codebook). (Mannheim: MZES, University

of Mannheim and ZUMA; and Cologne: Zentralarchiv für empirische Sozialforschung, 2001), 410–13.

31. *Eurobarometer 66*: Public Opinion in the European Union (Brussels: European Commission, 2006), 34.

32. European Industrial Relations Observatory Online, "Trade Union Membership1993–2003." http://eurofound.europa.eu/eiro/2004/03/update/tn0403105u.html (accessed August 12, 2008).

33. *Eurobarometer 66*, 34.

34. *Eurobarometer 66*, 34.

35. *Eurobarometer 66*, 39.

36. Isaiah Berlin, "Two Concepts of Liberty," in *Four Essays on Liberty* (London: Oxford University Press, 2002).

37. "Charter of Fundamental Rights of the European Union," *Official Journal of the European Union* 17 (December 16, 2004): C310/42.

38. *Eurobarometer 66*, 34.

39. Marcel Gauchet, *La démocratie contre elle-même* (Paris: Gallimard, 2002), 327.

40. See Harry Judge, "The Muslim Headscarf and France," *American Journal of Education* 111 (November 2004): 1–24.

41. Gauchet, *La démocratie contre elle-même*, 330.

42. Including George Bush, Richard Cheney, Tommy Franks, Colin Powell, and Norman Schwarzkopf.

43. Tocqueville, *Democracy in America*, 225.

44. Pierre Manent, *La raison des nations: Réflexions sur la démocratie en Europe* (Paris: Gallimard, 2006), 52.

45. International Institute for Applied Systems Analysis, "European Rural Develop Project," 2002. http://www.iiasa.ac.at/Research/ERD/DB/data/hum/dem/dem_2.htm (accessed August 12, 2008).

46. See Ayaan Hirsi Ali's recently published book, *Infidel* (New York: Free Press, 2007).

9

Democracy in Russia:
A Tocquevillian Perspective

Peter Rutland

There are at the present time two great nations in the world, which started from different points, but seem to tend towards the same end. I allude to the Russians and the Americans. . . . The American struggles against the obstacles that nature opposes to him; the adversaries of the Russian are men. The former combats the wilderness and savage life; the latter, civilization with all its arms. The conquests of the American are therefore gained by the plowshare; those of the Russian by the sword. The Anglo-American relies upon personal interest to accomplish his ends and gives free scope to the unguided strength and common sense of the people; the Russian centers all the authority of society in a single arm. The principal instrument of the former is freedom; of the latter, servitude. Their starting point is different and their courses are not the same; yet each of them seems marked out by the will of heaven to sway the destinies of half the globe.

—Alexis de Tocqueville[1]

Alexis de Tocqueville famously predicted that America and Russia would rise to dominate world politics, given that each country had vast resources, a large and rising population, and ambitious leaders.[2] He also saw Russia as doomed to servitude, just as America was destined for freedom. Tocqueville's *Democracy in America* (1835) is interesting not just for what it tells us about the American society of his day but also because it can be taken as one model for how a social scientist can go about studying a given society. In this and his other works, most notably *The Old Regime and the Revolution* (1856), Tocqueville showed an extraordinary self-awareness and sensitivity to questions of method and approach, one that truly marks him as one of the founders of modern social science. The goal of this chapter is to take up the framework that Tocqueville developed in *Democracy in America* and to use it to analyze the prospects for democracy in post–1991 Russia.

One problem with this exercise is that while Tocqueville was trying to explain the roots of democracy's *success* in America, with regard to contemporary Russia the challenge is to explain the *failure* of democratic institutions to take hold. Also, the circumstances of Russia in 2007 and the United States in 1830 differ so radically, and in so many dimensions, that the task cannot be one of direct "comparison." Rather, this will be an intellectual exercise to see whether Tocqueville's method can yield fresh insights into the political sociology of Russia today.

Tocqueville looked at America through the triple prism of "conditions," "mores," and "institutions." Our conclusion will be that geopolitical conditions and societal morals are indeed vital to explaining the duration of autocracy in Russia, yet these factors are often overlooked in Western analysis of contemporary Russia. Specifically, by "conditions" we have in mind factors such as a country's vulnerability to foreign attack, and by "morals" the role of religion. Tocqueville's analysis of institutions concurs with the mainstream of contemporary Western thinking about the importance of rule of law and civil society activity, the absence of which is held to account for the failure of Russia's democratic transition.

It is quite common for Russia to be compared to the other post-socialist countries, even to countries in transition from authoritarianism in Latin America. But few scholars now attempt a direct comparison between Russia and the United States. Back in the time of the Cold War, it was quite common to see studies written by Americans that stressed the *differences* between Soviet and American society—a natural outgrowth of the military-political rivalry between the two systems. The genre ranged from Hedrick Smith's dissection of daily life in *The Russians* (1976) to Paul Hollander's comparison of Soviet propaganda and American advertising.[3] However, the comparative approach (even a comparison grounded in difference) has fallen out of favor in America since 1991. Russia is now so widely reviled as the "other," a potage of poverty, crime, corruption, and extreme terrorism, that Americans no longer write books comparing Russia with the United States. There is, of course, a long tradition of Western literature treating Russia as the "other": an alien culture at Europe's door, dating back at least to the Marquis de Custine's trip to Russia in 1839.[4] Recent years have seen a somewhat surprising revival of the old arguments about Russian backwardness, based on a belief that Russia has followed a unique historical path that has "locked in" authoritarian political values and institutions.[5] At the same time, in Russia itself, the comparison with the United States remains a common point of reference, although analysis does focus more on contrasts than similarities—hence the publication of books explaining "Why Russia is Not America."[6]

The Sorry State of Russian Democracy

After 1991, most American observers quickly assumed that Russia was on a path to a Western-style market economy and liberal democracy. They took the Soviet collapse as vindication of Francis Fukuyama's prescient 1989 essay on "The End of History," which argued that liberal democracy was now unchallenged as a blueprint for national development and social progress.[7] In the 1990s, both the Russian and U.S. governments operated on the shared assumption that Russia was in the process of becoming a democracy, one that would take its rightful place among the Western family of nations—a status recognized by Russia's accession to the G8 group of advanced democratic nations in 1997.[8] Despite these initial hopes, however, Russia's political trajectory since 1991 has been a grave disappointment to Western observers (see table 9.1).

After seven decades of Soviet authoritarian rule, the perestroika reforms launched by Soviet President Mikhail Gorbachev after 1985 led to a degree of press freedom and partially contested elections in 1989–1990. But the social and ethnic unrest unleashed by Gorbachev's reforms led to the collapse of the Soviet Union in December 1991. The Russian Federation emerged as an independent state with a more or less free press, a spectrum of independent political parties and social movements, and an elected legislature and president. Ironically, Russia probably experienced its highest level of democratic freedom in 1991, when it was still part of the Soviet Union. Since then, the scope for political contestation has steadily contracted.

Russia's first president, Boris Yeltsin, won a fairly free election in June 1991.[9] But his decision to launch radical economic reform in January 1992 led to an ugly standoff between the reformist president and a Congress that opposed his "shock therapy." This confrontation culminated in September 1993 with Yeltsin's unconstitutional order disbanding the legislature. When

Table 9.1. A Tocquevillian checklist for Russia in 2008

	Impact on Democracy	
	Negative	Positive
Conditions		
Authoritarian past	XX	
Revolutionary legacy	X	
Vulnerability to attack	XX	
Former empire	X	
Ethnic fragmentation	X	
Economic structure	X	
Living standard		X
Education level		XX
Morals		
Lack of religiosity	XX	
Orthodox Church	X	
Individualism	—	—
Weak associational life	XX	
Equality of social status		X
Institutions		
Strong president	XX	
Strong security forces	XX	
Weak rule of law	XX	
Elected leaders		X
Universal suffrage		X
Weak checks and balances	XX	
Mixed system of government (presidential-parliamentary)		X
Federal structure		X
Lack of free press		X
Weak political parties	XX	

Note: X = present; XX = strongly present

the deputies refused to depart, Yeltsin ordered the army to storm the parliament building. A new constitution giving stronger powers to the president was adopted in December 1993, at the same time as voters elected a new parliament, the State Duma. But those elections were won by nationalists and Communists, so the political stand-off between the executive and legislative branches continued. In a bid to deflect political criticism, Yeltsin launched a brutal war to regain control over the rebel province of Chechnya at the end of 1994. Yeltsin narrowly won reelection as president in June 1996, after a campaign marred by biased media coverage and shady backroom maneuvering. Still, during the years of the Yeltsin presidency, (1991–1999) the media were more or less free, with some independently-owned TV and radio stations criticizing the government. Elections were held on schedule and the results broadly reflected the will of the voters.[10] In the course of coming to power, Yeltsin had struck deals with regional leaders, weakening the capacity of the federal government and allowing a de facto decentralization of power to the provinces.

Yeltsin resigned in December 1999, nominating his handpicked successor Vladimir Putin as "acting president," and Putin cruised to victory in the March 2000 presidential election.[11] President Putin moved quickly and decisively to roll back the nascent political pluralism of the Yeltsin years and recentralize authority in the Kremlin in what came to be called the "power vertical."[12] Within weeks of taking office, Putin tightened state control over the media, sending into exile two of the oligarchs who had controlled national television stations during the Yeltsin years. The restrictions on organized political opposition were gradually tightened. Putin removed the elected regional governors from the upper house of parliament, and in the December 2003 elections the pro-Kremlin United Russia party won more than two-thirds of the seats in the State Duma. Subsequent changes to electoral law made it even more difficult for opposition forces to win representation: the single-member seats that used to fill half the Duma were abolished, and the minimum threshold for representation in the proportional representation party-list race that now filled the whole body was raised from 5 to 7 percent. Putin also took steps to limit federalism, imposing legislative uniformity across Russia's regions; tightening central control of the state budget; and in 2004 abolishing elections for regional governors.[13] The erosion of democracy was due partly to the machinations of the presidential administration, and partly to the inability of opposition forces to coalesce behind coherent parties that offered a viable alternative to the Kremlin.[14]

Economic developments also played a role in the retreat of democracy. The economic slump of the 1990s, during which GDP and living standards fell by 30–40 percent, was inevitably associated in the public eye with the onset of democracy. One might then ask: What is the worth of democracy if it cannot protect citizens from such a fate? In Central European countries such as Poland or Hungary, the transitional state was able to do a better job at preserving the welfare state and thus to some degree ameliorating the costs of transition for the poor. The Russian state dismally failed in such a role in the 1990s. At the same time, the economy was going through a rapid process of privatization, with 70 percent of state assets being trans-ferred into legally independent corporations. A small group of "oligarchs" managed to seize control of about one-third of these former state indus-tries during the highly corrupt privatization process. This meant that the decentralization of power that one would have expected to follow from the introduction of capitalism failed to materialize. Most of the oligarchs maintained close relations with the Kremlin, and those that did not even-tually paid a price for their independence. The most striking example is that of Mikhail Khodorkovsky, the founder of the Yukos oil company, who was briefly the richest man in Russia with an estimated personal wealth of $16 billion. Khodorkovsky was funding opposition parties in the run-up to the December 2003 Duma elections, and he seemed poised to back a can-didate to challenge Putin in the March 2004 presidential election. Khodor-kovsky was arrested on trumped up tax evasion charges in October 2003, and subsequently sentenced to eight years in jail. The Yukos Oil Company was forced into bankruptcy and its assets divided up amongst the state-owned companies Gazprom and Rosneft. Putin also bought up some of the other private oil companies and pushed out foreign oil ventures, effectively renationalizing the crucial oil sector, which was driving Russia's post–2000 economic recovery. Observers started to argue that Russia was falling prey to the "resource curse," which refers to the fact that very few countries that are dependent on oil exports make a successful transition to democracy.[15]

The best known democracy index is that compiled by Freedom House. Countries are graded on a seven-point scale for the level of political rights (PR) and civil liberties (CL), with 1–2 being "free" and 6–7 "unfree." Free-dom House regarded the new Russian Republic as "partly free," ranking it 3 for PR and 4 for CL from 1993 through 1997 (see figure 9.1). Russia's grade slipped to 4 for PR and 5 for CL in 1999 and 5/5 in 2000–2003. In 2004, Russia was relegated to the category "unfree," with a 6 for PR and 5 for CL.[16] That ranking actually places Russia's political system *below* that of places like Afghanistan or Bahrain, which seems somewhat unrealistic, given the level of violence, the absence of contestation, and the seclusion of women in those countries. But even if the international comparisons may be shaky, the Freedom House index fairly accurately captures the trajectory of Russian democracy over time.

In terms of civil liberties, daily life for Russian citizens is quite free, with respect to freedom of movement and travel, freedom of religion, and so forth.

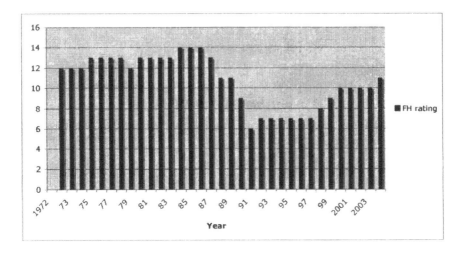

Figure 9.1. Freedom House ratings for Soviet Union and Russian Federation, 1972–2004 (political rights and civil rights added together).
Source: Freedom House, www.freedomhouse.org

For example, the Soviet registration system that required police permission to change one's place of residence was legally abolished. Non-governmental organizations (NGOs) have sprung up, and some have become an accepted part of the political scene—such as the Committee of Soldiers' Mothers. However, those that are seen as politically motivated or connected to foreign sponsors have been the target of state crackdowns.[17] Even under Yeltsin, in the 1990s some groups were harassed. For example, Western observers were alarmed by the 1997 law on religious organizations that forced all congregations founded during the previous fifteen years to reregister. The Putin administration got more serious about curtailing NGO activities after Georgia's "rose revolution" in 2003 and the "orange revolution" in Ukraine the next year, both of which were actively assisted by Western-funded NGOs.[18] A new, more restrictive law requiring all foreign-based NGOs to reregister came into effect in Russia in April 2006.[19]

The Tocquevillian Approach

Tocqueville divided the relevant factors shaping American democracy into three: historical and geographic conditions, the prevailing mores, and the ruling institutions. Tocqueville was not deterministic: he recognized the constraints of history and geography, but also gave ample room for human agency in choosing to live by certain moral codes and creating certain institutions. France and America had experienced revolutions as a result of which new moral codes and political institutions were brought into being, so Tocqueville did not see history as a vice. He was not a believer in "path dependency," a popular approach in contemporary political science that sees countries as "locked in" to certain institutional arrangements by the sequence of historical events they have experienced.[20] At the same time, as Tocqueville showed in *The Old Regime and the Revolution*, he was aware of the powerful continuities in human history, such that even after a revolutionary upheaval, a society will still carry many features of the preceding regime. This truth became all too apparent in Russia under President Putin, as, one after another, partially-submerged features of the Soviet system started to resurface.

Tocqueville's approach is deeply sociological: he does not dwell on contingency, or the chance sequence of events, though he does recognize that human interventions produce unintended consequences. Nor does he overemphasize the role of leadership. In contrast to most contemporary writing on America's origins, he does not provide a "Great Man" account of the role of the Founding Fathers in America's origin. Likewise, a majority of the books written on Russia's transition to democracy also take a "great man" approach, often being written as straight biographies of Gorbachev, Yeltsin, and Putin. Tocqueville reminds us that this is not the best way to write history.

Conditions

Russia lacks nearly all the conditions understood by contemporary political science as prerequisites for a successful transition to democracy. In its long history, there is no experience of democracy and barely any experience of civil society to draw on. Two centuries of the Mongol yoke (1240–1480) were followed by 400 years of the most oppressive autocratic rule in Europe. This was succeeded by seventy-five years of Soviet totalitarianism: the most innovative and deep-rooted system of authoritarian rule the world had ever seen.

In contrast, Tocqueville's America was a former colony of Britain, with 150 years' experience of rule of law and a degree of self-government that was high by contemporary standards. The United States itself came into existence through an act of rebellion and an assertion of self-rule against a central state. In contrast, Tsarist Russia and the Soviet Union that succeeded it were both multinational empires, different versions of an "empire-state" whose national identity was forged not in self-rule but in ruling over others. (The population of the Russian Empire in 1917 was only 44 percent ethnic Russian, while that of the USSR in 1989 was still only 53 percent Russian.)

It is true that Russia was not itself colonized and has never been under lasting foreign occupation since 1480. But this may be a liability rather than an asset, in the sense that among former colonies, experience of British rule positively correlates with democratization. And among former empires, U.S. military occupation was instrumental in the introduction of stable democracy in Japan, Germany, and Italy.

On the other hand, Russia shares with America the experience of being born out of revolution. The Soviet Union emerged from a revolutionary overthrow of the existing authorities in 1917, and today's Russian Federation came out of a quasi-revolution in 1991 whose slogans were democracy and sovereignty. However, from a Tocquevillian perspective, the revolutions of 1917 and 1991 have more in common with the experiences of France in 1789 than America in 1776. The Russian revolutions involved the breakdown of social order and a collapse into anarchy, rather than the positive affirmation of a new community. Russian public opinion itself is ambivalent over whether 1917 should be seen as a step forward, while an overwhelming majority regards 1991 in negative terms.[21] Famously, in his state-of-the-nation address on April 25, 2005, President Putin described the collapse of the Soviet Union as "the biggest geopolitical catastrophe of the century."[22] In contrast, in the United States, the revolution of 1776 continues to be regarded as an unadulterated good. Clearly, the Soviet collapse did not launch the Russian Federation in a spirit of optimism and self-determination; and a sense of defeat and despair is not conducive to the flourishing of freedom and democracy. Western observers usually dismiss this sense of historical loss as part of Russians' alleged nostalgia for empire, and they do not typically make the connection between this experience and Russia's subsequent lack of readiness to embrace democracy.

Tocqueville stressed America's freedom from foreign attack (a "nation without neighbors"), due to its fortuitous location behind the Atlantic ocean, as tremendously important in creating the space for a free society to develop. This happy situation continued for the United States throughout the nineteenth century. In the twentieth century, America's engagement in the two world wars did not bring any death and destruction to the civilian population of the continental United States. Russia's experience is quite the opposite: centuries of fending off foreign invasion culminating in the devastating "Great Patriotic War" of 1941–1945. That was followed by the Cold War, a decades-long institutionalization of vulnerability to total destruction. This fear of foreigners did not disappear with the dissolution of the USSR. In effect, the Soviet Union lost the Cold War, and in the wake of that defeat many Russians felt their country was weakened and even more vulnerable than before. From their perspective, all of Russia's *recent* enemies remained in place after 1991, from NATO to China; while *old* foes were stirring (Poland, Turkey) and *new* ones were rising (radical Islam). The men in charge of Russian security after 1991 were all born and bred during the Cold War: it was unrealistic to imagine that their fundamental assumptions about the character of the global system as a threatening environment would change overnight. And this sense of existential vulnerability, Tocqueville would tell us, is not fertile soil for the flourishing of freedom. Russians seem willing to give up a degree of political pluralism in return for the security of a strong leader.

Although Russia had been defeated, it still possessed the nuclear arsenal that had guaranteed its security during the Cold War. This led Russia's leaders to believe that its place at the table of the leading powers was assured, that it could and should be a rule-maker and not a rule-taker in the international system.[23] Even Yeltsin, who was making genuine overtures to the West, wanted Russia to be respected as an equal. Under Putin, the contradictions in Russia's position became sharper still, with Moscow resisting international pressures to embrace democratization when the latter came to be seen as deliberately intended to weaken the Russian state.

In terms of economic circumstances, Russia does have the vast land and resources that Tocqueville saw as giving America better living conditions and fewer social conflicts, than Europe. However, the economic preconditions for democracy have changed since the time of Tocqueville. Postindustrial and internationally integrated economies are now the most developed, and the most compatible with democracy. From the Soviet period, Russia inherited an economy that was predominantly industrial, but with 20 percent of the workforce still engaged in highly inefficient agriculture. These traditional economic sectors were held together by state subsidies and by hierarchical, patriarchal social relations: an economic structure highly inimical to liberal democracy.

Since 1991, the Russian economy has become more internationally integrated, with trade leaping from 10 percent to 25 percent of GDP. But this integration has been driven by the export of oil, gas, and metals, leaving Russia prone to the "resource curse." International experience suggests that resource dependency tends to distort the country's economic development, shrinking its manufacturing sector, but also makes it more prone to authoritarian politics since it is easy for a small ruling elite to capture the revenue flow from resource exports.[24] The term "resource curse" was unknown in Tocqueville's day, but he was clearly aware that the slave-owning, staple-exporting economy of the South was far less conducive to democracy than the family farms and manufacturers of the North.

Are there any conditions that are conducive to democracy in Russia? Most of the social infrastructure for modern life is in place. Russia has a highly educated, literate, and urbanized population, with a high degree of gender equality in terms of women's ability to access education and the labor market. However, very low life expectancy, especially for men (58.9 years), points to serious social pathologies that do not augur well for democracy.[25]

Tocqueville stressed America's advantages in being free of a landed aristocracy or an established church. This gave it a head start in providing a foundation of social equality, at least outside the South. Land was not concentrated in a few hands, as in Europe, and the absence of primogeniture would help prevent the accumulation of large estates. The open frontier would ensure that land ownership was an option for the masses. These material conditions were matched by an absence of strict social hierarchies, compared to Europe.

The Soviet Union did not have a landed aristocracy or church, having ruthlessly destroyed these institutions in the wake of the 1917 revolution. Soviet society was more egalitarian than nineteenth-century France—Tocqueville's point of reference—but it was not as open and equal as nineteenth-century New England. Its official ideology proclaimed social equality, and it was very difficult to acquire wealth in the form of property. But the Communist Party hierarchy was firmly in place, consisting of an elaborately graduated ranking of political status (the "nomenklatura") with accompanying privileges governing all aspects of life, from career opportunities, to vacations, to the purchase of sausage.[26]

In the course of the 1990s, Russian society has become more unequal at the same time that it has become more free. The nomenklatura system collapsed, though closed political elites remain in power in many regions. Market reform rapidly produced a new class of property holders, and the ownership of productive assets was highly concentrated in the hands of a new class of entrepreneurs and corrupt government officials. That perceived stalwart of democratic stability, the middle class, is but weakly present in contemporary Russian society. The old Soviet middle class of highly educated, state-employed professionals has eroded, and in its place a new middle class is slowly emerging, accounting for no more than one-fifth of the population.[27] Most of the middle class is still employed by the state, and these teachers and doctors have very low salaries. About one million small businesses have emerged, but that number has not risen for the past ten years, and they employ less than 10 percent of the labor force. Income inequality as measured by the Gini coefficient rose from 0.26 in 1991 to 0.409 in 1994 and 0.399 in 2004. [28] That is about the same as the United States, but well below the level of inequality to be found in countries such as Brazil or India. Although economic equality is conducive to democratic stability, the coexistence of high levels of inequality and a functioning democracy in countries as diverse as Brazil and India suggest that inequality is not necessarily a barrier to the spread of democracy in Russia.

Perhaps the strongest "conditions" argument in favor of Russia's democratic prospects is that of living standards. Tocqueville understood that the abundance of land and corresponding higher standard of living in the United States was highly favorable for democracy. If the poor have the hope of a comfortable life through their own efforts, they are less likely to use democratic institutions to expropriate the rich. Contemporary studies show that countries with per capita income above $5,000 per year are very likely to make the transition to stable democracy.[29] Russia dipped below that threshold in the 1990s, but is now rising well above it. In terms of purchasing power parity, Russian GDP per capita was close to $5,000 per head in 1990, fell to $3,000 by 1997, and had recovered to $9,900 in 2004.[30] At the current exchange rate, GDP per capita was $4,042 in 2004. GDP has grown at 5–7 percent per year since 1999, driven in large part by the boom in world oil prices. If this continues for another decade, then Russia's democratic prospects look fairly promising. Of course, it may turn out that Russia proves to be an exception to the correlation of wealth and democracy found in most other countries, due to a combination of the "resource curse" and the "Russian curse" (i.e., 1,200 years of authoritarian rule).

Ethnic homogeneity was not a prominent issue in Tocqueville's explanation of American democracy. America was a new community built on a shared identification with republican values, and consisting for the most part of English-speaking Protestants. (This homogeneity was assured by the exclusion of African and Native Americans.) But in the modern world, ethnic fragmentation is generally seen as a serious obstacle to democratic consolidation. Ethnic polarization has undermined democracy in countries from Sri Lanka to Lebanon—although there are some outliers, such as India, where ethnic fragmentation has not prevented the functioning of liberal democracy. Russia is fairly homogeneous by international standards, with 79.8 percent of the population registered as ethnic Russians according to the 2002 census.[31] However, about half of the non-Russian population (12–15 million people) are Moslem. The Moslems of the middle Volga (Tatars and Bashkirs) have lived under Russian rule for five hundred years and seem reconciled to their situation as a minority within the Russian state. They enjoy a substantial degree of autonomy through the system of Russian federalism, which grants self-rule to twenty-one ethnically designated "republics." Among the Moslems of the North Caucasus, however, the Chechen quest for secession triggered two brutal wars (1994–1996 and 1999–2003). The Chechen question has its roots in Russia's historical legacy as an empire. The Chechens preserved memories of their conquest in the 1840s and the entire nation's deportation to Central Asia by Stalin in 1944. Some observers argue that the treatment of Chechnya alone rules out any consideration of Russia as a legitimate democracy. The outbreak of the second Chechen war in 1999 was closely connected to Putin's rise to power and his subsequent ability to concentrate power in the hands of an authoritarian presidency.

Although open resistance ended by 2002, Chechen and Islamic resistance groups were still capable of mounting terrorist acts, which gave the Kremlin a pretext for tightening authoritarian controls. Thus, after the dreadful Beslan school siege in September 2004, Putin abolished the direct election of regional governors: instead, they are now nominated by the president.

Mores

Tocqueville made it clear that the success of democracy in America was closely connected to the prevailing social mores. He saw the American Revolution as animated by the spirit of liberty and the spirit of religion. In the absence of the internalization of norms of independence and responsibility among the common people, democratic institutions cannot be made to work effectively.

Centuries of Tsarist and Soviet rule seemed to leave Russian citizens sorely ill-prepared for the moral responsibilities of democratic citizenship. In the perestroika period, Russians were fond of citing the biblical experience of the Jews, who spent forty years in the wilderness after they left Egypt. Only a fresh generation with no experience of slavery would be capable of building a new, free society. Obviously, this did not happen in Russia. The accelerating pace of global integration meant they did not have the opportunity to stop history for forty years. Rather than wandering in the desert, for the past fifteen years the Russians have been frantically constructing a new society, with new social norms that were still heavily shaped by the preceding Soviet society. (One can also note that they have been following leaders who are somewhat less inspired than Moses.)

Russians do have a certain anarchic affinity for freedom, and there were moments when the spirit of liberty was abroad in 1989–1991, such as the televised debates of the first partly-freely elected congress in March 1989. But these were fleeting moments: 1991 was more a collapse than a revolution. Even Russian liberals would probably agree that fear of repression was a more powerful motivator than was an embrace of liberty. Even at the peak of mass mobilization in 1991, the demonstrations in Moscow were 200–300,000 strong—3 percent of the city's population—and smaller still in provincial cities, where they took place at all. Contrast this with the millions that took to the streets in Poland, East Germany, and Czechoslovakia.

Even during the perestroika period, opinion polls revealed a surprisingly strong well of public support in the Russian population for civil and political liberties.[32] Some skeptics argued that these polls were too abstract, in that ordinary Russians did not see those values embedded in the actual practices and institutions of emergent democracy in Russia.[33] Over the course of the 1990s, the rift between abstract acceptance of democratic principles and discontent with their practical realization in Russia grew more pronounced. But the fact that Russians continued to express their support for elections, free speech, and so forth was encouraging to those who argued that Russia could yet become a genuine democracy. One key difference is that in the United States, liberty was closely connected to property. This was not so in Russia, where property was historically monopolized by the state and there was no space to make the connection between property rights and individual freedom.[34]

Religious values feature prominently in Tocqueville's analysis of American democracy. ("It must never be forgotten that religion gave birth to Anglo-American society.") Protestantism cultivated a sense of equal worth and promoted individual responsibility for one's own fate, unmediated by priestly authority. Yet most published accounts of Russia's attempted transition to democracy barely mention the role of religion. In part, this was due to the fact that Russian society was indeed highly secular. For seven decades, the Soviet state had conducted a rigorous and effective campaign against religion, in the mistaken belief that modernity requires the abandonment of religious values. This dismissive attitude toward religion is shared by many Western liberals, which is another reason why religious values were usually absent from analysis of the prospects for democracy in Russia.

A further reason for downplaying religion is the fact that religious organizations did not feature prominently in the Russian transition. This is in stark contrast to the transition in East Europe. The Catholic Church was obviously pivotal to the anti-Communist resistance in Poland, while in East Germany, Protestant peace groups formed the core of the Leipzig protests. Indeed, in Russia, religious groups were invisible during the transition. The Orthodox Church was seen as a bastion of the state authorities, be they Communist or post-Communist. During the Soviet period, the Orthodox leadership, the Patriarchy, had made some significant compromises with the authorities in a bid to maintain the church's survival. The church also quickly established a cozy relationship with the Yeltsin administration, winning substantial concessions in exchange for its political support. (These ranged from the return of buildings to the granting of import/ export licenses for commodities from oil to alcohol.) Under President Putin, the church has been even more tightly embraced as the official ideology of the Russian state, with Putin introducing the practice of state officials attending church services. Since 1991, there has been a minor upsurge in religious identification and practice amongst ordinary Russians, but this is more a fashion than a spiritual revival, and has few political overtones— other than support for the Yeltsin-Putin regime.[35] More often than not, religion has achieved political prominence only in the context of the negation of liberty, as in the 1997 Russian Federation law that cracked down on "nontraditional" religions, including Protestantism and Catholicism.

Western analysts tend to regard Orthodoxy, in Russia and in southeastern Europe, as the least conducive to democracy of all the Christian denominations. Focusing on spiritual salvation rather than worldly deeds, it did not encourage the separation of church and state (something that enabled the church in the West to become an independent political actor), nor did it focus on the individual.[36]

Individualism (a word introduced into the English language via Tocqueville) was central to his explanation of the American breakthrough, and it is deeply rooted in the Protestant tradition of an individual responsible for his or her own fate, through study of the Bible. Russia is not a society devoid of prominent, and brilliant, individuals. It has more than its share of eccentrics, artists, holy men, and anarchists. So the contrast with America cannot be reduced to black and white. But Russian individualism was not grounded in a system of property rights, nor in a theological discourse, nor in a social contract to form a new society. The Protestant concept of the individual is above all tempered by a respect for the laws governing social life—which derive from God but are "etched in the minds of men." The weakness of religious belief in Russia thus correlates with lack of respect for the rule of law.

Protestant individualism was tempered by an urge to associate, which promoted awareness of common interests. Tocqueville's emphasis on the vigorous associational life of the early colonists has become a salient theme for contemporary political science, with the revival of interest in civil society and social capital.[37] Much effort has gone into studying incipient civil society in Russia, and researchers were dismayed to find that Russians were reluctant to join organizations and to participate in public life beyond the act of voting.[38] They had a low level of trust in public institutions and in their fellow citizens.

Closer analysis revealed that post–1991 Russian society did consist of dense social networks, but these were based on friends and family rather than public associations such as political parties, charities, clubs, and so forth.[39] Russian social networks were informal rather than formal, hidden rather than transparent, and based on manipulation and avoidance of state institutions. They had their roots in the networks of favors (*blat*) that evolved during the decades of central planning, when personal contacts were needed to secure resources from state authorities, which controlled everything from political life to personal careers to food and housing. These networks were built on the principle of inclusion and exclusion— "our" people (*svoi*) and "theirs" (*chuzhye*). "Ours" must be trusted and helped, "theirs" cannot be trusted and may be cheated with impunity. ("He who does not steal from the state, steals from his family.") This attitude was corrosive not just of civil society but of any concept of the rule and law, duty, and the public sphere. It still prevails in Russia today.

It turns out that just as there is "good" and "bad" cholesterol, so there is good and bad social capital. Russia in 1991 had deep reserves of social capital, but of the "bad" sort; and this actually flourished in the 1990s, finding new opportunities and tasks in the burgeoning but unregulated market economy. The Soviet state tried to compensate for the absence of public trust by stepping up bureaucratic monitoring and coercion. Under Yeltsin, the post-Soviet state had neither the capacity nor the political will to embrace those authoritarian methods. Instead, it turned to new "political technologies" of media manipulation. Under Putin, there has been more of a return to authoritarian techniques, invigorated by patriotism and xenophobia.

Institutions

Clearly, the odds were stacked against Russia becoming a democracy in terms of the geopolitical and economic conditions in which it found itself in 1991, and the moral universe it inherited from its "old regime." Only a vigorous set of new democratic institutions could drag it into a viable civil society—a development that was possible to imagine, not least because of the strong shift in the international climate in favor of liberal democracy that accompanied the Soviet collapse. Unfortunately, neither Mikhail Gorbachev nor Boris Yeltsin were able to build strong new democratic institutions. Their role was more that of destroying the old than creating the new. In the absence of strong institution-building from above, institutions were also slow to develop spontaneously, from below.[40]

Boris Yeltsin's Russia was an unstable combination of anarchy and authoritarianism. Yeltsin's priority was simple: to stay in power, to survive in a chaotic environment, and hopefully to set Russia on a path to a better future. He ruled through a mixture of threats and compromise, adapting some old Soviet-era institutions while closing others, and creating some new institutions on the spot. Powerful institutions that had ruled people's lives for decades disappeared almost overnight—not only state structures such as the Communist Party of the Soviet Union and the State Planning Committee (Gosplan) but also institutions that shaped social behavior down to its roots, such as the Young Pioneers or the elaborate customs that governed the practice of queuing for goods. Some feisty if unstable new institutions sprang up in their place: an elected parliament and president, a burgeoning capitalist class, markets, a free press, and even (perhaps) a free citizenry.

Although Western commentators are rightly critical of the poor quality of Russia's democratic institutions, in a broader historical context, it is still quite remarkable how quickly some of the core institutions of modern democracy were put in place. Russia now has a federal structure, a written constitution, universal suffrage, and a directly elected president and lower chamber of parliament—things that we take for granted today, but that were novelties in Tocqueville's time.

Free media became an important agent of change in the Gorbachev era, but this positive trend went into reverse as the Kremlin and its oligarchic allies used the media to rally support for Yeltsin's reelection in 1996.[41] However, under President Putin, media freedom was radically curtailed. By 2007, the television stations had become completely subservient to the Kremlin's political agenda. Independent voices can still be found in a handful of newspapers, on the radio station *Ekho Moskvy*, and on the Internet. During the Yeltsin period, elections were regularly held, and while there may have been some fraud in some regions, the results generally reflected the will of the voters.[42] The situation deteriorated under Putin; elections were still held on time, but the restrictions on the political opposition were stepped up. After the victory of the pro-government United Russia party in the 2003 elections, Putin established firm control over the parliament, which became to all intents and purposes an extension of the Kremlin.

Tocqueville put great store by the virtues of decentralization: democracy was rooted in free and self-governing local communities. Local government had never been a strong point of Russian political culture. Regional autonomy did receive a boost under Yeltsin, but Putin's recentralization drive has crushed most of what had been achieved in the 1990s.[43] Putin was also adamant in striving to restore the Russian state as the dominant institution in society and the agent of progress and modernity. This kind of centralization would have been anathema for Tocqueville, who would see it as leading inevitably to corruption from above and the stifling of initiative from below.

Still, the Russian political system is not yet a personal dictatorship as both Presidents Yeltsin and Putin did face some checks on their power. They had to contend with competing groups within the state bureaucracy and with the several dozen independent-minded wealthy businessmen who control about one-third of Russia's economy.[44] They were also constrained by the need to win elections (even with the help of fraud), to maintain a loyal majority in parliament, and to avoid popular protest by nonviolent means.[45] The main question mark hanging over the power structure that Putin solidified was whether it would survive the departure of its founder from office. Putin stepped down as president when his second term expired in May 2008, and handed over the post to his chosen successor, Dmitry Medvedev, who easily won election. However, Putin chose to stay on in the post of prime minister, and as of August 2008, it is unclear whether the "tandem" leadership of Putin and Medvedev will prove a stable arrangement.

Following the writings of Aristotle and Montesquieu, the Founding Fathers were convinced that the best form of government was a mixed system that dispersed power across different institutions that combined democratic, oligarchic, and monarchical elements. In a sense, the contemporary Russian political system fits the bill. It has a quasi-monarch (the president); it has direct elections for the presidency and the State Duma; and it has reinvented "oligarchy" in the sphere of economic management. There is little sign, as yet, of the emergence of a stable, closed ruling class, akin to the landed aristocracy that was for Tocqueville the major barrier to democratic rule. From 1997–1999, the dominant fear was that Russian democracy would collapse into rule by the economic oligarchy, but the 1998 financial crash and the subsequent arrival of President Putin laid that scenario to rest.[46] Nor has post–Soviet Russia yet developed an institutional structure equivalent to the old Communist Party of the Soviet Union that could reliably replicate the permanent suppression of democratic contestation.

Where modern Russian democracy would clearly disappoint Tocqueville is in the absence of rule of law. The rule of law was the unifying principle of American republicanism, but respect for the law is starkly absent in the Russian case.[47] Contemporary Russia is far from the Anglo-Saxon notion of law as an independent system that can serve as a check on the political authorities. And despite Putin's invocation of a "dictatorship of law," it is even some way from a Continental *Rechstaat*, in which the state obeys its own laws (while not subjecting itself to independent judicial review). The Russian state has shown a cavalier disregard of legal constraints: from Yeltsin's dissolution of the Supreme Court in 1993; to the waging of the war in Chechnya; to the persecution of Yukos in 2003–2005. The public correspondingly lacks faith in legal institutions—although polls show public support for the jury trials that have been steadily introduced across the country. The public disrespect for the law goes back to the Soviet period and is connected to the weakness of a religious moral code.

Western transitology has devoted more attention to institution-building in Russia than to preexisting conditions or morals. Institutions may be more interesting because they seem to be the most amenable to human agency (and Western intervention). But by the mid-2000s, even former exponents of the transition school were having second thoughts about the feasibility of a rapid transition to democracy in the post–Soviet states.[48] As of 2007, of the fifteen post–Soviet states, only the Baltic countries and Ukraine were rated as "free" by Freedom House, while Armenia, Georgia, and Moldova were rated as "partly free." The remaining eight are "unfree." Clearly, factors other than constitutional design were shaping the political trajectory of these countries, such as the absence of respect for rule of law or a political culture of give-and-take among the political elite.

Transitology assumed that any developed society was ripe for democratization, and that democratic institutions could quickly be designed and installed. Russians themselves were skeptical on this score. Having been burned once by the experience of revolutionary transformation, they take a conservative stance on the malleability of human nature and social institutions. A popular Russian homily from the perestroika era was the tale of the English gardener. When asked how to produce such a perfect lawn, he replies "It's easy, just roll it every day . . . for 300 years."

Were Tocqueville himself brought back to life and asked to comment on contemporary Russia, he would probably note both positive and negative features, and conclude that after fifteen years it is far too early to say what will be the long-term character of Russia's polity. It draws attention to some features that tend to be overlooked in the current pessimism about the state of Russian democracy, such as the presence of oligarchic and monarchic elements (balancing out the dangers of populist majoritarianism). But overall, the Tocquevillian perspective inclines one to be deeply skeptical about the possibility for the rapid introduction of democratic institutions in Russia.

Conclusion

Does it make sense to try to apply Tocqueville's approach to contemporary Russia? Tocqueville's analysis has stood the test of time as a brilliant dissection of some key features of the American political system. He was writing at a moment when America was just developing as a democracy—a stage not unlike Russia today. In the 1830s, of course, democracy was virtually unknown on the global stage, and America was an exceptional case. Now, at the dawn of the twenty-first century, democracy is the norm for developed, European countries, and Russia is the exception.

It is up to the reader to judge whether this is anything more than an empty intellectual exercise. One might say Tocqueville is irrelevant—that the world has changed since 1835, that giant bureaucracies like the KGB, or the welfare state, were unknown to Tocqueville, not to mention technologies like television. True enough. But some features of human society have stayed the same. The American political system itself still operates within an institutional structure created 225 years ago, in an age without modern bureaucracy, technology, and so forth.[49] Some of the key innovations of that time—a written constitution, rule of law, independent judiciary, individual rights, religious toleration, checks and balances, and so forth—are now being encouraged for other countries such as Russia. It thus behooves us to look back at the geopolitical, moral, and sociological context within which those institutions emerged.

Writing in the 1830s, Tocqueville failed to foresee some important developments in American society: the emergence of a powerful presidency and strong political parties; the Industrial Revolution and the rise of big corporations; and the role of money in politics, uniting these two trends. He only partly foresaw the cataclysm of civil war, although he did explore the differences between North and South and the conflicts they were engendering.

What does the Tocquevillian reading of Russian politics overlook? What, in the words of Donald Rumsfeld, are the "unknown unknowns" that we are omitting? No observer of Russian society would fail to note the strong presidency, the rise of big corporations, and the role of money in politics. Under the influence of Western democratic experience, U.S. political scientists have spent much of the past fifteen years anxiously awaiting the arrival of a strong party system in Russia. Suffice it to say that they are still waiting.

In contrast to the American case, a civil war is unlikely to explode on the scene. This was a widely discussed fear in Russia in the period 1987–1996, but it has largely disappeared since the consolidation of Putin's administration. Such a conflict would have been an ideological war for control over the state apparatus between Leftist and Rightist forces, as were its precursors in 1918–1921 and 1930–1937. Now, the only plausible civil war would be a widening of the Chechen insurrection to other Moslem regions of Russia, principally neighboring regions of the North Caucasus. This is a plausible and bloody scenario, but one that would probably lead to the further consolidation of Russian society around its leader.

Many observers have warned of the emergence of a hard-line fascist regime, drawing parallels with Weimar Germany.[50] However, that has not come to pass: there are fascists in Russia, but they are an extreme minority, not much more visible than in any other contemporary European democracy. And such thinking has not substantially influenced Russia's leaders: Yeltsin was not Slobodan Milosevic, invading his neighbors; and Putin has not reached the repression level of an A. Lukashenko in Belarus or Islam Karimov in Uzbekistan.

Perhaps the most valuable conclusion from this exercise is that Tocqueville reminds us of the interdependence between the domains of conditions, mores, and institutions. Foreign policy cannot be separated from domestic policy: the one feeds into the other. Western transitologists largely ignored Russia's sense of wounded pride due to its loss of superpower status, and hence the willingness of the people and the elite to support a leader who would act to restore that pride, even at the expense of democracy. Likewise, by overlooking the vacuum in religious beliefs, outside observers were overoptimistic in assuming that associational life and respect for the law would quickly and almost automatically take root in Russia.

Notes

I benefited greatly from conversations about Tocqueville with Stephen Engel, Boris Kapustin, and Aurelian Craiutu.

1. Alexis de Tocqueville, *Democracy in America*, vol. 1, trans. Henry Reeve (New York: Vintage Books, 1970), 434.

2. On Tocqueville and Russia, see Martin Malia, "Did Tocqueville Foresee Totalitarianism?," *Journal of Democracy* 11, no. 1 (2000): 179–86; Irena G. Gross, *The Scar of Revolution: Custine, Tocqueville, and the Romantic Imagination* (Berkeley: University of California Press, 1991).

3. Hedrick Smith, *The Russians* (New York: New York Times Books, 1976); Paul Hollander, *Soviet and American Society: A Comparison* (Chicago: University of Chicago Press, 1978).

4. Astolphe, Marquis de Custine, *Empire of the Czars* (New York: Doubleday, 1989).

5. Stefan Hedlund, *Russian Path Dependence: A People with a Troubled History* (New York: Routledge, 2005).

6. Andrei Petrovich Parshev, *Pochemu Rossiya Ne Amerika* [Why Russia is Not America] (Moscow: Krymskyi Most, 2000); see also Sergei Chugrov, *Rossiya i Zapad: Metamorfozy vzaimovospriyatiya* [Russia and the West: Metamorphoses of Mutual Perception] (Moscow, 1993).

7. Francis Fukuyama, "The End of History," *National Interest* 16 (Summer 1989): 3–18. The essay was "prescient" because it was written in the spring of 1989, three months before the Hungarians took down the border fences and six months before the fall of the Berlin wall.

8. Strobe Talbott, *The Russia Hand: A Memoir of Presidential Diplomacy* (New York: Random House, 2003).

9. Lilia Shevtsova, *Yeltsin's Russia: Myths and Reality* (Washington, DC: Brookings Institution, 1999).

10. Richard Rose and Neil Munro, *Elections without Order: Russia's Challenge to Vladimir Putin* (New York: Cambridge University Press, 2002); Timothy Colton, *Transitional Citizens: Voters and What Influences Them in the New Russia* (Cambridge, MA: Harvard University Press, 2000); and Michael McFaul, *Russia's Unfinished Revolution: Political Change from Gorbachev to Putin* (Ithaca, NY: Cornell University Press, 2001).

11. Lilia Shevtsova, *Putin's Russia*, 2nd ed. (Washington, DC: Carnegie Endowment for International Peace, 2005).

12. M. Steven Fish, *Democracy Derailed in Russia* (New York: Cambridge University Press, 2005).

13. For an overview, see Shevtsova, *Yeltsin's Russia* and *Putin's Russia*.

14. Henry Hale, "Why Not Parties? Electoral Markets, Party Substitutes, and Stalled Democratization in Russia," *Comparative Politics* 37, no. 2 (2005): 147–66.

15. Fish, *Democracy Derailed in Russia*, 118–36.

16. Robert W. Orttung, "Russia," *Nations in Transit 2005* (New York: Freedom House, 2005), http://www.freedomhouse.org.

17. Sarah Henderson, *Building Democracy in Contemporary Russia: Western Support for Grassroots Organizations* (Ithaca, NY: Cornell University Press, 2003).

18. Graeme Herd, "Colorful Revolutions and the CIS," *Problems of Post-Communism* 52, no. 2 (2005): 3–18.

19. Anastasia Kornya, "NGOs Fail the Test," *Vedomosti*, June 29, 2006.

20. Paul Pierson, "Increasing Returns, Path Dependence and the Study of Politics," *American Political Science Review* 94, no. 2 (2000): 251–67.

21. For example, in a 2002 survey, 27 percent gave a negative assessment of the October 1917 revolution, 33 percent said it "gave a push to socio-economic development," and 27 percent said it opened a new era (Levada Center Press Release, November 5, 2002), http://www.levada.ru. Opinions about August 1991 were more negative. In a July 2005 poll, only 10 percent saw the events as a democratic revolution, 36 percent saw them as a "tragedy for the country," and 43 percent characterized them as "the usual elite struggle for power" (Levada Center Press Release, August 18, 2005).

22. See www.kremlin.ru/eng/.

23. Andrei Tsygankov, *Russia's Foreign Policy: Change and Continuity in National Identity* (Lanham, MD: Rowman and Littlefield, 2006); Robert Legvold, ed., *Russian Foreign Policy in the 21st Century and the Shadow of the Past* (New York: Columbia University Press, 2007).

24. Michael L. Ross, "Does Oil Hinder Democracy?," *World Politics* 53, no. 3 (2001): 325–61; Ross, "The Political Economy of the Resource Curse," *World Politics* 51, no. 1 (1999): 297–322.

25. In 2004, out of 177 countries in the United Nations Development Project Human Development Index, Russia placed 65th. It ranked 33rd for education (88 percent school enrollment and 99.6 percent adult literacy), 59th for GDP per capita ($9,902), and 115th for life expectancy (65.2 years). It dropped from an aggregate score of 0.813 in 1990 to 0.771 in 1995, recovering to 0.797 in 2004. UNDP, *Human Development Report 2006*, http://hdr.undp.org/statistics/data/.

26. Mikhail Voslensky, *Nomenklatura: The Soviet Ruling Class* (New York: Doubleday, 1984).

27. Harley Balzer, "Russia's Middle Classes," *Post-Soviet Affairs* 14, no. 2 (1998): 165–86.

28. T. Yu. Bogomolova and V. S. Tapilina, "Ekonomicheskaya stratifikatsiya naseleniya Rossii v 90e gody," *Sotsiologicheskie issledovaniya* 6 (2001): 32–43, on p. 32. The 2004 figure is taken from the UNDP Human Development Report.

29. Carles Boix, *Democracy and Redistribution* (New York: Cambridge University Press, 2003); Adam Przeworski et al., *Democracy and Development: Political Institutions and Well-Being in the World, 1950–1990* (New York: Cambridge

University Press, 2000). The exceptions are oil-rich Islamic countries such as Qatar or Brunei.

30. UNDP, *Human Development Report 2006*.

31. http://www.perepis2002.ru/.

32. James L. Gibson, "A Mile Wide but an Inch Deep (?): The Structure of Democratic Commitment in the Former USSR," *American Journal of Political Science* 40, no. 2 (1996): 396–420; Timothy J. Colton and Michael McFaul, "Are Russians Undemocratic?," *Post-Soviet Affairs* 18, no. 2 (2002): 91–121; and Jeffrey W. Hahn, "Political Culture in Yaroslavl' Over Time: How 'Civic'?," in *Regional Russia in Transition*, ed. Jeffrey W. Hahn (Baltimore, MD: Johns Hopkins University Press 2001), 75–114.

33. James Alexander, *Political Culture in Post-Communist Russia* (New York: St. Martin's Press, 2000); Stephen White, Richard Rose, and Ian McAllister, *How Russia Votes* (Chatham, NJ: Chatham House, 1996); and Richard Rose, Neil Munro, and William Mishler, "Resigned Acceptance of an Incomplete Democracy: Russia's Political Equilibrium," *Post-Soviet Affairs* 20, no. 3 (2004): 195–218.

34. Richard Pipes, *Property and Freedom* (New York: Vintage, 2000).

35. Zoe Knox, *Russian Society and the Orthodox Church: Religion in Russia after Communism* (London: Routledge/Curzon, 2004); John Basil, "Church-State Relations in Russia: Orthodoxy and Federation Law, 1990–2004," *Religion, State and Society* 33, no. 2 (2005): 151–64.

36. Peter Berger, "Christianity and Democracy," *Journal of Democracy* 15, no. 2 (2004): 76–80.

37. B. Edwards, M. W. Foley, and M. Diani, eds., *Beyond Tocqueville: Civil Society and the Social Capital Debate in Comparative Perspective* (Hanover, NH: University Press of New England, 2001).

38. Marc Morje Howard, *The Weakness of Civil Society in Post-Communist Europe* (New York: Cambridge University Press, 2003); Al Evans and Lisa Sunstrom, eds., *Russian Civil Society: A Critical Assessment* (Armonk, NY: M. E. Sharpe, 2005).

39. Alena V. Ledeneva, *Russia's Economy of Favours: Blat, Networking and Informal Exchanges* (New York: Cambridge University Press, 1998).

40. Valerie Sperling, ed., *Building the Russian State: Institutional Crisis and the Quest for Democratic Governance* (Boulder, CO: Westview Press, 2000).

41. Laura Belin, "The Russian Media in the 1990s," *Journal of Communist Studies and Transition Politics* 18, no. 1 (2002): 139–61.

42. Rose and Munro, *Elections without Order*; Colton, *Transitional Citizens*; and McFaul, *Russia's Unfinished Revolution*.

43. Tomila Lankina, *Governing the Locals: Local Self-Government and Ethnic Mobilization in Russia* (Lanham, MD: Rowman & Littlefield, 2004).

44. According to a World Bank study, twenty-three large firms controlled by thirty-seven individuals accounted for 30 percent of Russia's GDP. See World Bank, *From Transition to Development* (April 2004), www.worldbank.org.ru.

45. Thomas F. Remington, *The Russian Parliament: Institutional Evolution in a Transitional Regime* (New Haven, CT: Yale University Press, 2001); Michael McFaul, Nikolai Petrov, and Andrei Ryabov, eds., *Between Dictatorship and Democracy: Russian Post-Communist Political Reform* (Washington, DC: Carnegie Endowment for International Peace, 2004).

46. Stephen Sestanovich, "Force, Money and Pluralism," *Journal of Democracy* 15, no. 3 (2004): 33–58.

47. Peter Solomon and Todd Fogelsong, *Courts and Transition in Russia: The Challenge of Judicial Reform* (Boulder, CO: Westview Press, 2000); Robert Sharlet, "Putin and the Politics of Law in Russia," *Post-Soviet Affairs* 17, no. 3 (2001): 195–234.

48. Thomas Carothers, "The End of the Transition Paradigm," *Journal of Democracy* 13, no. 1 (2002): 5–21.

49. Samuel P. Huntington rightly points out that most of these features actually evolved much earlier than 1787, in Tudor England, so the U.S. Constitution was enshrining a set of political practices that were already archaic. *Political Order in Changing Societies* (New Haven, CT: Yale University Press, 1965), 122–33.

50. Jeffrey Kopstein and Stephen Hanson, "The Weimar-Russia Comparison," *Post-Soviet Affairs* 13, no. 3 (1997): 252–83.

10

Tocqueville in Africa: Analyzing African Local Governance

James S. Wunsch

The remarkable insights Alexis Tocqueville brought to the analysis of eighteenth- and nineteenth-century American and French governance were not simply the product of random observations. Nor was the powerful theory of governance he developed. They grew instead from a creative analytical framework, animated by his assumptions about human behavior that guided his observations and analysis. The purpose of this chapter is to review that framework, those assumptions, and his theory of local governance, and explore how they are useful in analyzing recent and contemporary patterns of African local governance.

Tocqueville uses a configurational approach in his analytical framework and theory, much like that used by Theda Skocpol in *States and Social Revolutions*, and advocated by Charles Tilly in *Big Structures, Large Processes, Huge Comparisons*.[1] Tocqueville situates what contemporary social scientists would call rational individuals in a web of factors that structures their behaviors as they pursue their goals. For example, in volume II of *Democracy in America* in particular, Tocqueville leads the reader through a tour of American society: art, architecture, science and engineering, education, industry, family patterns, and so forth. Even where patterns have evolved from what he saw, as in science and education, those changes are consistent with his logic and what he saw as the variables critical to them.[2] The same applies to American political life. Tocqueville used his analytical framework to explain the vigor of much, though not all, of American local governance, as well as the lassitude he observed in France's local governance.

Several terms and assumptions need to be clarified. First, "effective local governance" refers to institutions that can mobilize community participation, identify local needs and problems, organize and implement appropriate collective action, manage conflict, and remain accountable to local residents. This could occur through both formal state-sanctioned (inorganic) institutions as well as unofficial community-based (organic) institutions, and on varying scales from small communities to large urban areas. Second, the chapter employs methodological individualism and a loose rational-choice model to predict/explain individual behaviors and ultimately general patterns, much as Tocqueville did. Third, as an analytical framework, it assumes that individuals will adopt personal behaviors, or "survival strategies," that will be powerfully influenced by the conjunction of and interaction among mores, physical circumstances, and laws and institutions.[3] Overall, it argues that these strategies strongly affect the sorts of local governance one finds in contemporary Africa. Whether and the extent to which these factors have truly altered Africans' mores is uncertain, as this chapter will suggest.

Tocqueville's analytical model emphasizes four dimensions:

- a people's historic circumstances;
- the mores ("habits of the heart") they generate;
- their physical circumstances; and
- their laws and institutions.

This chapter will also emphasize another complementary level of analysis as well:

- the behaviors produced as people, given their mores, to negotiate the opportunities and constraints the physical circumstances, laws, and institutions present.

In Tocqueville's dynamic and interactive model, individuals—influenced by their mores—attempt to negotiate the opportunities and constraints the latter two sets of factors offer, as they seek things they value. The outcome of this process are behaviors that generate patterns in social, economic, and political realms. Changes in laws, institutions, or physical context will generate *changed* behaviors as people seek to survive/flourish under new circumstances. These new behaviors generate successes and failures for individuals and for collectivities (though not necessarily the same outcomes they generate for individuals). Behaviors will also in turn change physical conditions and/or laws and institutions over time. Those changes in turn will affect individuals as they deal with the changed opportunities, costs, and problems they present. Eventually, these will likely affect mores, and then patterns of governance.

Animating this framework were Tocqueville's assumptions about human beings. While not expressed in the formal terms one sees in contemporary social science, Tocqueville points toward an implicitly rational-actor, self-interested model at numerous places in his analysis. Individuals learn from their experiences. They use this learning to try to develop strategies and tactics that succeed in achieving the things they value. According to Tocqueville's analysis, Americans love their local governments because they are useful and belong to them. In Tocqueville's model, individuals discern and pursue their perceptions of self-interest in ways that were conditioned by historical experience, physical conditions, laws and institutions, and mores. The combined factors might lead to individual actions growing from individual energy and enlightened self-interest that as collective behaviors would tend to produce cooperative behavior, reciprocity, prosperity, civil order, and stable mass governance. One aspect of that he called "self-interest, rightly understood." Alternatively, they might lead to individual actions based on passivity and/or narrowly construed self-centered interest, likely leading in turn to collective patterns of conflict, economic decay, civil disorder, and ineffective, unstable, and chaotic governance. He felt the latter existed in France. Tocqueville's work was driven by his search for answers as to why some peoples demonstrated the first pattern and others the second, and the implications this had for democracy and the quality of a people's governance.[4]

Tocqueville on Local Governance

For Tocqueville, local governance was the crucible of democratic mores. At the local level, human interactions molded citizens to sustain or lose liberty, and unleashed energy that could either stimulate or undercut economic development and prosperity, and counter or accelerate what he saw as inevitable centripetal political forces under conditions of democracy. Neither economic stagnation nor administrative centralization was conducive to maintaining political liberty. Local governance was critical because it offered the best hope to counter such negative tendencies at all levels of governance.[5]

Tocqueville argued that several factors had worked in the American situation to sustain effective local governance that created democratic mores and citizens, and fostered economic growth that countered the centripetal forces of democracy. For Tocqueville, effective local governance in America had several necessary preconditions. The absence of class divisions and conflict, and a religious heritage that emphasized individual responsibility, personal restraint, and an obligation to work for community improvement, were each important parts of America's historical experiences.[6] The mores of American society required that citizens be energetic, confident, knowledgeable about governance, and see their interests through a framework of enlightened self-interest, which led citizens to be aware of the need for self-restraint, the benefits of cooperation with others, and the value of law.[7] America's law and institutions reflected what some now call the principle of subsidiarity whereby collective problems were organized to be handled at the lowest level of society that might be expected to be able to deal with them. To accomplish this, local institutions had to have the authority to deal with these problems as well as stable legal-institutional frameworks within which to work. Regarding physical conditions, the then unlimited availability of free land, excellent river networks, coastal ports for commerce, and distance from Europe created an environment that stimulated personal optimism, local initiative, and general prosperity and offered protection from foreign wars.[8]

Tocqueville believed American local governance was an incubator and primary school for democracy and a dynamic institution that stimulated local development. In *The Old Regime and the Revolution,* he saw France in rather the opposite light.[9] An extremely centralized and elitist administrative system, state tutelage over localities, and stagnant and weak local governments taught Frenchmen to be subjects, not citizens, and engendered a pattern where Frenchmen commonly looked passively to Paris to take all initiatives and solve all problems. As a result, local economies stagnated and centralization continued apace. Not feeling themselves to be citizens and effective members of the political community, Frenchmen were prone to servile mores, where they would alternately act subserviently and then violently, depending on whether or not they felt intimidated by the presence of a powerful central government.[10]

Formal, legally sanctioned local government has not been an area of great success for post-independence Africa. There have been many false starts and not many clear successes in establishing formal local institutions that can deliver services, manage conflict, and generate development.[11] Institutional ineffectiveness and corruption, popular apathy, and failure in delivering services and generating development generally constitute the rule rather than the exception. However, at the same time that formal local governments have largely failed, small-scale local *governance* through unofficial and local, often organic institutions, has frequently been quite effective.[12] This chapter argues that these patterns can be explained through Tocqueville's theoretical perspectives on the preconditions of effective local governance and his four-part analytical framework.

Taking Tocqueville to Africa requires much more than seeing how Africa's local governance units do or do not duplicate the legal and institutional patterns typical of New England, the Old Northwest Territories, the South, and the prefects of rural France. The circumstances in Africa are radically different. Tocqueville's analytical framework, nonetheless, helps us to consider and understand how historical experience, mores, physical conditions, and laws and institutions have affected African local government, shaped Africans' survival strategies, and created structures that encouraged or discouraged Africans to act in ways that strengthened or weakened governments and governance.

This chapter has limited goals. It does not offer a comprehensive theory of African local governance, both because of the breadth and variety of sub-Saharan Africa's experiences and conditions, and because of the range of factors that have affected African local governance. It only proposes to explore the utility of Tocqueville's theoretical propositions and analytical framework in explaining general local governance patterns in Africa while providing a brief sketch of specific, recent local governance patterns in three African countries—Uganda, Ghana, and Chad—as a first step toward developing the rudiments of a Tocquevillian model for African local governance.

African Governance: Precolonial Patterns

Precolonial, sub-Saharan Africa contained an immense variety of political forms. These included the acephalous or stateless societies of the Igbo and many pastoral peoples (where there was indeed governance, but no discernible governments); the loose Yoruba confederation; the complex empires of Mali, Ghana, and the Ashanti; the powerful and centralized Hausa emirates; and Shaka's Zulu empire built on conquest. However, there is general consensus that most of these systems were constitutional regimes, based on law, and with power and authority widely distributed. Political leaders were checked, at times by formal processes of impeachment and removal, by secret societies that would assassinate abusive leaders, by strong age-grade systems, by strong legislative bodies, and/or by traditional understandings about the limits of any ruler's power. Individuals had rights, mediated often by kin groups to be sure, but rights nonetheless. Large-scale state structures existed to collect tribute and taxes and left local communities to handle local affairs. In most areas, local governance was quite strong. Localities were virtually autonomous in some regions, and in others worked within confederal or loose federal arrangements. Local publics were generally highly involved in their own governance, through systematic representation on councils, as active participants in community discussions, and as plaintiffs before councils. The African's conception of a spiritual realm, one that was lively and involved in this world, helped sustain a powerful moral ethos to guide and limit their political rulers and publics.[13]

One can only speculate about something that existed in a lost pre-colonial era. Nonetheless, there is substantial agreement among many scholars about precolonial mores, many of which are still present today in Africa. Africans throughout the continent exhibit a strong sense of responsibility—indeed, of obligation—to kin and to kinship structures. There is ample evidence to believe this sense existed long before colonialism, just as it continues today. Since kin groups are frequently the foundations of local representation systems, that strong sense of responsibility and obligation has frequently extended to broader local communities and their governance institutions. Respect for the aged, along with broader traditions of deference to all senior generations, reinforced these attitudes of responsibility and obligation. However, these were hardly the servile mores Tocqueville saw in France. Indeed, nor were they as individualistic as pre-revolutionary French mores seem to have been.[14] Instead, there continued to be strong communal mores of solidarity and reciprocity throughout the colonial, and even postcolonial, era. They were closer to the virile mores of the United States, where there was a general sense that law, obligation and hierarchy, and community responsibility were proper, and a person gained honor by accepting and fulfilling the duties these implied.

Given the above mores, Africans were generally highly engaged in their own governance. Despite the predominance of geroncratic government, women, men in different age-grades, various lineages, and clan groupings *were* generally represented one way or another; local affairs were governed by *law* and *precedent* (albeit often unwritten and therefore carried by oral traditions); and nearly all could aspire to a long life and eventual senior leadership roles—even women in most precolonial African societies.[15]

As a result of these patterns, African communities were characterized by broadly based, active, and usually effective engagement by most members in the core functions of governance: managing conflict and undertaking collective action. Broad participation in communal labor for community projects and the active engagement by local councils in managing conflict and allocating resources followed from these patterns. One could infer from these patterns that Africans' mores, at least regarding local affairs, had much in common with the American virile mores described by Tocqueville.

Since Africa is an enormous land mass with great cultural and institutional diversity, not all of Africa fits all or even most of these patterns. For example, the conquest empire of the Hausa-Fulani and the militaristically-based empire of Shaka and the Zulu provide exceptions to these patterns. Pastoral peoples, particularly areas organized through segmentary opposition, express their mores differently from agricultural peoples. Despite the great diversity of mores, one can identify broad patterns of mores that can be found across most of Africa.

The historical experience of colonialism had a catastrophic impact on Africa, though varying from one colony to another and even from different regions within the same colony. Despite the extraordinary persistence of mores noted by Tocqueville, it is unlikely this experience, and the fifty years of independence since then, left precolonial African mores unchanged. Nonetheless, scholars have demonstrated the ability of humans to engage in situational selection and carry and apply more than one set of attitudes and behavior as appropriate.[16] It is thus not easy to determine the extent to which mores have truly changed in this new context, or have been supplemented by alternative sets to use in different situations. While analyzing mores is difficult, what this chapter can do is explore a model of behaviors—survival strategies—that Africans developed to deal with their changed circumstances and the extent to which alternate sets of mores may have emerged under different circumstances.

In deference to the variability of conditions across the continent, the analysis will describe salient historical events for Africa and consider them as *variables* that affected Africans *more or less in proportion to their strength in any given area*. Similarly, the examination of physical conditions and laws and institutions might also offer some hypotheses as to how these variables might affect governance, *depending again on their strength/weakness in any given area*. This chapter does not presume to elaborate a complete model of this process. Instead, it utilizes the Tocquevillian analytical framework to identify factors that can help explain patterns and variance in African local governance. Every proposition it offers is a "more or less" proposition according to how powerfully the other factors it identifies were present in any given area.

Local Governance in Africa: The Impact of Colonialism and the Independent State

Tocqueville's analytical framework directs our attention to five sets of variables to explain the weakness of contemporary African local governance: historic circumstances; institutions and laws; physical conditions; by implication, the survival strategies that people fashion to deal with these factors; and, finally, the mores that these variables generate and influence.

Historic Circumstances

When one considers Africa's historic circumstances, it is clear that the cataclysmic—indeed catastrophic—event of the latter nineteenth and twentieth centuries for Africa was colonialism. While the impact of colonialism varied greatly, one can nonetheless identify a number of aspects that had great impact on Africans and offer hypotheses as to how they might have affected them. These aspects would include, but are not limited to, the following.

The distortion, corruption, erosion, and/or destruction of most indigenous institutions of local governance. For example, the Belgians were violent and ruthless in their treatment of indigenous institutions in the Congo.[17] They crushed anyone and anything that opposed them. While the British and French were generally less ruthless, their impact on local governance was still powerful. The French destroyed and replaced traditional institutions of governance with administrative frameworks reflecting those in France, while the British undermined and corrupted the integrity of traditional political structures they encountered through "Indirect Rule." British colonial incentive structures encouraged chiefs to tax and rule their subjects in unprecedented and arbitrary ways. As a result, the "indirect" rulers became accountable to the British colonial government, no longer to their subjects. While the particulars vary across Africa, a general consequence of colonialism was the erosion of the accountability of political and administrative institutional arrangements to the populace, which reduced the people's ability to resolve local problems and issues through historic social and political institutions and processes. Africans as a rule were fragmented among many small communities and what local institutions remained were limited in authority, scope, and resource base. In this regard, colonialism weakened or destroyed most larger-scale indigenous and publicly accountable formal institutions of local governance, those beyond villages and kinship structures.

The turbulence of the colonial economy. The introduction and expansion of cash cropping, the hut tax, compulsory labor, wage labor in urban areas, monopolistic commercial systems, and the vagaries and instability of the world-market economy redirected African economic growth and Africans' investments and occupational choices in ways that left most Africans poorer and vulnerable to economic forces well beyond their control. Land expropriation, forced cash cropping, and monopolistic colonial commercial practices pushed them in this direction. Historic economic survival strategies were frequently ineffective in this environment.[18] Under the independent governments, the situation usually did not improve or even grew worse.[19] While there were collective efforts to deal with these vulnerabilities through urban voluntary and ethnic associations, religious bodies and movements, these were for the most part local and small-scale efforts and really only palliatives.[20] Though Africans were subjected to the vagaries of world capitalism, colonial economic policy prevented the capitalist transformation of Africa. Opportunities in urban areas were relatively limited in comparison to the numbers seeking jobs or education, and kin networks and patron-clientage became very important ways to find and distribute what limited opportunities there were.[21]

The lack of accountability or moral limits on the colonial state. The colonial state was accountable to the metropolitan authorities and interests in London, Paris, Brussels, and Lisbon. Moral limits, which Africans generally imposed on traditional authorities by custom, law, segmentary opposition, religious sanction, or through secret societies, could not be imposed on the colonial state.[22] The colonial state crushed their historic governments and institutions, co-opted and corrupted their leaders, conflicted with (and sometimes destroyed) their patterns of governance (in such situations as segmentary opposition or acephalous societies), stole their land, and undermined their systems of status and authority. It behaved in ways that brooked no conventional limits, moral or institutional, to its authority by Africans. Furthermore, the colonial (and later the independent) state was distant from most Africans in ideology, language, space, status, and customs. New interlocutors were essential.

The transition from the colonial to the independent state. These patterns generally continued beyond the end of colonialism. Indeed, as the state grew rapidly in the postindependence era and pursued policies exploitative of agriculture (through both monopolies and monoposonies), colonial-era exploitative economic, social, and political trends continued. Rent-seeking behavior was the dominant form of capital accumulation in many states.[23] At the same time, newly independent leaders recentralized political power that had been dispersed to locally accountable governments. The international, institutional, and legal structure made elites virtually unaccountable to anyone.[24] Neopatrimonial and personalistic approaches to polities and governance have deep roots in many African societies and are at the heart of the "economy of affection" referred to by others. In this sense, precolonial practices and mores reasserted themselves under independent rule and further eroded the potential effectiveness of the independent states as agents of economic development. However, the wealth to be captured through the "swollen African State" led these patterns to reach unprecedented levels.[25] The concept of a neutral civic space where public interests were debated and public law was neutrally implemented was preempted and discredited by these processes.[26]

To summarize the consequences of colonialism and the postcolonial era for Africans, one might emphasize the following:

- Erosion and corruption of historic local political institutions, and of their capacity to resolve local problems, deal with threats to their populations' livelihoods, manage conflicts, take collective action, and exert cultural norms effectively to restrain the powerful;
- Centralization of formal political authority and the development of unconstrained sources of wealth and political power, often exploited by those who did not fit within community norms, nor were restrained by remaining structures of accountability and constraint;
- Development of a dys-synchronization between existing social capital (at the community level) and formal structures of governance (at districts and above) established by the colonial state and continued by the independent state;
- Sustained material poverty caused by the decline in the inclination and ability of the postcolonial state to provide public (collective) goods, the increase in rent-seeking behavior by state officials, and the general decline in economic growth;
- Appearance of institutions and classes with vast power, far beyond that of the vast bulk of Africans, accessible (if at all) through structures of patron-clientage and neopatrimonialism, but not through historic political structures or existing social capital, or moderated by market-driven capitalist economic accumulation strategies;[27]
- Continued or enhanced dependence on kin, extended family, and community ties for social and economic survival, and as media of collective action ("the economy of affection"); and[28]
- Erosion in the integrity and legitimacy of the postcolonial state.

Institutions and Laws

The institutional and legal patterns of most of Africa in the postcolonial era have been dominated by the following well-known and well-documented general patterns:[29]

- Growth of political factionalism, corruption, and erosion of administrative capacity and integrity, as well as erosion of rule of law at all levels of governance;
- Instability in national governance, caused by frequent and extra-legal regime changes, arbitrary and extra-legal rule by single-party and/or long-term dictatorial rule by neopatrimonial figures;
- National tax structures that systematically extract rural and village wealth and redistribute it as rents captured by urban areas and urban classes;
- Centralized and central institutional dominance of formal institutions of local government and their personnel, programs, budgeting and fiscal resources;
- Near complete fiscal dependence of local governments on national government and poverty of local governments;
- Inexperience of elected local government personnel;
- Institutional structures of local government that encourage executive dominance over locally elected legislative institutions;
- Substantial social distance between executive and professional local government personnel and local citizens;
- Scale of local government units that leave existing social capital and social infrastructure incongruent with and unable to engage with or hold formal local governments accountable;
- Pervasive resource shortages for government at all levels including great unreliability of transfers promised by the center to local governments; and
- Severe unpredictability of government resources from one year—and even month—to the next.

In Africa, there is thus a gross disconnect between the formal institutions of local government and the local populations. Formal local government in Africa is generally neither locally responsive nor accountable, which explains why the public invests so little time, energy, or resources in it in return. For the most part, even where some reforms in local government have been made, central governments have left key rules and institutions unchanged and local government continues, as Tocqueville might have expected, at best to limp along.[30]

These problems are compounded by an unfavorable national political context. National political instability and unpredictability in institutions, laws, administrative practices, and rule of law make it very difficult for institutions to begin to develop at local levels. Politics always involves risks, whether it is with time, resources, opportunity costs, or one's economic or physical security. An unstable or unpredictable national political context makes such risks intolerable for most people. Also, opportunities for corruption and abuse of office act as a political "Gresham's Law" that drive honest people from public life and empowers those who lack ethics and who are ruthless. Weak institutions and hierarchical accountability encourage opportunistic and corrupt behavior, which further degrades formal local government. "Principal-agent" and "moral hazard" issues abound.

Local governments in contemporary Africa resemble Tocqueville's description of local government in France. African local governments have little to no autonomy, little power, and do *not* belong to local populations. They are established in a top-down manner, their officials are accountable upwardly, usually regard local communities as under their tutelage, and treat the largely illiterate and poor populations in their district with disdain. They are weak institutions with little participation by local citizens in their management. They cost a great deal, provide few local public goods, and stimulate local factionalism and corruption over what benefits they do offer (generally as private goods).[31] Time invested in them is wasted, except for an influential few who can extract resources for themselves. A national tax structure extracts the people's resources and starves local government revenues because so little is redistributed. Needless to say, these conditions do little to enhance confidence in formal local governments.

Three major differences do distinguish local government in Africa from local government in Tocqueville's France. First of all, the state in France was much stronger, endowed with greater resources, and had the capacity to deliver public goods and services in an efficient manner. Second, the level of competency and authority of officials appointed by the French state was higher. Third, given the tight control exercised by the French state at the local level, there were few opportunities for organic communities in France (e.g., at the village level) to escape the grip of the state and develop effective self-governing institutions. The importance of these differences can be seen in the last section of this chapter.

Physical Conditions

Africa's ongoing physical and general contextual conditions reinforce weak local governments and popular disinvestment in them.[32] These include:

- severe poverty, particularly in rural, village, and smaller urban areas, and in most metropolitan neighborhoods;
- poor infrastructure, such as roads and communication networks;
- a challenging physical environment, particularly for agriculture and animal husbandry;
- general economic turbulence and decline since the 1970s; and
- continuing flow of the educated and skilled from rural and small urban areas into a few of the largest cities where there are rents and other opportunities.

These factors also work together to weaken the capacity and likelihood of popular involvement in local government. The general economic turbulence and decline, the outflow of the educated and skilled, and the challenging physical environment put great strain on what formal local government programs and projects do exist. There is little redundancy. Shortfalls in personnel, vehicles, or supplies cause rapid degradation in programs in this demanding environment. Poor communications, poor roads, endemic health problems, poor health facilities, few vendors to replace supplies, demands on personnel from poor relatives, all degrade local public programs and institutions. Resources are exhausted or diverted to meet these demands.

Overall, these factors (historic circumstances, laws, physical conditions) combine to create situations where the populace generally expects and gets very little from formal local governments. Indeed, they expect little from *any* level of formal government. Their survival depends on themselves, their families and kin, remnants of historic political institutions and processes, and the social capital that exists among small communities.[33] Public/collective goods are severely underproduced in this context, and whatever is provided and whatever social order there exists, is sustained through organic, micro, social institutions that remain independent of the state except for the state's role in providing basic order. Liberia, Sierra Leone, Somalia, Ethiopia, Nigeria, Rwanda, Congo, Zimbabwe, and the Ivory Coast are examples where the state has failed in this function, and disorder has broken out. Such disorder overcame the capacity of micro-institutions to sustain social and political peace.[34]

In general, local governments in Africa have failed miserably in the core functions of government: to provide collective goods and to manage conflict and maintain order. This reinforces local attitudes of distrust of and disengagement from local governments. Tocqueville would hardly have been surprised.

Survival Strategies

One might hypothesize that such circumstances would generate "survival strategies" quite different from those that worked in Africa's precolonial era or those that Tocqueville felt led to effective local government in the United States. Migdal supports this contention in discussing Sierra Leone in *Strong Societies and Weak States*.

In general, one might expect to see strategies such as these:

- Avoid the colonial and postcolonial states, unless one can capture or manipulate opportunities in them, usually through patron-client or kin ties.
- Withdraw from involvement in and interaction with colonially compromised historic political institutions and authorities unless one can capture rents and manipulate opportunities in them, usually through patron-client or kin ties.[35]
- Do not waste time or resources trying to organize collective action, deliver public goods, or manage local conflict through local governments.
- Emphasize micro social organizations and sustain social capital through informal structures and networks such as kinship, ethnicity, informal political structures, and new sorts of local associations.
- Increase economic and political individualism, though within— and in tension with—old and new micro and affective social organizations.
- Increase commitment to organizations (religious, voluntary, ethnic, labor, political) that were not destroyed or corrupted by the colonial state, and that address broadly shared concerns.
- Seek suprarational solutions to cataclysmic changes in the world that defy all known rational processes.[36]

In other words, most Africans turn inward and downward to survive, or create new, affective, informal social structures, but they all avoid the state.

Mores

Tocqueville's understanding of mores is that they are the "habits of the heart," which human beings gradually adopt and internalize in their attempts to flourish—or at least survive—in a given context. This chapter has proposed an intermediary concept—"survival strategies"—that reflects the behavioral dimension of mores as they encounter a dynamic and changing world. While mores are stubborn, their expression in daily life is always mediated by the need to find behaviors that offer the likelihood of survival. However, those behaviors must be expected someday to begin to affect those mores. Using this conceptualization, one would hypothesize that over time the colonial and ongoing postcolonial experiences in some measure altered mores regarding local government, as most Africans sought personal and social survival under unprecedented circumstances of rapid social, economic, and political turbulence and disempowerment. As new behaviors provided greater chance of survival, mores may gradually have followed. Given the previous discussion, one might hypothesize the following patterns of mores would emerge among those Africans most affected by these processes:

- Do not invest yourself or your trust in any formal political institutions or authorities beyond the kin group, village, or urban neighborhood.
- Do not expect moral behavior from the colonial or postcolonial state or any of its agents.[37]
- Take any advantage you can of the colonial and postcolonial state and its agencies since they do not embody any moral principles in their operations.
- Emphasize communal ties and reciprocity along with individual initiative, seek patrons ("big men"), and sustain micro social organizations in economic survival strategies.
- Continue to trust and invest in historic social infrastructure (e.g., kinship networks, neighborhood political infrastructure, voluntary and religious associations) that was not destroyed by the colonial state, and create new, organic infrastructure where you are able.
- Do not undertake collective enterprises beyond organic communities such as village and/or kin-mediated levels because weak larger-scale political institutions (like formal local governments and courts) mean that financial malfeasance, free-riding, and shirking cannot easily be controlled.

Implications of Africans' Mores for Local Governance

This tentative picture of Africans' postcolonial, emergent politically relevant mores suggests the following implications for governance:

- Africans will have great distrust for and a reluctance to invest in formal political structures (those created by and inherited from the colonial state).
- Africans will be prone to see such structures as legitimate targets to pursue for individual or group benefits, legal or otherwise.
- Africans will look skeptically upon collective enterprises beyond very small, localized, and affectively based groups and be suspicious of those proposed by formal institutions of governance, donors, and NGOs.
- Africans will pursue individualistic political and economic strategies, but will respect and support kin, local, communal, and associational social infrastructure as well, so long as they are useful.
- Africans will seek patronage, big-men, and luck as economic survival strategies beyond local social networks rather than invest in or develop long-term, institutional, and market-oriented enterprises since the economy is turbulent and since political institutions seem arbitrary, erratic, and beyond rational control.

These implications are not generally encouraging for effective local government along the lines drawn by Tocqueville. To the extent that they apply in a given area, formal political institutions are not trusted. Corruption of the state and the formal political processes is expected. Sinecures in the state and prebends are preferred over market-related investments. Long-term planning and occupationally focused work in the market are not seen as particularly likely paths to success while patrons, big-men, luck, kin, and affective networks are. At best, only local and limited social and political institutions are trusted, and therefore only small-scale collective action occurs. In general, formal political institutions at all levels dare not attempt to extract direct taxes from the populace because they would not be paid voluntarily, and if pressed there would be violent, public reactions.[38] As a result, formal local governments tend to be poor and weak. Furthermore, Africans remain uncaptured economically by the state and do not see the state as a tool to improve their lives. Finally, attempts at larger-scale community betterment are discouraged by the weakness of encompassing and integrating local political institutions, by passivity that looks to the central state to provide development and improvements, and by the pervasive belief that local communities are buffeted by powerful forces well beyond their ability to control.

To sum up, Africans living under these circumstances will not expect much of formal institutions of local governance, and indeed will often act in ways to evade and, in effect, erode them. Smaller-scale organic structures of governance are important to them, but those lack the resources and reach to accomplish substantial and long-term tasks. Larger-scale, official, and socially inorganic structures are not regarded as trustworthy nor as belonging to them, and as such are unlikely to accomplish anything of much value to them. Africans see them at best as possible common-pool resources, and take as much as they can from them before others draw them down first.[39] Most formal decentralization efforts, typically led by African governments and with international donor support, will not change these attitudes. Economic progress has been illusory for so long that even though local mores may include expectations of reciprocity among members of relatively small communities, they do not look beyond those small communities except with skepticism. Their attitude toward the national government continues to be negative and distrustful, though they will exploit it for resources beneficial to them or their localities anytime they are able. As a result, throughout most of Africa, formal local governments are weak or moribund. An unfortunate historical experience has been reinforced by national laws, institutions, and local physical conditions to lead to survival strategies and mores that are not supportive of local governments. These mores, consistent with Tocquevillian theory, in turn make viable local governments beyond the informal sector even less likely to develop. Is there any escape?

Alternate Patterns in African Local Governance: Three Cases since 1980

Events, reform efforts, and a few situations over the last two decades have suggested that alternate patterns of local governance are possible in sub-Saharan Africa. This section will briefly discuss such patterns in Chad, Uganda, and Ghana.

Chad

In rural Chad, local, nonformal institutions have become quite success-ful in establishing, funding, and managing local schools.[40] Communities raised general taxes, collected fees from students and their families, hired and supervised teachers, built and maintained school buildings, obtained supplies, and even networked with neighboring communities to share insights, pool scarce resources, and solve problems. These activities were carried out by local councils composed of traditional notables and other leaders of the local communities. These activities occurred across much of rural and village Chad, including many of its poorest areas.

These developments happened during and after Chad's civil war, when the central government had largely collapsed and lost all ability to admin-ister Chad beyond the capital and a few nearby areas. With all pretense of a national, educational administration gone, with no central adminis-trative or centrally directed local government scheme to prevent, co-opt, corrupt, or otherwise distort local initiatives, a clear locally felt need for education stimulated these efforts. Deep local poverty was clearly not an insurmountable obstacle to this, and efforts by relatively small localities using essentially historic political institutions and processes were more than successful in fulfilling a key local governance function—providing and managing education as a public/collective good for their communities, which was facilitated by a broad stock of social capital.

The key factors in Chad's local governance success seem to be the with-drawal of all central government activity from outside the capital; relative peace once the civil war had moved on from these areas; existing, his-toric political institutions and social capital at the community level; and a strongly felt need for a service—that is, education—that was best pro-vided collectively. This suggests that in the absence of national tutelage and enforced state monopolies in education and local governance, either rap-idly emerging new mores or a resurgence of precolonial mores and historic political and social institutions can give renewed birth to effective local and even regional governance. This reoccupied space was hitherto monopo-lized by state-sanctioned, formal governments. These patterns correspond to Tocqueville's conception of organic communities before the emergence of the centralized state. The ties that these small-scale communities volun-tarily developed with other communities to more effectively provide educa-tion suggest that small, organic units such as these can combine and provide goods requiring larger scales of production if they are allowed to negotiate freely with one another on the basis of shared values and self-interests.

Uganda

Wunsch and Ottemoeller found both encouraging and discouraging patterns in the multitier system of local governance established in the last two decades in Uganda.[41] While there are nominally five tiers of local governance, only three are really active: the village (tier one), the subcounty (tier three), and the district (tier five). The varying successes of the three tiers seem to follow predictably from various institutional and contextual differences among them.

The most apparently impressive tier to the casual observer is the fifth: the district level. At that level, there are buildings in reasonable repair, vehicles that work, and workers who show up at regular hours and seem busy at their assigned tasks. There is an able senior administrative staff, a knowledgeable planning department, apparently competent financial records, an elected and a seemingly effective district executive, and an elected legislative council that meets regularly, if infrequently. There is a planning and budgeting process, the legislative council meets and reviews plans and budget proposals and makes decisions, and there are actually minutes and records of these processes! If funding is not generous, there are nonetheless regular appropriations and distributions from the central government and the rudiments of a local tax system are in place. A local governance system appears to be alive, even at times energized, at the district level.

However, it is not clear that this local government really belongs to or is useful to local residents. Upon closer inspection, the evidence suggests that legislative councils have little to no effective input into the planning or budgeting process, and otherwise have no meaningful role in district governance. District plans are not locally driven, but are essentially the collation of sector ministry plans established in Kampala, the capital. The local executive is by far the most powerful local political actor, and there is no visible and effective public or civil society involvement in local governance. With the exception of a few notables, the public seems disengaged from governance at this level. Considering all these factors, this tier of governance seems to correspond to Tocqueville's French prefectures that were dominated by the state-appointed intendants/préfets.

The village level (tier one), on the other hand, was impressive in other ways. While villages lacked any permanent administrative presence, they were responsible at that level for dispute settlement and establishing and maintaining law and order. Villagers were enthusiastic about their local chiefs, whom they elected through universal suffrage at the village level, and their effectiveness in discharging these responsibilities.

They repeatedly reported that these leaders were a vast improvement over the corrupt and divisive chiefs selected by and accountable to the central government. Villages also were well involved in the grass-roots planning process, which begins at the village level. This level of government does seem to belong and is useful to its residents. These appear to be organic communities, but ones modernized through universal elections as a way to choose village leaders rather than inherited or externally appointed chiefs.

The weakest tier is the subcounty, or tier three. While this level does have a budget (from taxes collected locally) and several low-level, poorly trained professional personnel, the budget is very small, the trained personnel are few and without operational funds, and no cohesive or effective publics are organized to supervise this level of government. Furthermore, there is substantial social distance between tier-three administrative personnel and local dwellers (and even more, of course, between tier five and local people). Indeed, the entire tier-three budget is consumed by personnel expenses. The political leadership at this level seems moribund, and the administrative staff is discouraged and passive to the point of uselessness. Plans from the villages come to this level to die, and there are weak (to no) linkages between this level and level five, the district. It seems no more engaged with local residents than is the district level. It is in the worst of both worlds: the Ugandan state is not present in the way that it is to strengthen tier five, but it is too far removed from the villages to act as an organic community.

Thus, in a very interesting way, Uganda's local governance seems currently to demonstrate three different patterns. At the district level, a substantial and relatively stable flow of resources, along with a genuine deconcentration of trained administrative personnel, has added new vitality to local administration. Relative national political stability and consistency have encouraged political leaders, such as the district executives, to emerge and to begin developing coalitions among other local elites and civil servants, as well as administrative and political leaders in Kampala. However, the reality is that Kampala, either through the president's office, the ministry of finance, the donors or the sector ministries, essentially still controls this level of local government. This is facilitated by the weakness and limited role of the legislative councils and the distance between the public's existing social capital and political infrastructure and the district government. All this means that what Uganda has at the districts is really top-down control (tutelage), not *local* government. In that respect, there is nothing there that should change the average Ugandan's historic strategies for dealing with formal local government or mores regarding it. Nor is there evidence that it has. Much like the French prefecture of Tocqueville's time, while the district-level government seems largely competent, it is dominated by centralist, bureaucratic elites. Thus, the average Ugandan will ignore it.

The subcounty (tier three) is the weakest unit of local government. Too large to be congruent with existent structures of social capital; too formal to build on existing political infrastructure; too poor, costly, and ineffective to offer any useful services, it hangs suspended between the district and the village. It is poorly staffed, poorly organized, and poorly run. It is socially distant from the public, not responsive to it, and overall only reinforces public mores of distrust and disengagement from local government, all the more because it levies and collects taxes, from which the people see no benefit. It, too, diverges greatly from Tocqueville's model of effective local governance. Not only is it socially disconnected, it is incompetent.

The village level, utterly without professional staff, with no budget, and with only limited powers, seems to be the *most* effective level of local governance and government in Uganda. At this level, there is great public confidence in the village leadership's ability to resolve local disputes and problems, provide local security, and act with authority. Villages have organized to protect themselves from robbers and from errant military and police officials who formerly preyed upon them. Opinion surveys of villages showed great confidence in this tier of governance. This tier, of course, closely corresponds to remaining historic political institutions as well as to local communities and networks, ones likely to possess social capital. Governance at the village level belongs to local dwellers, and poor though it is, it is *theirs*. It is an organic community, along the lines discussed by Tocqueville as typical of the medieval, post–Roman Empire-era of Europe. Its greatest virtue, villagers report, is that it replaced the hitherto centrally appointed locality chiefs who were frequently corrupt, abusive, and ineffective.

Mores are likely affected in varying ways by these three levels of government. Levels three and five probably reinforce mores of distrust and disengagement. But level one, as currently fashioned, tends to encourage the opposite patterns among the populace, at least as they relate to that level of governance. Whether these are newly emergent mores, or a resurgent expression of socially embedded mores transmitted intergenerationally from precolonial times, is unclear. What happened at this level is, nonetheless, encouraging as well as consistent with Tocqueville's theory of local government.

Ghana

Ghana demonstrates a mixed picture, where some promising reforms of the early 1990s encountered problems a few years later.[42] The reforms initially appeared to establish local government units accountable to local legislative councils, civil servants accountable to local executives, and national fiscal transfers to fund all this. However, limited implementation of the reforms meant they did not bring about long-term change in local conditions, actions, or attitudes. Early enthusiasm was reflected in the large number of candidates standing for the elected legislative councils, high expectations among the populace that district governments could improve local conditions, and by remarkably high voter turnouts for elections. However, only a few years later, public confidence had plunged, incumbents were choosing not to stand for reelection, and electoral turnout dropped substantially.

The decline in public confidence had much to do with patterns of tutelage and bureaucratic domination consistent with Tocqueville's theory. Monies transferred from Accra rarely covered even the overhead costs of the newly established district governments; central government sector ministries did not relinquish control of sector specialists employed at district governments; and the structure of legislative council-executive relations was such that the executive (a person appointed by the central government) completely dominated budgetary, planning, and personnel issues. Taxes were assessed and raised locally, but most funds were consumed by salaries, vehicles, housing costs for professional personnel, and so forth, leaving very little for local capital projects or to fund local programs.

What few resources there were available for local projects stimulated strong—sometimes intense—competition among villages and other small communities to get their share. These, much closer to Tocqueville's organic communities than the districts, were mobilized by this structure to compete for resources, *not* (as in Chad) to work among themselves and with other communities to *produce* resources. The difference is striking.

In Ghana, then, local governments did not appear to be useful to local dwellers, were not independent of the control of others (the locally posted civil servants and national sector ministerial officers ran it), nor belonged to the local populace. Accordingly, they ceased investing in it. If new hopes had arisen with the decentralization reforms, subsequent events appeared to reinforce mores of distrust and disengagement toward local government. A few years later, prospects for a vibrant local government did not look much better.

Conclusion

This chapter has suggested that the four-part Tocquevillian analytical frameworks, as well as his core theoretical understanding about the nature of effective local governance, are useful in analyzing and explaining Africa's experience with local government in the postcolonial era. It has argued that Africa's most significant historic experiences of the nineteenth and twentieth centuries were with colonialism and the postcolonial state. It suggested that these factors, for the most part, would lead Africans to develop survival strategies unlikely to encourage flourishing, formal local governments. These in turn, over time, would encourage mores of distrust and disengagement from state-defined and formal local governments. However, it also noted that Africa's weak ("soft") states could accommodate local governance in organic communities, which France's strong state and often effective local administration prevented.

Finally, the chapter briefly explored cases in three countries where contextual conditions and/or institutions and laws appeared to have changed in the 1980–2000 era, to see if Tocquevillian understandings of local government would point to behavioral changes among Africans that would encourage effective local governance. In each case, such changes did alter popular actions, though the extent to which fundamental mores might also have changed (or precolonial, socially embedded mores, reemerged) will take more time to determine. In the case of Chad, where the greatest contextual and institutional/legal change occurred, the most dramatic and sustained changes in local governance followed. In many ways, the breakdown of order in Chad parallels the breakdown of order after the collapse of the Roman Empire, and the emergence of local governance in Chad parallels the emergence of organic, local self-governing communities during the European medieval era. As personal survival strategies altered with these changes, the vitality and effectiveness of local governance also changed. The scale and stability of these changes suggests that either precolonial, socially embedded mores reasserted themselves, or that local mores changed rapidly with these contextual changes. These patterns are fully consistent with Tocquevillian theory about local government, particularly his emphasis on the socially organic basis of effective local governance.

In Uganda, where genuine institutional changes occurred at the village level, substantial behavioral change also occurred. However, at the higher subcounty and district levels, the behavioral change was much less. There, the distance from local social capital and historic political infrastructure, the lack of institutional capacity at the subcounty level, the continued dominance of the districts by Kampala ministries, and the strong but not locally accountable district executive, seem to have led to few changes in institutional or public behavior. Recent studies indicate great popular distrust of the district level of local governance and little public organization at or engagement with the district or subcounty levels. Finally, in Ghana during the early years of its apparent reforms, behavioral changes were substantial. But, as the reforms were found by the public to be more appearance than substance, behaviors and attitudes quickly reverted to preform patterns. These patterns are consistent with Tocqueville's theory, particularly in contrasting public investment in governance at the organic level and its absence at the state-dominated, inorganic, district level.

Tocqueville's theory of local government and his analytical framework are useful and effective tools to analyze contemporary African local governance. As Tocqueville argued, mores develop from a people's historic experiences. Contemporary physical and institutional/legal conditions affect behaviors and thereby governance and can sometimes modify or reinvigorate historical mores. In some situations, they may stimulate people to develop new mores. It is not clear from the three cases considered briefly in this chapter whether behavioral changes there reflect rapidly emergent new mores, or the reappearance of socially embedded, precolonial mores, perhaps transmitted intergenerationally, or the simultaneous existence of both. What does seem to be clear is that individual behaviors were quite responsive to changes in context, and local governance patterns did change. In some cases (Ghana; Uganda's third and fifth tiers), they rapidly reverted to previous forms when changes in institutions or context were limited in scale or duration. In other cases, they have persisted (Chad; Uganda's village level). Thus, attempts to develop strong local governance in Africa must look carefully at laws and institutions as well as at the physical and other contexts. Incomplete or poorly considered reforms will likely only reinforce existing survival strategies and render democratic and effective local governance units a more distant goal. To encourage real, broadly based, and effective local governance, African governments must work to encourage survival strategies that stimulate mores of confidence and engagement in local governance. This would include reforms in laws and institutions as well as strengthening supportive physical conditions. Whenever possible, building local governance institutions that are not dominated by the state, but rest on the bonds of trust and reciprocity that may still exist at truly local—organic—communities, would seem to be an important foundation to rebuild local government in Africa. Reformers must be sure that these changes encourage Africans to behave in ways that contradict the mores of distrust with and disengagement from local government—and indeed the contemporary state—that are now several generations old. Tocqueville would, of course, suggest such new mores would support democracy and the rule of law throughout the state. He would also urge patience and persistence.

Notes

1. See Theda Skocpol, *States and Social Revolutions* (Cambridge, MA: Cambridge University Press, 1979); Charles Tilly, *Big Structures, Large Processes, Huge Comparisons* (New York: Russell Sage Foundation, 1984). Such an approach looks at recurring patterns of human interaction as produced by a large variety of factors that are unique to each case. However, once a case is considered in detail, factors that may appear quite different in different contexts can be seen to have important similar traits. Therefore, while each case is unique at one stage of analysis, general patterns may exist that explain similarities. The approach cannot easily be broken down into abstract variables, as these are rarely contextually sensitive enough to discern these patterns.

2. Alexis de Tocqueville, *Democracy in America* (Garden City, NY: Doubleday and Company, 1966).

3. Joel Migdal, *Strong Societies and Weak States: State-Society Relations and State Capabilities in the Third World* (Princeton, NJ: Princeton University Press, 1988). Migdal argues that under circumstances of rapid and substantial change, human beings will seek and adopt behaviors and life strategies that facilitate their personal survival. Dramatic and apparently permanent social transformation may eventually result from these strategies. Tocqueville is very clear that mores are the most important influence on social patterns such as governance and more powerful than laws and institutions or physical conditions. And yet, mores do change, even if gradually, as these other factors change. Otherwise, all humans would continue to maintain the same mores, which is clearly not the case. If indeed mores are not volatile, as Tocqueville argues, but human beings do adapt to changes in their legal, institutional, and physical environments, there seems to be implied transitional behavioral change. It also seems reasonable to hypothesize that mores gradually change as altered behaviors prove more or less successful in those changed contexts. Migdal's concept of "survival strategies" seems to reflect this idea and fill a logical gap in Tocqueville's theory. How *do* mores change? Do they change gradually, and are there stages when people hold multiple sets of mores, to be applied according to situation? Also, might one expect people closer to the margin of survival to change their behaviors and mores more rapidly if environmental factors change than people who are in more robust political and economic contexts?

4. Tocqueville, *Democracy in America*, 19–20.

5. Tocqueville, *Democracy in America*, 87–98.

6. Tocqueville, *Democracy in America*, 50–66, 277–86.

7. Tocqueville, *Democracy in America*, 301–11.

8. Tocqueville, *Democracy in America*, 277–94.

9. Alexis de Tocqueville, *The Old Regime and the Revolution* (Garden City, NY: Doubleday, 1955).

10. Tocqueville, *Democracy in America*, 311–15; and *Old Regime*, 61–81.

11. For a detailed analysis of this issue, see Dele Olowu and James S. Wunsch, *Local Governance in Africa: The Challenges of Democratic Decentralization* (Boulder, CO: Lynne Rienner, 2004).

12. There is a large and rich literature on this topic. A few of the most useful sources include: Kenneth Little, "The Role of Voluntary Associations in West African Urbanizations," *American Anthropologist* 59 (1959): 579–96; Michael Banton, *West African City: A Study of Tribal Life in Freetown* (Oxford: Oxford University Press, 1958); Abner C. Cohen, *Custom and Politics in Urban Africa: A Study of Hausa Migrants in Yoruba Towns* (Berkeley: University of California Press, 1969); Audrey C. Smock, *Ibo Politics: The Role of Ethnic Unions in Eastern Nigeria* (Cambridge, MA: Harvard University Press, 1971); and Stephen Bunker, *Peasants against the State: The Politics of Market Control in Bugisa, Uganda, 1900–1983* (Chicago: University of Illinois Press, 1987).

13. Peter Geschiere, *The Modernity of Witchcraft: Politics and the Occult in Postcolonial Africa* (Charlottesville: University of Virginia Press, 1997).

14. See Tocqueville, *Old Regime*; Skocpol, *States and Social Revolutions*.

15. Catherine Coquery-Vidrovitch, *African Women: A Modern History* (Boulder, CO: Westview Press, 1997).

16. For example, see Clyde J. Mitchell, *Tribalism and the Plural Society* (London: Oxford University Press, 1960); Smock, *Ibo Politics*.

17. Crawford Young, *The African Colonial State in Comparative Perspective* (New Haven, CT: Yale University Press, 1994).

18. Sara Berry, *No Condition is Permanent: The Social Dynamics of Agrarian Change in Sub-Saharan Africa* (Madison: University of Wisconsin Press, 1993).

19. Robert Bates, *Markets and States in Tropical Africa: The Political Basis of Agricultural Policies* (Berkeley: University of California Press, 1981).

20. Little, "Role of Voluntary Associations"; Thomas Hodgkin, *Nationalism in Colonial Africa* (New York: New York University Press, 1957), 84–92.

21. Goran Hyden, *African Politics in Comparative Perspective* (New York: Cambridge University Press, 2006).

22. Peter Ekeh, "Colonialism and the Two Publics in Africa: A Theoretical Statement," *Comparative Studies in History and Society* 19, no. 1 (1975): 91–112.

23. Larry Diamond, "Class Formation in the Swollen African State," *Journal of Modern African Studies* 25, no. 4 (1987): 567–96.

24. Robert Jackson and Carl Rosberg, "Sovereignty and Underdevelopment: Juridical Statehood in the African Crisis," *Journal of Modern African Studies* 24, no. 1 (1986): 1–33; Jeffrey Herbst, *States and Power in Africa: Comparative Lessons in Authority and Control* (Princeton, NJ: Princeton University Press, 2000).

25. Diamond, "Class Formation."

26. Hyden, *African Politics.*

27. Jean-François Bayart, *The State in Africa: The Politics of the Belly* (New York: Longman, 1993); Mahmood Mamdani, *Citizen and Subject: Contemporary Africa and the Legacy of Late Colonialism* (Princeton, NJ: Princeton University Press, 1996).

28. Goran Hyden, *Beyond Ujamaa in Tanzania: Underdevelopment and an Uncaptured Peasantry* (Berkeley: University of California Press, 1980); Berry, *No Condition is Permanent.*

29. For a good recent overview of this subject see Hyden, *African Politics.*

30. Olowu and Wunsch, *Local Governance in Africa.*

31. Richard Crook and James Manor, *Democracy and Decentralization in South Asia and West Africa: Participation, Accountability and Performance* (Cambridge: Cambridge University Press, 1998).

32. In this chapter, this concept is broadened to include the general economic context Africans face as well as Tocqueville's more strictly physical and environmental factors.

33. Hyden, *African Politics*; Bunker, *Peasants against the State*; and Berry, *No Condition is Permanent.*

34. Amos Sawyer, "Violent Conflicts and Governance Challenges in West Africa: The Case of the Mano River Basin Area," *Journal of Modern African Studies* 42, no. 3 (2004): 437–63.

35. Ekeh, "Colonialism and the Two Publics."

36. For example, see Peter Geschiere and Cyprian Fisiy, "Domesticating Personal Violence: Witchcraft, Courts and Confessions in Cameroon," *Africa: Journal of the International African Institute* 64, no. 3 (1994): 323–41.

37. Ekeh, "Colonialism and the Two Publics"; Bayart, *State in Africa.*

38. For more details on this phenomenon, see I. Livingstone and R. Charlton, "Financing Decentralized Development in a Low-Income Country: Raising Revenue for Local Government in Uganda," *Development and Change* 31, no. 1 (2001): 77–100.

39. Ekeh, "Colonialism and the Two Publics."

40. For Chad's decentralization efforts, see Simon M. Fass and Gerritt M. Desloovere, "Chad: Governance by the Grassroots," in Olowu and Wunsch, *Local Governance in Africa*, 155–80.

41. For more details on Uganda's decentralization experience, see Wunsch and Ottemoeller, "Uganda: Multiple Levels of Local Governance," in Olowu and Wunsch, *Local Governance in Africa*, 181–209.

42. For more on Ghana's decentralization experiences, see Crook and Manor, *Democracy and Decentralization*; Joseph Ayee, "Ghana: A Top-Down Initiative," in Olowu and Wunsch, *Local Governance in Africa*, 125–54.

11

Roots of Democracy in Burma

Tun Myint

When Tocqueville came to America in the 1830s, he was greatly impressed by the general equality of conditions he found there and its influence on society. In his introduction to *Democracy in America,* Tocqueville wrote, "Among the novel objects that attracted my attention during my stay in the United States, nothing struck me more forcefully than the general equality of conditions."[1] Tocqueville further asserted that "the more I advanced in the study of American society, the more I perceived that the equality of conditions is a fundamental fact from which all others seem to be derived, and the central point at which all my observations constantly terminated."[2] Tocqueville considered the general equality of condition as the root of democracy in America.

When I first read Tocqueville's *Democracy in America*, it was quite difficult for me to accept his premise concerning the general equality of conditions in America after having been exposed to American history and learning about racism, the treatment of Native Americans, and the continuous struggles for women's and civil rights. My reaction to Tocqueville then was that there was no "general equality of conditions" in America when he visited the country. How could he identify equality of conditions as the key to understanding the essence of American democracy?

After reading through *Democracy in America* more carefully, I began to appreciate that Tocqueville's observations concerning the "general equality of conditions" in America led him to delve beyond the shallow layer of power politics and to reveal that the associational life of the people enabled by the general equality of conditions constituted the foundation of politics in America. He was describing a general equality of conditions based on people's spiritual, behavioral, and associational relationships to each other rather than power politics and wrote: "I confess that in America I saw more than America; I sought the image of democracy itself, with its inclination, its character, its prejudices, and its passions, in order to learn what we have to fear or to hope from its progress."[3] Tocqueville's work on democracy in America provides an analytical framework that can be applied to observe any society on this planet. To some extent, the continuous struggles of human societies for human rights, democracy, and open societies around the world reflect the tensions and conflicts between equality and power politics. For some political scientists and observers, politics revolves around power politics conducted by elites. Tocqueville looked at politics from the perspective of the associational life of the people.

Having observed Burmese politics, society, and the ongoing struggle for democracy, I assert in this essay that the general equality of conditions must either be altered or suppressed by creating or capturing governmental institutions embodied in the state in order for power politics and elite rule to prevail.

Much of the political science literature on Burmese political development has mainly focused on the state, elitist politicians, and efforts to build a strong nation-state in Burma based on the Westphalian model.[4] The analysis underscores the continuous failure of efforts to build a strong and viable state in Burma. The people's uprising of 1988 in Burma, better known as the 8.8.88 people's movement, is widely understood as a democracy movement, that is, a movement calling for the establishment of a multi-party democracy. However, taking the analytical lens of Tocqueville and on closer examination of the political, social, religious, linguistic, and cultural factors leading toward the 8.8.88 people's uprising, it has to be understood that this uprising was part of a long struggle to reconstitute the general equality of conditions in all aspects, including equality among different ethnic groups, relevant to Burmese society.

The literature on Burmese politics contains little analytical discourse concerning the extent to which the continual domination of power politics consumed by elites contradicts social, religious, linguistic, ethnic, and cultural conditions of Burmese society. There is a serious need to question intellectually whether the contradiction between power politics, which minimizes general equality of conditions, and people's politics, which enhances general equality of conditions, is a necessary condition for the survival of the Burmese military regime and the continuation of elitist power politics. The military dictators' brutal suppression on the 8.8.88 people's movement, their refusal to accept the results of the 1990 democratic election, their brutal crackdown on the protests of Buddhist monks in 2007, and ongoing struggles of ethnic minorities to gain greater self-determination highlight the differences between the people's politics based on equality norms and those of the military regime based on forceful domination. Can the elitist power politics be guided by the general equality of conditions fostered by Buddhist philosophy and norms in Burma and not the other way around? This normative question is the central question that scholars and Burmese political practitioners must consider if Burma is to overcome the legacy of authoritarian regimes and elitist power politics. To put it in the context of this essay, for Tocquevillian democracy to reach the shores of Burma requires addressing and resolving this question if Burma's political system is to evolve toward greater self-government and democracy.

The prevailing view of Asian societies is that individuals are normally confined to different social hierarchies and classes at birth; few examples of classless societies exist in Asia.[5] This view is held widely not only among the majority of observers from outside Asia but also reflected among the majority of scholars and politicians in Asia.[6] This view perceives that the general equality of conditions does not exist in Asia because a person's social and political status is determined at birth. A deeper and closer observation of Burmese society challenges the validity of this sweeping generalization. If Tocqueville were to observe Burma at the time he visited America, he would have found two fundamental institutions of Burmese society: (1) the state under the king and (2) the people's institutions imbued with Buddhist teaching and cultural traditions largely detached from the king and his state. Sometimes, these institutions coexisted peacefully along parallel lines; at other times, they clashed violently. The longest-surviving kings and governments in Burma mastered maintaining a balance between the logic of the state and the logic of the people. Tocqueville would have observed that Burmese society had social elements that tended to promote the general equality of conditions in the realm, while the king and his state tended to limit the movement toward equality in order to ensure his power over the people through the state.

In this essay, I will apply Tocqueville's analytical lens to examine the state of general equality of conditions in Burmese society. In so doing, I will focus on (1) Burmese beliefs and behaviors in relation to orders of life and human associations imbued with Buddhist teachings, (2) the structure of language as a reflection of political socialization toward equality, and (3) the social foundations of the concept of government and legal institutions. This essay will be guided by three questions: (1) How is Tocqueville relevant to analysis of the Burmese struggle for the general equality of conditions?, (2) What are the elements of social conditions and Burmese behaviors that define "equality of conditions" in Tocquevillian terms?, and (3) How does this equality of conditions explain ongoing power politics and persistent failures in state building in Burma?

Taking the 8.8.88 people's uprising as a historic and symbolic declaration of Burmese people against the Westphalian state and power politics that have little concern for improving the well-being of the people and the development of Burmese civilization, I will explain how the tide of democracy as understood by Tocqueville could eventually reach the shores of Burmese civilization again, and how it might revitalize elements of the general equality of conditions in Burmese society.

Foundations of General Equality

What Tocqueville called "the general equality of conditions" has to be understood as the equality that existed a priori in human associational societies. This inherent equality is above all the other forms of equality such as ethnic, economic, social, and political equality. All other equalities have to derive from the maximization processes of the "general equality of conditions" of a society. Tocqueville carefully articulated his intention of what he meant by the "general equality of conditions" when he stated that "the equality of conditions is a fundamental fact from which all others seem to be derived, and the central point at which all my observations constantly terminated."[7] If individuals in a society respect and treat individuals as equal human beings regardless of their identity based on citizenship, race, gender, economic status, religion, beliefs, and cultures, such a society respects the equality of conditions. This Tocquevillian analytical view of the general equality of conditions is an important framework to connect to the general equality of conditions fostered by Buddhist philosophy and cultural norms in Burmese society, which I will elaborate in the remainder of this essay.

To assess the foundation of the equality of conditions in Burmese society as put forth by Tocqueville, one has to understand the influence of the philosophy of the teaching of Buddha on Burmese social thinking. While social thinking may not match social action exactly, social thinking does guide the social action of individuals in society. Understanding the dynamics of social thinking among individuals and groups in their associational life is crucial for assessing the general equality of conditions of a society.

The Logic of Associational Society

In Burma, it is fair to state that the mainstream society is imbued with Buddha's teaching. Aung San Suu Kyi, a careful observer of the foundation of Burmese society, in her *Freedom from Fear* and other essays, asserted that the "one single factor which has had the most influence on Burmese culture and civilization is Theravada Buddhism."[8] This assessment is especially true in rural Burma today. In order to understand the behavioral logic of associational life in Burma, one must investigate the sources of Burmese social thinking concerning the existence of the physical world and human orders.

One of the major understandings put forth by the teaching of Buddha is that human individuals and events do not possess intrinsic reality and absolute independent existence in the order of nature. This notion is drawn from the theory of emptiness. The theory of emptiness construes that "things and events are 'empty' in that they do not possess any immutable essence, intrinsic reality, or absolute 'being' that bestows independence."[9] The reality of events and the existence of things are afforded by "emptiness" of those. For instance, as an individual with a physical nature and mind and carrying a name, I am "independent" only because the world all around me exists. I am "empty" if there is no surrounding world. Even if I build a surrounding world out of my "empty" existence and slowly cultivate the world around me, who I am in my intrinsic and independent existence can only be defined through my surrounding world.

The theory of emptiness taught Burmese to see the relationality and rationality of individual existences along with other human beings, non-human beings, things, and events in the world. In Burma, any social or communal events that involve Buddhist monks include recitation of what is called *ngar bar thila* or the five precepts of ethical conduct. The five precepts of ethical conduct for lay people are: (1) abstain from killing (preserve and respect existence of life), (2) abstain from stealing and robbery, (3) abstain from unwholesome sexual conduct, (4) abstain from incorrect speech or lying, and (5) abstain from consuming intoxicants.[10] These five precepts are viewed in Burmese social conduct as the basis for cultivating respect for other individual human beings and nonhuman beings. Both relationality and rationality are embedded in the construction of these five precepts. Thus, these five major rules of daily intentions and actions for individuals instructed in Buddhist teaching encourage Burmese to cultivate a relational and rationalized practice of sympathy to others' feeling and thinking.

The cultivation of sympathy begins with thinking for the self, meaning that one should associate with and treat others, as one would want to be associated with and treated by others. This is closer to the notion of what Adam Smith called "moral sentiment." The consequences of the practices of sympathy that Burmese consider are major factors in their calculus of karma. Karma can be viewed as a subtheory of emptiness that provides relational and rational grounds for the "empty" individual to be creative in associational society. The concept of karma establishes a mechanism for individuals to be creative and productive individuals who would relationally and rationally consider avoiding negative or bad things against oneself and others in society. This process permits empty individuals to become meaningful and well-intended individuals who create associational society. In essence, this mechanism of enabling empty individuals to become intrinsic and independent individuals affirms that the existence of the individual self and intrinsic independent individual is not a given privilege by God from the beginning of an individual's life but has to be earned and created by the individual herself or himself. Burmese people consider that the existence of self and their freedom in associational society are grounded on self-driven intentions and actions that are governed by the rules of relationality (precisely sympathy) and the calculus of karma.

In most interpretations of karma, the concept of karma is taken as an explanation for "rebirth" of the individual as the sum of the consequences of actions taken in previous lives. However, this is only half of the meaning of karma for Burmese Buddhists. For Burmese Buddhists, karma also explains the progress of the stages of an individual's active life as the sum of the consequences of intentions and actions taken in previous days, weeks, months, and years. This broader understanding and perception of karma has led individual Burmese Buddhists to consider karma as the guiding principle for their daily intentions and actions. Thus, the concept of karma serves as the guiding principle of self-interest rightly understood in Burma.[11]

The Calculus of Self-Interest Rightly Understood

Understanding the notion of individual self-interest is crucial for understanding associational society that is composed of individuals. While it is almost impossible to know everyone's individual self-interest, it is possible to observe the framework of individual self-interest based on the foundations of socialization. Burmese people believe that the sole "Creator" of an individual is the individual himself. An individual is responsible for his or her own intentions and actions, which are eventually judged by the karma of the individual. The similar concept of karma is found in Isaac Newton's Third Principle of Force, which states that when object A hits object B with a certain force, object B would respond with the same measure of force that comes from object A. Thus, all good and bad actions of individuals would result in their respective (not in a computational sense) ways according to the principle of karma. This concept of karma is a guiding principle of individual self-interest among Burmese people.

For Burmese, the calculus of karma is fundamentally concerned with the consequences of intentions and actions of a human being. A state of pure thought exists before intention enters one's mind. When the pure thought of mind begins to interact with the reality of the surrounding environment, the pure thought begins to generate intention. When the state of mind interacts with the surrounding environment such as smell, sound, light, other objects, and beings, pure thought travels from the pure state to a state of interaction with others, and the journey of intention begins.

One of the ways that Burmese Buddhists attempt to unpack this process is through meditation. Meditation is fundamentally concerned with setting the boundaries between the state of pure thought of mind and the state of interaction with the surrounding environment clearly. Thus, meditation focuses on zooming in on pure thought in order to guide the mind not to travel beyond the boundary of state of pure thought and not to engage in intentions. It is important to understand this distinction because the intention is the beginning stage of the calculus of karma when one measures the consequences of intention and actions. Without intention, a mere movement is not considered an action. Action is defined closely with intention in calculating the consequences of karma. Intentions and action thus comprise the two major elements affecting karma.

Intentions

The state of intention is the state of mind that begins after crossing the boundary of the state of pure thought of mind leading up to decision for an action or inaction. This state of mind in Burmese is coined as *setana* (pronounced "say da nar"). *Setana* can roughly be translated as volition or will. *Setana* is an essential parameter that Burmese apply to measure one's action to evaluate whether a person has good intentions or bad intentions in enacting an action. Illustratively speaking, *setana* is like a software component in a calculator for the equation of karma that renders judgment whether the intended action produces positive or negative consequences for that individual. When a Burmese makes a judgment concerning the actions of people, they use *setana* as a primary parameter. Approving or disapproving one's behavior and action in Burmese society for any type of relationships and associations is based on how good or bad the *setana* behind the intention and action of people is. Burmese people tend to disapprove an action that is caused by bad *setana*.

In the associational life of Burmese families and communities, *setana* is applied to evaluate the state of a person's trustworthiness, respect, affection, and moral standing demonstrated by his relationships with family and community. *Setana* stands above the physical and social identity of people in Burmese social behaviors in the sense that racial identity, gender, color of skin, formal educational level, economic status, or the physical look of a person does not come first in the judgment of a person. *Setana* comes first in measuring behavioral aspects of a human being whose intentions and actions are believed to produce transformative consequences to human society.

Actions

Is there a possibility that action can occur without intention? It is possible to give an affirmative answer to this question. However, according to Burmese Buddhist philosophy, it is almost impossible that an action would occur without intention. This degree of measurement "almost" is important because it indicates the existence of mechanisms of ultimate control of the mind within the self except for the constraints resulting from medical conditions. Burmese call this mechanism *thadi*, meaning mindfulness in English. *Thadi* is applied to draw a line between action with intention and action without intention. *Thadi* can be closely interpreted as mindfully aware or fully cognizant of one's state of mind and its potential movement through the thinking process. *Thadi* has to be active all the time to check the balance between two states of mind—one pure thought and the other intention. By serving as a mechanism of checks and balances, *thadi* can steer the pure thought to travel to the territory of positive (desirable) intention toward the surrounding environment and minimize the mind's travels to the negative (undesirable) intentions toward the surrounding environment. When a Burmese person leaves for daily chores or says goodbye at the end of a visit, parents or elders usually remind that person not to forget about *thadi*. In daily ceremonies of donation and offering to Buddhist monks, the monks always remind people about *thadi*, which will serve an individual not to allow the mind to produce negative intentions that can potentially lead individuals to commit negative and bad actions.

The question of how one decides whether an intention or an action is negative and bad is linked to the level of enlightenment of an individual and the level of enlightenment of the people in the environment in which this question is considered. In other words, the negative and bad or positive and good are to be understood within the contextual and social condition of associational society in which an individual conducts intentions and actions. Thus, there are no universal bads and goods in Burmese thought. There are particular goods and bads in a case-by-case basis. However, there is a universal belief that every intention and action has both good and bad forces attached, and the challenge for an individual is to minimize negative and bad forces and to maximize positive and good forces in all possible intentions and actions.

Emptiness and Karma as the Foundation
of the General Equality of Conditions

The preceding discussion of the classical theory of emptiness, calculus of karma, intention, and action of the world of the individual is crucial for understanding the general principle of how equality among individuals is perceived as the foundation of Burmese society. The individual's world of intentions and actions, according to the framework of karma, includes five regions: (1) the state of consciousness and pure thought, (2) the state of intention and decision, (3) the state of action, (4) the state of outcomes of actions, and (5) the state of consequences of the outcomes of actions. The existences of these regions within the framework of karma are possible due to the theory of emptiness that generates the logic of individual existence in associational life in Burmese thought. If the intrinsic reality of events and the absolute independence of individuals are upheld in opposition to emptiness, there is no need for individuals to associate in society and there is no causal mechanism that serves as a foundation for the science of explanation and prediction.[12] If there is no causation among events and things, there is no need to discuss the general equality of conditions.

However, there is a danger in misunderstanding the theory of emptiness and reaching the sweeping conclusion that every event and every individual are connected. This can lead to the overall elimination of the general equality of conditions by reasoning that these connections need to be governed by some authority. In fact, some of the politically conservative elements of Burmese society have reached this conclusion. They have been the main force behind the establishment of the Hobbesian Leviathan state, which is justified by the need for a state or supreme authority to ensure order in a chaotic and complicated world that makes it difficult for individuals to interact with each other peacefully and to solve their problems through association. Under these conditions, the Leviathan state suppresses the general equality of conditions and imposes its will through an authoritarian state as we have seen in Burma under successive military regimes. The danger of power politics taking control over associational life and undermining the general equality of conditions is a major challenge and threat to Burmese civilization.

The Self-Created Individual

The general equality of conditions is understood as based on the coherent understanding of the theory of emptiness and the framework of karma, which upholds the individual's equal footing with others and provides reasons to become an egalitarian member in ex ante human society. This general equality of conditions is accorded to all human beings, not just to the believers of a Buddhist philosophy or Buddhism as "religion." The embodiment and existence of the individual in Burma's associational life under this notion of the general equality of conditions means that the individual is self-created.

The individual is not created by anyone but the individual himself. The existence and essence of self-created individuals are defined through the theory of emptiness and the framework of the karma of an individual rather than through creation by some supernatural force. This classical Buddhist concept of the individual is different from the mainstream Western notion of the individual who is created by a supernatural force. In the mainstream Western notion, because the individual is created by God, this individual does not embody individual freedom ex ante human society. Logically, God guarantees her existence and freedom ex ante human society. In mainstream Burmese social and political thought, the individual is self-created according to the following logic.

The notion of the self-created individual paves the social foundation for nullifying the existence of social class or ethnic prejudices in terms of inheritance of individual freedom in the mainstream thinking of Burmese society. At the same time, karma also provides the rationale for individuals to be different due to self-created paths, intentions, and actions that produce consequences for individual existence in accordance with the calculus of karma of that individual. The self-created individual and the notions of independence and differences among individuals are reflected in both the structure of genealogy and naming system of individuals in Burmese social and cultural practices. The structure of genealogy and naming system reflect fundamental notions of Burmese thought that individuals within a family, even if biologically related, are born to the world on an equal footing with independent paths of self-creation.

Structures of Genealogy

In the mainstream Burmese culture, a family is a joint unit of two parents without anyone taking the dominant "head" position in functions and ideas. Burma, in fact, is the only society in modern Asia that does not recognize the male domination of family structure and lineage. There is a danger in making sweeping generalization to claim this for Burmese society as a whole. However, it is legitimate to assert that the majority of Burmese people, including some minority ethnic cultures and traditions, reject male domination in Burmese family structures. The influence of Indian and Chinese cultures among Burmese people of Indian descent and Burmese people of Chinese descent, however, differs from the mainstream Burmese thinking. While Chinese-Burmese and Indian-Burmese women may not change their family names to their husband's family names, the practice of male domination in their family structure is more prominent than those within mainstream Burmese families.

Within the mainstream Burmese society, when a woman marries a man, she does not need to change her name. Their children are given individual names without the family name. Burmese individual names are not meant to construct a lineage system of domination by either parent. For instance, my name Tun Myint is independent of my father's name U Khin Maung or my mother's name Daw Phwa Gyi. This idea of family structure and lineage is very much reflective of mainstream social beliefs and cultures that are deeply influenced by the ideas of the emptiness of individual and the framework of karma, both of which define individual existence and independence. This also reflects the respect of Burmese for the self-created individual. However, for the sake of sharing and depicting parental love and the family unit, some Burmese have named their children in combining words from each parent's name or grandparents' name. For example, Burmese Nobel Peace Laureate Daw Aung San Suu Kyi is named with a combination of words from her father's name U Aung San, her mother's name Daw Khin Kyi, and her paternal grandmother Daw Suu. The term "Daw" is a respectful title for a female in Burma.

Government and its Responsibility in Protecting Equality

In the preceding sections, I have presented mainstream Burmese social thoughts that are fundamental to the concept of the equality of conditions. The first-level struggle for Burmese society is to examine whether these fundamental thoughts for equality match reality so as to bring about greater equality of conditions. To check the extent to which the equality of conditions is present in Burma, one must consider the reality of the political life of Burmese society. When one considers the reality of the political life of Burmese society, one must carefully examine the relationship between the state and people.

One of the sources of unlocking the positive side of karma of Burmese people in their political life is found in the Buddhist Burmese view of kingship or government or state. Burmese Buddhists consider the government or the king or the state as one of five enemies in their lives. When Burmese worship and pray at temples and pagodas, or before going to bed, as one of their daily activities, they willfully pray to be away from five enemies of life—fire-related disasters, water-related disasters, wind-related disasters, the king or state, and thieves and robbers. Therefore, it is necessary to understand the Buddhist view of kingship or the state.

The Buddhist view of kingship (government) does not invest the ruler with the divine right to govern the realm as he pleases, which is in contrast to the Chinese view of the legitimacy of government based on the "Mandate of Heaven." The king or government is expected to observe the Ten Duties of King or Government, the Seven Safeguards against Decline, and the Four Assistances to the People, and to be guided by numerous other codes of conducts stated in Buddha's teaching.

During the people's movement in 1988, a number of speakers including a famous Burmese scholar, astrologer, and novelist Min Thein Kha widely quoted the Ten Duties of Government in his public speeches. The Nobel Peace laureate and opposition leader Daw Aung San Suu Kyi also discussed the importance and relevance of the Ten Duties of Government to democracy in *Freedom from Fear*. Since the Ten Duties of Government or King are highly regarded by Burmese people as guidelines to judge their government, it is necessary to discuss how the concept of the Ten Duties of Government works in the context of modern politics and legal system in Burma.

The Ten Duties of Government are: charity (*dana* in Parli), morality (*sila*), self-sacrifice (*paricagga*), integrity (*ajjava*), kindness (*maddava*), austerity (*tapa*), patience (*akkodha*), nonviolence (*avihamsa*), forbearance (*khanti*), and nonopposition to the will of the people (*avirodha*). The first duty of charity (*dana*) demands that a ruler should contribute generously to the welfare of the people, and makes the implicit assumption that a government should have the competence to provide adequately for its citizens. In the context of modern politics, *dana* means that one of the prime duties of the people's government would be to ensure the economic security of the people, such as creating jobs and eliminating unemployment.

The second duty of government, morality (*sila*), is based on the observance of the Five Precepts of Buddha's teaching, which entails refraining from destruction of life, theft, adultery, falsehood, and indulgence in intoxicants. The Burmese believe that the ruler must have a high moral character to win the respect and trust of the people and to serve as a proper role model for society. Moral rulers thus ensure the happiness and prosperity of society. When the king or the government does not observe *dhamma* (the rule of morality or ethics), state functionaries become corrupt; and when state functionaries are corrupt, the people are subjected to suffering.

Self-sacrifice (or *paricagga*) is the third duty of government. *Paricagga* is sometimes translated as generosity and sometimes as self-sacrifice. The former would overlap with the meaning of the first duty, *dana*, so the latter, meaning self-sacrifice as the ultimate generosity that gives up all for the good sake of the people, would appear to be the more appropriate interpretation. The concept of selfless public service is sometimes illustrated by the stories of the hermit Sumedha who took the vows of Buddhahood. In so doing, he "who could have realized the supreme liberation of nirvana in a single life time committed himself to countless incarnations that he might help other beings free themselves from suffering."[13]

The fourth duty of government is to observe integrity or *ajjava*, which implies incorruptibility in the discharge of public duties as well as honesty and sincerity in personal relations. Burmese believe that those who govern should be wholly bound by the truth in thought, word, and deed. According to the fourth duty, to deceive or to mislead the people in any way would be an occupational failing as well as a moral offense. The ruler, therefore, has to observe the truth that is "as an arrow, intrinsically straight, without warp or distortion, when one word is spoken, it does not err into two," as Buddha has compared the meaning of truth to a straight arrow.[14]

The fifth duty of government is to practice kindness (*maddava*). A ruler has to have the courage and sensitivity to feel concern for the people's welfare. With this courage, the ruler has the mind and heart to take care of public services. To care is to take responsibility and to dare to act in accordance with the dictum that the ruler is the strength of the needy and helpless. Not just "a few good men" but many good men are needed in the government of the people in order to observe the fifth duty of government.

The sixth duty, austerity (*tapa*), implies that a ruler must adopt simple habits, develop self-control, and practice spiritual discipline. This duty prevents rulers from abusing public properties and taxpayers' money. This duty is to safeguard against corrupt practices of the government. The seventh, eighth, and ninth duties—patience (*akkodha*), nonviolence (*avihamsa*), and forbearance (*khanti*)—are similar and are related in most of the interpretations of Burmese culture. Rulers must not allow personal feelings of enmity and ill will to erupt into destructive anger and violence. It is incumbent on a ruler to cultivate true tolerance, which serves him/her to deal wisely and generously with the shortcomings and provocation of even those enemies he could crush with impunity. Violence is inhumane and absolutely contrary to the Buddha's teachings. A good ruler relinquishes ill will and anger with loving kindness, wickedness with virtue, parsimony with liberality, and falsehood with truth. These are all relevant to the seventh, eighth, and ninth duties of rulers.

The most significant duty among the Ten Duties of Government is the tenth duty, which states that the ruler must not oppose the will of the people. *Avirodha*, or nonopposition to the will of the people, is the Buddhist endorsement of democracy. This principle has been supported by numerous stories of the kings during the Buddha's time in the ancient world. For instance, Pawridasa, a monarch who acquired an appetite for human flesh, was forced into exile because he would not heed the people's demand that he should abandon his cannibalistic habits. Another different kind of ruler was the Buddha's penultimate incarnation on earth, the pious King Vessantara, who was also sent to exile when, in the course of his striving for perfecting generosity, he gave away the white elephant of the state without the consent of the people. The true meaning of the tenth duty, nonopposition to the will of people, is a reminder that the legitimacy of government is founded on the consent of the people who have the power to withdraw their mandate at any time if they lose confidence in or creditability of the ruler or his ability to serve their best interest.

The Ten Duties of Government or King in the tradition of Buddha's teachings greatly influences the hearts and minds of the Burmese people. The concept of these duties is not very different from the concepts comprising representative democratic norms currently practiced in democratic countries. We are faced with the puzzle as to how the current military regime is able to remain in power in a Burmese society in which the concept of the Ten Duties of Government is so widely accepted. To understand the answer to this question, one must first understand the concept of karma and how it plays out in Burmese social life, as discussed earlier.

The social and legal theory discussed above still plays an important role in the daily lives of Burmese beliefs and practices. However, their underlying concepts are difficult to translate into contemporary legal terms or to be incorporated into the modern rule of law system. The challenge for citizens and future governments in Burma is to find ways to incorporate these elements into the political and legal system.

The Empirical Reality of the Equality of Conditions

In the majority of Asian societies, when it comes to considering the social foundations of the polity, there are subtle differences from the mainstream Western societies. In the mainstream Western societies, individual liberty or freedom takes precedence over the general equality of conditions in discussing political associational life. Perhaps this is one of the major reasons why most Western scholars and readers of Tocqueville do not pay sufficient attention to the implications of Tocqueville's focus on the general equality of conditions as constituting the foundation or the roots of democracy. The general equality of conditions and individual liberty are closely connected. Indeed, it is impossible to have one without the other. It may be a matter of epistemic choice of language or terminology as to why the West places liberty before the equality of conditions in discussing the attributes of democracy. To me, the major difference between the East and the West is this epistemic choice of language in considering the foundation of political institutions.[15] The East prefers the general equality of conditions as the mobilizing force, while the West prefers individual liberty as the mobilizing force in structuring orders in their respective societies.

As I have discussed in this essay that focuses on Burmese social and political concepts and thinking, individual existences and freedom in the polity are possible due to the existence of the general equality of conditions ex ante formation of political society. The elite-manufactured hierarchical foundation of social structures in Asia and the dominant culture of "we" over "I" are not conducive to putting individual liberty before the general equality of conditions in determining the nature of the polity and its political institutions. Perhaps this is the reason why some Asian democratic revolutions that should have succeeded in transitioning to promoting more freedom and equality in the late 1980s and early 1990s have continued to lag behind in this area. The failure of the 8.8.88 movement in Burma and the Tiananmen Square movement in China in 1989 provide examples of this phenomenon. Alternatively, the slow evolutionary transformations in Indonesia, Malaysia, Singapore, South Korea, Taiwan, and Thailand toward Tocquevillian democracy constitute other examples where there were not abrupt revolutions like those that occurred in Eastern Europe and the former Soviet Union. The question as to why the people's power movement in the Philippines was successful in overthrowing the Marcos regime in the mid-1980s can be answered from the sociological and anthropological point of view by analyzing the general condition of the dominant part of Filipino society that closely followed Western traditions, particularly Roman Catholic traditions.

The empirical reality of political association in Burma today is that both the general equality of conditions and individual liberty have been suppressed in order for the power politics of a few to survive. Oppression does not just come from the military regime's brutal practice of raw power. The opposition democracy movement's failure to articulate a vision and alternative institutional design for the Burmese polity based on Burma's Buddhist social and cultural context is also partly responsible for the longevity of the dictatorial regime whose patterns of governmental power are rooted in British colonial state traditions fostered by the logic of Leviathan.

The epistemic choice of the ongoing democracy movement in Burma focusing on "Free Burma," rather than on the equality of conditions that would empower Burmese communities to manage their affairs, is another subtle reason why most Asian neighbors and even the majority of Burma's population, especially those supporting the regime, regard the democracy movement as inspired primarily by Western ideals and concepts. The factors hindering a shift from the paradigm for democracy, based primarily on Western notions of individual liberty to a paradigm for democracy based on the general equality of conditions as articulated in Buddhism, merit further investigation. Such an enquiry would help us to explain the crucial role of the general equality of conditions as the roots of democracy not only in Burmese society but also in most Asian societies where the epistemic choice underlying the foundation of associational life is not individual liberty but the general equality of conditions.

Concluding Remarks on Tocqueville and Burma

Like Tocqueville, who saw the general equality of conditions in America as the foundation for democracy, I have examined the general equality of conditions in Burma. Despite the similarities in the concept, there are major differences in the elaboration of the concept and the empirical realities found in Tocqueville's America and Burmese contemporary society. Given these major differences, it is legitimate to raise the question as to what extent Tocqueville's concept of the equality of conditions and his analysis of American social structures are relevant in illuminating our understanding of the prospects for democracy and the shape democracy might take in Burma. While the general concept may be similar, the empirical data are fundamentally different.

There are at least three differences between the data I drew from Burma and the empirical data Tocqueville drew from France and America. First, individuals and their existence in Burmese society are perceived and practiced as self-created, while individuals in France and America were perceived as created by a supernatural force, namely God. Second, Burmese society did not regard the existence of races and classes as a priori associational forms of human life, while French and American societies did. Third, the general equality of conditions Tocqueville found in America applied only to white males, which Tocqueville by extension applied to all humanity, while the general equality of conditions in mainstream Burmese thinking did not distinguish people by the color of their skin or their family origins. While it is important to recognize these differences, these differences should not nullify the basic validity of Tocqueville's concept of the general equality of conditions as a key element for the foundation of democratic societies even in non-Western countries like Burma where the social, cultural, and religious contexts are markedly different from those found in America and Western Europe.

This essay has focused primarily on the ideas and concepts rooted in Buddhist principles and Burmese culture contributing to promoting the general equality of conditions in Burma. This assessment raises an important question about the contention between the general equality of conditions and power politics in Burma's political development. The ongoing struggle of the Burmese people to topple the military regime and elitist politics in Burma illustrates the major contention between power politics and the general equality of conditions.

Notes

1. Alexis de Tocqueville, *Democracy in America* (New York: Bantam Classics, 2000), 3.
2. Tocqueville, *Democracy in America*, 3.
3. Tocqueville, *Democracy in America*, 15.
4. For example, see Mary P. Callahan, *Masking Enemies: War and State Building in Burma* (Ithaca, NY: Cornell University Press, 2003); Robert Taylor, *The State in Burma* (Honolulu: University of Hawaii Press, 1987).
5. Sombat Chantornvong, "Tocqueville's *Democracy in America* and the Third World," in *Rethinking Institutional Analysis and Development: Issues, Alternatives, and Choices*, ed. Vincent Ostrom, David Feeny, and Hartmut Picht (San Francisco, CA: ICS, 1988), 73.
6. The exceptions are John S. Furnivall, *Colonial Policy and Practice: A Comparative Study of Burma and Netherlands India* (Cambridge University Press, 1948), chaps. 4–6; Victor Lieberman, *Strange Parallels: Southeast Asia in Colonial Context, c. 800–1830* (Cambridge University Press, 2003), 21–23, 37–59, chap. 2.
7. Tocqueville, *Democracy in America*, 3.
8. Aung San Suu Kyi, *Freedom from Fear* (London: Penguin Book, 1991), 66.
9. Dalai Lama XIV, *The Universe in a Single Atom: The Convergence of Science and Spirituality* (New York: Morgan Road Books, 2005), 47.
10. David R. Loy, *The Great Awakening: A Buddhist Social Theory* (Boston, MA: Wisdom Publications, 2003).
11. The expression "self-interest rightly understood," coined by Tocqueville in *Democracy in America*, corresponds with Buddhist concepts concerning the obligations of Buddhists in dealing with others.
12. Dalai Lama, *Universe in a Single Atom*, 47.
13. Aung San Suu Kyii, *Freedom from Fear*, 171.
14. Aung San Suu Kyii, *Freedom from Fear*, 172.
15. The logic of Leviathan formulated by Thomas Hobbes and the Theory of Emptiness formulated in Buddhist philosophy are two views of East and West.

12

The Road to Democracy in China: A Tocquevillian Analysis

Jianxun Wang

With the remarkable economic development in China in the past three decades, many observers are wondering if and how the country will move forward politically. Although the Tiananmen movement in 1989 left few to doubt that democracy was out of the question at least for the moment, China scholars are now curious about the direction the country will take. Given the nature of the political system under the party-state regime, it is very difficult to predict whether China will become a democracy in the near future. What are the major obstacles to democracy in China? Are there any developments and changes in the past three decades that might help a democratic transformation in the country?

This chapter addresses these questions by engaging in an analysis from a Tocquevillian perspective. As the foremost student of democracy, Tocqueville's understanding of the processes of political development is more profound than many other scholars of democratization processes. Many of his political assessments and predictions are highly regarded in the literature on democratic transformation. Tocqueville's keen observations and judgments can help us to better appreciate the challenges China faces in moving from an authoritarian to a democratic regime and China's prospects for democracy. Drawing upon Tocqueville's insights and analytics, this chapter looks into the political conditions and changes in contemporary China that might influence its trajectory.

A Tocquevillian Diagnosis of China's Transformation

China is an ancient country with a distinctive civilization. Although the society has many remarkable achievements in its long history, it has never established democracy in terms of citizen self-governance. Instead, the country has been governed by various autocratic and authoritarian institutions that have been responsible for numerous uprisings and revolutions in Chinese history. Since the mid-nineteenth century, China has been forced to open its doors to the West, and has tried to learn democracy and science from the West. Efforts to build a democratic regime, however, have failed again and again, and resulted in new rounds of rebellions and revolutions. China's frequent revolutions have led to what is frequently called the "cycle of dynasties"—a unique phenomenon among the world civilizations.[1]

What factors are responsible for the problem of "cycle of dynasties"? Or, in other words, what are the obstacles to democracy in China? Some scholars argue that the major obstacle to democratic transformation in China is the regime's lack of legitimacy. Since political leaders are not elected by the people, their authority has no legitimacy. Thus, the introduction of national elections would solve this problem.[2] Others assert that the major obstacle to democracy is the weakness of the communist party-state in terms of its monopoly of the use of force, extracting and regulatory capacity, resource redistribution mechanisms, institutional coherence, and ability to shape national identity.[3] Still others maintain that the one-party system, the will and role of political elites, the strength of the conservative leaders, and the sheer scale of the country are other important obstacles to China's democratization in the short or long run.[4]

These assertions certainly capture some truth in investigating this complex authoritarian regime, which presents contradictory trends and confusing signals. It is true that the Chinese Communist Party is still powerful and dominant; the political authority lacks legitimacy; political leaders still prefer stability and unity to liberty and democracy; and the size of the country with 1.3 billion people has an inevitable impact on the transition. All of these might well pose enormous challenges to democratization in China.

Although the constraints listed above are all important, I argue that centralization, especially administrative centralization, is one of the key obstacles to democracy in China. According to Tocqueville, administrative centralization tends to undermine and diminish local liberty and local spirit that is the foundation of national democracy.[5] In other words, for

Tocqueville, administrative centralization is the major obstruction to democracy because the foundation of democracy lies in local institutions and grassroots self-governance.

This judgment by Tocqueville can help us better understand the problem of "cycle of dynasties," since administrative centralization has predominated the multimillennia Chinese history. In Imperial China, emperors and their households were the central and supreme authority, and all laws and significant policies came from the center, especially the emperors. All magistrates were appointed by the emperors, and thus identified themselves with the imperial authority rather than local interests. Although there was no formal unit of government below the county level, the imperial authority, especially the late dynasties, tried to control local society by instituting various systems, including *baojia*, *lijia*, and *xiangyue*.[6]

Tocqueville himself commented on the high degree of administrative centralization in Imperial China. In a footnote, he remarked:

China appears to me to present the most perfect instance of that species of well-being which a highly centralized administration may furnish to its subjects. Travelers assure us that the Chinese have tranquility without happiness, industry without improvement, stability without strength, and public order without public morality. The condition of society there is always tolerable, never excellent. I imagine that when China is opened to European observation, it will be found to contain the most perfect model of a centralized administration that exists in the universe.[7]

Since the late imperial era, China has witnessed a deliberate and far-ranging trend toward centralization of power in building a modern and strong state.[8] As Kuhn put it, the twentieth-century politics of China is "a story about the relentless march of the central state."[9] If the imperial state had physical difficulties in penetrating villages, the state during the Republican era (1912–1949) took advantage of modern improvements to reach local society. In particular, the rapid development of mass communication and transportation in the early twentieth century made it easier for the state to intervene in local affairs. Efforts to build a strong and modern state greatly transformed rural areas as the state began to penetrate local society more deeply and moved toward bureaucratization, rationalization, and administrative extension.[10]

Shortly after 1927, the Republican government began to model subcounty administration upon the system that Yan Xishan, governor of Shanxi, had been operating in that province since 1917. The system was

based on a four-level hierarchy of units below the county.[11] In 1941, the
Kuomintang enforced the "large township" (*daxiang*) system, consisting of
one thousand households, which was aimed at replacing the administrative functions of villages. The establishment of townships was an important
step taken by the central state to penetrate and control local society, and
the penetration worsened the problem of "state involution," which means
the state cannot develop systems of bureaucratic responsibility at a rate
faster than the entrenchment of the informal apparatus of extraction.[12]

Although the Communist regime fiercely attacked the Nationalist
government from every angle, they did share one goal—building a modern and strong state. In fact, when the Communist Party came to power
in 1949, it claimed it was building a "New China." This "New China" was
more centralized than its predecessor because it was intended to be an
omnipotent and tutelary state. The tutelary power was much like what
Tocqueville well articulated:

> That power is absolute, minute, regular. . . . It would be like the authority
> of a parent if, like that authority, its object was to prepare men for man-
> hood; but it seeks on the contrary to keep them in perpetual childhood;
> it is well content that the people should rejoice, provided that they think
> of nothing but rejoicing. For their happiness such a government willingly
> labors, but it chooses to be the sole agent and the only arbiter of that hap-
> piness; it provides for them security, foresees and supplies their necessity,
> facilitates their pleasures, manages their principal concerns, directs their
> industry, regulates the descent of property and subdivides their inheri-
> tance: what remains but to spare them all the care of thinking and all the
> trouble of living?[13]

Following the Marxist-Leninist doctrines, Mao was prepared to utilize
a highly centralized state to reshape the whole society and the minds of
the people. Where the imperial state claimed only the power to tax and to
maintain order, the party-state asserted its right to restructure society.[14] In
the 1950s and 1960s, Mao began to centralize the country through collec-
tivizing farming in rural areas and factories in urban areas.[15] At the same
time, the communist regime established party branches in every working
unit and community while administrative power was centralized in the
hands of party secretaries. Although the communist regime, from time to
time, evoked the concept of "democratic centralism," this was nothing but
a façade behind which only centralism was accepted. Thus, Mao's era wit-

nessed one of the most centralized periods in Chinese history. The central-ized administration under Mao led to numerous disasters and catastrophes that claimed tens of millions of lives.[16]

Since Mao's death and the reform and "open" policies in the late 1970s and early 1980s, the country has moved away from a totalitarian regime. Although the center loosened its control over society somewhat, and espe-cially the economy, the party-state, however, remained highly centralized under a unitary system. An institutional analysis of the central-local power structure will demonstrate how the system worked.

First, the legislative power was almost totally vested in the center under the 1982 Chinese Constitution. As the supreme authority, the National People's Congress (NPC) can make whatever laws it wishes concerning national sovereignty, governmental organization, civil laws, criminal stat-utes, the economic system, and legal procedures. In other words, the legis-lative power of the NPC is unlimited, at least in principle. In contrast, the legislative power of local people's congresses is very limited. According to the Constitution and the Legislation Law (2000), provincial and some met-ropolitan people's congresses can make local regulations (*difang xing fagui*) under only two circumstances: (1) in order to enforce laws made by NPC and NPC Standing Committee and administrative regulations (*xingzheng fagui*) and (2) to deal with local affairs.

The first circumstance is actually not an independent legislative power, since local regulations based on this power were aimed at implementing national laws and regulations. The second circumstance vested provincial and some metropolitan congresses with independent legislative power regarding local affairs, but the scope of local affairs here was actually very narrow, because many important affairs, especially those closely related to the everyday life and basic rights of citizens, were legislated by the center (see table 12.1).

Second, the personnel power can be used as an important indicator of centralization in China. As many Chinese scholars know, the personnel power is crucial to the party-state regime. The communist party has long controlled government personnel through the *nomenclatura* system, which is called "*dang guan ganbu*" in China. The center, through the Communist Party Politburo and the Communist Party Central Committee (CPCC), controls high-ranking leaders, including those at the provincial level. The membership of the CPCC is often regarded as an indicator of central-local relations, since some members are from the central government and others from local (mainly provincial) governments.

Table 12.1. Comparison of central-local legislative power in contemporary China

The Center (NPC and NPC Standing Committee)	The Localities (Provincial and Metropolitan People's Congresses)
(1) National sovereignty	(1) To specify national laws and administrative regulations in order to enforce them
(2) Establishment, organization, and authority of all levels of people's congresses, governments, courts, and procuratorates	
(3) Minority regional autonomy, special administrative regions, and grassroots mass self-governance	
(4) Crimes and punishments	
(5) Disfranchisement and coercive measures and punishments on personal freedoms	
(6) Expropriation of non-state property	(2) To make local regulations regarding local affairs
(7) Basic civil affairs	
(8) Basic economic policies and financial, tax, customs, banking, and foreign trade policies	
(9) Legal and arbitral procedures	
(10) Others	

Source: Articles 8 and 64, Legislation Law of the People's Republic of China (2000).

A recent study by Sheng finds that from 1978 to 2002, provincial shares in the full membership of CPCC declined and that the center's control over top provincial leaders was much greater than generally thought.[17] In 1978, provincial officials constituted about 44.77 percent of the full CPCC membership, while this percentage by 2002 dropped to only 23.12 percent (see table 12.2).

Finally, fiscal power is often regarded as the most important indicator of central-local relations in China.[18] Based on the reforms of the tax system in the past two decades, many China scholars argue that the fiscal system has been decentralized, which gives local officials incentives to

Table 12.2. Provincial share of the full Central Committee membership (1978–2002)

Year	Provincial Share (%)
1978	44.77
1982	32.23
1987	37.08
1992	31.68
1997	24.31
2002	23.12

Source: Adapted from Yumin Sheng, "Central-Provincial Relations at the CCP Central Committees: Institutions, Measurement and Empirical Trends, 1978–2002," The China Quarterly 182 (2005): 349.

develop local economy.[19] Some even maintain that China is moving toward "market-preserving federalism."[20]

Although it is true that, in contrast with the Maoist era, fiscal power is relatively more decentralized, decentralization is still very limited. More importantly, the 1994 tax reform, in fact, recentralized the fiscal system.[21] Under the tax system, the central share of national revenue increased considerably while the local share decreased. On the other hand, the central-local sharing of expenditures has not changed much. In 1993, for instance, the center shared 22.0 percent of the revenue, while the local shared 78.0 percent. In 1994, however, after the tax reform, the center's share of the revenue increased to 55.7 percent, while the local share decreased to 44.3 percent. The central-local percentages of revenue share have changed little in the past ten years. At the same time, the central share of expenditure remained steadily around 30 percent from 1993 to 2004, while the local share of expenditure was around 70 percent during the same time span (see table 12.3).

The discussion above indicates that China has been a highly centralized country. The center has been the supreme and ultimate authority, while localities have been the delegates or obedient agents of the center. In Imperial China, the power of local magistrates came entirely from the center, and they were nothing but the representatives of the imperial

Table 12.3. Central-local shares of revenue and expenditure

	Shares of Revenue (%)		Shares of Expenditure (%)	
Year	Central	Local	Central	Local
1993	22.0	78.0	28.3	71.7
1994	55.7	44.3	30.3	69.7
1995	52.2	47.8	29.2	70.8
1996	49.4	50.6	27.1	72.9
1997	48.9	51.1	27.4	72.6
1998	49.5	50.5	28.9	71.1
1999	51.1	48.9	31.5	68.5
2000	52.2	47.8	34.7	65.3
2001	52.4	47.6	30.5	69.5
2002	55.0	45.0	30.7	69.3
2003	54.6	45.4	30.1	69.9
2004	54.9	45.1	27.7	72.3

Source: *China Statistics Yearbook 2005*, http://www.stats.gov.cn/tjsj/ndsj/2005/indexch.htm

court. Today, the authority of local governments derives completely from the central party-state, and local cadres are the disciplined servants of the center. Magistrates and cadres might be aware of local concerns, but their authority was and is based entirely upon their identification with the central authority. In the bureaucratic hierarchies, local officials are expected to act only according to directives from above.[22]

Administrative Centralization versus Democratic Governance

Why does administrative centralization tend to obstruct the establishment of democracy? What is the rationale? Tocqueville's classic argument asserts that administrative centralization, which concentrates decision-making power over local affairs in the center, has a tendency to destroy local institutions and local liberty that is the very foundation of democracy. Tocqueville eloquently argues that:

> Municipal institutions constitute the strength of free nations. Town meetings are to liberty what primary schools are to science; they bring it within the people's reach, they teach men how to use and how to enjoy it. A nation may establish a free government, but without municipal institutions it cannot have the spirit of liberty.[23]

The logic of Tocqueville's argument is that democracy originates in the everyday practices of citizens in dealing with public affairs in their local communities. In the localities, citizens learn how to cooperate with one another and how to solve their common problems. When every community becomes a local republic, the society will become a democracy that is sustainable. Democracy, in Tocqueville's view, is a bottom-up and gradual process, and is based on the everyday practices and experiences of citizens in local communities. Thus, for Tocqueville, national elections or the modern party system does not constitute the heart of democracy, as many contemporary scholars, like Huntington and Linz and Stepan understand.[24] Instead, democracy means citizens themselves govern public and private affairs. Or, in Tocqueville's own words, democracy means "society governs itself for itself."[25] In short, democracy is better understood as citizen governance or simply self-governance.[26]

Hayek's work on knowledge and information supports Tocqueville's argument.[27] According to Hayek, every person possesses only limited knowledge, and no single person is able to combine all of the fragments of knowledge. Hayek also finds that rational decision making often relies on one important type of knowledge, that is, the "knowledge of the particular circumstances of time and place."[28] Without the knowledge of specific people, local conditions, and special circumstances, appropriate and reasonable decisions are difficult to be made. Nevertheless, the knowledge of the particular circumstances of time and place is dispersed among numerous individuals. Every individual has some advantage over all others in that he/she possesses some unique information, and thus it is better to let the individual make decisions that depend on the unique information.

From an anthropological perspective, Geertz supports Hayek's approach to knowledge by asserting that many types of knowledge, including law and politics, are local.[29] The localness of knowledge requires the understanding of local conditions and vernacular characterizations and imaginings. According to Geertz, to reduce local knowledge to abstract commonalities prevents us from appreciating diverse human experiences and legal rules.

Based on this understanding of the nature of knowledge, it can be said that decision-making arrangements are better decentralized or polycentric than centralized, because no central authority is able to obtain all the necessary knowledge possessed by every individual. As Tocqueville comments:

> However enlightened and skillful a central power may be, it cannot of itself embrace all the details of the life of a great nation. Such vigilance exceeds the powers of man. And when it attempts unaided to create and set in motion so many complicated springs, it must submit to a very imperfect result or exhaust itself in bootless efforts.[30]

At the same time, centralized administration inherently prefers the unitary system and uniform laws and policies. Consistent with Hobbes's theory of sovereignty, centralized administration is aimed at the unity of the state, which in turn requires the unity of power and law.[31] Under the unitary system, local authorities are instituted by the center and thus depend on the center for their power. In order to maintain the unity of the state, the unitary system governs through uniform laws and policies and disregards diverse local conditions.

One of the most striking examples of the unitary system is China, which is a vast continent with enormous diversity in its ecological, economic, and cultural conditions. South China is based on rice culture, while North China is based on wheat and millet traditions; East China is related to massive cities and their distinct economic interests, while West China is close to a nomadic culture. As Pye points out:

> Yet for all of these striking differences, which reflect a geographically diversified land, at no time in history has Chinese politics revolved around them. Political issues have usually emanated from the center; but if pressing concerns are raised in one part of the country, they are either quickly suppressed or are taken over by the central authorities and made into national concerns, relevant for the whole country.[32]

Actually, the unitary system has been elevated to the level of a cultural myth in China, which holds that the country has always had a unitary system and that no other system is consistent with Chinese tradition and culture. The distrust of pluralist decentralization is the fear of independent kingdoms, warlords, or separatism, which is regarded as the breach of conformity and submission to the supreme power. A regime that loses strong central control would be considered weak and might soon collapse.[33] This myth assumes that the center, in most cases, makes good policies and takes care of the people, while local authorities are full of corrupt officials and often fail to enforce central policies.

With the centralized administration, local authorities have to play the game of feigned compliance with the center, a game similar to that of cat and mouse.[34] When the center issues their absolute orders or promulgates their uniform policies, the local authorities pretend to obey and follow them. Nevertheless, the local authorities know that they cannot follow the policies because they are not tailored to local conditions. Whenever there are complaints from the people, the center will blame the local authorities for failing to enforce the policies. Thus, the center and the localities have always been in a state of tension.

Consistent with the unitary system, the contemporary Chinese government is fond of making numerous uniform codes of law to govern the society, without considering diverse local conditions. Despite the slogan of establishing the rule of law, the uniform laws are inherently incompatible with this goal since they are not able to provide individual justice based on local customs and particular circumstances. Thus, citizens regard these uniform laws as arbitrary obstacles to justice and try to avoid them. It is not difficult to understand the fact that while hundreds or even thousands of laws are made by Beijing every year, the society is moving no closer to the rule of law.

Further, without the appreciation of local knowledge and local conditions, centralized administration often engages in large-scale social engineering and planning in order to reshape the society fundamentally, which has led to numerous disasters and catastrophes. The centralized planning economy and collectivized farming in former communist countries and China paved the road to serfdom and were responsible for tens of millions of deaths. Elsewhere, the large-scale social engineering regarding scientific forestry, high-modernist cities, and rural settlement failed badly due to the simplifications of complex social facts and the disregard of "practical knowledge."[35]

Although centralized administration can "bring together at a given moment, on a given point, all the disposable resources of a people," as we have seen in Mao's China or Stalin's Russia, the administration "injures the renewal of those resources."[36] Moreover, while the administration "may ensure a victory in the hour of strife, . . . it gradually relaxes the sinews of strength." The administration "may help admirably the transient greatness of a man, but not the durable prosperity of a nation."[37]

Finally, centralized administration tends to distort the concept of citizenship and create passive citizens, which is fatal to democracy. Under a centralized regime, the center becomes "an indefatigable mentor" and "keeps the nation in quasi-paternal tutelage."[38] The country changes without citizens' concurrence and knowledge. Thus, citizens become indifferent to the fate of their communities, their localities, and their country, since the citizens think that they are unconnected with the so-called government, especially the central government. When citizens are in danger, they will fold their arms and wait rather than take the initiative to deal with their problems. Soon, citizenship, the bedrock of democracy, will fade, and servitude will grow.[39]

In sum, centralized administration is liable to obstruct democratic governance since it fails to appreciate local knowledge, subjugates the people under uniform laws, and makes citizens passive subjects. Democracy relies on a polycentric system that allows multiple decision-making units at different levels to formulate policies based on the diverse physical, socioeconomic, and cultural conditions.[40] Under the polycentric system, policymaking depends on local people's participation because they usually know better about local conditions than those at a distance. Indeed, local initiatives and efforts constitute the bedrocks of democratic governance.

Local Governance, Civil Society, and Bottom-Up Democratic Transformation

Can China move away from administrative centralization to establish democracy? Are there any changes and developments under the post–Mao regime in the past three decades that provide some hope for a democratic transformation? If we focus on Beijing and the Communist Party, it is clear that the authoritarian nature of the party-state regime has not changed much during the post–Mao era. However, if we, following Tocqueville, pay close attention to localities and initiatives of citizens, we can find some interesting developments in local governance, the remarkable efforts and creativity of citizens, and the emergence of civil society. If we agree with Tocqueville's judgment concerning the foundations of democracy, these changes and developments in contemporary China might offer some hope for a bottom-up democratic transformation. With the loosening of control in post–Mao China, the country has moved toward a relatively more pluralist society. One of the extraordinary changes has occurred in tens of thousands of villages. With the dismantlement of collectivized farming in the late 1970s and early 1980s, the decision-making power of party cadres has declined, and villages have been experiencing changes and reforms in many rural areas.

Struck by poverty and hunger, a group of peasants in Anhui province pioneered an important experiment in family farming by allocating their collective land to each household. The success of the experiment soon led to its spread to other villages and rural areas. In the early 1980s, the collectivized farming system was dismantled, and the "household responsibility system" was established throughout the country. The demise of collective farming undermined the central state's economic control over the villages, and individual households took back their decision-making power over farming.[41]

At the same time, with the dissolution of communes and brigades, peasants began to reorganize villages in the early 1980s. Some peasants in Guangxi province formed "Villagers' Committees" as village governing bodies to provide public goods, such as defense and fire control. Later, many villages in other regions followed them to establish similar kinds of committees. In some villages, peasants selected the members of the committees by election. When the post–Mao government recognized that elections might be an effective way to mitigate the tensions between peasants and cadres, it supported the practice and experiment.[42] In 1987, the government passed the Organic Law on Villagers' Committee (experimental), and the organization of the committee and village elections became institutionalized.

Thus, villages in post–Mao China have been moving in different directions and becoming enormously diverse in terms of decision making and development. For instance, despite the national policy of the thirty-year farming land contract, villages follow different patterns of allocating and reallocating their land. In some villages, they reallocate their land every five years, while in others, they reallocate land every three years or less. In still others, they have rarely reallocated their land since land was allocated to each household in the early 1980s.

Also, in contrast with Mao's era, local decision-making structures have become vastly diverse in today's China. Although Party Secretaries still play a dominant role in making decisions over public affairs in some villages, their power has been decreasing in many others. In some communities, the Villagers' Committees have played an active role in public affairs, while, in others, lineages have been making efforts to share the decision-making power with the cadres. In still others, some or many villagers have chances to participate in the decision-making process over public affairs in one way or another.[43] In short, in post–Mao China, some

villages have developed relatively more open and self-governing structures and a large number of villagers have been actively involved in public
affairs, including disbanding brigades, organizing Villagers' Committees,
electing members of the committees, attending public meetings, urging
the publication of fiscal records, declining the payment of "illegal" fees,
and suing corrupted leaders.

Moreover, the more open decision-making structures and greater
peasant participation have a positive influence on governance performance in terms of providing local public goods and services. The villages
with more open governing structures and peasant participation perform
better in terms of providing roads, education, land management, and fiscal management. The rationale for the significance of peasant participation
is that peasants have extraordinary local knowledge and time and place
information, which is indispensable for rational decision making over
public affairs. Villagers know better about local conditions than cadres or
the state because they have lived in their communities for a long time. The
villagers have accumulated much wisdom and know-how based on many
generations of experience. They know what kinds of crops are compatible
with local soils, where their roads should be built, who the good teachers in
their village schools are, what kind of land system is consistent with demographic changes, and whether public funds are mismanaged.

Greater peasant participation also helps enhance the transparency
of decision-making processes and the responsiveness and accountability
of local cadres. Public participation gives peasants chances to be familiar
with decision-making processes, articulate their preferences, and, to some
degree, limit the cadres' decision-making power. Peasant participation
facilitates public deliberation and preference revelation through which
peasants articulate their needs and urge the cadres to be responsive to the
needs. When peasants are involved in decision-making processes through
public meetings or other means, it becomes relatively more difficult for
local cadres to engage in behind-the-scenes practices. When peasants are
part of the decision-making events, the decisions become more transparent, and the cadres are more likely to be held accountable.

My field research in four rural communities—Minlu, Beishuai, Xin,
and Linhai—revealed that villages with more peasant participation in
decision-making processes over public affairs performed better in terms
of providing public goods and services, such as roads, schools, land management, and fiscal management. In Minlu village, the Party Secretary
alone dominated decision making over public affairs, and villagers had few
chances to participate in the decision-making process. The village's per-

formance in providing public goods and services was the worst among the four communities. It had a dirt road, and no arrangements were made for its maintenance. School facilities were also bad in the village. Electricity and water were often not provided in the school in a timely manner, while the Party Secretary had a hand in the schools' hiring of unqualified teachers. The Party Secretary also took advantage of his dominant role in allocating land and leasing to enrich himself and his close friends, which led to many violent conflicts. Moreover, thanks to his poor fiscal management, village finances suffered and incurred heavy debts.

In Beishuai village, several cadres controlled decision making over public affairs, and villagers, like those in Minlu, had few opportunities to be involved in the decision-making process. The village's performance in providing public goods and services was similar to Minlu's. Although Beishuai has tar roads, their construction involved misappropriation of public funds. Although the village's school facilities were better than Minlu's, the school often failed to supply electricity and water. The cadres in Beishuai sparked many land conflicts because they took advantage of land allocation to benefit themselves. As in Minlu, the lack of transparent fiscal management resulted in the village's incurring heavy debt.

In contrast, in Xin village, the institutional structure was more open, and some lineage leaders and senior villagers in many cases participated in decision-making processes over public affairs. Xin's performance in providing public goods and services was much better. The village built gravel roads and established arrangements for regular maintenance. Its school facilities were also better than Minlu's and Beishuai's. At the same time, land allocation and reallocation were relatively fair, and there were much fewer land conflicts here. Further, the village's fiscal management was more transparent, and there was no public debt.

Among the four communities, Linhai's institutional structure was most open, and here many villagers participated in decision making over public affairs in one way or another. The village had the best performance among the four in providing public goods and services. Its main road was made of cement, and regular maintenance was undertaken. Its school facilities were also the best among the four villages. Meanwhile, land allocation and reallocation was relatively fair in the village, and there were fewer land conflicts. The village's fiscal management was more transparent, and there was no village debt (see table 12.4).

At the same time, village elections have been held in many rural areas for a decade or so. Although the practice is uneven across regions and even villages, the studies on village elections indicate that grassroots elections

Table 12.4. Governance performance of four villages in China

Village Name	Villager Participation	Roads	Schools	Land Management	Fiscal Management
Minlu	Little	Earth	Worst	More land conflicts	Less transparent
Beishuai	Little	Tar	Worst	More land conflicts	Less transparent
Xin	Some	Gravel	Better	Fewer land conflicts	More transparent
Linhai	Much	Cement	Best	Fewer land conflicts	More transparent

have an empowering effect by enabling villagers to remove corrupt and unresponsive cadres, exercise their rights as citizens, and raise consciousness. Village elections helped facilitate more active and widespread political participation, enhanced the responsiveness of village cadres, improved village governance, promoted higher-level reforms, and restructured the political landscape in rural China.[44] According to Schubert, grassroots elections helped bring democratic training and idealism to Chinese peasants and will most probably facilitate a stable democracy in the future.[45] He suggests that Taiwan is a good example, where local elections since the 1950s helped propel its democratization in the 1980s. Village elections heighten peasants' consciousness of their political rights, which is fundamental to a democratic process.[46] The cumulative effect of the piecemeal reforms, including village elections, might change the very nature of the party and mode of governing. Once the people become used to approving their leaders, the authoritarian regime will have to change.[47]

While rural China has achieved the above significant changes and improvements, urban communities have also been making some progress in terms of self-organization since the 1990s. During Mao's era, urban residents were organized and tightly controlled by their working units, which were like a small paternal state. Residents relied on their working units for almost everything, including housing and other welfare benefits. With the collapse of many state-owned enterprises and urban reforms in the past two decades, residents have bought commercial apartments and begun to reorganize urban communities. As homeowners, the residents have begun to administer community affairs together and to protect their property rights.

Despite hostility from the party-state, thousands of urban communities have organized homeowners' associations or committees to protect their property and to provide public goods and services such as waste disposal, road maintenance, and security. In many urban communities, the residents have elected the leaders or representatives of their associations or committees, participated in public meetings to discuss community affairs, and contributed various resources to their communities. Some residents have become community leaders and public entrepreneurs, while urban communities have become an important arena for citizens to practice collective action and democratic experiments.

A recent high-profile case, involving the community of Meiliyuan in Beijing, provides some clues concerning the interesting development of community governance in urban China. Consisting of 1,378 households, the Meiliyuan community was established in 2002. At that time, its properties were managed by a company that had been hired by the developer of the community. Residents in this community soon found that the developer and the property management company had deceived them and had collected excessive fees for their services. In August 2004, the residents organized a homeowners' association and a committee to protect their property rights and to administer their community affairs. Under the leadership of the committee, the community decided to sue the property management company for its high service fees in March 2005 and lost the case. The community then appealed to a higher court, and won the case in December 2005. The company, however, requested a retrial of the case on the grounds of new evidence in May 2006, and again the community won. This case was regarded as one of the most important cases in which communities and residents defeated powerful property management companies and developers.[48]

After winning the legal battle, the community has continued to attract the attention of the people due to ongoing developments and experiments. First of all, the property management company abruptly left the community, leaving residents without electricity and water for more than ten hours. Thanks to the intervention of local government, the provision of electricity and water was restored. Second, some residents proposed to oust certain committee members by voting them out. In October of 2006, the temporary Assembly of Homeowners in the community convened; however, supporters for removing the committee members failed to do so because they did not constitute a quorum.

Third, the community selected a new property management company
through a public bidding process.

In addition to the development of more democratic rural and urban
modes of community governance, the emergence of numerous civic associations, NGOs, and other types of organizations and groups in today's China
offers some evidence of movement toward democratization. Although
few political associations are tolerated by the authoritarian regime, many
nonpolitical organizations have been formed over the past ten years or so.
These organizations' orientations and aims are multifarious and include
a wide variety of activities such as environmental protection, HIV/AIDS
prevention, poverty reduction, support for education, cultural exchanges,
religious activities, animal rights, and legal aid. Many public intellectuals
and lawyers have been involved in these civic or quasi-civic organizations
and have frequently acted as organizers, speakers, advisers, or consultants
for these organizations.

Although some associations and organizations have registered with the
government, many others have not, because the threshold for registration
is very high or because the government is hostile to them. Many associations considered to be sensitive by the government have to be registered in
the name of corporations. Some associations, such as house churches, are
not tolerated by the party-state and have to remain underground.

Given the underground nature of many organizations, it is difficult to
know the exact number of civic associations, NGOs, and other types of
groups in today's China. It was estimated that there were about three million NGOs in China in 2005, although only 280,000 of them registered
with the government.[49] At any rate, civic and quasi-civic associations have
been spreading in China and have contributed to the emergence of a civil
society under the authoritarian regime.

Meanwhile, various civic networks have come into being and have been
very active in post–Mao China, especially with the rapid development of
the Internet since the late 1990s. It was reported that China had around
132 million Internet users by the end of 2006,[50] making it the second largest user of the Internet behind the United States. Recently, blogging has
become very popular among Internet users. By the end of 2006, there were
20.8 million bloggers and 101 million viewers.[51] Many Web users have been
using the Internet to develop networks for various aims such as finding
friends, discussing hobbies, sharing news, lodging complaints, launching
protests, and so forth. Actually, innumerable networks are Internet-based
or using the Internet to share information, which indicates that a Web-
based civil society is under way.

To sum up, the development of more democratic rural and urban community governance, the extraordinary initiatives of citizens, and the emergence of civil society are some of the most important changes in contemporary China. These changes, from a Tocquevillian perspective, are fundamental to the establishment and sustainability of democracy. Despite the authoritarian and centralized party-state, these changes on the ground could help undermine the foundations of administrative centralization in China. Although the rural and urban communities are still far from democratic, they are moving toward self-organizing units. In the process of change, local citizens have demonstrated their remarkable capabilities for governing public affairs. The formation of civic and quasi-civic associations has contributed to the gradual emergence of a civil society. When the grassroots communities become "local republics" and a vibrant civil society takes root, a democratic transformation from the bottom up will be in sight.

Conclusion

If Tocqueville came to China today, what would he see and suggest in terms of democratic transformation? This chapter is partly an effort to shed some light on this hypothetical question. Following Tocqueville's insights on administrative centralization, I have provided a diagnosis of the obstacles to democracy in China. Despite its splendid civilization, the country has never moved out of the "cycle of dynasties" and established a democratic regime. This analysis has suggested that administrative centralization has been mainly responsible for the autocratic or authoritarian rule throughout China's long history because the concentration of decision-making power in one place has undermined local liberty and citizen self-governance, which constitute the very foundation of democracy.

This study has discussed how China can move away from the centralized administration to establish a democratic system. It has indicated that some significant changes, including the developments of both rural and urban community governance, the initiatives of local citizens, and the emergence of civil society, provide some hope for a bottom-up democratic transformation in the future. Local communities have become schools for the ordinary citizens to learn the artisanship of organizing collective actions and administering public affairs in contemporary China. Many citizens have actively participated in the process of reforms and experiments in their communities, which might eventually evolve into grassroots republics. At the same time, in organizing numerous civic and quasi-civic associations and networks in post-Mao China, the people have clearly promoted the emergence of a civil society.

Democracy means that citizens—rather than the government, national leaders, or political parties—govern. Thus, it is crucial to understand how citizens on the ground organize and govern their private and public affairs since democratic governance relies on the self-organizing and self-governing capabilities of ordinary citizens. Based on such an understanding, I suggest that China's movement out of the cycle of dynasties toward democracy will depend, to a large degree, on the construction and development of citizenship in everyday life. When every citizen has learned how to cooperate with their fellow citizens to solve problems, we can expect a genuine democratic transformation in this millennia-old country.

Notes

1. See John Meskill, *The Pattern of Chinese History: Cycles, Development, or Stagnation?* (Lexington, MA: D. C. Heath, 1965).

2. See Yang Gan, "Gongmin geti weiben, tongyi xianzheng liguo" [Based on Individuals, State-Building with Unity and Constitutionalism], *Ersehiyi shihi* [Twenty-First Century] 35 (June 1996): 4–14.

3. Shaoguang Wang, "The Problem of State Weakness," *Journal of Democracy* 14, no. 1 (2003): 36–42.

4. See Michael Oksenberg, "Confronting a Classic Dilemma," *Journal of Democracy* 9, no. 1 (1998): 27–34; Bruce Dickson, "China's Democratization and the Taiwan Experience," *Asian Survey* 38, no. 4 (1998): 349–64; Robert A. Scalapino, "Current Trends and Future Prospects," *Journal of Democracy* 9, no. 1 (1998): 35–40; Maxim Pei, "Contradictory Trends and Confusing Signals," *Journal of Democracy* 14, no. 1 (2003): 73–81; and Jacques De Lisle, "Democratization in Greater China: Introduction," *Orbis* 48, no. 2 (2004): 193–203.

5. Alexis de Tocqueville, *Democracy in America*, vol. I, ed. Philips Bradley (New York: Vintage Books, 1990), 86–97.

6. *Baojia* was a system of police control—a device to watch and check the number, movements, and activities of the people—through local agents, while *lijia* was a system of tax collection through which the imperial authority extracted revenue from local society. *Xiangyue* was an ideological control system over local society by requiring the people to learn the imperial orders and edicts. See Kung-Chuan Hsiao, *Rural China: Imperial Control in the Nineteenth Century* (Seattle: University of Washington Press, 1960) and Philip A. Kuhn, "Local Self-Government under the Republic: Problems of Control," in *Conflict and Control in Late Imperial China*, ed. Frederic Wakeman Jr. and Carolyn Grant (Berkeley: University of California Press, 1975), 260–61.

7. Tocqueville, *Democracy in America*, vol. I, 90.

8. See T'ung-tsu Ch'ü, *Local Government in China under the Ch'ing* (Cambridge, MA: Harvard University Press, 1962); John R. Watt, *The District Magistrate in Late Imperial China* (New York: Columbia University Press, 1972); Robert E. Bedeskie, *State-Building in Modern China: The Kuomintang in the Prewar Period* (Berkeley: Center for Chinese Studies, China Research Monograph no. 18, 1981); Philip C. Huang, *The Peasant Economy and Social Change in North China* (Stanford, CA: Stanford University Press, 1985); Prasenjit Duara, *Culture, Power, and the State: Rural North China, 1900–1942* (Stanford, CA: Stanford University Press, 1988); and Xin Zhang, *Social Transformation in Modern China: The State and Local Elites in Henan, 1900–1937* (New York: Cambridge University Press, 2000).

9. Philip A. Kuhn, *Origins of the Modern Chinese State* (Stanford, CA: Stanford University Press, 2002), 132.

10. Duara, *Culture, Power, and the State*.

11. Kuhn, "Local Self-Government under the Republic," 284–85.

12. Duara, *Culture, Power, and the State*, 223–25.

13. Tocqueville, *Democracy in America*, vol. II, 318.

14. Philip C. Huang, *The Peasant Family and Rural Development in the Yanzi Delta, 1350–1988* (Stanford, CA: Stanford University Press, 1990), 321.

15. David Zweig, *Agrarian Radicalism in China, 1968–1981* (Cambridge, MA: Harvard University Press, 1989); Dali L. Yang, *Calamity and Reform in China: State, Rural Society, and Institutional Change since the Great Leap Famine* (Stanford, CA: Stanford University Press, 1996); Jonathan Unger, *The Transformation of Rural China* (Armonk, NY: M. E. Sharpe, 2002); and Andrew G. Walder, *Communist Neo-Traditionalism: Work and Authority in Chinese Industry* (Berkeley: University of California Press, 1986).

16. Jasper Becker, *Hungry Ghosts: Mao's Secret Famine* (New York: Free Press, 1996).

17. Yumin Sheng, "Central-Provincial Relations at the CCP Central Committees: Institutions, Measurement and Empirical Trends, 1978–2002," *China Quarterly* 182 (2005): 338–55.

18. See Christine P. W. Wong, "Central-Local Relations in an Era of Fiscal Decline: The Paradox of Fiscal Decentralization in Post–Mao China," *China Quarterly* 128 (December 1991): 691–715; Wong, "Central-Local Relations Revisited: The 1994 Tax Sharing Reform and Public Expenditure Management in China," *China Perspectives* 31 (2000): 52–63; Shaoguang Wang, "Central-Local Fiscal Politics in China," in *Changing Central-Local Relations in China: Reform and State Capacity*, ed. Hao Jia and Zhimin Lin (Boulder, CO: Westview Press, 1994), 91–112; Jae Ho Chung, "Studies of Central-Provincial Relations in the People's Republic of China: A Mid-Term Appraisal," *China Quarterly* 142 (June 1995): 487–508; Chung, "Beijing Confronting the Provinces: The 1994 Tax-Sharing Reform and Its Implications for Central-Provincial Relations in China," *China Information* 9, nos. 2–3 (1995):

1–23; and Pak K. Lee, "Into the Trap of Strengthening State Capacity: China's Tax Assignment Reform," *China Quarterly* 164 (December 2000): 1007–24.

19. See Jean C. Oi, "Fiscal Reform and the Economic Foundations of Local State Corporatism in China," *World Politics* 45, no. 1 (1992): 99–126; Oi, "The Role of the Local State in China's Transitional Economy," *China Quarterly* 144 (1995): 1132–49; Oi, "The Evolution of Local State Corporatism," in *Zouping in Transition: The Process of Rural Reform in North China*, ed. Andrew G. Walder (Cambridge, MA: Harvard University Press, 1998), 35–61; and Oi, *Rural China Takes Off: Institutional Foundations of Economic Reform* (Berkeley: University of California Press, 1999).

20. Gabriella Monitola, Yingyi Qian, and Barry Weingast, "Federalism, Chinese Style: The Political Basis for Economic Success in China," *World Politics* 48, no. 1 (1995): 50–81; Barry Weingast, "The Economic Role of Political Institutions: Market-Preserving Federalism and Economic Growth," *Journal of Law, Economics, and Organization* 11, no. 1 (1995): 1–31; Yingyi Qian and Barry Weingast, "China's Transition to Markets: Market-Preserving Federalism, Chinese Style," *Journal of Policy Reform* 1, no. 2 (1996): 149–86; and Hehui Jin, Yingyi Qian, and Barry Weingast, "Regional Decentralization and Fiscal Incentives: Federalism, Chinese Style," *Journal of Public Economics* 89, nos. 9–10 (2005): 1719–42.

21. Yongnian Zheng, "Political Incrementalism: Political Lessons from China's 20 Years of Reform," *Third World Quarterly* 20, no. 6 (1999): 1157–77.

22. Lucian W. Pye, *Asian Power and Politics: The Cultural Dimensions of Authority* (Cambridge, MA: Harvard University Press, 1985), 183–84.

23. Tocqueville, *Democracy in America*, vol. I, 61.

24. For example, see Samuel P. Huntington, *The Third Wave: Democratization in the Late Twentieth Century* (Norman: University of Oklahoma Press, 1991); Juan J. Linz and Alfred Stepan, *Problems of Democratic Transition and Consolidation: Southern Europe, South America, and Post-Communist Europe* (Baltimore, MD: Johns Hopkins University Press, 1996).

25. Tocqueville, *Democracy in America*, vol. I, 57.

26. For the concept of self-governance and Tocqueville's understanding of this concept, see Vincent Ostrom, *The Meaning of American Federalism: Constituting a Self-Governing Society* (San Francisco, CA: ICS Press, 1991) and *The Meaning of Democracy and the Vulnerability of Democracies: A Response to Tocqueville's Challenge* (Ann Arbor: University of Michigan Press, 1997).

27. See Frederick A. Hayek, "Economics and Knowledge," *Economica* 4, no. 13 (1937): 33–54 and his classic work, *The Road to Serfdom* (Chicago: University of Chicago Press, 1944).

28. Frederick A. Hayek, "The Use of Knowledge in Society," *American Economic Review* 35, no. 4 (1945): 519–30.

29. Clifford Geertz, "Local Knowledge: Fact and Law in Comparative Perspective," in *Local Knowledge: Further Essays in Interpretive Anthropology* (New York: Basic Books, 1983).

30. Tocqueville, *Democracy in America*, vol. I, 90.

31. Thomas Hobbes, *Leviathan*, ed. Edwin Curley (Indianapolis, IN: Hackett, 1994).

32. Pye, *Asian Power and Politics*, 184.

33. See Pye, *Asian Power and Politics*, 190; Michael Davis, "The Case for Chinese Federalism," *Journal of Democracy* 10, no. 2 (1999): 125.

34. Lucian W. Pye, "China: Erratic State, Frustrated Society," *Foreign Affairs* 69, no. 4 (1990): 59.

35. James Scott, *Seeing Like a State: How Certain Schemes to Improve the Human Condition Have Failed* (New Haven, CT: Yale University Press, 1998).

36. Tocqueville, *Democracy in America*, vol. I, 87.

37. Tocqueville, *Democracy in America*, vol. I, 87.

38. Alexis de Tocqueville, *The Old Regime and the French Revolution* (Garden City, NY: Doubleday & Co., 1955), 41.

39. Tocqueville, *Democracy in America*, vol. I, 92–93.

40. For more on the concept of polycentricity, see Vincent Ostrom, "Polycentricity," in *Polycentricity and Local Public Economies: Readings from the Workshop in Political Theory and Policy Analysis*, ed. Michael D. McGinnis (Ann Arbor: University of Michigan Press, 1999), 52–74, 119–38.

41. See Daniel Kelliher, *Peasant Power in China: The Era of Rural Reform, 1979–1989* (New Haven, CT: Yale University Press, 1992); Kate Xiao Zhou, *How the Farmers Changed China: Power of the People* (Boulder, CO: Westview Press, 1996).

42. Daniel Kelliher, "The Chinese Debate over Village Self-Government," *China Journal* 37 (January 1997): 63–86.

43. For a detailed analysis of village governance reforms, see Jianxun Wang, "Political Economy of Village Governance in Contemporary China" (PhD diss., Indiana University, 2006).

44. For more details on village elections, see Kevin J. O'Brien, "Implementing Political Reform in China's Villages," *Australian Journal of Chinese Affairs* 32 (July 1994): 33–59; O'Brien, "Villagers, Elections and Citizenship in Contemporary China," *Modern China* 27, no. 4 (2001): 407–35; O'Brien and Lianjiang Li, "Accommodating Democracy in a One-Party State: Introducing Village Elections in China," *China Quarterly* 162 (June 2000): 465–89; Lianjiang Li and Kevin O'Brien, "The Struggle over Village Elections," in *The Paradox of China's Post-Mao Reforms*, ed. Merle Goldman and Roderick MacFarquar (Cambridge, MA: Harvard University, 1999), 129–44; Lianjiang Li, "The Empowering Effect of Village Elections in China," *Asian Survey* 43, no. 4 (2003): 648–62; Sylvia Chan, "Research Notes on Villagers' Committee Election: Chinese-Style Democracy," *Journal of Contemporary China* 7, no. 19 (1998): 507–21; Tianjian Shi, "Village Committee Elections in China: Institutionalist Tactics for Democracy," *World Politics* 51, no. 3 (1999): 385–412; and Melanie Manion, "The Electoral Connection in the Chinese Countryside," *American Political Science Review* 90, no. 4 (1996): 736–48.

45. Gunter Schubert, "Village Elections in the PRC: A Trojan Horse of Democracy?" (Duisburg, Germany: Institute for East Asian Studies, Project Discussion Paper no. 19, 2002).

46. Chan, "Research Notes on Villagers' Committee Election."

47. Kelliher, "The Chinese Debate over Village Self-Government."

48. Many reports on the case of Meiliyuan can be found on the Meiliyuan Community Blog at: http://www.focus.cn/~mly or at: http://house.sina.com.cn/bbs/bbsmeiliyuanwq/index.html (accessed January 22, 2007).

49. See *nanfang zhoumo* [Southern Weekend], May 19, 2005.

50. *Xinhua News*, December 28, 2006. http://news3.xinhuanet.com/english/2006-12/28/content_5544561.htm (accessed January 22, 2007).

51. *Xinhua News*, January 10, 2007. http://news.xinhuanet.com/hlw/2007-01/10/content_5587999.htm (accessed January 22, 2007).

13

Tocqueville and Japan

Reiji Matsumoto

Reception and Relevance

The title of this chapter can be interpreted in two ways. It can mean the Japanese reception of Tocqueville's works and ideas. When and how were Tocqueville's ideas introduced to Japan and what kind of intellectual influence did they have on the people? It may also be taken as a reflection on the following questions: To what extent and why is Tocqueville useful for understanding Japanese society and history? If so, is he more relevant or less for that purpose than other European social theorists such as Karl Marx and Max Weber?

The two questions are different, though related to each other. A European thinker who has nothing to say about Japan can still be widely read in certain historical situations by the Japanese. The most remarkable example is the case of Herbert Spencer, who was probably the most popular European thinker in Meiji Japan. His books were widely read and not a few intellectuals went to Britain to see him. It would be impossible to write an intellectual history of modern Japan without referring to his influence. But today, no one tries to draw on Spencer to analyze Japanese society. His popularity in the Meiji era reveals something important about the nature of the society at the time, but his social theory itself is of little use for understanding the country. That is the reason why his fame was limited to the nineteenth century and rapidly declined later in Japan as well as in Europe.

On the other hand, one can successfully use a foreign theoretical framework to investigate the Japanese society. Robert Bellah's *Tokugawa Religion* makes a brilliant use of Parsonian paradigms to reveal an important aspect of Japanese society.[1] When the book was first published, however,

Parsonian theory was almost unknown to Japan. Maruyama Masao's long review of the book was the first substantial essay that introduced to Japan the sociology of Talcott Parsons.[2] Nevertheless, Bellah's thesis triggered the strong interest of Japanese scholars and caused subsequent debates about the nature of Japanese modernization.

In many cases, however, the two questions are more closely connected. Indeed, no social theorist could have an enduring influence on a foreign country, unless its people find in him or her a theoretical guide to their self-recognition. The publication of numerous Japanese studies on Marx and Weber is a result of the fact that Japanese scholars have found in both thinkers theoretical frameworks useful for considering their own society.[3] The intellectual influence of Tocqueville in Japan is not comparable to that of Marx or Weber. Although his works, in particular *Democracy in America*, were widely read and referred to in the era of the Movement for Freedom and People's Rights (in the 1870s and the 1880s), he has never become as popular in Japan as Herbert Spencer once was (before fading in obscurity). This does not discourage us, however, from examining the relevance of Tocqueville to Japan in the historical context of democratization and from our present point of view.

This chapter is not concerned with the Japanese reception of Tocqueville per se; it deals mainly with the relevance of Tocqueville to Japan. However, I shall also touch upon several points that early Meiji intellectuals learned from Tocqueville and advanced in the public debates of their time. So far as these issues are concerned, the problem of reception must inevitably be addressed. How and why did early Japanese readers of Tocqueville— Fukuzawa Yukichi or Tokutomi Sohō, for example—pick up those issues? At the same time, I shall also consider other Tocquevillian ideas and arguments that might throw fresh light on certain aspects of our society and history, although they have not been taken seriously in Japan thus far.

I would like to underline the universality of Tocqueville's theory of democracy, which is a source of inspiration for rethinking the nature of democracy in Japan. Moreover, Tocqueville's ideas did have a significant impact on the Japanese people's political understanding in the past and inspired some Japanese thinkers in their attempts to reform their own society. In a paper presented at the 2005 Tocqueville conference held in Tokyo, Françoise Mélonio showed that Tocqueville's political theory and his historical thinking found a wide resonance in the mid-nineteenth century throughout continental Europe, including not only Germany and Italy but also Russia, where the issue of the anticipated emancipation of serfs was hotly debated.[4] Not surprisingly, *The Old Regime and the Revolution* was enthusiastically discussed in terms of the task of how to abolish the Russian old regime without the risk of revolution. Why not broaden the same comparative perspective to the Far East and examine the relevance of Tocqueville to Japan, the country that desperately attempted at the time to transform its old regime into the first modern state in Asia?

Equality and Egalitarianism

A basic reason for Tocqueville's relevance to Japan is that its society is democratic. There is no doubt that Japan is one of the most egalitarian countries in the world. Except for a few people belonging to the royal family and their *entourage*, there remains no aristocracy. Every statistical report tells us that wealth and income are relatively equally distributed in comparison with other advanced economies. The economic equality of Japan is probably smaller than that of some European countries, Denmark or the Netherlands, for example, but far greater than that of the United States.[5] Thus, in the 1980s when the Japanese economy was at its zenith, more than 90 percent of the population was reported to consider themselves as belonging to the middle class, although recently there has arisen a controversy about new inequality, or "disparity," and the new lower classes.[6] Social mobility is perhaps less dynamic than in America, but greater than in most European countries.

In terms of culture and education, the equality and homogeneity of the Japanese society is even more remarkable. Japan gave the first successful example of modernization outside of Europe and North America, and its success depended largely on the educational system through which social and political elites were competitively recruited and basic knowledge was propagated to the common people. Under the effective meritocracy of higher bureaucrats recruited from the graduates of privileged colleges, aristocracies, intellectual as well as political, have disappeared and the postwar egalitarian reform of the school system, drawing every family into a bitter competition for a better school for its children, has completed "status democracy" (*shusse minshushugi*). Certainly, the spread of basic knowledge among the common people, which was already noteworthy in the Tokugawa period,[7] and the success of universal education in modern Japan afford a good testimony of Tocqueville's claim that a certain amount of shared knowledge and learning is a necessary condition for the function of democracy.[8] The other side of the coin of this intellectual egalitarianism is the spread of "diploma disease"[9] and the dissolution of high culture. Indeed, many of Tocqueville's remarks about the intellectual tendencies of democracy, the preponderance of technology over science, practical use over pure theory and others, are equally applicable to modern Japan and Jacksonian America.

Egalitarianism is not only a feature of contemporary Japanese society but also a historical tendency noticeable in modern Japan. Equality was celebrated in the early Meiji period, when Tocqueville found his first audience in Japan. The Meiji Revolution abolished legal distinction between samurai and commoners and declared "the equality of four peoples (samurai, peasants, artisans and merchants)" (*shiminbyōdō*). Thus, Fukuzawa Yukichi, one of the first and greatest Japanese readers of Tocqueville, began his famous tract, *An Encouragement of Learning*, by articulating a Jeffersonian philosophy of equality.[10] Nakae Chōmin, who might have read Tocqueville in the original French text, translating Rousseau's *Du contrat social*, became a representative ideologue of the Movement for Freedom and People's Rights. Tokutomi Sohō, a journalist and a second-generation Meiji intellectual, heavily drawing on Spencer, Guizot, and Tocqueville, regarded as a distinctive hallmark of modern European history the rise of middle classes, which he thought also underlay the transformation of Japanese society before and after the Meiji Revolution. While he did not endorse Tocqueville's skepticism about the bourgeoisie of the July Monarchy, it is obvious that Sohō's notion of "the society of commoners" (*heiminshakai*) was inspired by Tocqueville's idea of democratic society.

Moreover, equalization should not be regarded as a modern phenomenon that abruptly emerged in the Meiji era. Under the Tokugawa Regime, historians underline, a certain process of equalization was already going on. With the advance of the money economy, the samurai class on the whole became relatively impoverished and both central (*shogunate*) and local (*han*) governments became more and more dependent on financial aid from prominent merchants. Cultural equalization was even more remarkable. In the cultural history of Japan, the Tokugawa period is characterized as the epoch of the rise of bourgeois culture (*chōnin bunka*).[11] Since the late seventeenth century, various kinds of art and culture flourished in the big cities (Osaka, Kyoto, and Edo), attracting urban middle classes. Most Japanese traditional arts—musical (*jyōruri*), theatrical (*kabuki*), poetic (*haikai*), and others—attained perfection during this time. These artistic works and plays represented the lives and sentiments of townspeople, and the audiences were pleased to find there a sophisticated expression of their own outlook: materialism, secularism, hedonism, and sentimentalism. Compared with French classical literature, Japanese literature of that period was probably more democratic according to the standard by which Tocqueville characterized the democratic literature in contrast to the aristocratic one. Yonosuke, the hero of a famous novel by Ihara Saikaku and the Japanese counterpart of Don Juan, had no aristocratic ambition to intentionally violate social morality and religious teachings. In the end of his sexual odyssey, he was sent not to hell but to a legendary island of women. Not a small number of samurai, bored with the rigorism and stoicism of their class ethics, wished to imitate the pleasant lifestyle of urban middle classes and some were glad to change their status by adoption or marriage. But few rich merchants would have shared Monsieur Jourdain's enthusiasm for learning aristocratic culture.

Even in the ruling class that was itself hierarchically organized, the process of equalization was inevitably going on. Under a growing difficulty of administration and finance, a kind of meritocratic appointment of lower-class samurai to higher offices became fashionable in the late Edo period. Toward the end of the era, this tendency increased and the political crisis triggered by the arrival of Commodore Perry sharpened the struggle between the traditionalist upper classes and the reformist lower classes. As a result of this struggle for political hegemony, which was remarkable in several big anti-bakufu *han* like Chōshū and Satsuma, a loose coalition was formed among radicalized lower-class samurai coming from various *han* that played a major role in carrying out the Meiji Revolution. It was in a sense the final result of this inner class struggle within the ruling people, and historians agree that most of the revolutionary leaders came from lower-ranking samurai.

So, in spite of an enduring system of legal distinctions, a process of social, economic, and cultural equalization was apparently going on in Tokugawa Japan, just as Tocqueville observed the similar progress of equality in France of the Old Regime. The Meiji Revolution was a consequence of this long process as well as the starting point that opened a new stage for further equalization. In short, it was a democratic revolution in the full sense of Tocqueville's use of the term and therefore comparable with the French Revolution.[12] There was ample reason why early Meiji intellectuals were so attracted by Tocqueville's works, for they lived in a post-revolutionary era similar to the one in which Tocqueville himself had lived.

The Postwar Reform after the defeat of 1945 did away with all the remnants of inequality in Japanese society. The Land Reform destroyed large landowning and abolished absenteeism, eliminating the factors that had nurtured the peasants' political radicalism, on the Right or on the Left.[13] The revised law of inheritance, which abolished primogeniture and imposed on every proprietor the principle of equal partition, divided property into an infinite number of fragments. Indeed, postwar Japanese society confirmed once again Tocqueville's prediction about the social effects of the law of equal inheritance: an infinite fragmentation of landed property and the disappearance of the hereditary spirit of the family.[14] And finally, the unprecedented growth of the Japanese economy since the mid-1950s involved everybody in the exclusive pursuit of happiness and thus made our society more and more similar to Tocqueville's ideal type of democratic society. Not surprisingly, one finds in the present society of Japan several important features that Tocqueville considered characteristic of democratic society: individualism and privatization, absorption in the pursuit of material well-being, psychological restlessness, and so forth.

Centralization and Public Spirit

The second focal point of Tocqueville's democratic theory is liberty. Early Japanese readers of Tocqueville did not miss this central issue. The first Japanese publication of his text was the translation of chapter 3 of the second part of the first volume of *Democracy in America*, dealing with the freedom of the press,[15] and the second contained the chapter on public spirit in America. The Japanese title of the first entire translation of the first volume of *Democracy in America* meant *A Fundamental Theory of Freedom*.[16] These facts eloquently show in what context Tocqueville was introduced to Japan. At the high tide of the Movement for Freedom and People's Rights, he was referred to above all as a proponent of freedom and political democracy.

It is no wonder that one of the frequently discussed topics was his argument on public spirit and patriotism. Indeed, his insistence on the necessity of uniting public spirit and individual rights was extraordinarily attractive to those involved in the movement. Living in a time, "when ancient customs were transformed, mores decayed, faiths were shaken, memories lost their prestige, but enlightenment had yet to complete its work and political rights remained insecure and limited,"[17] early Meiji intellectuals took seriously his argument that the only way to develop civic spirit and to substitute a rational and reflective patriotism for an instinctive and passionate one was to make people participate in politics. It was only natural that they should find in Tocqueville's proposition an urgent task for a country in which, in Fukuzawa's words, "there was a government but no nation (meaning the aggregate of free and independent citizens)."[18]

Another related issue seriously discussed was his notion of centralization. Here also Fukuzawa was a leading player. Drawing on Tocqueville's theoretical distinction between two centralizations, the governmental and the administrative, he warned against the danger of the latter to freedom, while emphasizing the necessity of the former as imperative for the country.[19] Only a decade after the Meiji Revolution, which had destroyed the poly-governmental Tokugawa Regime and established a new national government instead, the Japanese people should make every effort to centralize governmental power, Fukuzawa argued, so as to maintain their national independence against the menace of Western imperialism. In fact, a series of policies and legislations successively introduced by the new government, the abolition of semi-sovereign *han* governments and the institution of the local unit of the prefecture, the creation of national land tax and others, marked inevitable steps toward governmental centralization. The transition from the Tokugawa Regime to the Meiji state was a dramatic process of governmental centralization through which the feudal division of sovereignty was revolutionarily overcome and the country was transformed into a modern nation-state. In the midst of this rapid progress of centralization, Fukuzawa rightly understood Tocqueville's warning against administrative centralization and was in agreement with Tocqueville when writing: "I cannot conceive that a nation can endure, much less prosper, without a high degree of governmental centralization. But I think that administrative centralization serves only to sap the strength of nations that are subjected to it, because it steadily weakens their civic spirit."[20]

Fukuzawa's argument against administrative centralization was all the more remarkable because the government at the time was planning its own local administrative system. In the prefectural system of Japan, which was established in 1890 and existed until 1945, every prefecture was governed by an omnipotent prefect, appointed by the Ministry of Interior Affairs, and elected local assemblies had no real power. In a word, it was a local administration system *à la française*; its ideal was the enlightened and benevolent government of the local people under bureaucracy. It is surprising that higher bureaucrats like Ōmori Shōichi, who played an important role in the creation of the system, made a different use of the same Tocquevillian distinction between government and administration.[21] Drawing on the French aristocrat, he insisted on the importance of keeping local communities immune from the ideological and partisan struggle of national politics. Whether truly a Tocquevillian argument or not, this became a dominant political philosophy of Japanese conservatives.

After 1945, the Japanese system of local government was greatly changed under the U.S. Occupation. The Ministry of Interior Affairs was divided and its local government section was transformed into the Min-

istry of Self-Government (*Jichishō*).²² The appointive office of prefect was
replaced by the elective one of governor. Local assemblies, increasing their
legal and financial competence, gained in importance. In short, the old
system *à la française* was largely Americanized. Officially, His Majesty's
magistrates became civil servants. But it was doubtful that their mentality
and behavior changed overnight. In spite of the institutional reorganization, financial autonomy was only insufficiently accorded to local governments so that the national government might easily control them. Without
the allocation of tax grants and other subsidies from the national government, most prefectures and municipalities could not avoid bankruptcy.
The main job of governors or mayors was to get as much money as possible from the national government, and a considerable part of the routine
activity of local administration was devoted to "transferred matters" (*inin-
jimu*), namely, the administrative tasks imposed upon municipalities by
the national government. The limited financial autonomy of local government and administration has led critics to voice their complaint about "30
percent self-government" (*sanwari-jichi*).

Of course, the national government has not utterly been deaf to this
critique. Following the Comprehensive Decentralization Law that had
come into force in 2000, the Koizumi Administration launched the "Trin-
ity Reform Package": the reform of local tax, local allocation tax grant, and
national government disbursement, aiming at giving a greater deal of fiscal and financial autonomy to local governments. In spite of the Koizumi
people's enthusiasm for reform, however, it seems to have only resulted in a
massive wave of municipal mergers and the increase of economic disparity
between metropolitan and local areas, which is said to have been a cause of
the drastic defeat of the Liberal Democratic Party at the 2007 national election of the Second House. Ironically, this decentralization promoted by the
Ministry of Interior Affairs reminds us of Tocqueville's remark:

> Centralization may, then, in despair, call upon citizens for help. But it
> speaks to them in these terms: You shall do what I want, just as much as
> I want, and in precisely the way I want. You shall assume responsibility
> for the details without aspiring to direct the whole. You shall work in the
> dark, and later you will judge my work by its results.²³

Another aspect of the postwar system of local government is the
coalition of party politicians and administrative bureaucrats. Under the
so-called 1955 Year Regime, the predominant conservative party, the Liberal Democratic Party, which has generally retained the majority in most

prefectural assemblies as well as in the National Diet, has frequently chosen a career bureaucrat as their candidate for governor, in many cases, an ex-official of the Ministry of Self-Government. In election campaigns, they have consistently pointed to the advantages associated with strong ties between bureaucrat governors and the national government, and won in most cases. As a result, three-fifths of the forty-seven governors are ex-bureaucrats[24] and most of them have been easily reelected with the strong support of the majority of local assemblies and with the financial aid of interest groups. Bureaucrats, politicians, and business elites—connected by the bond of vested interests—constitute a powerful interest group complex that dominates local politics and functions as a local unit of national interest politics.

This coalition or fusion of bureaucrats and party politicians that is characteristic of Japanese interest politics has certainly been useful in reducing the administrative instability that Tocqueville considered as peculiar to democratic government.[25] But it is doubtful whether it has provided a favorable political culture for cultivating public spirit among ordinary citizens. With the disappearance of the anti-LDP municipalities of the 1960s and the early 1970s that had mobilized to some extent nonpartisan urban voters, the percentage of those voting in local elections has tended to decrease and the influence of political clientelism has become greater. The emergence of many types of citizens' movements and the development of the theory and practice of civil society have not had a profound and enduring effect on professional politics in Japan, a country that still lacks, for example, a green party, despite the growing importance of environmental issues.

In 2000, Tanaka Yasuo, a best-selling writer and media celebrity, who had gained popularity as an organizer of volunteers helping the victims of the Kōbe Earthquake in 1995, ran for the Governor of Nagano Prefecture against the seemingly strongest candidate, the former vice governor designated as the successor to the six-time reelected governor and supported by almost all established parties and interest groups. Thanks to his popularity in the media and the enthusiastic support of grassroots people looking for a dramatic change, Tanaka Yasuo won the election and introduced a new style of local government during his two terms in office that solicited the participation of ordinary citizens and abandoned some public construction projects. In the 2006 elections, however, various groups of people benefiting from conventional interest politics—party politicians, members of the prefectural assembly, and business managers—united in order to oust the new governor and finally succeeded in defeating him.[26] Another example of a successful challenger to the established clientelism of local administration is the present Governor of Shiga Prefecture, a female environmental scholar who surprisingly defeated the incumbent governor supported by all political parties except the Communists in the 2006 elections. These rare cases certainly bring to light not only the accumulated frustration of the common people with conventional interest politics but also the persistence and resilience of the latter.

Interest politics and political clientelism are consequences of the democratization of Japanese postwar politics that has become vulnerable to political corruption after 1946. This is not to say that Japanese politics used to be clean. Since the early Meiji era, political scandals have continuously emerged and some of them caused serious governmental crises. Naturally, muckraking also has a long history in Japanese journalism. In prewar politics, however, it was mainly ministers and party politicians who were blamed for corruption. Higher bureaucrats, especially those responsible for local government, were in general less vulnerable to criticism. Prefects sent from the Ministry of Internal Affairs might have been unpopular and authoritarian, but they were rarely involved in money scandals. As shown above, the postwar reform of local government did not properly cultivate the public spirit of citizens and extended political corruption from the national to local levels. The office of elected governor with formidable competence, unless properly checked by the prefectural assembly, has thus become a good target of bribery and manipulation. The rapid expansion of the budget and the growing amount of subsidies from the national government has only aggravated this danger. Thus, since the 1960s, there have been so many political scandals in both local and national politics that the term "structural corruption" (kōzōoshoku) was coined. In 2006, three governors were arrested for bribery and a couple of others were severely criticized for their activities.

Although this prevailing corruption can be seen as a consequence of a certain form of democratization of politics, it will in the end discredit politicians and administrators in the eyes of ordinary citizens and will spread cynicism and apathy that might undermine democracy in the long run. In this sense, Tocqueville's brief reflection on democratic corruption is highly relevant to contemporary Japanese politics. As he wrote in *Democracy in America*:

> What is to be feared, moreover, is not so much the sight of immorality in the great as that of immorality leading to greatness. In a democracy, ordinary citizens see a man step forth from their ranks and within a few

years achieve wealth and power. This spectacle fills them with astonish-
ment and envy. They try to understand how a man who only yesterday
was their equal today enjoys the right to rule over them. To attribute
his rise to talent and virtue is inconvenient, because it requires them to
admit to themselves that they are less virtuous and clever than he. They
therefore ascribe primary responsibility to some number of his vices,
and often they are right to do so. This results in I know not what odious
mingling of the ideas of baseness and power, unworthiness and success,
utility and dishonor.[27]

The Democratic Family

The scope of Tocqueville's theory of democracy is not limited to politics
but covers a wide range of social and cultural phenomena. In his analysis
of the influence of democracy on mores, he addressed many important
topics, including the democratic family. Tocqueville's sociological account
of the historical transition of the family type from the aristocratic to the
democratic is extremely insightful as an early attempt to understand the
meaning of the transformation of family relations in modern times.[28]
Sociohistorical studies of the family have touched upon most of the issues
and tendencies on which Tocqueville himself focused: the weakening of
paternal power, the independence of children, the domestication of mar-
ried women, the growing intimacy based on the natural bond of the family,
and so forth. It is true that recent studies tend to consider these phenomena in the context of modernization and industrialization and are skeptical about Tocqueville's explanation of social phenomena as consequences
of democratization. Present-day gender historians and feminist theorists,
for example, tend to be critical of his view of the domestication of women
as compatible with the democratic principle of sexual equality, while confirming it as the historical description of the American family in the Victo-
rian age. Nonetheless, Tocqueville's holistic approach to the various aspects
of the family testifies to the radical and deep transformation occurring in
family life in his era. His attempt to consider changing family patterns as
a result of the democratization of society at large is quite understandable
against this background and would sound interesting to other people experiencing a drastic transformation of society comparable to that of his age.

In particular, the democratization of family relations became a subject
of intense debate in Japan as the country experienced a profound social
transformation in the postwar era. Among various reforms introduced

under the Occupation, the drastic revision of the family law in 1947 was one
of the most important, for it attacked the ideological basis of the old society
and at the same time exerted a direct influence on everyone's life. The revision was inevitable because the old patriarchal principle of the Japanese
family was not compatible with the New Constitution, which declared the
dignity of the individual and the equality of men and women.

The traditional household of Japan, called "*ie*," legally established by
the Civil Code in 1898, was not simply a kinship group but also a social
organization for maintaining its property and continuing its hereditary
occupation. It constituted as such the bottom unit of the whole nation that
was considered as a big family headed by a benevolent patriarch-monarch,
the Emperor. In this ideology of the family-state (*kazokukokka*), the virtue
of benevolent paternalism was extolled as a consistent principle of Japanese society from the family through corporations to the state, and every
form of leader-follower relation was compared to the relation between the
father and his children (*oyabun-kobun* relation). This ideological extension of the family spirit to political society was possible only because the
family structure itself was politicized. The head of the family, usually the
father, was always supposed to consider the collective interest of the family
and consequently every member was expected to obey him faithfully. Marriages were arranged for the benefit of the family and the future of every
child was in many cases determined by parents. Neglected in this instrumental family relation was the freedom and rights of individuals, especially
of female members. Also missing was the tender and affectionate sentiment that should have naturally been shared by the members of a family
united by true and reciprocal love.

It was only natural that in the postwar atmosphere of the total negation
of the past, the Japanese came to challenge the patriarchal structure of the
family and called for its democratization. Kawashima Takeyoshi's famous
essay, "The Family-Like Structure of Japanese Society,"[29] blaming Japanese
family structure for providing the basis for the feudal mentality of the people, had a wide appeal, although it was later severely criticized for its inac-
curate historical understanding. The argument was that in postwar Japan,
democracy and democratization could not be confined to politics but had
to be extended to the private sphere as well, including family life. The revision of the family law was endorsed and welcomed by most people as a
springboard for the creation of a new type of family. Not surprisingly, this
family pattern had many things in common with Tocqueville's notion of
the democratic family; the only difference was that the conventional type
of Japanese family was not called aristocratic but feudal or feudalistic.

It would be wrong, however, to imagine that the Japanese people's frustration with the old family system erupted after the defeat under the influence of the policies carried out by the occupation forces. It was born almost at the same time as the *ie* system was legally established, and subsequently grew together with the increasing contradictions of its ideology. Tocqueville's keen observation that the natural bond of heart is overshadowed in the aristocratic family by the social bond of interest[30] is also true of the traditional Japanese family. In fact, its ideology of benevolent paternalism was often discredited by the resistance of the underprivileged members of the family. Modern Japanese literature is filled with such themes and stories revealing serious problems of family relations: conflicts between fathers and sons, the subjection of wives, the unhappy destiny of love marriages, and so forth. These literary fictions reveal the dark side of traditional family relations and represent the accumulated frustration of the people with them.

It should be noted, however, that already before the war, the real family life of the people contradicted to some extent the legal and ideological fiction of the traditional patriarchal family. With growing urbanization, the number of nuclear families increased and modern family sentiment based on love and intimacy prevailed in urban areas. Hence, in a certain sense, the postwar revision of the family law legally justified a certain tendency that had already been apparent before the war, which explains why it was welcomed and little resisted. Once firmly established, no one dared to doubt the virtue of the democratic family. This was a remarkable phenomenon all the more that some of the political and economic reforms implemented in the early years of the occupation were severely attacked later. The democratization of family relations was not a result of the policies favored by the occupation forces, but a consequence of an irreversible change of social life in Japan, which started in interwar years and became highly noticeable in the postwar period.[31] Here also Tocqueville's remarks are relevant to the Japanese experience of the changing family patterns: "Democratic mores are so mild that even partisans of aristocracy find them attractive, and after savoring them for a time, they are not tempted to revert to chilly and respectful formalities of the aristocratic family."[32]

If Tocqueville's view of the family is relevant for thinking about the Japanese case, why has it not drawn the attention of Japanese readers so far? Was the consequence of the Meiji Revolution so restricted to the political sphere that early readers of Tocqueville were not interested in his discussion of the family and mores? That was certainly not the case. The social transformation caused by the revolution was much greater and far more radical than that of the postwar era. Its long-term effects were so wide and deep that manners and mores, including family life, changed irreversibly.

One reason for this neglect of the topic of the family is that only the first volume of *Democracy in America* was translated into Japanese in the Meiji era. The Japanese version of the second *Democracy* was not available until after World War II. Even those Meiji intellectuals who read the book in English or in French were not much attracted to the second volume, probably because in the age of political enthusiasm they regarded the author as a proponent of freedom and political democracy and could not discover Tocqueville as a moralist. In addition, the true value of the second volume was not appreciated at that time even in Europe and the United States.

In any case, it is regrettable that Fukuzawa Yukichi, who carefully read the first volume in Reeve's translation, did not go on to the chapters on the family and women. Experts of Fukuzawa studies, examining his private copy of Reeve's version filled with many marginal notes, infer that he stopped reading somewhere in the early part of the second volume. If he had read those chapters carefully, he would assuredly have been attracted by Tocqueville's argument, for he extensively wrote about the same issues. He argued for the right and independence of women and severely criticized Confucianism as the doctrine of the subjection of women. He wrote many articles on the education of girls and would have resonated in particular with Tocqueville's discussion about good morals in democratic society.

Obviously, among Meiji intellectuals, Fukuzawa was one of the most consistent and decisive proponents of the equality of men and women, although he stopped short of being a feminist. Interested in the British movement for women's suffrage, he introduced to the Japanese reading public John Stuart Mill's *The Subjection of Women*. But Fukuzawa, not being a fellow traveler of feminism like Mill, would have been more comfortable with Tocqueville's view of the family and women.

Two Revolutions: The French and the Meiji

I have already pointed out that the Meiji Revolution was a form of democratic revolution comparable to the French Revolution. This similarity was recognized from the early period of Meiji. Tokutomi Sohō was probably the first who called the Meiji Revolution egalitarian. Marxist historians have discussed the similarities and differences between the two revolutions for over half a century.[33] They had as a common frame of reference the notion of bourgeois revolution formed on the model of the French Revolution, but they greatly differed in their assessment of how and to what extent the Meiji Revolution was bourgeois. Some took it for granted that it was a revolution necessarily brought about by the historical transition from feudalism to capitalism and tried to gather historical evidence to support this thesis. Others more sensitive to historical particularities emphasized differences between the two events and regarded the Meiji Revolution as a limited and partial revolution. This debate among Marxist historians addressed a number of important issues such as the nature of the class struggle undergirding the political process of the revolution, its economic background, the growing crisis of governmental finance, the relative impoverishment of the ruling samurai class, and the rise of the commercial class. Historians also touched upon other related topics, including the accumulated frustration of the peasants and its social and political consequences, the nature of the Meiji government (absolute monarchy or constitutional monarchy?), the development of liberal and democratic movements (the Movement for Freedom and People's Rights), the transformation of class structure (the dissolution of the samurai class and the polarization of the agricultural population into big landowners and poor peasants), and so forth. Under the heavy influence of Marxism, the Tocquevillian approach has rarely been referred to and regarded as useful for the comparison of the two revolutions, although some Marxist experts of the French Revolution called historians' attention to Tocqueville's thesis concerning the preponderance of peasant proprietors before the Revolution. However, under the impact of François Furet's critique of the Marxist approach to the French revolution (a critique that destroyed the notion of bourgeois revolution itself), it now seems to be out of fashion to consider the Meiji Revolution in the light of the French Revolution.[34]

Watanabe Hiroshi, a leading scholar of Japanese political thought, has recently made a creative use of some arguments of *The Old Regime and the Revolution* to shed new light on historical parallels between the two revolutions.[35] After showing structural similarities between the French Old Regime and the Tokugawa Regime, he pointed out that the process of administrative centralization was going on in the latter as well as in the former, thus paving the way for the revolution. His second point concerned the similar social position that French *philosophes* and Japanese Confucian scholars occupied. Like the *philosophes* and men of letters in general in eighteenth-century France, Watanabe argued, Confucian scholars and National Learning scholars in eighteenth- and nineteenth-century Japan were intellectually active and influential but had no real political power. Although some of them were hired as instructors of *hankō* (schools for samurai run by *han*) or as advisers to higher officials, their policy proposals were rarely adopted. They were men of letters living in an intellectual community of their own, in which they debated with one another and exchanged ideas among themselves without being involved in public affairs with the exception of a few rare cases. As Watanabe pointed out, these individuals were quite different from the Chinese mandarins who were men of letters and bureaucrats at the same time. By contrast, they had much in common with the inhabitants of the French "Republic of Letters." This distance from the world of real politics in the absence of political liberties, as Tocqueville suggests about the French case, is supposedly a reason for their political radicalization in the last years of the Tokugawa era.

Finally, Watanabe remarked that Tocqueville's famous thesis that belated reforms from above cannot stop the collapse of a corrupt regime but only accelerates it is perfectly true of the rapid breakdown of the Tokugawa Regime that had peacefully survived for two and a half centuries. The sudden visit of Commodore Perry's squadron in 1853 forced the shōgun's government to reconsider its traditional policy of closing the country and even to consult local lords' opinion on the issue. This unprecedented reformist action inevitably triggered the attention and interest of many samurai and emboldened them to voice their views from below that brought about an uncontrollable political situation. Indeed, the growing political crisis triggered by Perry's visit showed a typical revolutionary process in which successive actions and reactions, always producing unexpected consequences, rendered the situation unmanageable for everybody. It resulted in a final catastrophe beyond anyone's expectation, thus confirming Joseph de Maistre's famous claim that "It is not that men lead revolution, but that revolution employs men."[36]

But Tocqueville's argument went further than that. However unexpected and uncontrollable a revolutionary process is for the people involved in it, a true revolution occurs only when conditions for it have been prepared for a long time without drawing people's attention. A revolution is perfectly understandable when one considers it in a proper and long-term historical context. This is exactly the case with both the Meiji and the French Revolutions. No wonder then that the first paragraph of *The Old Regime and the Revolution* sounds to Japanese ears very much like a reference to their own Meiji Revolution: "There is nothing more suited to instilling modesty in philosophers and statesmen than the history of our Revolution. Never was such a great event, with such ancient causes, so well prepared and so little foreseen."[37]

Appendix 1: Some Notes on the History of Modern Japan

Tokugawa Regime (1603–1867). Japanese historians generally refer to the political system of Japan before the Meiji Revolution (1867–1868) as *Bakuhan Taisei*, while it is usually called the Tokugawa Regime in English. In this regime, founded by Tokugawa Ieyasu (1542–1616), the country was divided into close to three hundred domains (*han*) of rural lords (*daimyō*) and territories called *tenryō*, which were directly governed by the central government (*bakufu*), including big and strategic cities (Edo, Kyōto, Osaka, and Nagasaki) and important mines. The *shōgun*, who was at the same time the head of the ruling Tokugawa clan and that of *bakufu*, reigned over the whole country and treated all *daimyō* as his vassals. However, the administrative power of *bakufu* did not extend inside the *han*, which kept a great deal of autonomy in legislation and jurisdiction. The former exercised only indirect control on the latter and the *shōgun* was far from an absolute king but the greatest of all *daimyō*, namely, *primus inter pares*. This polycentric regime was abruptly destabilized by the arrival of Commodore Perry's squadron (1853) and collapsed after the subsequent fifteen years of turmoil.

Meiji Revolution. The historical process, through which the Tokugawa Regime was abolished and the new Meiji state was founded, is called in Japanese the *Meiji Ishin* (*ishin* means a total renewal). The conventional English translation—the Meiji Restoration—is misleading and based on the fact that the revolution began by the new Emperor's declaration in 1867 of "imperial restoration." The emperor, who had just acceded to the throne at the age of fifteen, had no real power at that time and was just a puppet king manipulated by Chōshū and Satsuma. While this transfer of sovereignty itself was conducted without revolutionary violence, it immediately caused a bloody civil war that continued for a year and half (1868–1869). After the civil war, the new government took a revolutionary turn, issuing a series of important laws and decrees that eventually destroyed the old regime and abolished the status-based social system. These radical policies inevitably encountered the strong reaction of the people and provoked the rebellion of a significant number of former samurai who had been deprived of their privileges. In the mid-1870s, several revolts against the government broke out that eventually led to the greatest civil war in modern Japan, *Seinan Sensō*, in 1877. Crushing this last samurai rebellion led by Saigō Takamori, the very hero of the Restoration, and responding to the challenge of the Movement for Freedom and People's Rights (see below), the new government gradually consolidated its power until the promulgation of the Constitution of the Great Empire of Japan in 1889. Throughout the entire period of these succeeding historical mutations, the Japanese people experienced a fundamental change in all spheres of social life: law and political system, socioeconomic structure, manners and customs, even language and vocabulary. It is quite legitimate to call the historical process of such a drastic transformation the Meiji Revolution.

The Movement for Freedom and People's Rights (or *The Popular Rights Movement*). In January 1874, Itagaki Taisuke (1837–1919) and others, all of whom had just stepped down from governmental offices, addressed to the government a "Memorial on the Establishment of a Representative Assembly" (*Minsengiin Setsuritsu Kenpakusho*). This triggered off the political activities of the people asking for freedom and participation, which developed into a large-scale opposition movement called the Movement for Freedom and People's Rights (*Jiyū Minken Undō*). The Popular Rights Movement was born from political struggle among governmental leaders for hegemony and started as a strategy adopted by the defeated party. At the outset, it was a political movement of the ex-members of the government mobilizing the frustrated former samurai class. With the progress of the movement, however, it involved a wide range of people and gained ground in particular among the upper-middle class of the agrarian population. Under the growing influence of liberal and democratic ideas of the West and in the general atmosphere of social emancipation, it became a major opposition movement in the 1880s that prompted the government to establish a constitution and introduce parliamentary politics.

Postwar Reform. This refers to a series of legal and political reforms introduced in Japan under the Occupation (1945–1952). Apart from the drafting of a new constitution and the immediate task of demilitarization, it extended to various fields of social and political life: agrarian land reform, education reform, the dissolution of *zaibatsu* (financial cliques) and the encouragement of trade unions, the revision of family and inheritance laws, and so forth. All of these changes were imposed by the GHQ on the Japanese government, which sometimes resisted and accepted them only reluctantly. Two exceptions stand out in this regard: land reform and the revised family law. Both were enthusiastically welcomed by the people and produced significant effects.

Appendix 2: Glossary of Personal Names

FUKUZAWA Yukichi (1835–1901). Educator and journalist, the most important and influential thinker in Meiji Japan. The founder of Keiō University, he worked hard to foster in the Japanese people the spirit of individual independence and self-respect, which he considered as the founding principles of Western civilization. Major works available in English translation: *The Autobiography of Fukuzawa Yukichi*, trans. E. Kiyooka, with a preface and afterword by Albert Craig (Lanham, MD: Madison Books, 1992); *An Encouragement of Learning*, trans. David A. Dilworth and Umeyo Hirano (Tokyo: Sophia University, 1969); and *An Outline of a Theory of Civilization* (Paris: UNESCO Collection of Representative Works, 1973).

IHARA Saikaku (1642-1693). Poet and writer in the Tokugawa period. Together with the dramatist, Chikamatsu Monzaemon (1653-1724), Saikaku is one of the most important literary artists in the *Genroku* era (1688-1704, in the narrow sense), the epoch of the rise of *chonin bunka* (bourgeois culture). *Koshoku Ichidai Otoko* (*The Life of an Amorous Man*), published in 1682, is an erotic life story of a rich merchant, Yonosuke.

KAWASHIMA Takeyoshi (1909-1992). Professor of law at the University of Tokyo. Together with Maruyama Masao and others, he played an important role as an opinion leader of the so-called Postwar Enlightenment. In particular, his critical analysis of the "feudal or pre-modern" structure of the Japanese family had a wide resonance at the time.

MARUYAMA Masao (1914-1996). Professor of political science at the University of Tokyo. Political theorist as well as intellectual historian, Maruyama is the most influential social scientist in postwar Japan. His major works are available in English translation and highly regarded by Western scholars: *Thought and Behavior in Modern Japanese Politics*, ed. Ivan Moris (Oxford: Oxford University Press, 1963); *Studies in the Intellectual History of Tokugawa Japan*, trans. Mikiso Hane (Tokyo: University of Tokyo Press; Princeton, NJ: Princeton University Press, 1974).

NAKAE Chōmin (1847-1901). Political thinker and philosopher. On returning from several years' stay in France, he founded a private school dedicated to French learning (*Futsugakujuku*) and became the first Francophile philosopher in Japan. His translation of Rousseau's *Contrat social* earned him an enormous influence on the Movement for Freedom and People's Rights.

ŌMORI Shōichi (1856-1927). Bureaucrat and prefect in the Meiji and Taisho era. As an able aide to Yamagata Aritomo (1838-1922), one of the central figures of the Meiji oligarchy and the second prime minister succeeding Ito Hirobumi (1841-1909), Ōmori played a major role in building up the local government system under the Meiji Constitution, which was designed in reaction to the Movement for Freedom and People's Rights as an institutional device for keeping local communities immune from political radicalism.

TOKUTOMI Sohō (1863-1957). Journalist and historian enjoying an exceptionally long career. Starting as a young radical under the influence of the Popular Rights Movement, Sohō became, after the Sino-Japanese war, increasingly nationalistic and expansionist and, in the end, fanatically supported Japan's military invasion of China and its catastrophic war against the United States.

Notes

In this chapter, I owe many of my arguments about the Japanese reception of Tocqueville to several experts of the history of Japanese political thought: Anzai Toshimitsu, Matsuda Kōichirō, Miyamura Haruo, and Watanabe Hiroshi. Particularly helpful was the information and inspiration that I have received through discussion with Professor Watanabe over the years. All Japanese personal names are given in Japanese order except that of the present author.

    1. Robert N. Bellah, *Tokugawa Religion: The Values of Preindustrial Japan* (Glencoe, IL: Free Press, 1957).

    2. Maruyama Masao, "Bellah, *Tokugawajidai no Shūkyō ni Tsuite* [On Bellah's Tokugawa Religion]," in *Maruyama Masao Chosakushū* [Collective Works of Maruyama Masao], vol. 7 (Tokyo: Iwanami Shoten, 1996–1997), 247–89. The essay was first published in *Kokkagakkai Zasshi* 72, no. 4 (April 1958). Bellah accepted most of Maruyama's critical arguments. See Bellah's response, "Reflections on the Protestant Ethic Analogy in Asia," *Journal of Social Issues* 19, no. 1 (1963): 52–60.

    3. On the Marxists' debate about Japanese capitalism, see Germaine A. Hoston, *Marxism and the Crisis of Development in Prewar Japan* (Princeton, NJ: Princeton University Press, 1986). On the Japanese reception of Max Weber, see Wolfgang Schwentker, *Max Weber in Japan: Eine Untersuchung zur Wirkungsgeschichte 1905–1995* (Tübingen: Mohr, 1998).

    4. Françoise Mélonio, "Tocqueville, ou la conscience malheureuse européenne." This paper, a development of her article, "Tocqueville européen: la France et l'Allemagne," originally published in the *Tocqueville Review* 27, no. 2 (2006): 517–32, was translated in a Japanese journal together with three other papers and the *compte-rendu* of the conference written by the present author; Françoise Mélonio, "Tocqueville, aruiwa Yōroppa no Fukōna Ishiki," trans. Miura Nobutaka, *Shisō* 979 (November 2005): 36–50. The Tokyo conference celebrating the bicentennial of the birth of Tocqueville was held in June 2005 at the Maison Franco-Japonaise of Tokyo, with the participation of five American scholars and the same number of the French: Olivier Zunz, James T. Schleifer, Rogers Smith, Stephen Holmes, and Alan Kahan on the American side; Françoise Mélonio, Lucien Jaume, Denis Lacorne, Agnès Antoine, and Nancy Green on the French. All the papers submitted will be published in Japanese book form in 2009 from the University of Tokyo Press.

    5. According to the Government's *Annual Report on the Japanese Economy and Public Finance* (2006), the Geni Coefficient of income of Japan is near the average of OECD countries. It is greater than that of most continental European countries, but smaller than that of the United States and the United Kingdom. The report maintains that the country's poverty rate, absolute as well as relative, is comparatively low, although it admits that the income gap has increased since the 1980s. Although it is certain that economic inequality has increased in Japan in

recent decades, this phenomenon occurred after the economy had attained a high degree of equality and affluence.

6. Miura Nobuo, *Karyūshakai: Aratana Kaisōshūdan no Shutsugen* [Low Society: The Appearance of a New Group of Class] (Tokyo: Kobunsha, 2005); Tachibanaki Toshiaki, *Kakusashakai; Nani ga Mondaika?* [Society of Disparity: What is the Problem?] (Tokyo: Iwanami Shoten, 2006). In fact, "kakusa (disparity)" is now a big topic for debate in Japan.

7. Ronald P. Dore, *Education in Tokugawa Japan* (London: Routledge & Kegan Paul, 1965).

8. Alexis de Tocqueville, *Democracy in America*, trans. Arthur Goldhammer (New York: The Library of America, 2004), 348 ff.

9. Ronald P. Dore, *The Diploma Disease: Education, Qualification, and Development* (Berkeley: University of California Press, 1975).

10. Fukuzawa Yukichi, *Gakumon no Susume* (Tokyo: Iwanami Shoten, Iwanami Bunko), English translation by D. A. Dilwirth and U. Hirano, *An Encouragement of Learning* (Tokyo: Sophia University, 1969). The first essay of the book was first published in 1871.

11. Tsuda Sōkichi, *Bungaku ni Arawaretaru Waga Kokuminshisō no Kenkyū* [A Study of Our National Thought Expressed in Literature] (Tokyo: Iwanami Shoten, Iwanami Bunko, 1978), vols. 5-7. The book was first published in 1916-1921.

12. This does not mean that there is no difference between the two revolutions. The Meiji Revolution represented the nation's reaction to the influence of Western values and principles and is therefore rightly called "a nationalist revolution." See Andrew Gordon, *A Modern History of Japan: From Tokugawa Times to the Present* (New York: Oxford University Press, 2003), 62. The challenge and menace of foreign countries were absent in the French case before the revolution. French nationalism was born in the process of the revolutionary war.

13. On the political process of the Land Reform and its social effects, see Ronald P. Dore, *Land Reform in Japan* (Oxford: Oxford University Press, 1959). Although the reform policies were formulated and implemented under the U. S. Occupation, there had been before the war a long history of debates about the necessity of agrarian land reform on the part of policymakers of the Ministry of Interior Affairs as well as among revolutionary social critics.

14. Tocqueville, *Democracy in America*, 53-57.

15. *Jyōboku Jiyū no Ron* [On the Freedom of the Press], trans. Obata Tokujirō, 1873.

16. *Jiyū Genron*, trans. Koizuka Ryū, 1881-82.

17. Tocqueville, *Democracy in America*, 270.

18. Fukuzawa, *Gakumon no Susume*.

19. Fukuzawa, "Bunkenron (On Decentralization)," in *Fukuzawa Zenshū* [Complete Works of Fukuzawa], vol. 4 (Tokyo: Iwanami Shoten, 1952), 231-93. The essay first appeared in 1877.

20. Tocqueville, *Democracy in America*, 98.

21. Here I am indebted to Professor Matsuda Kōichirō's paper presented at the above-mentioned Tokyo Conference on Tocqueville, "Public Spirit and Tradition: Tocqueville in the Discourse of Meiji Intellectuals." For more information, see the proceedings of the conference, *La France et les Etats-Unis, deux modèles de démocratie?*

22. Since the total reorganization of ministries and governmental agencies in 2001, the Ministry has been called *Sōmushō* and its official English name is the Ministry of Internal Affairs and Communications. The Ministry of Self-Government is the literal translation of the former Japanese name, *Jichishō* (it is worth asking if self-government could ever be regulated and supported by a ministry?). The prewar *Naimushō* was much bigger, for it was at the same time the national police headquarters. The most appropriate translation in Western language would be the French *le Ministère des Affaires Intérieurs*.

23. Tocqueville, *Democracy in America*, 103.

24. After the gubernatorial election of Miyazaki Prefecture in January 2007, in which a media celebrity unexpectedly defeated the LDP candidate, taking advantage of the political scandal of the former governor, twenty-nine of all the forty-seven governors are still ex-bureaucrats. The greatest number of them (fifteen) come from the former Ministry of Self-Government and the second greatest (nine) from the former MITI.

25. Tocqueville, *Democracy in America*, 237–38.

26. Later he founded a political party and was elected to the Second House in 2007.

27. Tocqueville, *Democracy in America*, 253.

28. Reiji Matsumoto, "Tocqueville on the Family," in *Tocqueville Review* 7/8 (1987): 127–52.

29. Kawashima Takeyoshi, *Nihonshakai no Kazokuteki Kōsei* (Tokyo: Gakuseishobō, 1948).

30. Tocqueville, *Democracy in America*, 689.

31. Andrew Gordon is right to show a certain continuity of social life in Japan, including family relations, from the 1920s to the 1950s. See Gordon, *A Modern History of Japan*, 251 ff.

32. Tocqueville, *Democracy in America*, 690.

33. For the review of the discussed issues, see Kawano Kenji, *Furansu Kakumei to Meiji Ishin* [The French Revolution and the Meiji Restoration] (Tokyo: Nihon Hōsō Kyōkai, 1966).

34. François Furet, *Penser la Révolution française* (Paris: Gallimard, 1978). For an English translation, see Furet, *Interpreting the French Revolution* (Cambridge: Cambridge University Press, 1981).

35. Watanabe Hiroshi, "The Old Regime and the Meiji Revolution," paper presented at the above-mentioned International Conference on Tocqueville in Tokyo and included in the proceedings of the conference *La France et les Etats-Unis, deux*

modèles de démocratie? The enlarged Japanese version of this paper, "Anshan Reji-imu to Meiji Kakumei," was published in *Shisō* 979 (November 2005): 51–70.

36. Joseph de Maistre, *Considérations sur la France* (Paris: Imprimerie Nationale, 1994), 41. The translation is mine.

37. Alexis de Tocqueville, *The Old Regime and the French Revolution*, vol. I, trans. Alan S. Kahan (Chicago: University of Chicago Press, 1998), 93.

Index

Custine, Marquis de, 201
customs, 41, 44, 46, 120
Cyprus, 189
Czechoslovakia, 212

Dahl, Robert, 164
dang guan ganbu (nomenklatura), 275.
  See also nomenklatura
Dareste, Antoine (de la Chavanne),
  65, 69
daxiang ("large township"), 274
decentralization, 2, 3, 13, 48, 128, 186,
  216, 241, 277; of administrative
  responsibility, 180; pluralist, 280; of
  power, 203; radical, 148; reforms, 246
Declaration of Independence, 20, 98,
  104, 105, 107
De la Réorganisation de la société
  européene (Saint-Simon), 178
De la Rua, Fernando, 153
democracy, 2, 5–7, 9, 12, 23, 33–34,
  37–38, 44, 57, 61, 120, 158, 162,
  164, 173, 183, 203–4, 206, 269,
  271; American, 5, 7, 9, 23, 33, 38,
  44; dangers of, 12, 57; delegative,
  162; dilemmas of, 6, 17n25; direct,
  164; economic preconditions for,
  206; to educate, 3, 6; egalitarian,
  173; electoral, 120, 158; elusive,
  12; erosion of, 203; flaws and
  vulnerabilities of, 7; ideal, 34;
  majoritarian, 183; minimal and
  procedural definition of, 37;
  participatory, 2; plural definitions of,
  61; prospects for, 269, 271; Russian,
  204; shape of, 269; successful
  transition to, 206; vibrant, 38;
  Western style, 34. See also self-
  government, democratic
Democracy and the Organization of
  Political Parties (Ostrogorski), 23
Democracy in America (Tocqueville),
  1–3, 6–7, 9–10, 12–13, 15, 33, 35, 38,

  39, 40, 44, 55, 58, 59, 60, 63, 72, 76,
  85, 95, 96, 107, 118, 120, 164, 173–
  74, 199, 200, 225, 253, 296, 300, 308
Democracy in Europe (Siedentop), 177
Democracy Movement in Burma, 13
democratic age, 25, 85, 87, 91
democratic revolution, 6, 8, 10, 14, 19,
  38, 86, 89
democratic society, 9, 10, 14, 19, 41
democratic soul, 61, 88
democratic transition, 8, 147
democratization, 6, 10, 14, 33, 207,
  208, 271, 288, 305–7; China's, 272;
  of family, 305; political, 156, 157; of
  politics, 304; of society, 305
Denmark, 188, 297
despotism, 1, 2, 11–12, 38, 174;
  democratic, 11, 35, 173, 174; gentle,
  5; of the majority, 120; state, 120
dictators, 120, 125
dictatorship, 34, 194; domestic, 96;
  of law, 217; military, 24, 126, 158;
  personal, 48, 216; of the proletariat,
  24; temporary, 132
Dillon's Rule, 22
dissent, 11, 101, 102
dissenters, 93
Dominican Republic, 153
Drescher, Seymour, 7, 17n16, 17n25,
  60
Drolet, Michael, 15n2, 71, 72, 73
Duchatel, Tanneguy, 71, 72
Du Contrat Social (Rousseau), 298
Duma, 202–203, 216; elections, 204

Eberly, Don, 4, 16n13, 16n15
Ecuador, 148, 150
Edo, 298–99
Egypt, 211
Eisenhower, Dwight, 2
elections, 10, 35, 38, 151, 158, 203,
  246, 255, 283, 303–4; democratic,
  125, 126; free, fair, and open, 37;

Larkin, Emmet, 119
Las Casas, Bartolome de, 129
Lasswell, Harold, 28
latifundia, 45
Latin America, 6, 8, 9, 11, 33, 40, 45, 47, 48, 117, 120, 125, 145–60, 165, 200
Latinobarómetro Report, 151–53, 157–58
Latvia, 189
Law and Revolution (Berman), 25
Le Globe, 71
League of Nations, 26
Lebanon, 210
Legionnaires of Christ, 130
Leo XIII, 184
Letter on Pauperism in Normandy (Tocqueville), 75
Lettres sur l'Amérique du Nord (Chevalier), 71
Liberal Democratic Party, 302
Liberia, 42, 102, 103, 104, 237
Lincoln, Abraham, 98, 105
lingua franca, 177
Linhai, 284–85
Linz, Juan L., 279
Lombards, 179
Lukashenko, Alexander, 219
Lula da Silva, Luiz Inacio, 153, 160–61
Luxembourg, 189

Macarel, Louis-Antoine, 65
Mack, Helen, 134
Madison, James, 19, 97
Maistre, Joseph de, 310
The Making of Tocqueville's Democracy in America (Schleifer), 63
Malaysia, 268
Mali, 229
Malta, 189
Malthus, Thomas, 74
Manchester, 121, 127, 139
Manent, Pierre, 15n2, 58, 61

Mao, Zedong, 274–75, 281, 286
maquiladoras, 127
Maruyama, Masao, 296, 313
Marx, Karl, 2, 6, 43, 58, 71, 295–96
Massachusetts Bay, 92, 98
Mayan culture and religion, 11, 117, 124, 129, 130, 141
Medvedev, Dmitry, 216
Meiji, Japan, 295; era, 304, 308; government, 309; intellectuals, 296, 300, 308; period, 298; Revolution, 14, 298–301, 307–11. *See also* Japan; revolution
Meiliyuan community, 287
Mélonio, Françoise, 296
Memoir on Pauperism (Tocqueville), 7
Menchu, Rigoberta, 134
Menem, Carlos, 157
mestizo, 117, 118, 120, 124
methodology, 5, 8, 10, 34, 40, 44, 56, 57, 58, 120
Mexico, 11, 124, 147, 157, 161, 164
Middle East, 33, 40, 47
Mill, John S., 2, 16n7, 58, 308
Milosevic, Slobodan, 219
mini-fundia, 124
Minlu, 284–86
modernization, 47, 147, 155–56, 164–65
Moldova, 217
monarchy, 38, 39
Monnet, Jean, 177
Mont, Efrain Rios, 129, 131
Montesquieu, Charles de Secondat, 56, 61, 216
Montgomery bus boycott, 106
monts-de-piété, 75
Morales, Evo, 161
mores, 6, 89, 95, 101, 130, 136, 137, 200, 211, 226–27, 229–31, 234, 239–42, 245–46; African, 231; democratic, 227, 307; fundamental, 247; new, 249; precolonial, 230, 242,

Contributors

Barbara Allen is professor and former chair of the Department of Political Science at Carleton College, Northfield, Minnesota. Professor Allen writes extensively on applying Tocqueville's theories to contemporary politics and policy. Her most recently published book is *Tocqueville, Covenant, and the Democratic Revolution: Harmonizing Earth with Heaven* (2005). Other publications include her research on Martin Luther King Jr.'s contributions to American political thought. She has served as a contributing editor for the Martin Luther King Jr. Papers Project at Stanford University and as a fellow at the Mondale Policy Forum at the Hubert H. Humphrey Institute of Public Affairs.

Krister Andersson is assistant professor in environmental policy at the University of Colorado at Boulder. He received his Ph.D. in Public Policy from Indiana University in 2002. In 2007, he was awarded the Giorgio Ruffolo Research Fellowship by Harvard University for his research on public policy reforms and their mixed effects on rural development and natural resource governance in Latin America. His work has appeared in several journal articles and in three books—the latest one is coauthored with Gustavo Gordillo de Anda and Frank van Laerhoven and is entitled *Local Governments and Rural Development: Comparing Lessons from Brazil, Chile, Mexico, and Peru* (University of Arizona Press, 2008).

Aurelian Craiutu is associate professor in the Department of Political Science at Indiana University, Bloomington. He is the author of *Liberalism under Siege: The Political Thought of the French Doctrinaires* (2003), which won a 2004 CHOICE Outstanding Academic Title Award; *Le Centre introuvable* (2006); and *In Praise of Moderation* (2006; in Romanian). Dr. Craiutu also edited Guizot's *History of the Origins of Representative Government in Europe* (2002). He is currently working on a book on political moderation entitled *The Extremism of the Center: Faces of Moderation* *in Modern Political Thought,* exploring various aspects of moderation in modern political thought. Professor Craiutu has translated and edited (with Jeremy Jennings) a new volume of Tocqueville's writings, *Tocqueville on America after 1840: Letters and Other Writings* (Cambridge University Press, 2009), and co-edited (with Jeffrey C. Isaac) a volume entitled *America through European Eyes* (Penn State University Press, 2009). He also edited a new translation of Madame de Staël's *Considerations on the Principal Events of the French Revolution* (Liberty Fund, 2008).

Frederic Fransen received his Ph.D. in 1996 from the Committee on Social Thought at the University of Chicago, under the direction of the late François Furet. He is the author of *The Supranational Politics of Jean Monnet* (2001). Dr. Fransen is president of Donor Advising, Research, and Educational Services, which assists philanthropists with their higher education and other major gifts, and a Visiting Fellow of the Center on Philanthropy at Indiana University. From 1996 until 2006, he was variously a program officer, fellow, and senior fellow at Liberty Fund Inc. From 2001 to 2006, he also served as director of grants for the Pierre F. and Enid Goodrich Foundation. In 2001, he was a Visiting Fellow at the International Centre for Economic Research in Turin, Italy. From 1988 to 1991, he worked in Brussels, Belgium, as a researcher studying European Community and NATO security policy. Fransen has spent extensive time living and studying European politics and culture, having conducted research in Belgium, France, Germany, Switzerland, and Italy.

Sheldon Gellar is a research associate at Indiana University's Workshop in Political Theory and Policy Analysis. One of the first scholars to systematically apply Tocqueville's methodology to the analysis of non-Western societies, Gellar is the author of *Democracy in Senegal: Tocquevillian Analytics in Africa* (2005), *Structural Changes and Colonial Dependency: Senegal 1885–1945* (1976), and *Senegal: An African Nation Between Islam and the West* (1995). He is currently completing a book-length manuscript on religion and politics in Africa for Lynne Rienner Publishers. Dr. Gellar has taught at Indiana University, Michigan State University, and the Hebrew University of Jerusalem and was a research associate at Princeton University (1982–83) and the Harry S. Truman Institute for the Advancement of Peace (1989–2001).

Gustavo Gordillo de Anda has been a practitioner, academician, and policymaker in agriculture, rural, and regional development issues. As a practitioner, he has been co-founder of a seventy-five rural organizations network in Mexico (UNORCA–La Unión Nacional de Organizaciones Regionales Campesinas Autónomas). Dr. Gordillo de Anda holds a "Doctorat de Troisième Cycle" from the École Practique des Hautes Études, Paris, France. He has been a visiting professor at various universities in Mexico and the United States and is author of more than twenty books and eighty articles. From 1988 to 1994, he served as Vice-Minister of Agriculture and Undersecretary of Agrarian Reform to the Government of Mexico. Between 1995 and 2005, he served as Director for Rural Development in FAO's headquarters and Assistant Director-General, Regional Representative of FAO for Latin America and the Caribbean based in Santiago de Chile. Dr. Gordillo de Anda was a visiting scholar at the Workshop in Political Theory and Policy Analysis at Indiana University from 2006 to 2008.

Reiji Matsumoto is professor of political science at Waseda University in Japan where he teaches political science and the history of political thought. Educated in Japan and France, Professor Matsumoto was a Fulbright Scholar at Yale University (1984–1986) where he worked on the Tocqueville papers at the Beinecke Rare Book and Manuscript Library. Matsumoto's major academic interest has always been in Tocqueville studies, but he has also written several articles on other issues such as the French image of America and the comparative study of French, American, and Japanese intellectuals. He is the author, among others, of *A Study on Tocqueville: Family, Religion, State and Democracy* (in Japanese, 1991). In 2008, he completed his four-volume translation of *Democracy in America*.

Tun Myint is assistant professor of political science at Carleton College, Northfield, Minnesota, and was previously a research associate at the Workshop in Political Theory and Policy Analysis at Indiana University. He left Burma after the September 18, 1988, military coup that cracked down on the people's movement for democracy in which he was involved as a student activist. He came to Indiana University in 1993 after he was awarded a scholarship by the United States Information Agency-funded Burmese Refugee Scholarship Program administered by the Office of International Programs at Indiana University. Myint is also a research fellow at the Institutional Dimension of Global Environmental Change (IDGC) program, which is a core science project of the International Human Dimension Program that strives to achieve scientific understanding of the human dimensions of global environmental change.

Vincent Ostrom is Arthur F. Bentley Professor Emeritus of Political Science and founding director of the Workshop in Political Theory and Policy Analysis at Indiana University, Bloomington. Professor Ostrom has been a fellow of the Social Science Research Council and the Center for Advanced Study in the Behavioral Sciences, contributed to the drafting of the Alaska Constitution, has received honors from the American Political Science Association, and was a co-recipient of the Atlas Economic Research Foundation's Lifetime Achievement Award. He has been president of the Public Choice Society and has served on the editorial boards of *Constitutional Political Economy, International Journal of Organization and Behavior,* and *Publius: The Journal of Federalism.* His books include *The Meaning of American Federalism: Constituting a Self-Governing Society* (1991), *The Meaning of Democracy and the Vulnerability of Democracies: A Response to Tocqueville's Challenge* (1997), *The Intellectual Crisis in American Public Administration* ([1973] 2008), and *The Political Theory of a Compound Republic: Designing the American Experiment* ([1971] 2008).

Charles A. Reilly is a research fellow and professor at the Joan B. Kroc Institute for Peace and Justice of the School of Peace Studies at the University of San Diego where he teaches courses on civil society, peace-building, and development. He also serves as senior adviser to the New Americans Immigration Museum and Learning Center. Dr. Reilly was a research fellow at the University of Notre Dame and a Fulbright fellow at the University of Ireland, Galway. Previously, Dr. Reilly taught at Georgetown, UCSD, the Federal University of Pernambuco in Brazil, and Landivar University in Guatemala. From 1998 to 2003, he was Peace Corps Director in Guatemala. Dr. Reilly has edited or authored several books, including *Peace-Building and Development in Guatemala and Northern Ireland* (2009), *New Paths to Democratic Development in Latin America: The Rise of NGO-Municipal Government Collaboration* (1995), and *Inquiry at the Grassroots,* co-edited with William Glade (1993).

Peter Rutland is professor of government and chair of the College of Social Studies at Wesleyan University where he teaches courses on comparative politics and political economy. In 1995–1997, he was assistant director (research) at the Open Media Research Institute in Prague. In 1997–1998, he chaired the Olin Security Studies Seminar at the Davis Center for Russian Studies, Harvard University, and in 1999–2000 he was executive director of the Caspian Studies Program at the Kennedy School of Government, Harvard University. He is the author of two books on Soviet political economy—*The Politics of Economic Stagnation in the Soviet Union: The Role of Local Political Organs in Economic Management* (1991) and *The Myth of the Plan: Lessons of Soviet Planning Experience* (1990)—and the editor of *Business and the State in Contemporary Russia* (2000).

Jianxun Wang is associate professor of law at China University of Political Science and Law in Beijing and has been affiliated with the Workshop in Political Theory and Policy Analysis at Indiana University since 2000. Wang has law degrees from Lanzhou University and Peking University and earned his Ph.D. at Indiana University, Bloomington. His research interests include Tocqueville, federalism, institutional analysis, and constitutional choice. Wang has published several journal articles and book chapters in Chinese, and translated a volume on American federalism into Chinese (2003).

James S. Wunsch is professor and director of the African Studies Program at Creighton University. A specialist in comparative politics, public administration, and Third World development, Wunsch also teaches courses on African politics, West European politics, democratization, ethnicity, public policy, and political theory. Wunsch has published articles on Third World development, African government, ethnic conflict, and public administration, his areas of primary research interest. Professor Wunsch has authored or coauthored nearly forty articles and reviews in professional journals or chapters in anthologies. He is also the co-editor with Dele Olowu of *The Failure of the Centralized State in Africa: Institutions and Self-Governance in Africa* (1995) and *Local Governance in Africa: The Challenges of Democratic Decentralization* (2004).